Advance Praise

"Straight from the creators of the highly influential Imago Relationship Therapy, this book presents the wonderful treatment method to clinicians. It's the epitome of authoritative finality and needs to be on every couples and family therapist's bookshelf. Buy it!"

—**John M. Gottman, Ph.D.**, author of
The Seven Principles for Making Marriage Work

"You might buy this book because you loved the lessons from *Getting the Love You Want*. You might buy this book because you will personally profit from the knowledge, expertise, and experience of two extraordinary teachers. You might buy this book because your couples will love your increased wisdom and interventions. You might buy this book to increase your ability and confidence to handle your toughest cases. Whatever the reason, you won't be disappointed by this terrific book and its fresh perspectives on the extraordinary complexities of relationships."

—**Peter Pearson, Ph.D.**, cofounder of The Couples Institute

"Relationships can be healed from the interwoven wounds of historical ruptures. Harville Hendrix and Helen LaKelly Hunt, the architects of Imago, one of the primary schools of contemporary therapy, provide a thorough, comprehensive, and scientifically-based program that brings relational living to life."

—**Jeffrey K. Zeig, Ph.D.**, Director, The Milton H. Erickson Foundation

"The book could be an entire college course in couples therapy! Every couples therapist can celebrate the groundbreaking discoveries Harville Hendrix and Helen LaKelly Hunt make in this foundational text. They dissect what really happens in the couple experience—the interactive fields of energy, particles, and waves and how, in practical, applicable steps, the positive connectivity of the Space-Between ultimately creates relational wellbeing."

—**Stan Tatkin, Psy.D., MFT**, author of *Wired for Love* and *We Do*

DOING
IMAGO
RELATIONSHIP
THERAPY

IN THE SPACE-BETWEEN

A Norton Professional Book

A Clinician's Guide

DOING

IMAGO

RELATIONSHIP THERAPY

IN THE SPACE-BETWEEN

HARVILLE HENDRIX, PH.D.
HELEN LaKELLY HUNT, PH.D.

W. W. NORTON & COMPANY
Independent Publishers Since 1923

Note to Readers: Standards of clinical practice and protocol change over time, and no technique or recommendation is guaranteed to be safe or effective in all circumstances. This volume is intended as a general information resource for professionals practicing in the field of psychotherapy and mental health; it is not a substitute for appropriate training, peer review, and/or clinical supervision. Neither the publisher nor the author(s) can guarantee the complete accuracy, efficacy, or appropriateness of any particular recommendation in every respect.

For information about permission to reproduce selections from this book, write to Permissions, W. W. Norton & Company, Inc., 500 Fifth Avenue, New York, NY 10110

For information about special discounts for bulk purchases, please contact W. W. Norton Special Sales at specialsales@wwnorton.com or 800-233-4830

Manufacturing by Lake Book Manufacturing
Book design by Vicki Fischman
Production manager: Katelyn Mackenzie

Library of Congress Cataloging-in-Publication Data

Names: Hendrix, Harville, author. | Hunt, Helen, 1949- author.
Title: Doing imago relationship therapy in the space-between : a clinician's guide / Harville Hendrix and Helen LaKelly Hunt.
Description: First edition. | New York : W.W. Norton & Company, [2021] | "A Norton Professional book." | Includes bibliographical references and index.
Identifiers: LCCN 2020035054 | ISBN 9780393713817 (hardcover) | ISBN9780393713824 (epub)
Subjects: LCSH: Imago relationship therapy.
Classification: LCC RC488.5 .H47 2021 | DDC 616.89/156—dc23
LC record available at https://lccn.loc.gov/2020035054

W. W. Norton & Company, Inc., 500 Fifth Avenue, New York, N.Y. 10110
www.wwnorton.com

W. W. Norton & Company Ltd., 15 Carlisle Street, London W1D 3BS

1 2 3 4 5 6 7 8 9 0

Contents

APPENDICES

FIGURES

TABLES

Acknowledgments

Until now, *Getting the Love You Want: A Guide for Couples*, was the major source of Imago theory and practice for students, graduate schools, therapists, and couples. *Doing Imago Relationship Therapy in the Space-Between* adds a comprehensive, in-depth academic and clinical Imago text.

From our hearts, we express our thanks personally to all the persons and communities who have received, read, shared, taught, and practiced Imago globally for over 30 years. We would love to be inclusive with names, but the list would be too long, so we list Imago communities instead, with a few exceptions.

Oprah Winfrey: thanks for making *Getting the Love You Want* and *Imago Relationship Therapy* visible internationally with those 18 appearances on The Oprah Show.

Couples and other readers: thanks to the four million of you who have read *Getting the Love You Want: A Guide for Couples* and passed it along to other people.

The Imago Faculty of the Imago International Training Institute: thanks for dedicating your careers to comprehending, expanding, and distributing Imago theory and therapy by training over 2,500 therapists in 59 countries and counting.

Imago therapists: thanks for helping couples in diverse cultures globally transform their relationships and experience full aliveness, joy, and wonder.

Imago Workshop Presenters: thanks for increasing the number of couples and individuals who have access to the Imago process by leading Imago educational workshops around the world.

Imago Relationships International: thanks for supporting the faculty so it could focus on teaching and Imago therapists so they could help couples connect and for supporting and monitoring the research process to move Imago towards evidence-based status.

To a short list of early adopters of Imago: Thanks for showing up at the beginning to help decide to name the system Imago Relationship Therapy, to organize the first training groups, to become the first practicing Imago therapists, to be the first trainers of Imago therapists and the first contributors to Imago theory, and to stay for the long haul. These include but are not limited to: Gay Jurgens, Gene Shelly, Bruce Wood, Wendy Patterson, Francine Beauvoir, Maurine Brine, Sophie Slade and Pat Love, Joyce Buckner, Maya Kollman, Bruce Crapuchettes, and Sunny Shulkin who became Master Trainers.

To Randy Mason, my (Harville's) first clinical supervisor and first employer at the Greater Chicago Pastoral Counseling Center, and Robert Elliott, my senior colleague at Perkins School of Theology, Southern Methodist University—now both deceased—I want to express my awe and appreciation that, early on in the Imago journey—before Oprah and before visibility—they both became my students and members of the faculty of our training institute. Their support and participation has been a long-time inspiration and a model of humility.

To writers, editors, consultants and assistants: thanks to Mo Hannah for the first draft; Jean Staeheli for parts of the second; Wade Luquet for consultation, references, and footnotes; Sally Lindsey for graphs and charts; and executive assistant Mollie O'Neal for helping take it the last mile.

Sanam Hoon: our deep and special thanks is reserved for you for being on our team for nearly three decades, for your amazing intellect, writing talent, endurance, organizational and management skills, and without whom the book would not have been any fun, and might still be in utero.

Deborah Malmud, Vice President and Director of Norton Professional Books: thanks for your warm welcome to Norton and your validation and patience so we could get it done just right.

Mariah Eppes, Project Editor: thanks for bringing such expertise to managing the project. And to Trish Watson for her developmental editing, Julie HawkOwl for her copyediting, and Sara McBride Tuohy for her editorial assisting. All of you contributed toward a more perfect manuscript.

Preface

A BRIEF INTELLECTUAL AUTOBIOGRAPHY

We wrote this book to answer a question: why do couples fight? We asked the question about forty years ago, right after we met. Both of us were troubled about our divorces, given that we were committed to marriage. In discussing our discomfort with our relational status, we expanded the question to: Why does the dream become a nightmare? And eventually, we asked: "why does anyone fight?" And finally, "what is the source of human conflict?" These questions sent us on a personal quest and research process that eventuated in "Imago" as an intellectual system operationalized as a couple's therapy, a relational education process, and a social movement. And, to the conclusion that the answer to the "why" of couples conflict is the answer to the "why" of human conflict, and the solution to both is the same.

Although we come from opposite ends of the social and economic spectrum, we have similar childhood experiences which contributed, from the beginning, to a very complex and conflicted relationship that provided the perfect (though unplanned) laboratory within which we incubated ideas, invented new processes, and practiced new behaviors. The contribution each of us made was a function of our unique gifts, needs, resources and personal history, and therefore, in all respects, like having children, Imago is a co-creation that could not have developed without constant collaboration around the tension of our differences, and our mutual commitment to co-create a connecting, thriving relationship and a more effective therapeutic process for couples. The success of our relationship is largely a product of the experiments we developed to improve it. After testing them in the clinic, those that repeatedly worked became core theory and the practices that contributed to success of the Imago system.

Forty years ago, when we began our conversations, the field of couples therapy practiced what we now call parallel or therapist-centered psychotherapy. Since couple's therapy is a derivative of psychotherapy, it made sense that the therapist would primarily interact with each partner to discover their history and their view of the problem, and then help them learn better communication skills that would resolve conflict and solve problems. However, the success rate of couples therapy then was about forty percent (Grande, 2017).

We decided to try something different. We created what we now call couple-centered therapy. In this type of therapy, the couple is the center and the therapist is at the periphery, facilitating a conversation between partners rather than talking to each partner in the presence of the other partner. The outcome of that was Imago Relationship Therapy, which we present in this book.

In these pages, we share a brief narrative of the sequence and process of our discovering and developing the core concepts and practices of Imago, with credits to couples who became our teachers.

IMAGO DIALOGUE

Our first discovery led to the creation of Imago Dialogue, the singular therapeutic intervention of Imago. We were about seven months into our relationship, which had always been intense and not always positive, when in the middle of an altercation, Helen stood up and adamantly said: "Stop! One of us talk and the other listen," which we did. The deceleration of our negative feelings was so dramatic that it aroused our professional curiosity and we took the "taking turns talking" process to the clinic. As a precis to couples centered therapy (or Imago Therapy) we asked couples to face each other and then facilitated a conversation between them rather than with us. To structure the conversation and regulate affect, we eventually developed sentence stems. We asked the speaking partner to repeat the sentence stem and then to complete the sentence with their own content. The content exchanged was also regulated by asking couples to speak from their experience and refrain from any descriptions of their partner, either negative or positive, and to mirror accurately, and without comment, what their partner said.

The results were immediate. Couples calmed down and began to talk—and more importantly, listen—to each other at deeper and deeper levels. As the energy between them changed from negative to positive, their glare was replaced with a gaze, anger gave way to tears, and avoidance was replaced with engagement and touch. We eventually developed "taking turns" into the three-step process: mirroring, validating, and empathizing—called Imago Dialogue—which has become Imago's central intervention. The most exciting and unexpected consequence of the dialogical process that we observed was the creation of safety. In a predictably safe environment, couples were enabled to relax their defenses, practiced since childhood, and become vulnerable and present to each other, effecting profound intrapsychic changes because of changes in the quality of their interactions with each other.

ZERO NEGATIVITY

Our second discovery was the necessity and power of Zero Negativity, removing all negativity from the relationship. We discovered the importance of this concept 18 years into our marriage, when we found ourselves at the brink of divorce. While separated, we decided to go on a date to a bookstore, our favorite activity. As a lark, we went to the esoteric rather than the psychological or philosophical sections we tended to haunt. There we discovered a book of essays on relationships between persons with different astrological signs. When we turned to Virgo–Aquarian relationships, we were shocked that the description of the intense negativity of couples with our astrological signs so accurately described our relationship. Taking it as a sign, Helen proposed that we begin the practice of eliminating negativity and use a calendar to record the days when either or both of us engaged in negative exchanges. If either experienced a negative message, we would quickly restore connection. Six weeks later, we began to experience dramatic change. And in nine months, we were ready for a recommitment ceremony and a new, dream marriage which has grown in richness and excitement ever since.

The lesson we learned from our experiment, and from observing the impact of negativity on other couples, was that negativity is fatal in relationships, and needs to be removed entirely. To implement its removal, we asked couples at the beginning of therapy to emulate what we were doing: remove all negative statements—shame, blame, guilting, etc.—from their relationship and to keep track of their success with a calendar. After observing that all couples who committed to the process began to move through their impasse, we invented the concept of Zero Negativity, a clinical process of removing all negativity, and a reconnecting process to quickly restore connection when they failed. We then added the theory of Zero Negativity and the Zero Negativity process to the core of Imago theory and practice.

THE AFFIRMATIONS PROCESS

Very shortly afterwards, we discovered that most couples initially made great progress—sometimes falling in love again—but then had great difficulty sustaining their gains and, mysteriously, became very anxious when trying to do so. Without going into much detail here, we discovered in brain science research that our brains have a negativity bias that has been a primary defense for as long as there have been brains. And when couples removed negativity, the brain lost its homeostatic balance, and without its evolutionary weapon of protective paranoia, it did not know what to do to survive, so it became anxious and reengaged its defenses.

That raised the question of what could replace negativity and remove anxiety so that couples could sustain connecting. Further research and experiments led to our understanding that the chaos and anxiety the brain experienced could be changed by giving it something new and positive to do. Since Helen had changed from using bedtime to help me improve to engaging in a mutual exchange of three appreciations—which helped us experience intimacy—we decided to pass that information on to couples. What made this successful, we learned, was that the daily exchange of positive energy made it predictable, a feature the brain needs in order to integrate it. And if they failed, we provided them with a quick reconnecting process so they would not be habituated to disconnection. With repeated practice, couples learned that positive energy expressed as appreciations, acknowledging caring behaviors, and engaging in surprises and spontaneous play equipped the brain with the tools it needed to create the safe environment required by the survival directive. We called the new concept and process the Affirmations process.

Over time, as we facilitated Imago Dialogue for all conversations and the replacement of negativity with affirmations as the culture of the relationship, we discovered a near total reduction in anxiety and defensive behaviors. Upon exploration with couples about that effect and examining our own relationship, we came to the conviction that safety was the nonnegotiable quality of a thriving relationship.

THE SPACE-BETWEEN

One day we found ourselves thinking a previously unthinkable thought: *The problems couples bring to our offices are not located inside themselves, where they have been since the founding of psychotherapy in the late nineteenth century. They are located in their interactions with each other, in the space between them.*

We then surmised, if problems are precipitated by interactions with others, then change has to be initiated from the same place—from the interactive rather than the intrapsychic space. We further posited that change in the interactive space produces new experiences which are recorded in the memory configurations of the hippocampal library.

Thus, the content of "inside" is the experience of the "outside." If the outside is dangerous, then the inside will reflect it. If the outside is safe, then memory stores that experience. It also followed, logically, that changing memory requires changes in the interactive space which in turn, like the original constellations of memory, would change the intrapsychic space. Since the oscillation between the interactive and the intrapsychic space seems to be how life works, interventions should be activated at the source of experience, which is relocated to interactions with the outside social world rather than the interior of the psyche.

Coming to the conclusion that what transforms couples' relationships is not the depth of their internal explorations, nor historical exploration nor insight, but the quality of their interactions with each other led to the question of the necessary conditions for relationship transformation. It turned out to be simple: the requirement for all thriving organisms is Safety. The mechanisms of safety turn out to be structured conversations called Imago Dialogue, a commitment to and practice of Zero Negativity, and the exchange of at least three daily affirmations.

We eventually called the interaction between partners "the Space-Between," informed and inspired by the I–Thou constructs of Martin Buber, a Jewish mystical theologian, and Harry Stack Sullivan, a psychiatrist who posited that what happens between people is what matters, not what happens within them.

Over time, we became clear that life is lived in the Space-Between, which populates the Space-Within. The quality of relationship is the active agent of change.

FROM THE INDIVIDUAL PARADIGM
TO THE RELATIONAL PARADIGM

Then we came to another conclusion: the roots of psychology (which is the logos of the psyche) is the separate self of western culture and was modeled after the atom—which Newton proclaimed was that out of which everything is made. Freud converted this separate self into the psychological self by endowing it with an interior world called subjectivity. That is the client we meet when we begin our therapeutic work. Couples, from that perspective, are two individuals, essentially separate, who are trying to live together without conflict and hopefully with satisfaction and, sometimes, joyful aliveness. To overcome their alienation, they were directed to explore their inner world of feeling and memories in order to acquire insight which would restore them to their pre-neurotic condition. This autonomous self eventually became the centerpiece of civilization, giving birth to the Individual Paradigm.

For us, the discovery of the centrality of relationship conflicted with this perspective, which was and is the orthodoxy of our profession. Since we were certain that the formation, challenge, and transformation of the self is in relationship, we needed a scientific grounding for "relationship as reality" that matched the ground of the separate self. Our search began with a review of Freudian literature and the history of psychotherapy where we discovered, serendipitously, a relational thread in Freud (see Chapter 1) that was woven into a tapestry by the end of the twentieth century, and led to the formulation of a new paradigm we call the "relational paradigm."

Essentially, this paradigm makes relationship central and the individual peripheral; distinct from the individual paradigm which makes the self the center of reality and relationship peripheral or optional. Therapy in the individual paradigm is understanding leading to insight and the release of internal constraints. In the relational paradigm, therapy is a function of resonance and connecting made possible by safe exchanges in the Space-Between that lead to the experience of connecting, full aliveness, joy, and wonder.

FROM THE RELATIONAL PARADIGM
TO THE QUANTUM FIELD

Since relational reality has no ground in psychology (since by definition, psychology is about the self), we proceeded to ask the question: if the paradigm of the individual is grounded in the hardcore science of Newtonian atomism (and since that paradigm does not contain data of the foundational reality of relationship) is it possible to ground the relational paradigm in another hardcore science, quantum physics, that posits the interconnectivity of everything?

When we began dating in 1977, both of us were reading about quantum theory. Through the lens of quantum theory, we learned that reality is a connecting field of energy–information–consciousness in which all forms—including the universe itself—arise and dissolve. In quantum theory, this is called the particle–wave duality. This perspective posits the field as primary and the form as secondary, and interconnecting as the primary feature of nature. We began to language our thoughts that quantum physics is the ground of the relational paradigm and of Imago Relationship Therapy.

One day we woke up and realized that our relationship was an instance of the particle–wave duality. That showed up in the way we posed answers to the question of why couples fight. Helen had long lists, making suggestion after suggestion. Harville had a short list, which he minimally refined. Helen was the wave with an infinity of answers, Harville was the particle who distilled all the answers into one: because those particles cannot tolerate difference. Following up on this process, Helen queried: can't we think of every couple as a particle–wave duality? That clinched the shift from classical physics, the ground of psychology, to the quantum field as the ground of Imago.

With this understanding, our formulation of the Space-Between became less a metaphor and more an instance of "real space," a manifestation of the quantum field containing the same energies that constituted the space between subatomic particles and galactic forms. In this Space-Between, everything arises and disappears in a never-ending process of information exchange. It is the same field that is inside every cell of our bodies; it is the synapse between each of the billions of cells in our brains; it is the "between" of the double helix that constitutes our DNA, as well as the DNA in all other life forms. The polarities interact with each other in a continuous exchange of energy that offers an infinite number of possible outcomes until one is chosen.

When couples shift the focus from themselves as discrete entities vying for need satisfaction to creating safety in their relationship, when they stop competing for emotional resources and focus on the quality of the Space-Between, their unmet needs from childhood, plus their yearnings unsatisfied in their marriage, dissolve into the flow of "being present" to each other without judgment—a condition created by reliable safety in the Space-Between. Couples discover that connecting is their essence, and disconnection is their problem and the source of their complaints. Connecting appears to be what they want and is thus the goal of therapy. Moving away from the abstract of the Space-Between to these concrete activities made us feel that Imago Relationship Therapy was finally complete.

As contemporary psychotherapy and couples therapy was grounded in classical physics, we view the quantum field as the ground for the reinvention of our view of humanity as a whole and the person as a location in the whole. Looking at reality in general and humanity in particular through the lens of ontological connecting can lead not only to the reconstruction of all our disciplines, like psychology and therapy, but to the reconstruction of all our philosophies and social institutions.

Introduction

We have a stealthy purpose in writing this book! And we welcome your joining us on this journey of discovery and wonder.

We think a fundamental cultural shift is underway in how we look at the world, at our view of others, how we *interact* with them, what suffering is, why we suffer and how to respond to it, and how to go beyond surviving to thriving. We share it because we think it has radical implications for our profession as therapists, as well as for the human sciences in general. Our hope is that you might embrace and use this new perspective to guide your interaction with those whom you see as clients, especially couples.

Our intention is to introduce this new worldview as the theoretical foundation of a couples therapy called Imago Relationship Therapy, and to show, through the concreteness of a therapeutic process, the relevance of this new perspective to how we live everyday life.

The central narrative of Imago therapy is our answer to the question we posed at the beginning of our personal relationship and our exploration of the purpose, function, and dynamics of couplehood. The question is: Why do couples fight? That question evolved into several other questions. 1) Why does anyone fight? 2) What happens when they do? 3) What can be done about it? While we will offer our answers to these important questions, most of this book is a response to the last question.

Our work is rooted in decades of attempting to understand the human condition, especially suffering, and to find effective ways to ameliorate it. When Imago is embraced as a theory and operationalized as a therapy, it helps couples transform conflict into connecting*, thus concretely situating them in the new perspective as a new way of life. And it not only works for couples in therapy—it works for everyone.

Our intended audience includes all clinical professionals, college and

---

* We use the gerund "connecting" as the process that is happening in Imago therapy. Although it may seem awkward at first reading, it describes our state of being: active, vibrant, and interrelating at all times. Therapy is needed, as you will read in the pages, when the experience of this reality is ruptured in the developmental process.

university faculties who are teaching and engaged in research, graduate students in all fields of mental health (especially marriage and family therapy), undergraduate students in psychology, other professionals interested in relationship education and social change, as well as anyone who is curious about "relationships," especially intimate ones.

In this Introduction, we give you a bird's eye view of the primary assumptions, or metatheory, behind the clinical theory and clinical practices we will elaborate. If you know the why, which is the metatheory, then the what of clinical theory and practice may make more sense to you.

WHAT IS IMAGO?

At the linguistic level, "Imago" is Latin for the English word "image." Our use of the term goes back to our first training group in 1980, in which our trainees contributed to naming the therapy system we were developing that focused on how the "image" we all develop in childhood, while interacting with our caretakers, influences whom we choose as an intimate partner in adulthood. Since "image therapy" was not attractive to any of us, we decided to use the Latin word for image and call the new therapy Imago Relationship Therapy.

At the clinical level, "Imago" is a composite image of our caretakers. While it is unseen and unconscious, the Imago is the template created in childhood of the person to whom we will be drawn as our intimate partner in adulthood. When there is similarity between the memory constellation and the traits of a potential partner, the positive energy generated is called romantic love. We call the relationship that evolves out of this attraction an "Imago-Match." This is the person with whom we will experience our deepest hurts and our most profound transformation. Later, when the positive energy is replaced by negative energy, partners experience intense emotional pain and polarize and enter a second stage called "the power struggle." The purpose of this book is to understand these patterns in all intimate relationships and to describe what can be done about them to help couples move from an unconscious relationship to another stage that we call conscious partnership.

As an intellectual system, Imago theory is a new way of thinking about "relationship" itself and proposes that being-in-relationship is our primary reality. Or, to put it another way, there is no "being" outside of relationship. We are not only relational creatures, possessing relational interests and needs, we *are* our relationships; *we are* "relating." It is our nature. This perspective differentiates Imago theory from other psychological and therapeutic systems that place "self," with relational features, as primary reality. As we will discuss later, the "self" that has been the foundational construct in western psychology and therapy, was modeled after the separate and unchangeable atom in classical physics. As a complement to the idea of the separate self, self as being-in-relationship as our primary reality is rooted in quantum cosmology about how the universe works, and in quantum field theory which posits "reality" as a "field of energy–information–awareness" in which every "thing" is interconnected and connecting. We believe that looking at our world and at ourselves through the quantum lens has profound implications for revising our view of ourselves and how we need to interact with others, and also offers a process for doing it—deeply impacting how mental health practitioners conceive of and do our work.

While the focus in this book is expressed operationally as doing couples therapy, teaching relationship education, and launching a social movement, Imago as an intellectual system grounded in the quantum field has implications for how all relationships work. The processes in the micro world of the couple are operative in the macro world of society and culture, which means that processes that occur clinically with couples impact the culture and the processes that occur in culture impact the couple. While the elaboration of the personal–cultural complementarity will not be done in this book, it will be implied and referred to, and appears as a vision and proposal in the Conclusion.

You may be an expert (or on your way to becoming one) who has taken on the task of reducing friction and increasing positive engagement between partners in couples therapy, or some other form of therapy, in the service of cultural transformation. We (Harville and Helen) present, as *our* perspective, a structured process that we think can encourage dialogue in the service of replacing an unconscious relationship with a conscious partnership, and an individualistic culture with a relational civilization. We invite you to consider *your* perspective on these issues and how you might want to relate to ours.

Since this is a ponderous book and very long, in this Introduction we provide you with an overview which we hope will entice you to read every chapter. If not, you will have an outline of what it contains. If you find it repetitive in some places, we think the point is important enough to remind you of it.

THE ISSUE OF PERSPECTIVE

Let's start with the idea of perspective.

It is fascinating to us that, according to the sciences of perception, there are no colors in the physical universe. There are only photons, which are particles of light, and light is "white." White exists and is visible only because of the blackness of the universe in which the photons appear. All the color we see is a function of receptors in our eyes that send signals to the visual centers of the brain which translates them into a spectrum of colors.

According to brain science, this is how it happens:

> *In humans and a number of other mammals, light enters the eye through the cornea and is focused by the lens onto the retina, a light-sensitive membrane at the back of the eye. The retina serves as a transducer for the conversion of light into neuronal signals. This transduction is achieved by specialized photoreceptive cells of the retina, also known as the rods and cones, which detect the photons of light and respond by producing neural impulses. These signals are transmitted by the optic nerve, from the retina upstream to central ganglia in the brain. (Visual Perception, n.d)*

So far as *our experience* is concerned, our *world view* of the physical world is that color is a feature of physical reality. Without knowing how our visual system works, we would assume that what we see is what is there, and what we believe—our world view—is that color is a feature of the universe, rather than a function of the way our brain is structured and how it receives information and what it does with it.

Parallel to the physical sciences (which tell us that we receive information from the wave field of the environment and put together a story about how the universe looks and how it works) are the human sciences, which posit the same process in the social and psychological world. They posit that our brains cannot not see the world "as it is." Instead it receives signals from the natural and social environments and weaves those signals into a composition that becomes "our social world," a picture about how humans organize themselves as groups, how they are organized inside, the challenges that constitute human experience, their potential, and the transformative processes that help them achieve it. Since this is the way our brains work in nature and society, that is how it works in our interaction with our clients.

In effect, when we sit with our clients, we do not see them as they are. We see them as we are. Every observation we experience as a perception is an interpretation. Experiencing reality objectively is not an option, because objectivity is not a capacity of the human brain. Perception appears to be receiving what is presenting itself, but the receptive mechanisms of the brain limit it to *interpretation*, therefore all perspectives are relative to the position of the observer and how the observer interacts with the observed. Just as everyone unconsciously looks for a partner through a lens shaped by childhood memories, we therapists unconsciously look at our clients through a lens shaped by our own personal history—and the implicit assumptions which are embedded in our professional training—and by the unconscious assumptions of the culture that inhabits our mental content as "reality"; our belief system. This is normal, of course, but it is an important observation to make, because we influence our clients by the very fact of observing them, and how we observe them influences how they show themselves to us.

In our opinion, as therapists, it is extremely important that we know our perspective, because we cannot NOT have one; and it is important that you know yours, because you cannot NOT have one. You may or may not choose to join the Imago perspective, but it is important that you know you have one and are intentional in selecting it.

What all this means for us is that we want to acknowledge that Imago is a lens through which we look at couples and interact with them. Before we get into an overview of Imago theory and practice, we want to take a short detour to describe that *Imago lens* through which an Imago therapist looks at the client couple and the therapy process. We call it Imago "metatheory."

METATHEORY AS PERSPECTIVE

Metatheory is the "why" perspective behind the clinical theory and clinical practices. It is the theory behind the theory or the foundation upon which the clinical system is based.

Given this book is about therapy, it makes sense to us that a book on therapy should have a theory of suffering: what it is, what causes it, and how to resolve it. At the outset, it is important to emphasize that the answer to those questions—like the answer to all significant life questions—are always rooted in a sociocultural context that defines who we are, as humans, as well as what suffering is and how it can be resolved. Since Imago offers a theory of suffering and a method of intervention, it is important to locate Imago in the historical discussion of suffering and its amelioration.

Who Are We and Why Do We Suffer?

Over historical time, we have collectively redefined ourselves, our human identity, and our view of suffering and its mitigation only twice. In all the ages of human speculation on our fate, suffering itself (as a phenomenal experience) has been identified as anxiety, but the cause of and relief from anxiety has been connected to two world views based on the physics of the time. From our perspective, a third perspective of who we are and our existential situation is emerging from our collective consciousness as a result of the emergence of a new view of physical reality called quantum field theory. As an onramp to the present, we will mention all this here and elaborate in Chapter 1.

The first theory of physical reality is called the geocentric view, or the

Ptolemaic universe. This theory is named after Ptolemy, who is designated by historians as the world's first physicist and lived in Greece around 100 AD. In a geocentric universe, the earth is at the center of all the heavenly bodies. Theologically, it is also at the middle sphere of a three-tiered space where humans live, an upper tier inhabited by divine powers, and a lower sphere which was the fate of anyone who did not obey the tenets of the occupant of the upper sphere. In the Ptolemaic universe, humans were *special creations of transcendent powers* to whom they belonged and to whom they owed allegiance. Suffering was anxiety caused by disobedience of divine powers in the upper sphere, and the alleviation of suffering was simple: remorse and abject obedience expressed through various rituals of sacrifice.

This view remained unchanged until the sixteenth century, when *we became creatures of nature*, not of mythological gods. This radical redefinition of our human identity replaced faith with reason as the primary mode of knowing, the communal self of classical antiquity with "separate" self that was modeled after the separate and uncuttable atom of classical physics, and a primarily instinctual nature based on evolutionary biology. By the nineteenth century, we were no longer children of the gods nor creatures with a pristine rationality, but a creature of nature driven as all other creatures by survival instincts that placed us in perpetual competition for our resources.

Into this new model of the self, Sigmund Freud, the founder of psychotherapy, injected a tripartite inner world—id, ego, and superego—that mirrored the social forces of the culture at that time: reason, instincts, and morality. The push of the instinctual life force against the resistance of the internalized cultural value system produced feelings of guilt that triggered anxiety, as suffering, about the potential punishment of the id by the superego. This conflict was managed by hiding our animal nature from ourselves. To find relief, it became necessary to discover and to bring our instinctual nature out of its hidden place and restore it to full functions without activating the self's punitive moral structure.

In the late nineteenth century and the early twentieth, Ptolemaic physics was replaced by Newtonian physics, which included a new theory of physical reality called quantum mechanics. Instead of identity as a tribal member or an individual self that is separate from and in competition with others in the natural order, human beings, in quantum field theory, can be viewed as citizens of a conscious and connecting universe with a cosmic identity. In this universe, in which we are intrinsically connecting, suffering is anxiety about the actual or possible rupture of the experience of our cosmic belonging that happens when connecting with a significant other is ruptured. Rupture at the cosmic level is simultaneous with rupture at the personal level. Anxiety is about the possibility that relational rupture will result in the loss of the experience of being; i.e., of non-being.

This model of the self and its problem has not yet been adopted by the human sciences and psychotherapy. We present it for consideration.

From Metatheory to Clinical Theory

Let us move now from metatheory to clinical theory and share our perspective on how the human story evolves in a connecting universe, who we are as human beings in that universe, why we suffer, and how we can respond to it effectively.

OUR RELATIONAL IDENTITY

In the middle of the twentieth century, in the fields of psychology and psychotherapy, a relational *feature* of the self was discovered that eventually evolved into the construct of *a relational self*, in whom autonomy and independence was replaced with essential interdependence and interpenetrating subjectivities, which led to a view of the self as "relationship." Given the emergence of this relational paradigm and the availability of quantum field theory as a resource for redefining human identity, the human situation, and the problem of suffering, Imago theory posits that human beings are born experiencing connecting to Being through an attuned caretaker. The baby and caretaker are two poles in a seamless, harmonious bond called resonance. The caretaker smiles and sings, and the baby laughs and coos. The baby's survival depends upon this mutual intuition they share with their caretakers. As long as the caretaker stays resonant with the child's experiences, the child's connecting to the caretaker is sustained and, through the caretaker, the child's connecting to the universe. To achieve that, the caretaker must "know" what the baby needs and act on that knowingness to keep the child safe and happy. The challenge to the caretaker and the fate of the child is the ability and willingness of the caretaker to sustain connecting across the developmental stages so that as the child becomes an adult, the experience of connecting with Being is sustained. The caretaker is the conduit to our relational identity as human beings and to our "cosmic identity" as participants in a connecting universe. The caretaker is the conduit to the cosmos.

Our Problem: Ruptured Connecting

We posit that every child who was ever born, in all caretaker–infant relationships in all of human history, has experienced a rupture with their caretaker that simultaneously ruptured the child's experience of connecting to the universe. The connectional rupture replaces the sensation of full aliveness, that is intrinsic to us, with anxiety about the local connection to the caretaker and distally to Being itself. That rupture follows the child into adult life and into intimate partnerships.

Why do we say that loss of connecting is universal? Because we humans have not evolved to the point that we know how to sustain connecting with our children, or our partners, or anyone else. Given the limits of all caretakers for all of human history, rupture occurs early, and our first and most profound losses occur in childhood. These ruptures are inevitable. It does not mean that our parents were ogres (although some are). For most people it just means that our parents were flawed human beings. (Surprise!) As the child grows through the stages of development, if the ruptures are constant or permanent, they experience these losses as a disruption of their universal sense of belonging—of Being—although they wouldn't be able to put it that way. They might not be able to recognize that they are angry or depressed or feel worthless because of the sensation of connecting. This leads to self-absorption, loss of empathy, and objectification of Other. During the teenage years, they start searching in all the wrong places for stimulation that they hope will calm their anxiety and allow them to recover aliveness and joy.

We will spend some time later in this book learning about childhood ruptures and how they are likely to manifest in relationships, and therefore how to treat them. But for now, let us follow one thread that begins in these large and small ruptures and winds itself around everything that happens after. This unraveled thread is our search to find other intimate connections that are as life-giving as the ones that are now broken. We spend our lives looking for the same safety as our first secure connections. We don't know that's what driving our decisions and our behavior, but for most of us, trying to establish positive intimate connections is thematic.

Our Search for Restored Connecting

The search for safety and connecting begins in the early school years when we start auditioning BFFs (best friends forever). In adolescence, we venture into the risky territory of crushes and infatuations and romantic skirmishes. When we get older, we start looking for romantic love. When we find it, we feel like we are home free as we experience the bliss of romantic and sexual attraction. All of a sudden, we are more happy, creative, energetic, and, most of all, more beautiful than we have ever been in our entire life.

The Imago

One of the most important elements of Imago theory is that we are attracted to potential partners who have the same traits as the parent with whom we had the most difficulty. We say they are an "Imago-Match." Who could imagine that we would want to be with a man who is as unavailable as our father was, or as intrusive as our mother? It is unconscious, of course, and it defies logic that we would want to replay the drama we experienced with our mother who was overly controlling or, conversely, dependent. The traits are not gender-specific, but our propensity for the familiar conflict or obstacle or injury is undeniable. Never underestimate the power of the unmet needs that slumber fitfully in the unconscious.

Romantic Love: Temporary Restoration of Connecting

Romantic love, which is discussed in Chapter 6, is so magnificent because it is a transient recovery of the experience of connecting and the sensation of joyful aliveness. It is so powerful, and the lover is so beautiful or handsome, because they are the conduit to experiencing Being. But the connection between the two is not in our awareness. And, because we have not evolved enough as a species to know this and to sustain it, it is transient. Like the rupture in childhood when the caretaker was not reliably available emotionally or physically, or both, the romantic partner triggers this primal memory, and we find ourselves battling it out with our partner in a power struggle. In a cruel paradox, our beloved has become our enemy, the dream has become a nightmare.

How could this have happened?

The Power Struggle: Connecting Is Lost Again

The seeds of marital conflict are sown unwittingly in childhood through moments of neglect, anger, and insensitivity. We can add to this legacy of early deficit parenting all the other baggage both partners bring to their romantic relationship, including the childhood challenges, defenses, and character flaws they developed when they were younger. As the partners' frustration with each other escalates, the emotional symbiosis they formed during the romantic stage is ruptured. And they react with the same unconscious and automatic defensive adaptations that they developed in childhood. Spontaneous feelings of romantic love are replaced with negativity that triggers anxiety and defenses. Increasingly, they use negative reactions and other forms of coercion to get their needs met. And they end up unconsciously reexperiencing and reacting to each other in the same ways they did toward their imperfectly attuned caretakers during childhood.

From Conflict to Connecting

It is a paradox that our beloved becomes our enemy. But it is a double paradox that our beloved enemy can in turn become the source of our transformation. Estranged partners have the potential to be each other's best resources for restoring connecting. Warring partners can become allies. They can lose their sense of alienation, reform their defenses, change their behavior, and reexperience the safety that will restore connecting and love. In fact, in Imago we say that the *unconscious purpose of marriage is to finish childhood* and go on to live your best life.

The Process of Restoring Connecting

It is important now to introduce the ground from which this healing begins to take shape. A guiding principle for the therapist is the concept of the *Space-Between*. It is a way to focus attention on the atmosphere the couple has formed around them. From the quantum perspective, there is a field of energy between partners that holds them in a certain position in relation to each other, and their bond is strong in some ways and weak in others. We want to help them change the energy and the elements that make up their bond, and thereby, change their relationship—and then their interior world changes.

The basic tenet of Imago is: ***Being present and connecting through relationship is ultimately what transforms both partners, not attempting to change themselves or their partner as separate individuals.*** One of the therapeutic implications of this tenet is that *the important action takes place between the partners, not between the partners and the therapist.* And at this point, the therapist is an invaluable guide, but not the resource for their transformation. Developing the concept of the Space-Between makes it possible for the therapist to redirect the partners to look to their tripartite reality for the solutions they seek. By paying attention to the atmosphere they have created around themselves, each partner is de-pathologized as the focal point of the problem, and the emphasis is placed on the attitudes and feelings that will allow them to experience safety so they can work together in ways that are collaborative, cooperative, co-creative, and appreciative rather than competitive and controlling.

THE NONNEGOTIABLE CONDITIONS FOR RESTORING AND SUSTAINING CONNECTING

All Imago tools and techniques have the establishment of safety as their stated outcome or their intended effect. The partners have to know that they will never be attacked, discounted, or dismissed. *Their safety has to be absolutely reliable and predictable.*

The three practices that create and sustain safety include:

1. **Imago Dialogue:** Imago Dialogue is a three-step, structured way of talking that proceeds with a sequential use of specific sentence stems. The structure makes the Space-Between a safe place to talk; the sequential use of specific sentence stems helps

the brain know what is coming next; and the sentence stems, in the process, integrate the cognitive and emotional regions of the brain so that reactivity is eventually replaced with intentionality and safe social engagement.

2. **The Zero Negativity Process:** Going Zero Negative is the central challenge in establishing safety and restoring connecting. One of the most important functions of the therapist is to educate couples about these unconscious negative reactions, helping them recognize on their own when they are guilty of assault and helping them learn the Dialogue process, which when properly practiced makes rampant negativity impossible. You will find a thorough vetting of this process in Chapter 15.

3. **The Affirmations Process:** Two things that help couples increase safety and deepen engagement are curiosity and affirmations. When couples replace a negative response (such as criticism) with curiosity, they engage their prefrontal cortex rather than their lower reptilian brain. Once they are curious, if they then express strong affirmations of the value of the other, and do that reliably, protective systems in their brains will relax and the partners can connect. Since the brain has a negativity bias because of the millions of years we humans lived in unsafe environments (Vaish et al., 2008), it is not enough just to banish all negativity. That leaves the brain without its primary defense. When the affirmations process replaces negativity, and the brain experiences safety and assurance of survival as a consequence, the brain eventually replaces negativity with positive social engagement as a lifestyle.

If the rules are followed and the techniques are actively and consistently practiced, Imago Dialogue, Zero Negativity, and Affirmations will be the engine of transformation that leads to brain integration and a conscious partnership. As a therapist, you are undeniably a huge part of the movement to transform lives when you facilitate all of this.

HOW TO USE THIS BOOK: THE PARTS AND THE CHAPTERS

In the first two chapters, which constitute Part I, we present the metatheory of Imago in which the clinical theory is grounded. In Part II we present Imago clinical theory in which the clinical processes are grounded. Part III is a description and illustration of the core Imago process—Imago Dialogue— and explores the mechanics and artistry of being an Imago therapist. In

Part IV, you will find six chapters on clinical practices. For now, it is important to get to know the general terrain of Imago and to follow the path from metatheory to clinical theory to clinical processes to clinical practice. We will do that by walking you through the Parts and Chapters. They constitute the Imago narrative.

In the Introduction, which you have just read, we have discussed perspective—what is and why it is important. We invite you, as reader and therapist, to reflect on the lens through which you look at the world and imagine how it impacts how you think about and interact with couples. Moving forward, in Chapter 1, our first intention is to portray metatheory as the fundamental assumptions behind clinical theory and practice. We start our Imago narrative with a discussion of perspective itself and state that all perception is mediated through a perspective. Then we share the Imago perspective.

Our second intention in Chapter 1 is to situate Imago metatheory in the context of the history of psychology and psychotherapy. Our interest is to trace the intuition of the relational nature of the human psyche from Freudian subjectivism to Imago's interconnectivity. Along the way, we develop the concept of the relational paradigm as foundational.

In Chapter 2, we ground Imago metatheory in the relational paradigm, which itself is grounded in quantum field theory. The core thesis of Imago metatheory is that we live in a "connecting" universe in which everything and everyone is connecting, and that connecting is our nature, or essence. *Connecting is Being and Being is Connecting.* This is the lens through which we "look" at our clients, their problems, and their potential.

In Part II, Clinical Theory, Chapter 3, we describe how our brains work with special reference to relationship. In Chapter 4, we posit that our deepest desire is to sustain original connecting, which is possible only when we constellate *safe* relationships. Developmental arrest at any developmental stage results in a symbiotic consciousness—a mental condition that merges others with the self—and that is the problem that is brought into our adult relationships. In Chapter 5, on Ruptured Connecting, we identify and discuss the human problem as ruptured connecting. Connecting itself is ontological—a reality that cannot be lost—but the "felt sense" of connecting is fragile and can be lost from our awareness in a negative exchange. Chapter 6 introduces the Imago and describes romantic love as temporary reconnecting and the power struggle as the second loss of connecting. Chapter 7 describes the conditions that must be met to create a conscious partnership which recovers and sustains our original condition of connecting. Chapter 8 is a description of the developmental stage issues that will help you, as therapist, distinguish the nuances of developmental challenges in the couple's relationship and how those challenges are overcome in a conscious partnership.

In Part III, Imago Clinical Processes, Chapter 9 introduces and describes the Imago Dialogue Process. This is the singular intervention that Imago therapists facilitate and the singular required skill that couples must learn and practice to create and sustain a conscious partnership. In Chapter 10 we define the Imago therapist as a facilitator and engage you, the reader, in some reflection on your identity, beliefs, and function as a couples therapist. Chapter 11 is about the mechanics and art of the therapy process between therapist and the couple. What should therapists do? What are the best Imago practices? What should the couple do?

In Part IV, Imago Clinical Practices, we introduce the six steps to conscious partnership and the practices used to facilitate the process and achieve the therapeutic goal of Imago therapy: restoring connecting. We present the six steps in a linear fashion because there is a logical sequence to the flow. But we do not prescribe nor mandate that linearity be the guide for the sequence. Although the logic of the sequence provides coherence to the therapy process, life and the therapy sessions do not always follow our road map, and we have to adjust.

In fact, the flow of therapy tends to be like a spiral rather than a circle or a line. The spiral shows therapy as returning to the beginning as experience deepens and then moving to higher, or deeper, levels of experiencing as therapy progresses. Nevertheless, the value of the sequence is that it describes the essential ingredients of a completed therapy process, so you know when you are finished!

Each chapter that follows begins with a description of a specific topic—like the couple's vision for their relationship—the rationale for that topic, and how to facilitate the conversation about that topic. Each chapter includes a lengthy illustration of the details of facilitating the Imago Dialogue process and the necessity and value of the regular use of specific sentence stems. While it is acceptable to follow the sequence of processes below or invoke them as needed in real time as the therapy process proceeds, in Chapter 12 we advise Imago therapists to start couples with Revisioning, which both defines the goal and outcome of therapy, and then shift (Chapter 13) to Recommitting to help them become intentional and also to remove any impediments to achieving their goal. Chapter 14 describes processes that invite couples to replace their symbiotic consciousness with differentiation and to deepen connecting, and Chapter 15 guides the therapist to help couples remove the most powerful impediment to their success: negativity. To operationalize Zero Negativity (Chapter 16) clients discover the wish embedded in the frustration and learn to express the wish instead of the frustration. And we close out the process, in Chapter 17, with processes that help couples reexperience and sustain connecting: the recovery of romantic love.

These processes focus on the quality of the Space-Between partners. The emphasis is not on solving each person's particular problems but on sowing seeds of harmony in the psychic space that unites them. This harmony creates presence and resonance, and since these were resources missing in childhood that ruptured connecting, their recovery dissolves the source of symptoms, thus the core cause, and restores connecting, which is the core solution. By doing these practices, first with the facilitation of the therapist and later on their own, couples will come to love the resultant flourishing accompanied with sensations of full aliveness, joyful relaxation and wonder, and are now in the territory of real love.

THE ULTIMATE GOAL

Humans cannot exist joyfully without connecting. It is our nature. It is the substance of our being, and without it the world seems empty and dark, like a vast ocean. Universally, couples desire to have the relationship of their dreams. No matter what their complaint or symptom or the details of their vision, embedded in every couple's vision of their dream relationship will be the desire to experience connecting. Their bodies are exquisitely designed for the sensation of full aliveness, relaxed joyfulness, and wonder. Since that is what they really want, the intention of the Imago therapist is to facilitate their creating that. While one of these exercises, Revisioning, focuses on designing it, and Re-romanticizing restores and sustains it, connecting and the sensation of aliveness and joy are the ultimate goals of the whole therapy process.

We encourage you to read the chapters sequentially because each is a continuation of the flow. If you are not interested in metatheory, you might skip the first two chapters. If you just want to know the "how," you may skip to Part IV, where you will find guidance for Imago Clinical Practice in the last several chapters. The only problem with opting for this is that the rationale of all the other chapters will be missing, so you may not know "why" you are engaging in the clinical practices!

It is an honor to walk with you on the journey through Imago theory, processes, and practices. Thanks for joining us on this mission.

Part I

IMAGO METATHEORY

INTRODUCTION TO METATHEORY

When you are sitting with partners who are glaring at each other, how you will respond to them depends upon your metatheory, your unconscious assumption about who couples are and why couples fight. We remind you that we cannot see couples as they "are," but only through our interpretative filter. We call this metatheory.

Imago metatheory, to which we turn in a moment, is the ground of clinical theory, which is the ground of clinical processes, which are operationalized in clinical practices. Think of metatheory as a **vision** that gives form to the whole, within which all the parts fit and without which they would not exist. In one sense, metatheory is the highest level of abstraction, but in another it is the most concrete because it is expressed in every interaction we have with our clients, and everyone else.

To show the extent and profundity of the world view change we see coming, in the sections below, we provide a brief contrast between the old worldview we currently inhabit and the new one that is emerging. Notice that both of them are rooted in physics and the transition from our current worldview to a new worldview is a shift from classical mechanics to quantum physics.

OUR CURRENT WORLDVIEW IN A NUTSHELL

In the first chapter on Imago metatheory, Chapter 1, we review and analyze the worldview in which Imago was birthed and lived its early life. We show that we began our careers and constructed the first model of Imago therapy, without awareness that we were doing so, through the lens of Newtonian atomism which portrayed our universe as made of atoms that are unchangeable and essentially separate from each other (Rutherford, 1911). The "cultural self" that evolved in western civilization was modeled after the atom of classical physics and became the psychological self when Freud gifted it with an interior world. This located experience in human subjectivity, which we will refer to as the Space-Within, which is also the location of suffering. Initially the cause of suffering was the tension between internal dynamics of the structures of the substantive self, and later, suffering was assigned to a negative internalized caretaker, and finally to the quality of nurturing provided by caretakers. From the beginning of psychotherapy, the Space-Within (subjectivity) has been the source and location of experience and suffering and the process of exploration and interpretation of the inner world has been assigned as the mechanics of the cure. In this worldview, the individual is the primary reality; relationship is secondary and optional. At the paradigm level, we call this the paradigm of the individual.

THE EMERGING NEW WORLDVIEW

In our second chapter, we present our perspective on the emerging new worldview that is an expression of quantum physics, with special reference to quantum field theory which becomes the new foundation for Imago theory and therapy. In this new worldview, the source of all experience shifts to interactions in the Space-Between. The self is not a substance with features that can be observed; it is a constantly changing oscillation between focus and flow. The source of experience is the focus–flow oscillation, and whether this brings suffering or transformation is determined by whether the relational energy generated by the oscillating poles is safe or dangerous. We call this the relational paradigm and see it as an ontological shift away from the individual paradigm rooted in classical physics.

We relocate life as happening in the Space-Between and remembered in the Space-Within. The quality of our interactions in the Space-Between determine whether we remember joy and aliveness or pain and suffering. We are born in relationship, live in relationship, suffer in relationship, and are transformed in relationship. In this world view, relational wellbeing is the source of emotional and mental wellbeing rather than the other way around. Given that, all therapeutic interventions need to be redirected from the Space-Within to the Space-Between because that is where joy or anxiety happens and where the deepest transformations take place.

Imago Relationship Therapy embodies this new worldview and contributes to its implications for a transformation of therapeutic interaction. Imago is an expression of the relational paradigm and its ground has been shifted, in this book, from the world of separate objects to quantum field theory, a world where everything everywhere is interconnecting with everything everywhere. The primary posit of Imago theory is: Connecting is Being.

1
The Space-Within

Why do couples fight? That question launched our work and the search for an answer has been our passion. We have been impressed that couples polarize and hurt each other for significant and sometimes insignificant reasons. And they will do this for years, even decades, and generally without remorse, for the pain they cause each other. Since we belong to that population of challenged couples, we ask it of ourselves.

Our response to this question, after decades of personal exploration, clinical interviews, and literature research is that couples fight because they object to "difference." To elaborate: couples object to difference because they live in a symbiotic consciousness in which they unconsciously expect their partner to relate to them in such a way that a primitive need from childhood is met without resistance and with prescience—so that a request is unnecessary—and with predictability so that it can be counted on. But none of this is in their awareness. The second objection to difference is connected to an expectation, again unconscious, that their partner lives in the same "world" in which they live, sees things the same way, and wants what they want with minimal deviations. This is called the "symbiotic illusion." When either or neither of these conditions occur, "difference" is experienced. Anxiety is triggered; defenses are activated, and a pattern of mutual pain infliction ensues that follows a predictable course that will be repeated over and over again, until they decide to break the pattern by divorce or engaging you, the therapist.

From the Imago perspective, the unmet need is universal, and has happened with different degrees of intensity to all human beings in all of human history. The need is for the restoration of an original condition of connecting that was attended at birth by relaxed joyfulness and the sensation of full aliveness. Because of resonance failure with caretakers, this condition was short lived, being ruptured in different time frames in different familial and cultural contexts and replaced with anxiety and defenses. Since anxiety is not just a fear of some discomfort, but the imagination of the possibility of extinction—of not being at all—the complaint about an unmet need and the willingness to inflict pain to get it met makes sense. It is human and universal. And, nature seems to have constructed a variety of ways (but not many) to restore that original condition, one of which is intimate relationships. And that is what gives importance to the conflict and makes its resolution seem non-negotiable. The trauma of childhood is replayed as the drama of marriage and other intimate relationships, and universally as the human drama of conflict and suffering.

We see couple's conflict as a special instance of the universal human condition, just intensified by the special meaning partners have for each other and their proximity. Couples conflict is an instance of the global conflict. The agenda that feeds the tension between partners is the agenda that feeds the tension between everyone—to restore original connecting. The conflict resides in the fact that the person, local or global, who is supposed to be doing it is not doing it the way *I* need it to be done. There is no other way but my way. However, behind all the diversity of forms of desire is the universal desire to experience connecting. And that means, for us, that the solution that works for couples will work for everyone, with some adaptations to context. While we will focus in this book on the proximate conflict between intimates, we will indicate instances of distal application whenever appropriate.

A PERSPECTIVE ON HUMAN SUFFERING

Behind the question "why do couples fight? (or anyone, for that matter)" is the function of the suffering behind the conflict, and the suffering the conflict produces, which makes the conflict seem necessary on the one hand, and on the other hand, the conflict is sometimes a welcome distraction from the suffering; a sort of negative engagement that is, in its own way, satisfying.

As our interest in couples conflict led to the construction of a couple's therapy, we became aware that any theory of therapy needed a theory of the self: who are we? And it needed a theory of suffering consistent with the theory of the self that answered the question: what is the experience of suffering; what is its source? What can be done about suffering is both a theory and an intervention that may or may not be called therapy.

Before we proceed to the Imago theory of human nature, its theory of suffering and its mitigation, we set the conversation in a cultural and historical context. Our interest is the phenomenology of suffering in human history, and in therapeutic disciplines in particular, where suffering is experienced: where is the source located, what causes it, and how suffering has been mitigated in the human story.

In a summary overview of what is to come, we will posit that in all of human history to the present:

1. the experience of suffering is anxiety about one's existential condition;
2. the location of the source of suffering has shifted only three times;
3. the solution to suffering has changed only three times;
4. the Imago view of the phenomenal experience of suffering as anxiety about Being is identical to the historical one, but the cause of suffering and its solution is different.

We are particularly interested in the location of the source of suffering. It appears that it has to be on the inside—in our subjectivity—or on the outside, in our relationships.

Our thesis is that the source of suffering in history tends to be located on the inside, our subjectivity. It is a function of the dynamics within the self that has implications for the self's interaction with its context, but the source of suffering is not the relation to the context itself. In Imago, we posit that the source of suffering is the outside, in what we will discuss in the next chapter, as the Space-Between. We also hypothesize that "suffering as anxiety" is such a profoundly painful phenomenal experience that its universality makes sense. But, as we shall see, the explanation of its source seems to change with the dominant theory of physics at a particular time.

Suffering is both an existential reality and a personal experience, but who we are that suffers and how we deal with it have no objective answers. Our understanding of the universe in which we live unconsciously informs and shapes our view of who we are as citizens in that universe, what we have to do to survive and thrive in it, and why we suffer and what we can do about it, if anything. Our answers are context determined. Suffering always takes place in a view of the universe in which such suffering *can* or *does* happen, and the mitigation of suffering is defined by the laws of that universe, and if effective, the methods of amelioration must be consistent with the definition and cause of suffering. In other words, the cure must relate to the nature of the suffering.

We start with a generic definition of suffering and then look at its specific meaning and amelioration in couple's therapy and psychotherapy. We follow a theme in the history of psychotherapy that evolves into a new perspective on our humanity, on our suffering and its mitigation.

Human Social Evolution and Changing Views of Suffering
It is interesting that the lens through which we humans in western civilization, have looked at ourselves regarding who we are and our existential situation is dictated by the physics of the day. Over course of our history, there have been only three views of the nature of physical reality: Ptolemaic

cosmology, Newtonian atomism, and currently, quantum mechanics. We begin with Ptolemy.

Suffering and Restitution in the First Stage of Human Evolution
To set Imago theory of suffering and its resolution in historical context, we need to briefly review what happened in the fourth century B.C. with the Greeks, our intellectual ancestors and the source of our current worldview in western civilization. The context has to do with the questions about who organized the universe, what the features of its organization are, and how humans were related to it. Answers to these questions were given by the Hellenistic astronomer and the world's first physicist, Claudius Ptolemy (100-170 AD). It was Ptolemy who finally standardized geocentricism, in which the Earth was considered the second story of a three storied universe. Human beings lived on the middle floor of this universe, and all the heavenly bodies revolved around them. The upper floor was occupied by some sort of transcendent energy, and the lower floor was reserved for people who were out of favor with the occupant of the top floor. Human beings were viewed as the creation of the divine agency on the top floor, who owns and cares for them and regulates how they should live and relate to others, and to the divine agency. Regulatory power over humans was assigned by the transcendent to a special order of religious and political authorities, who also claimed ownership and control of humans as their right because they were representatives of the transcendent agency. Since this story is a product of the agrarian age, these authorities owned all the land and animals and also humans, whom they turned into serfs whose responsibilities were to obey, serve, and sacrifice for the political and religious leaders who identified themselves as representatives of the transcendent powers on the third floor.

In this universe, suffering was anxiety about one's relationship to the beings who inhabited the transcendent realm. The source of fear was "up-there." Whether physical, mental, emotional, or circumstantial, anxiety as suffering had a spiritual explanation and a cure. Anxiety as suffering was self-inflicted: the consequences of a willful act of disobedience, a turning away from the transcendence which ruptured the relationship between the human and the transcendent, resulting in exclusion from the transcendent agency; exclusion from its presence, feelings of guilt, and fear of exile to the third floor of punishment and other horrors. There was only one cure: confession of the willful act, ridding oneself of preoccupation with oneself, pledging total obedience to the laws of the culturally imaged transcendent, and resuming the practice of obedience by engaging repetitively, and for a lifetime, in a range of reparative and shaping rituals.

Suffering and Its Relief in the Second Stage
of Human Social Evolution

The Ptolemaic universe endured from the second century B.C. until the sixteenth century A.D., when it was toppled by the rediscovery of Greek philosophy, by the rise of the physical sciences (especially astronomy), and by two famous astronomers, Copernicus and Galileo, who informed us all that the universe is not three-storied with the Earth as the center, and that we could not view ourselves as special creations of a divine source, thus ending the hegemony of theology as an explanation of human experience. With the end of the Dark Ages and of the feudalism and slavery that preceded it, a 1,000-year period (476 AD–1453) of social, emotional, and mental repression by religious and secular authorities was replaced by the rise of the early capitalist structures of the Renaissance and, later, the Enlightenment. This led to the second stage of human social evolution and its new view of human nature and human suffering, called the "age of reason," a total transformation of human thought, a total reorganization of social institutions, and the emergence of a new culture based on reason and science rather than on faith. *But the ancient spiritual view of human nature and of suffering and its cure remained intact in the new worldview,* until the nineteenth century.

The prelude to this transition was begun in the seventeenth century, when Sir Isaac Newton, the world's next great physicist after Ptolemy, proposed a new picture of the universe which became a new lens through which to look at the human situation, and eventually, a new way to look at the cause of suffering. When science came down to earth, the location of interest was "out there." This epistemology was borrowed from a fourth century Greek philosopher named Democritus, whose theory of nature was that everything is made of separate, uncuttable, interactive atoms. He created a new physics of motion in which separate objects interacted according to fixed laws of nature, but those objects had no intrinsic connection to each other. Newton's separate, unchangeable, and autonomous atom was used in the eighteenth century by the social sciences as the model for the construction of an autonomous "self," which was independent and self-sufficient, to replace the shackled "serf" of the Middle Ages, who neither belonged to themselves nor had any freedoms. To this picture of the separate self, René Descartes added autonomous reasoning as the primary human faculty (to know what was "out there" directly and without mediation) giving birth to the rational self with a mind–body split.

Interest in the internal world was initiated by Charles Darwin in his evolutionary biology. Darwin countered the autonomy of the rational self with his view of the instinctual self, which he considered to be located mainly in the emotional and reactive lower brain that fights for survival by adapting to changing circumstances. The combination of all these features created a naturalistic and materialistic worldview of nature, and of humans living in a universe that may have been created and set in motion by the gods, but not needing their supervision or control—the gods retreated to let it run on its own. The concept of the human as a self that was separate and isolated became the foundational cultural value for whom all the institutions of western civilization were designed to protect and promote, including psychology and psychotherapy.

The Emergence of a New View of Suffering in Psychotherapy

A new source and location of suffering was offered by Sigmund Freud, in the late nineteenth century, who used an eclectic assemblage of ideas that included the Newtonian view of the separate, independent self, the Darwinian instinctual self, and Descartes' rational self. This became the psychological self, whose primary feature was an inner world, creating for the first time in human history the SPACE-WITHIN as the location of reality.

Into this isolated self, Freud posited three interacting structures in conflict with each other—the superego, the ego, and the id—which interestingly mirrored the Ptolemaic three-tiered universe. Since the transcendent forces were no longer involved in human affairs, for the first time in history, the source of anxiety (as suffering) was located in the SPACE-WITHIN this newly minted subjectivity. It was triggered by the tensions between the demands of the id and the superego, the instinctual push of the life force to survive and experience pleasure, and the attempt by internalized social prohibitions to repress its expression. Guilt about violating social prohibitions and anxiety about punishment and survival makes suffering implicitly relational, but not explicitly. The explicit character of suffering as relational emerged with the discovery of relational features of the self.

DISCOVERY OF A RELATIONAL THREAD
IN FREUD AND PSYCHOANALYSIS

While the focus of psychotherapy for the last 150 years has been on the internal world of the individual, it has been accompanied by the recognition that relationships may impact the systemic problems of the self—but few therapy systems indicated those problems were *caused* by relationships. Given the interiority of the goal, it makes sense that therapy has logically been directed at relieving the tensions of the inner world by excavating and understanding the mental content of memory, dreams, and the imagination, and returning that information to the conscious self with an explanation of what it all means, with the assumption that insight can restore the conditions that preceded the onset of the symptoms.

Our thesis is that there is an implicit relational thread in Freud's model of the self and in his therapeutic relationship with his patients that was woven into a tapestry by his successors to create the concept of a relational self, and that concept was a bridge to a shift to the "self as relational." By relational, we mean that the problematic is assigned to stress in relationships with significant others and that the resolution is a change in the relationships, and it is that change that produces a change in the interior of the self. Our goal in the remainder of this chapter is to trace those implicitly relational features of the self, in Freud's earliest formulations, to their full expression in the major psychotherapy systems and to show that those disciplines have been moving implicitly in the direction of relationality since their inception by Sigmund Freud. Our thesis is that the "self as relationship" revealed itself sequentially, over the last century or so, in small indicators of the importance of "relationship" which therapists who were theoreticians assembled into a new entity called the "relational self." This was a bridge concept to the self as relationship, which is a bridge to the self as a quantum phenomenon.

This thesis contrasts with other views that assign adaptive and defensive functions to human relational interests rather than those interests being innate. This contrary view posits an evolutionary origin to social interest, and thus posits relational adaptation for survival as an acquired interest and skill at an early age (Atzil, Gao, Fradkin, & Barrett, 2018). In our view, this locates relationality in the separate self and sustains that outmoded view which has haunted psychotherapy since its inception. Our intention is to show that the human interest in relationship is an expression of our nature, and not an adaptation to social context for survival.

At the outset, we asked the question: why did the relational intuition of early psychotherapists not get developed? From our perspective, two constraints prevented the implicit relational features of psychotherapy from being explicit. One is that Freud was a medical doctor and used a medical lens to respond to psychological suffering. Seeing emotional symptoms as medical problems that have an onset, a treatment, and a cure makes sense when you consider that psychotherapy was founded by a physician with no psychological training. The second constraint was the value system of the culture itself, and its view of the self. The autonomous self and its subjectivity were primary values that gave birth to most of the institutions of western civilization, and it makes sense in that mindset that the self would be the source of all experiencing, and thus of suffering. Both constraints prevented Freud from seeing the relational source of the trauma of his patients. We posit, however, that his individualistic psychotherapy treatment was implicitly relational, as was his model of the separate self, and his therapy process.

Following the relational thread from the early period of psychotherapy to the present will lead to our view that amplifying the relational features of the self leads to the quantum self we discuss in the next chapter. Quantum theory offers couples therapy, for the first time in history, the possibility of an independent ground for theory and practice.

As we begin to trace the history of psychotherapy from Freud to Imago, we discern a softening of the boundaries of the separate self and an increased attention to interactions with and shaping by the self's social environment, a process that eventually shifts the identity of the self from being a substantial and separate entity to being a process of constant interaction with its environment.

The Relational Essence of the Individual Self

One powerful relational thread was Freud's reversal of his diagnosis of one of his first clients. In this famous story, his client confessed that her father sexually abused her, and for a while, Freud professed to believe her. When he spoke about this in a public lecture, more than a third of his audience objected, stating that no professional gentleman of Vienna would sexually abuse his daughter, and left in disgust. Afterward, for reasons that have been examined in several books, Freud reframed his diagnosis and assigned the cause of her symptoms to her wishful fantasy that she could be sexually involved with her father. The fate of Freud's decision to shift from a relational diagnosis to attributing the source of his client's neurosis to a sexual fantasy was that he established psychotherapy as a discipline devoted to exploring the complexity and richness of the inner world with little commerce with the world of others, and he missed becoming the world's first relational therapist. Had that happened, psychotherapy might not have made its detour into the fantasy of the separate, individual, and autonomous self (Rush, 1980).

The second thread was the function of the superego. In its purest form, all experience in the Freudian self was generated inside the self as a result of internal dynamics between the three structures of the self—ego, superego, and id (or unconscious). All relationality was between the internal systems, and anxiety as suffering was a result of how the ego managed conflict between those systems. If the ego failed to pacify the id, with its laundry list of instinctual demands, the push of the survival instincts of sexuality and aggression would be repressed by the restrictive superego, giving birth to emotional problems, such as hysteria and the anxiety neuroses. Freud claimed that the bias of the superego against instinctual content and subsequent repression came from the internalized parents of his patients, making him the first to discover that the dynamics between his patients and other people (including him) were directly derivative of a conflicted relationship between the client and their parents. Anxiety about the punishment of the superego (as surrogate parent) about instinctual desires led to the repressive defense that gave birth to all psychological and physical symptoms that became interesting to psychotherapy.

Freud's Discovery of the "Talking Cure"

Perhaps the most impactful relational phenomena in the Freudian corpus has to do with Freud's relationship to women.

In the late seventeenth century, women suffered from a condition doctors called hysteria, which spread throughout Europe. The Salpêtrière Hospital was founded as part of the Great Confinement of the seventeenth century, which included these women. It housed prostitutes, female adulterers, and women suffering from hysteria. In the nineteenth century, the hospital became an asylum. This one institution housed 5,000 to 8,000 women. The symptoms of hysteria were hallucinations, ticks, falling down, and "a tendency to cause trouble." Among the "cures" used to treat these women's mental illness were bloodletting, induced vomiting, application of leeches, solitary confinement, straight-jacketing, and clitorectomy.

Doctors began to work with the women in the asylum. These women were among Freud's first patients, three of which were rather notable. The most famous is Bertha Pappenheim, known in case studies as Anna O., to whom Dr. Breuer, a colleague of Freud, listened while she talked rather than implementing the other "cures" for hysteria. She reported she felt so much better in the "collaborative act" of telling him her feelings without him touching her body that she coined the term "the talking cure." Although Dr. Breuer was the main doctor working with Anna O., Freud galvanized the treatment and for 13 years kept pushing Breuer to publish the case study. Freud referred to Anna O.'s case frequently in his letters and more than 40 times in his collected works.

Elizabeth von R. was the second patient to whom Freud just listened. He wrote that he had no idea what he was doing, but just sat and listened. After listening for a while, she seemed to get over her symptoms, and he was extremely curious about the results he was seeing just by listening.

A third client was Emmy von N. While Freud was listening to her, he noted that family secrets were central to her illness, and that she had "unfilled possibilities and suffered hysterical neurosis of a consequence." In his notes about the way Emmy von N. gave Freud feedback, he recorded: "She said in a definite grumbling tone that I was not to keep asking her where this and that came from, but to let her tell me what she had to say." "I fell in with it," he said (Freud & Breuer, 1895, p. 139). Once healed, Emmy von N. became a patron of the arts and helped fund one of the nineteenth century movements about temperance.

Noting that talking had a cathartic effect, Freud surmised that talking released pent up instinctual energy that the ego had failed to regulate and, therefore, had been repressed by a punitive superego, which the ego also failed to constrain, giving birth to suffering in the form of anxiety and guilt attended by fears of punishment that become physically symptomatic. Since his patient did not understand what was happening because the dynamics were unconscious, Freud directed the aim of his new intervention of listening to the patient's inner world by allowing the women to explore buried memories and cathartically release the energy attached to them. He evoked a shift of awareness out of the unconscious into the ego, which allowed the patient to achieve an insight. With greater insight, in his view, the patient could eventually return their thoughts, emotions, and their life to rational management.

Freud later adopted the term "the talking cure" as the listening stance in his new methodology, which he called psychoanalysis. According to Freud, listening to his patients' suffering ideations and interpreting them helped his patients acquire insights that effected a cure that transformed debilitating anxiety, resulting in greater calm.

Although his female patients' illnesses could be linked to painful relationships with men at the start, Freud reversed his position to one that gave him greater dignity and status in early nineteenth-century Vienna. He ignored the relational context as an active agent in the causation or cure of suffering and asserted that the client's suffering is caused by internal dynamics of the interaction of the structures of the psychic edifice with the life force. The only contextual variable is the analyst, who provides the therapeutic space and waits for the patient's productions of memories. As psychoanalysis began to evolve, the analysand became dependent on the psychoanalyst.

Emotionally, the client was dependent upon the therapist for relief, as a patient is dependent upon a medical doctor. When tension was discharged, a rational therapist offered an interpretation that integrated the client's memories into their life, which simultaneously removed the accompanying painful emotions. Near the end of his life, Freud's claim of what psychoanalysis achieved for the patient was that it helps them move from neurotic misery to the misery of everyday life.

Freud's creation of psychoanalysis established a new chapter in the story of suffering, which accidentally gave birth to a new cure for emotional distress that is the stance behind most forms of psychotherapy today.

Psychoanalytic Process as an Implicitly Relational Therapy

An important relational thread was the psychoanalytic process itself. While Freud prided himself on his objectivity, invoked by facing away from his clients so as not to distort what he thought was the purity of their free asso-ciations, he became aware that because of the intensity and carefulness of his listening and the empathic way he delivered his interpretations of his cli-ents' free associations, they tended to develop affectionate feelings for him, which he referred to as transference—and which he saw as a hinderance to successful analysis.

On the other hand, Freud believed that it was the hovering and care of the therapist that healed the patient. It is interesting that he discovered, but did not recognize, the therapeutic power of the relational aspects of the therapeutic relationship. What Freud forbade, Carl Rogers—founder of cli-ent centered psychotherapy—later discovered as the active agent in success-ful therapy: empathy.

The Relational Thread and Theory of Suffering in the Post Freudians

Although the influence of social context on the quality of experience began to be included in descriptions of subjectivity by post Freudians Alfred Adler, Karen Horney, and Abram Kardiner, the dynamical interactions of that structure (now influenced but not determined by the external environment) continued to dominate the definition of the self and its experience of suffer-ing. According to ego analysts David Rapaport, Heinz Hartmann, and Anna Freud, the conscious ego required a relational context that influenced devel-opment, but it retained its focus on internal experience and a biologically given inner structure.

Erik Erikson

Perhaps the most significant among Freud's detractors was German-born psychoanalyst Erik Erikson (1959), who contributed a valuable relational component to the notion of human development. Overall, Erikson claims that personality structure adds up to the sum of the bio, psycho, and social exchanges with everyone we interact with inside our cultural context. He posited that human beings develop partially as a result of the increasingly complex demands we face from our interactions with those around us. Erik-son posited eight stages of psychosocial development and proposed that relationship experiences at each stage, whether negative or positive, deter-mine the outcome of sense of self. His theory described how these social experiences impacted the self across the whole lifespan.

However, in his classic description of the developmental stages from birth to death, Erikson kept Freud's atomistic self, but now this self was viewed as embedded in a social environment as it progresses through the developmental stages from birth to death.

Harry Stack Sullivan

Although Sullivan retained the atomistic Freudian structure of the self, he developed a theory of psychiatry based on interpersonal relationships in which he softened the self's rigid boundary. But his distinction from Freud was his adamant claim that the cause of suffering was not tension and conflict between the structures of the self, but the impact of interactions with other people on those structures. He was convinced, and loudly proclaimed, that the outside is responsible for the inside (Sullivan, 1953). In his view, our emotional life is not written in cement during childhood, "we write each chapter as we go along." But his stance was that the progress and outcome of this evolutionary journey was the power of relationship on shaping the self. As he so eloquently said, "It is a rare person who can cut himself off from mediate and immediate relations with others for long spaces of time without undergoing a deterioration in personality" (Sullivan, 1953, p. 33).

In his idea of a permeable self, Sullivan's theory of the source of suffering as anxiety is a disturbance within the interpersonal context, which for him is the etiology of all psychological dysfunction. He proposed that this anxiety came in two different types, each with its own negative impacts: 1) anxiety picked up by a child from his mother, like a flu virus she passes on unknowingly, interferes with the child's ability to integrate his experience; 2) anxiety transmitted to the child not by the mother but by others within his interpersonal context that threatens the quality of his relationships with others.

And this negative impact was especially the case with *significant others*, a term Sullivan introduced into our psychological vocabulary. Significant others determine the sense of security, sense of self, and the dynamisms that motivate the child's behavior. This included mental illnesses, like schizophrenia, which he saw as not so much a sick psyche but a function of sick relationships—a shift from biology-as-cause to relationship. One of Sullivan's most famous sayings is: "It does not matter what happens with an individual, what matters is what happens between persons." Another that distinguishes him as a relational therapist is: "When the satisfaction or the security of another person becomes as significant to one as one's own satisfaction or security, then the state of love exists."

Besides making the first mention of the *significant other* in psychological literature, Sullivan developed the idea of the "self-system," a configuration of personality traits developed in childhood and reinforced by positive affirmations and the security operations created to avoid anxiety and threats to self-esteem. Sullivan further defined the self-system as a steering mechanism toward a series of I–you interlocking behaviors; that is, what an individual does is meant to elicit a particular reaction. He and

Jewish theologian Martin Buber were the inspiration for the Imago concept of the Space-Between as the source of the Space-Within.

Object Relations Theory

Object relations theory is an offshoot of psychoanalytic theory that is interested in inner images of the self and others and how these images manifest themselves in interpersonal situations in adult life. Object relations theorists include Donald Winnicott, Melanie Klein, and Ronald Fairbairn, (Winnicott, 1960; Klein, 1952; Fairbairn, 1952), who did their work from the 1960s through the 1980s. Although object relations theorists kept Freud's atomistic self, they replaced the sexual and aggressive drives, proposed by Freud to be the primary sources of motivation, with our need for contact with others and to form relationships. The explanation of motivation shifted from biology to relationship.

Viewed through this lens, our maladaptive behaviors as adults ultimately have relational sources. The suffering of anxiety is caused by a caretaker's failure to meet the infant's need. The infant defends against anxiety by "splitting" the caretaker into good and bad, and without remediation, that polarity becomes the lens through which they will look at all of life.

Heinz Kohut and Self Psychology

Around 1960, Heinz Kohut, the founder of Self Psychology, wrote a seminal paper on empathy, which became the centerpiece of his work. The theme of the paper related to the foundations of psychoanalysis: the ability of one human being to potentially gain access to the inner state of another human being. From this he evolved a therapeutic intervention he called "vicarious introspection," which was his attempt to understand individuals from within their subjective experience: "without empathy, the mental life of man is unthinkable" (Mitchell & Black, 1995).

Later he developed a concept of a fully permeable self and a relational therapy based on his perspective that empathy from the caretaker was essential to the developing child. He also saw their interactions as co-creating each other. They are each other's "self-objects." He was certain that the failure of the caretaker to respond was at the root of all pathology.

This principle is relevant and prescient to everything else we will discover within the pages of this book. Valued empathy from the caretaker is essential to the developing child. The interactions between the child and parent co-create both parent and child. This offers beautiful and unique imagery from the way most humans view couplehood, especially when things start to wane. If we are co-creating each other, we create the problem we are complaining about, and we are now a part of the solution!

These insights led Kohut, later in his career, to replace the drive theory that drove the built-in three-part structure of the Freudian self with a relationally constructed tripartite self that develops only when "state specific" needs are met in relationship with another. This radical position posited the source and fate of the self as dependent on the vicissitudes of relationship, not just the fate of its internal drives or the structure of the self. This idea of a self that is literally the sum of the person's interactions with intimate others, as revolutionary as it sounded, would eventually become the foundational thesis for the next wave of relationally oriented theories coming from the field of psychology, including the concept of mirror neurons in our brain. Not only has the self's boundary become permeable, its internal structure has become relationally created, and with that advancement, steps toward the self as a quantum phenomenon seem to have been taken without anyone intending to do so!

Carl Rogers

At the time all this was happening, in the 1960s, Carl Rogers emerged as an influential humanistic psychologist known for his client-centered therapy that sought to help clients engage in self-actualization processes to develop their personalities. While he included interpersonal relationships in one of his books and his interest seemed to be on communication, he is not known for his relational theory (Rogers, 1959).

Along with Kohut, Rogers introduced empathy into the therapy process not as a shared emotion, but as an activating energy that supported emotional growth—an early, powerful, and intuitively strategic contribution of the relational field. What he is famous for is his challenge to the Freudian practice of analysis and insight as therapeutic interventions. Instead, he offered that therapists must have three attributes to create a growth producing environment so people can move forward toward becoming their true self: 1) congruence, 2) unconditional positive regard, and 3) accurate empathy.

Attachment Theory

The roots of attachment theory can be traced back to Freud's two theories about love, which John Bowlby, the developer of attachment theory, defined as "lasting psychological connectedness between human beings." In the second of these two theories, Freud had mentioned "the internalization of the other" that can happen when one loves another. This condition, according to Bowlby, is a function of the confidence the child has that the caregiver will be present as predicted, because the caregivers have been so in the past. If that confidence is there, it tends to be relatively permanent throughout life (Bowlby, 1988).

Mary Ainsworth, a colleague of Bowlby, developed a research tool called the Strange Situation that she used to identity the four attachment styles of defenses: secure, avoidant, anxious, and disorganized (this last style was added by Mary Main). Implied in the attachment styles is a theory of suffering as the experience of anxiety triggered by the lack of confidence in the expectation of a secure relationship with the caretaker. And that style will likely remain unchanged in their lifetime without intervening experiences.

Without interventions, the style will likely show up in intimate relationships as unfinished business; if not identically, they will be similar. Attachment research states that the best predictor of adult attachment styles is the perception formed in childhood about the quality of their relationships with their parents. This was a significant "wake-up call" to the mental health field at the time: that the quality of the "attachment" or "connecting" between one person with another has a tremendous influence on one's mental health.

Relational Psychoanalysis
In the mid-1980s, Steven Mitchell and his colleagues, most notably Robert Stolorow, created relational psychoanalysis. The adjective "relational" in front of psychoanalysis signaled a "paradigm shift" in which the concept of drives as biological and innate motivators of behavior was replaced with the thesis that the primary motivator of people is relationships with others (Mitchell & Aron, 1999).

When relational analysts do therapy, they include "waiting" for the client's presentation and the therapist's interpretation, and spontaneous engagement of the client's presentation in a lively, genuine relationship with their clients. They believe the healing process works better with a combination of insight and a healing relationship—combining the classical with the relational.

From our perspective, the relational thread in Freud's early work was woven into a relational tapestry by Sullivan and Kohut and became foundational reality in relational psychoanalysis.

Feminist Psychology
The tapestry of relationship as foundational was woven larger and more beautiful by a group of feminist psychologists. The first was Jean Baker Miller, who developed relational-cultural theory and therapy. She was joined by Judith Jordan, Irene Stiver, Janet Surrey, and Amy Banks as they formed the Stone Center for Developmental Studies at the Wellesley College in 1981 (Miller & Stiver, 1997).

This group of courageous and creative women scholars and therapists encouraged the shift away from the "separate self" in western psychology and asserted there is no such thing as a self, there is only a "self-in-relation."

They effectively replaced the substantive self with the paradigm of "self -in-relation" as more representative of experience. In this model, relationship is the basic goal of development: that is, deepening the capacity for relationship and relational competence across the developmental stages. It assumes that other aspects of self (e.g., creativity, autonomy, assertion) develop, but they evolve within a relational context.

As a group, they attempted to study and document the way women differ from men in the way they relate. The major difference was the centrality and continuity of relationships throughout women's lives. It was their perspective that we all have a natural drive toward relationships and that we long for acceptance in these relationships. And, they were adamant that any attempt to clarify women's development adds to our understanding of human development. For them, suffering is relational; it is anxiety about the failure to become a self-in-relationship.

The work of the relational-cultural therapy developed at the Stone Center challenges another dominant norm in our culture that values knowledge and authority as important goals for individuals—striving to be the best, win the debate, and out-perform others. They emphasized that the drive to gain power and authority isolates us from one another because it makes us believe that our individual development is in competition with the development of others. This belief prevents us from resolving conflicts because we are so certain that we know what is right and we are so quick to judge our partners for thinking differently than us. By reminding us of the relational essence of the self, these psychologists emphasize that while there is value in being an authority on things, an important part of relationship is learning how to "not know," stressing the importance of "not knowing" in the creation of healthy relationships. As Jean Baker Miller said, "In order for one person to grow in relationship, both people must grow." In order to grow together, relationships require vulnerability and uncertainty, a willingness to not know. This means that a strong relationship skill is shifting from judgment to curiosity and wonder. When one shifts from criticism or blame to wondering why a person does what they do or thinks what they think, the other person feels seen and respected, creating healthy connection.

Carol Gilligan, a colleague at the Stone Center, also contributed to the relational view of the self with her classic book *In a Different Voice* (1982). It challenged the dominant paradigm in mental health, advocated by the work of Gilligan's mentor Lawrence Kohlberg. Gilligan noticed that Kohlberg's moral development studies that viewed autonomy and individuation as the highest stage of moral development had used only men as subjects. Drawing on interviews with women, Gilligan argued that an ethic of care and responsibility (which is attentive to the relational aspect of ethics) should also be understood as a fully developed form of moral reasoning. Gilligan does not argue that this mode of moral reasoning is exclusive to or universally descriptive of women. Rather she reveals the limits of thinking that any single group can stand in for all of humankind. By focusing on women, as a supplement to Kohlberg's studies of men, Gilligan uncovered a different aspect of moral development, "a different voice," and contributed to an understanding of humans as not only individuals, but as relational beings.

Interpersonal Neurobiology
Interpersonal neurobiology is an interdisciplinary approach to healthy relationships, developed by Dan Siegel and a large group of his colleagues, who assign the achievement of healthy relationships to the intersection of brain–mind and relationships. Although heavily rooted in attachment theory, interpersonal neurobiology is not a therapy, as such, but a researched and highly developed resource for therapists interested in the interface of the mind–brain dyad, its impact on relationship, and the impact of relationship on the mind–brain system (Siegel, 2006).

In Siegel's work, the boundaries between self and relationships soften and tend to become indistinguishable. Siegel, who works closely with his wife Caroline Welch, turns the conversation to the concept of an intrinsic "linkage" between mind–brain and relationship and between self and others. In his elaboration of the concept of linkage, Siegel suggests a new term for the self: the "me" becomes a "MWe."

Relationships, mind, and brain are not different domains of reality. They are each about energy and information flow, and the mechanism is the exchange between the brain, subjective impressions, and the conscious mind. In this triad, relationships are defined as the flow of energy and information between people. This makes the mind an "embodied and relational process." We do not own "mind," it is shared between people and this makes us profoundly interconnected.

This integrated space forms the mind and the brain, which in turn form relationships which, reciprocally, form the mind and the brain in a continuous oscillation of information and energy. Relationships are the way we share that flow. The natural outcome of integration is compassion, kindness, and resilience. Such a state creates the possibility of sensing our connection to a larger world. On the other hand, the failure of integration activates anxiety, which mounts the defense of a rigid self.

The emerging field of interpersonal neurobiology has grounded what the mystical and transpersonal traditions have taught forever: that we are undeniably interconnected and interdependent. This assertion locates interpersonal neurobiology at the intersection of biology, psychology, and spirituality, and on the doorsteps of the quantum field.

SUMMARY

Our thesis is that an implicit relational thread can be discerned in Freud's therapeutic interventions and partly in his theory of the self. These include the internalization in the superego of family and cultural values; in psychotherapy, the relational phenomena were his attitude toward his patients, his listening style, and his initial clinical impression that his client's trauma was interpersonal rather than imagined.

Over the next 100 years, an erosion of the features of this isolated, biological self was replaced with a reconstruction of the structure of the self as increasingly relational and relocated in the social environment. In the first phase of the transformation, the fact of having relationships that influenced the insulated and isolated self made relationships important. As the concept evolved the adjective "relating" became attached to the insulated self as something it "did." It related. In the next phase, emphasis on the biologically given instinctual drives was reduced and a relational drive toward human engagement was emphasized. In this phase, "relational" became a characteristic of the self, expanding something it *did* to something it *was* as a chronic activity—from an action to a feature. In the final stage of this evolution the construct of "self-in-relationship" made relationship essential to the self, without which it could not "be." The concept of the self has now moved from being intrinsically instinctual to being intrinsically relational, thus context-dependent rather than context-independent (Table 1.1). The individual paradigm has morphed fully into the relational paradigm, replacing the self as the center of gravity to the status of being secondary to relationship. This development retained its relational features as extrinsic but not intrinsically. Imago takes the final step and shifts the self-*in*-relationship to self-*as*-relationship.

Ontologically, the self *as* relationship makes relationship the primal reality and those phenomena called "self" become derivatives of relationship, thus moving from "self as center" to "relationship as center." However, since the subject of psychology and psychotherapy is the self, as primary reality, there is no way to account for nor any place to locate the self as relational. Just as the substantial self of psychotherapy was rooted in the atom of classical physics, we need a new physics for the self *as* relationship. Quantum field theory comes to the rescue. Its thesis that interconnectivity is the nature of nature provides the scientific basis for the self as relationship, and that as the bridge to the quantum self and, by extension, lays a quantum foundation for revisioning couplehood, and for positing our cosmic identity.

The concept, in quantum field theory, that is the basis for the quantum self, quantum couplehood and our cosmic identity is the *wave–particle*

Table 1.1: Individual vs. Relational Paradigm	
Individual	**Relational**
The individual is primary and creates relationships. Psychology focuses on the "me."	The relationship is primary and creates individuals. Psychology focuses on the "we."
The self is a material substance with boundaries.	Relating and connecting are foundational realities in which the self is a derivative.
Psychological development is an internal process.	Psychological development is an interpersonal process.
The human psyche is fixed.	The human psyche is in constant oscillation, (between two opposing polarities and between energy and information) and in constant change according to its context and as a result of interactions.
Problems are inside the individual, and thus solutions are created from the inside.	Problems are created in relationship, and thus co-created solutions happens in the Space-Between partners.
The individual defines what is his/her subjectivity and memory as "truth" and is not influenced by its context or observation.	Interpenetrating subjectivities co-create each other, intrapersonal subjectivities intertwine. (Pure static experience and memory are illusionary.)
Autonomy, self-sufficiency, self-soothing, and self-care are the therapeutic goals.	Interdependency, safe, connecting and attuned relational-care are the therapeutic goals.

duality—also known as the *wavicle*. This construct becomes the new frame for understanding the interacting self as a polarity—a wavicle—with another wavicle which in combination constitute quantum couplehood (Eisberg & Resnick, 1985). In this frame, couplehood as a "union of opposites" is a relational reality grounded in the quantum field.

2

The Space-Between

We intuit that our collective humanity, and each of its members individually, is on the verge of something big, something
beyond our imagination, which we can dimly but not clearly
see. Here is what we think it is.

The universe in which psychotherapy arose was a universe inhabited by
disconnected objects ontologically separated from each other. One of those
objects was the autonomous and psychological self, the client of psychotherapists for the last one hundred and fifty years, that has been modeled after
Newton's isolated and uncuttable atom. In this model, the location of the
source of human experience was generally viewed as human subjectivity, on
the "inside," which we call the Space-Within, and therapeutic intervention
was inserted into that internal space of memory, dreams and imagination to
discover patterns of thoughts, feelings and behaviors and achieve insight into
their source and purpose, generally with the assumption that such outcomes
were healing and productive of constructive behavior change.

Over time, as a result of clinical experience and research in the neurosciences, evidence has been collected that suggests that humans have a
plastic, not a fixed nature, as implied in Newtonian atomism, and they are
shaped, not just by, but in, their social environments. With that information, the field of therapy gradually evolved a relational theory of the self
and suffering that placed human beings as interactive agents in social contexts that shaped, injured and transformed them, and which they in turn
shaped and transformed. The discovery of this foundational interactivity
and its growing appreciation relocated the source of experience from the
inner world to social engagement with "others," from *knowing about* them
through memory and imagination to *being with them* in lived experience.
This amounted to a paradigm change, in psychology and psychotherapy,
from the individual paradigm to the relational paradigm.

From the Particle to the Wave in Physics and Psychology
It is interesting that, in adjacent geographies in western Europe, and at
approximately the same time, when Sigmund Freud was exploring the

unconscious realm of the human psyche and its relationship to the conscious ego, quantum physicists were exploring the subatomic world and its relationship to the macroworld, using in different sciences the same method of exploring the interior of the psyche and particle. It is also an interesting parallel that in the same time period, quantum physicists were discovering the wavelike qualities of the particle and locating its origin in the quantum field, and, as if choreographed, Freud and his protégé Carl Jung were discovering the complexity and permeability of the conscious ego and locating it in a vast energy field of dreams and memories. The discovery by quantum physicists of the wavelike qualities of the particle resulted in the establishment of the quantum field as reality and of its primary feature as interconnecting. The discovery by Jung of the unconscious (wavelike) features of the formerly isolated self resulted in the establishment of the collective unconscious as the ground of the personal unconscious discovered by Freud. It is interesting to note that the exploratory methods of the soft sciences of human experience and the hard sciences of nature were the same—see what is inside a particular phenomenon, not the company it keeps! And, simultaneously, in both fields, a shift from the part to the whole is occurring— self to context and particle to the wave. For us, this suggests an evolution in human consciousness that is species wide. Although this evolution from part to whole has not occupied the consciousness of everyone, yet, the direction toward a more inclusive conscious is highly suggestive of our future.

On this basis, we view the ascendance of quantum physics to primary status and classical physics to secondary status as a part of the next step in our human social evolution. The transition in the human sphere from the separate self to the self as a quantum phenomenon seems supported by the sciences of nature. And that makes sense, since we humans are nature embodied. The implications of this transition are huge; it is on the scale of the shift from Ptolemy to Newton. For, just as western civilization was built on the model of the autonomous and separate self as foundational reality, a new relational civilization will be modeled on the quantum view of reality as a network of relationships, an interconnecting whole.

At the cultural level, we see this as transitioning *from* an individualistic civilization focused on the "self" as a discrete entity, separate from and in competition with all other selves, *to* a relational civilization which will support our experiencing our true nature as relational creatures by collaborating, co-creating and cooperating with others. At this point, when the quantum view of an interconnecting universe is transcending and including the Newtonian view of a universe of separate objects, our model for the reconstruction of all our social institutions will transcend, transform and include those built on the individual paradigm, ushering in a new value system, as primary personal and cultural values for human civilization that will be housed and expressed in those institutions that include: universal equality, celebration of difference and total inclusiveness, the value system of a relational rather than an individualistic civilization.

Before we discuss the theory of the quantum field, in which these human values are implied, and the implications of the quantum field for Imago theory and therapy—and by extension, the human sciences and therapies—two questions have arisen for us. Because of their centrality and significance, we want to ask them and comment on them as an onramp to the discussion of quantum theory for Imago.

Is the Universe Evolving and Taking Us Along?

Here is the first question: Is the energy propelling this transition from the self to relationship, from the particle to the wave, from an individualistic to a relational culture coming from the quantum field, within which all forms—from particles to people to galaxies—arise and in which they all remain? Or, are we imagining the next stage in our social evolution and seeing the relevance and implications of quantum field theory for our emerging vision of who we are and can become? Or, has our consciousness evolved to the point that we can see more of the universe than Newton saw, and we are re-visioning ourselves in this new quantum universe as the ancestors re-visioned themselves, replacing Ptolemy's earth-centric with Copernicus' sun-centric and Newton's atomistic universe? Or, is the universe itself a conscious entity or organism that is evolving, and since we are in it, it is evolving us with it? If so, is our evolution contributing to cosmic evolution? In other words, are we the source or conduit, or the energy that propels us toward the next stage of our social evolution? Or, are we separate and isolated from the processes of the universe, as classical physics would have it; pawns in a deterministic, mechanical system upon which we have no influence, and certainly no control?

Believe it or not, while most quantum physicists are too humble (and too wise) to answer those questions, they are brave enough to have an opinion, based both on their thought and experimental evidence. And the response by many (enough to be significant) distinguished quantum physicists is astonishing, sobering and challenging. Their position is that not only can we imagine the new possibilities of our approaching social evolution, we are *participants*, not passive objects, in the cosmic process, and our imagination contributes to it whether we are intentionally or unconsciously visioning. John Wheeler, who coined the term "black hole" says, "We are not only observers. We are participators. In some strange sense this is a participatory universe." (Wheeler, 2001, p. 127). And Wheeler remarked to physicist/science writer Jeremy Bernstein in 1985, "I do take

100 percent seriously the idea that the world is a figment of the imagination," (Horgan, 2018).

Along with Wheeler, many other quantum scientists and philosophers of science share the view that nature responds to our observation and to our imagination, thus making us co-creators of our destiny and, mind challenging, the direction and destiny of the universe itself. We are actors on the stage with a script we did not write and to which we can object. Or, we can by choice participate in the cosmic drama and fulfill our destiny as cosmic citizens. In other words we have a cosmic identity behind the psychological and social identity with which we are familiar. But here is the most daunting position of all: we are so embedded in the universe as a thread in the tapestry of being that we influence the cosmic process whether we know about it or not, or whether we are conscious of our participation or not or whether or not we want to. We cannot escape our cosmic responsibility, and how we participate shows up in our human contexts, and how we participate in our human contexts impacts cosmic consciousness and evolution—because this interconnecting is our nature.

> "Participant" is the incontrovertible new concept given by quantum mechanics. It strikes down the "observer" of classical theory, the man who stands safely behind the thick glass wall and watches what goes on without taking part. It can't be done, quantum mechanics says it . . . May the universe in some sense be "brought into being" by the participation of those who participate? (Misner, Thorne, & Wheeler, 1973, p. 1217)

To emphasize this amazing perspective, a large body of physical scientists, and philosophers of science, posit that when the universe and our intention and imagination are in flow, we all move towards greater cohesion which, in turn, impacts our experience of ourselves. In their view, the cosmos is evolving as a result of our engagement with each other and we are evolving as a result of our engagement with the cosmos (Schwartz & Woollacott, 2019).

The implications of the participant theory for all the human sciences are currently undeveloped but huge, and the contribution to Imago and to couples is the next chapter in what we are calling Imago 2.0.

Is the Universe Conscious?

Now here is where it gets really interesting! According to quantum science, you do not have to use your imagination or have faith that you share the features of a conscious quantum universe to have agency in it. Because, as Wheeler wrote:

Behind it all is surely an idea so simple, so beautiful, so compelling that when—in a decade, a century, or a millennium—we grasp it, we will all say to each other, how could it have been otherwise? (Wheeler, 1984, p. 304).

To Wheeler, "the universe gives birth to consciousness, and consciousness gives meaning to the universe." This position is based on the oldest and most reliable quantum experiment that has been repeated thousands of times since the early 1800s and that has had the same outcome: the observer and the observed are connected and influence each other.

The concept is very simple, and the outcome is beyond everyone's explanation, but it is accepted as the most reliable fact in quantum physics, and thus a defining feature of nature. This tried and true experiment, called the double-slit experiment, consists of the following: in the background is a screen. In front of the screen is another screen but this one has two slits in it which is called "double slit." An experimenter has a device that can fire as few as one photon (an elementary particle that is the smallest conceivable unit of light) at a time at the card with the double slits. Now here is the mystery: when the experimenter "looks" at the double slit screen when the photon gun is fired, the each photon passes through one slit only and makes a pattern on the background screen that looks it was hit by a multitude of rifle pellets, or like a particle. This happens whether the observer is human or a mechanical measuring device. If the experimenter does *not* look at the photon when it approaches the double slit screen, the pattern on the background screen is all spread out, like the multiple pellets in a shotgun shell. The photons go through both slits at the same time as is indicated by a wave like pattern on the screen behind the screen with the double slit. This always happens, *if no one is looking.* The particle effect always happens if someone is looking, even a mechanical device. This asks the question: is the photon a particle or a wave? The only answer quantum physicists have offered is that it depends upon whether someone is looking, on whether or not there is an observer (Ananthaswamy, 2018).

Quantum scientists draw several conclusions from this experiment. First, they posit that every quantum phenomenon is both a particle *and* a wave (which is collectively called a wavicle). This duality is an ontological feature of all quantum phenomena and its name is the principle of complementarity. This complementary character of this duality is not a feature reserved for the subatomic world. It is not only expressed in the constant oscillation between particle and wave, field and form; it is presumed to be an indigenous feature of all the larger forms of nature in the Newtonian universe that are visible to the eye, such as the left and right hemisphere of brains, the conservative and progressive views of social systems, the complementary characteristics—found in all intimate relationship, in the space between heartbeats in the pulse, and the general tension of the opposites.

For our purposes in Imago, we see, in the future of all therapies, the wavicle as the model and essence of the quantum self that includes and transcends the separate autonomous self that is based on the atom in classical physics. The principle of complementarity as an ontological foundation presents itself in the couple dyad, including their character defenses, adaptations, and opposing functions of socialization. In Imago theory, this tension of opposites is the engine for attraction.

Second, some scholars of the quantum world posit an alchemical bond (McTaggart, 2011) between the observer and observed, which they call the "observer effect." The presence or absence of an observer determines whether the photon shows up as a wave or a particle. The observer effect—this interaction between a photon of light and a human or mechanical observer—is an indication, not proof, that the energy and information that constitutes the quantum field, as foundational reality, is Consciousness Itself, thus making consciousness primary reality (Kafatos & Nadeau, 1990). This is the foundation of our thesis that *our personal consciousness is a local instance of quantum consciousness.* The collective consciousness that was postulated by Jung is a container and expression of information in the field of quantum consciousness postulated by quantum theory. When Einstein blurred the distinction between matter and energy with his famous equation "energy equals mass times the speed of light squared," he made the point that when a point of consciousness, myself, is interacting and communicating with another point or consciousness, someone or something else, the outcome of the communication *depends on how I observe the interaction. It becomes what I see.* The implications of this for couples is obvious; we can postulate that consciousness can impact matter and, therefore, how we look at our partner impacts how they show up for us. As therapists, this has enormous implications for how we regulate the energy in the Space-Between with our interactions.

The third conclusion from this experiment is that the primary feature of the universe is interconnectivity between the micro of all quantum phenomena—electrons, photons, mueons which are invisible and the macro of all things in the visible universe of classical physics, such as organisms, people, plants, the earth, and galaxies. While a "theory of everything" that would bridge or combine these two realms of nature has not been developed, there is a strong sentiment that the macro world of visible things is "made" of the micro world of "invisible" things, so that their connection is a seamless manifestation of cosmic oneness. One physicist calls the invisible and cosmic unity, in which everything is connecting, the "implicit" order, and locates it behind the visible and finite realm of everyday experience which he calls the "explicit" world (Bohm & Hiley, 1995.) This is expressed in the axiom that everything everywhere is connecting with everything everywhere. In Imago we translate this into the axiom: Connecting is Being; Being is Connecting.

Before we proceed to an elaboration of the quantum field theory and the quantum theory of consciousness, we feel it imperative to say that the relationship of consciousness to the brain (which we will discuss later) and the place of consciousness in the universe, which we are now discussing, are both controversial and polarized, and the answer depends upon your point of view, which is culture-bound. Some scientists and some philosophers of science on both sides of the discussion are clear and vehement that consciousness is an epiphenomenon of the brain and that it emerged as an evolutionary achievement over eons of time. Others are just as certain that the brain is an epiphenomenon of consciousness; that everything, including the brain, is "made" of consciousness, thus consciousness is reality, and consciousness evolved a brain over time that was complex enough that the universe could become aware, then become self-aware, and then aware of its awareness, so that the universe became self-aware in *us*. Those who believe that consciousness is an epiphenomenon of the brain are called materialists, either scientific or philosophical. Materialists believe that physical matter is the only or fundamental reality and that all being and processes and phenomena can be explained as manifestations or results of matter. They do not believe there is anything "behind" the forms of matter—particle, molecules, people, trees, planets, galaxies— except atoms. Consciousness is reserved for biological life and somehow, evolved out of matter with the capacity to experience "qualia," subjective experiences like smell, seeing rainbows, and feelings like love, fear, and hate. As an advocate of this position said: "Consciousness, like sleep, is of the Brain, by the Brain, and for the Brain. A new day is dawning" (Laureys & Tononi, 2008, p. xi). As an instance of the particle–wave duality, materialists occupy the particle side of that duality, and since the eighteenth century, they have occupied the center of attention as they reported their explorations of the material, physical world. And their achievements are astonishing; western culture is their product.

Those who believe that the brain is an epiphenomenon of consciousness have been called idealists, or anti-materialists, whether they are scientists, philosophers, or both. They believe there is *something* "behind" all physical forms of matter; a formless, boundless, infinite realm that gives birth to all forms in our material world. Since consciousness is a feature of biological life that cannot be accounted for as arising out of a material object of matter, like a physical brain, they imagine that all biological forms, as well as in some way all inorganic forms, participate in consciousness in some way. They imagine consciousness is all the way up and all the way down, so consciousness is reality, and all things are made of consciousness. This means that consciousness in biological forms is a local manifestation of cosmic consciousness; human consciousness is a derivative of cosmic consciousness (or the Field) rather than our brains. From a research perspective, they posit that the observer effect discovered in the double-slit experiment is empirical evidence of consciousness as the primary feature of nature, if not Reality Itself; or, Consciousness as Being.

What is really interesting is that this conversation between the materialists (or realists) and the anti-materialists (or idealists) has been going on for a long time. These two world views have dominated the conversation in western civilization for around 2,500 years. All other world views can be considered derivatives of these. If you want to know what you believe, just answer whether you believe that the physical world is made of material things—that the universe is bounded and finite—and that is all there is. Or, perhaps you believe that all things in the material world are made of an immaterial "something," behind or above or beyond it, that is boundless and infinite.

Whichever you chose, you join a conversation, according to the historical record, that began with the Milesian school of pre-Socratic Greek philosophers in the fifth century BC. They were divided on the issue. Some assigned reality to the "boundless," and their colleagues assigned reality to what you can see: earth, air, fire, and water. A hundred years later Plato took the anti-materialistic, or idealistic, position that the world of physical forms were appearances from a formless, transcendental realm. A hundred years after that, his student Aristotle took the other, essentially materialistic, side by stating there is no transcendental realm; that the actual, visible world of things includes the essence that Plato assigned to them in the transcendent realm. The conversation continues to this day with the tension between Newtonian physics, which states that everything is made of atoms, and many advocates of quantum field theory, which posit that everything is made of consciousness. More specifically, David Bohm—among the most famous quantum minds—divided reality into an "explicit" world of polarities, which like Aristotle's view of natural objects arises from a formless "implicit" realm, but unlike Plato's transcendental world, the essence of things is inherent in their form.

The most impressive and defining contemporary data point, to us, is the double-slit experiment, from which came the posit that the defining feature of all quanta is the particle–wave duality (the wavicle); the view that all matter is a compaction of energy (Einstein: $E=mc^2$) and that light=energy–information–consciousness is the invisible and infinite realm behind the world of visible things. But the consciousness that is Reality is not in a transcendent realm; it is natural. The natural world, available for experimental study, as in the double slit experiment and many others, reveals itself to as a polarity in tension. Therefore, a choice or prioritizing of one pole over the other would be to distort reality. Instead, the evolutionary process progresses by holding the polarities in tension, a tension that gives birth to another set of polarities, and so on, in the cosmic process. Thus, to us, the materialism-idealism debate is pointless, since both are correct, but only as the polarities engage each other. It is interesting that an experiment in the quantum sciences suggests that both Plato and Aristotle were correct, but only when seen as a natural polarity. In the double slit experiment, the observer influences whether the quantum object shows up as a wave or a particle, and if there is no observer, it presents as a wave. This biases us toward the position that nature, when a brain is not looking, shows up as a wave, and thus prioritizes for us that the wave as consciousness is the source of the brain, and of all material forms.

For all this musing may be worth, we see it as extremely relevant to couples whose conflicts tend to be expressions of polarities of perspective as well as opposite personalities. We will return to this later when we talk about the quantum features of couplehood.

Now let's move into quantum field theory and its implications for Imago.

A SHORT OVERVIEW OF
QUANTUM FIELD THEORY

In the last century or so, quantum field theory, a subfield of quantum theory, was developed, and this theory provides a new vision of REALITY. This new perspective is our basis for the proposition of an interconnecting quantum self that will replace the separate and isolated psychological self and become the foundation for what we will call quantum couplehood. This new perspective on the self and couplehood will provide a new view of the source and solution of suffering in a quantum universe, all as preparation for the development of a new version of Imago Relationship Therapy.

Quantum science assents to the reality of the visible world as described by Newton and classical physics and concedes that it operates as described at the level of our conscious experience. But, they assert, this is not the whole story.

The Quantum Field as Reality

Behind every visible "thing" that is in the universe (like a plant, a person, the sun, or a galaxy) or invisible (like a particle, or a molecule, or energy), there is a larger "something" out of which it arises that contains and supports it and with which it interacts. Then, there is the universe which holds all.

Is there something behind the universe itself? Quantum physicists say "yes" (Bohm & Hiley, 1995). To account for all the visible things we can see and the invisible things we know exist, like particles and energy, and our universe itself, quantum field theory posits a "field" in which all things arise and disappear, which they call the "quantum field," which philosophically can be called REALITY: that which is behind—or the ground or source of—everything, but there is "no-thing" behind it. Like an ocean, it is both flat and seamless, and like drops of water that constitute the ocean, it consists of "quanta," the smallest conceivable packet of conscious–energy– information. But unlike the ocean, it has an infinity of possible forms— from quarks, to molecules, to humans, to the universe, and possibly to other universes.

According to quantum field theory, this "field" is invisible, infinite, and without boundaries. If it could be described, it would be "consciousness creating forms," (Kafatos & Nadeau, 1990) but that is not something that it "does," it is something that it "is." Cosmic creativity is energy oscillating between field and form, constantly giving birth to an infinity of entities that are diverse, unique, equal, and finite, and then dissolving them back into the field, within which new forms are constantly being constellated in a never-ending cycle of creation, dissolution, and re-creation. Since the quantum field is the foundation of the visible world, this process is occurring everywhere in the universe, including the human level.

Since everything that is constellated in the field remains in the field, and since all things are constituted by the field, the field is in them and they are in the field. And given that "everything" consists of energy–information–consciousness, not only is everything made of the same substance, everything is also connected to everything in continuous oscillation called the particle–wave duality, or the wavicle. As we indicated earlier, quantum scientists attribute that feature to every quantum, and thus, oscillation between wave-like and particle-like features of all quantum phenomena is the primary feature of every "thing," including humans, and is expressed in couples' relationships as complementarity and known as the tension of the opposites.

Analytically, in all of this, four things stand out about how "reality" is structured and how the constituents of the field interact:

1. The field is primary—it gives birth to form—and form is a polarity (particle–wave duality) in the field.

2. Form is secondary, although essential because its creation is the function of the field.
3. Connecting is the nature of the field—not a mere feature, but its very essence.
4. Humans are quantum phenomena and have a cosmic identity.

Having a cosmic identity means that we live in a universe that inhabits the quantum field, and that universe inhabits the galaxy that inhabits the field; every organic and inorganic form on the planet, including humanity, inhabits the quantum field, and each person in the body of humanity is a quantum phenomenon, and everything is connecting in the field.

Furthermore, because the quantum field is conscious–energy–information, the universe and all its inhabitants—galaxies, solar systems, planets, the Earth—and all organisms that comprise nature constitute a sentient/aware universe, which itself is an organism in the quantum field (Goff, 2019). Sentience, which has been assigned to the quantum (smallest conceivable instance of energy) means that we are not only interacting and interconnecting in the quantum field but, at a primal level, we and everything are "aware" that we are interconnecting, and in fact, we are that organism in which self-awareness appears in the quantum field. When any organism in the field becomes self-aware, it not only participates in the field but also impacts it. Reflective consciousness as knowing "with" (con) could be, perhaps, the intention of the field; and our awareness that we are an intrinsic part of the tapestry of being, residing at a specific location in a conscious universe with which we are interacting, is the telos of humanity.

The implications of all this are profound for humanity and for our discipline. It calls for a revisioning of what it means to be human, to experience living with other people, to love and relate to others, to suffer, and to be transformed.

Since we intend to deal with those implications throughout the book, here is a summary of them now to set the landscape and provide a foundation as we explore together.

- If the quantum field is consciousness and all things arise out of the field, then the universe, and everything that constitutes it, is consciousness, all the way up and all the way down. Consciousness *IS* REALITY, not a feature of the universe.
- If we are conscious, and it is obvious that we are, our consciousness is a derivative of the consciousness that constitutes the quantum field.
- If consciousness, as the essence of the field, preceded the brain,

then the brain is not the source of consciousness, but a receiver and a conduit.

- If the brain is a receiver and a conduit, then we can access the information that constitutes the quantum field and transmit it to others.
- If the information in the quantum field is accessible and can be transmitted to others, then coherence of information between others is simultaneous participation in the source.
- If the quantum field is conscious creativity, then our creativity is an expression of the creativity of the field of consciousness.
- If the quantum field is conscious creativity and creativity is the oscillation between field and form, then change is constant and infinite and mirrors the oscillation that characterizes the field.
- If the wavicle (the particle–wave duality) is an inherent feature of all quanta, and the quantum is the source of everything, then complementarity is an ontological feature of nature and thus of human beings.
- If everything is connecting in the field, then any interaction between forms influences all other forms in the field, locally and nonlocally.
- If coherence is an indicator of connecting, then conflict with others about how things work or should work, or what something is or is not, produces incoherence and chaos, indications that both or all involved are attached to a preferential form and no one is receiving information from the field.
- If the observer in the double-slit experiment "sees" a photon (a particle) when they watch, and a wave pattern shows up when they do not watch, then observation influences how something shows up to the observer, and consciousness impacting matter is a fact of nature.
- If every "thing" is connected to every "thing," then any local action has a cosmic impact on things at a distance. This is the basis for a morality of responsibility of each for the whole.
- If all forms that constellate in the field are infinitely diverse and equally valuable, then diversity, equality, and difference are quantum features that should be the foundations of all human institutions, which are themselves derivatives of the field.
- If the field occupies the space between forms, then the Space-Between everyone is a local instance of the quantum field.
- If the field occupies the Space-Between in all forms, then interactions in the Space-Between impact and are impacted by the field.

· If the universe is an interconnecting organism, then the creation of a relational universe is the next stage in human social evolution.

NOTE: We are aware that you did not pick up this book for a lesson in quantum physics; more likely, you selected it to satisfy your curiosity or deepen your knowledge of a couples therapy called Imago Relationship Therapy. So, you may have a question like: What does this have to do with couples therapy? What should this mean to me? Yes. Good questions. Our answer: we have attempted to base Imago Relationship Therapy, as a theory and a therapy of couplehood, on the principles that govern the workings of the universe. Just as the model of the separate self and the practice of psychotherapy (living in a universe of separate objects with implications for suffering and therapy) was based on Newtonian physics, Imago theory and therapy is a model of the self, suffering, and resolution that we are grounding in the quantum field of interconnectivity. Let's look a little more closely.

THE QUANTUM FIELD AND IMAGO

Imago theory is a seamless and elegant synthesis of theoretical systems emerging from a diverse range of fields, including psychology, eastern and western religious traditions, philosophy, neuroscience, relativity, and, most importantly, quantum physics. These disciplines might seem to make strange bedfellows, especially quantum field theory, but underneath their diversity is a common theme: interconnectivity. Everything everywhere is connecting with everything everywhere at all times. This is a description of its nature, not a feature that it could have or not have.

Using quantum field theory as the foundational source, we define and discuss the type of universe in which we live, and given that universe, who are we, how and why we suffer, what our agenda is—is it built in or chosen?—for ourselves and for others, and what relationship, couplehood, and marriage mean in the quantum universe.

Quantum Principles in Imago Therapy

Through years of studying couples closely, as well as reading widely in science and philosophy, we are now clear, at least to ourselves, that human relationships mirror the principles that operate in the universe as a whole. For instance, throughout this book, we will show you how discoveries in brain science illuminate both the mechanism and the observable phenomena of couple behavior. We will illustrate how discoveries in quantum physics, epigenetics, and biology have led to a new relational paradigm for understanding what happens between partners and what needs to happen to restore their partnerships. We are biological and spiritual beings, or bio-spiritual beings without division. It is a polarity, like a wavicle, not a duality. We are of nature and in nature in ways we have just begun to grasp.

We have based Imago theory on three fundamental features of the quantum field that scientists understand apply to Everything There Is. In a neat example of the unity of things, these principles have direct application to our understanding of how couples connect and rupture connecting—that is, why couples fight—and how connecting can be restored. The micro view of the universe turns out to be relevant to the macro view of us poor, struggling humans.

1. Energy

The first principle is that matter can be understood as energy and energy as matter. Einstein built a whole cosmology on this premise: $E=mc^2$. Human beings are, like everything else that exists, an expression of cosmic energy, magnificent specks that are made from the same elements that make up everything else.

We are energy fields, not psychological metaphors. We are led to see ourselves as dynamic and interactive rather than static and separate. We partake of the dynamism that is present in every area of science: the vibration of violins strings, the firing of neurons in the brain, the slow oscillation of a swinging pendulum.

On a practical level, this means that the Imago therapist is sensitive to the energy each partner brings into the room, the energy they generate together, and how this energy is changed and transmuted into something else by the interactions that occur. Partners often come in anxious, depressed, and angry, sleepwalking through their days, automatically reacting to the things that happen without any real stirring of genuine feeling. They say they feel chaotic, scared, or like the walking dead. The core techniques of Imago are designed to transform negative energy into open energy and then positive energy, so that connecting is restored.

It must be said that therapy is hard work. So where will the energy needed for transformation come from? At first, the fuel that powers the work must come from the cognitive decision the partners make to engage in the process, regardless of how much enthusiasm they may or may not feel for it. But after that? It is generated from the moments of being heard and hearing, being accepted and accepting, being cared about and caring. The oscillating flow begins again. Thinking of your clients as energy fields rather than discrete constructions with absolute identities reminds you that change is your milieu. You are working with live, fluctuating, oscillating forces that you will be challenged to facilitate and help regulate so they can focus their energy and operate out of their prefrontal cortex.

2. Consciousness

Early founders of quantum mechanics, Max Planck, Niels Bohr, and Werner Heisenberg, made a radical contribution to Einstein's "matter equals energy" and "energy equals matter" thesis by positing "consciousness" as the essence of energy, thus of matter, and thus of the universe. In an interview, Max Planck put it this way:

> *I regard consciousness as fundamental. I regard matter as derivative from consciousness. We cannot get behind consciousness. Everything that we talk about, everything that we regard as existing postulates consciousness. (Sullivan, 1931, p. 17)*

This declaration by one of the preeminent founders of quantum physics that everything existing postulates consciousness supports the view that, since consciousness is "reality," the quantum field referenced above is a "field of consciousness." Equal declarations from distinguished scientists state that the primary feature of consciousness is creativity which constantly expresses itself in the creation of forms—quarks, atoms, molecules, us, galaxies, universes—all of which arise out of, and participate in, the conscious field and are in a constant flow of interconnecting interactions. Therefore, we are "made" of consciousness; we are participants in the conscious field and the conscious field lives in us. Thus, our personal consciousness is an instance of quantum consciousness, not an epiphenomenon of our brains, but its source.

And this, perhaps, establishes that our purpose and function, as a part of an evolving universe which has become conscious, is to be the location through which that universe is discovering Itself. The experience of becoming aware that we are THAT and that our connecting to the whole is expressed in the sensation of full aliveness pulsating through the fibers of our neurophysiology, which is experienced emotionally as joyful relaxation and a state of wonder. This is the experience of our true nature. From the perspective of Imago, our access point to the cosmos, and the sensation of full aliveness, joy, and wonder that attends it, is the quality of our significant relationships. We do not seek to be in thriving relationships because it is "something" that we "need"; we seek relationships and suffer dreadfully when we are not "in" relationship because not being in a thriving relationship is not "natural." That is why they are so important, and to get them right is so compelling.

This can be summarized as six fundamental propositions:

1. Since the "observer effect," in which particle behavior has been shown to be influenced by the observer implies particle

awareness, Imago incorporates the view that consciousness, as nonreflective awareness, may be not simply the predominant feature of the universe but the essential "stuff" of which the universe is made. That is, the universe does not have a conscious feature; the universe *is* consciousness itself.

2. Since awareness/consciousness is a property of everything, from stars to particles to cells and thus of humans, our consciousness is derivative of consciousness itself.

3. Since we are not only aware but also possess self-awareness, we are the part of the universe through which the universe is conscious of itself. This argument about our essential nature as self-reflective consciousness is the basis for the possibility of a "conscious partnership," which we shall propose and discuss in Chapter 7.

4. Since consciousness is "reality" and we are a manifestation of consciousness, we are not just endowed with consciousness as a feature. Our personal consciousness exists as a derivative of the field of consciousness, like a baby exists as a derivative of its mother or ice as a derivative of water. The substance is the same; the shape, form, and capacity are different. By the way, this parallels our discovery about the evolution of the self from the individual to the relational paradigm in which the self's relational features morphed into the self *as* relationship.

5. Given that "con" in *consciousness* means "with" and "scious" means "knowing," the literal meaning of consciousness is "knowing with" (Zeman, 2004). This replaces the general theory of consciousness as a quality or feature of the brain with a view that consciousness is a quality of relationship, not just a feature of the brain. In this cosmology, essential human nature is full aliveness, and our energetic patterns and deepest emotions are ecstatic and relaxed joyfulness and wonder.

6. If quantum consciousness is inherently benign and creative—without any qualities related to good versus bad, positive or negative, desirable or undesirable—then it inevitably follows that human beings, too, as a manifestation of the conscious universe, are intrinsically benign and creative.

3. Connecting

And that brings us to our third point about the ontological reality of the universe: connecting. Consistent with, and simultaneously, consciousness is the medium of connecting. Just as consciousness is our nature, so is connecting. We could call it conscious connecting. Except for the fact that we can lose awareness of connecting, but not connecting itself, there is no other reality than conscious connecting. We can neither start it nor stop it. It is our participation in Being. Connecting is Being.

The entire universe is contained in each of its parts, like the entirety of the human genome that resides in every cell of the body. And like the human body, the universal organism is aware of aspects of itself, and it brings energy to the points where attention is focused. We call the interconnectivity and interdependency of all aspects of this universe the tapestry of being. Because every segment of this tapestry is connecting with all other segments, each one influences, and is influenced by all of the others. Therefore, interconnecting—as the essential feature of human life and of everything else in the universe, from the interactions of massive star systems all the way down to the way nanoparticles react in concert with each other—denotes an ever-flowing exchange of conscious energy and information, a dynamism that allows seemingly discrete entities to influence and, even more, to cocreate each other.

Therefore, there can be no intrinsic autonomy of any part of the universe or, by implication, any person. Like the DNA lying within each cell that comprises and unites every organ within the human body, each part of the universe contains, and is contained within, every other part. In a letter to a grieving father who recently lost his son to illness, Einstein wrote:

A human being is a part of the whole, called by us "Universe," a part limited in time and space. He experiences himself, his thoughts and feeling as something separate from the rest—a kind of optical delusion of his consciousness. The striving to free oneself from this delusion is the one issue of true religion. Not to nourish it but to try and overcome it is the way to reach the attainable measure of peace of mind. (Calaprice, 2005, p. 206)

In human terms, our ontological connections are easy to see; after all, we live them day to day. As biological beings, our mind and body are connected in contrast to the Descartian illusion with which we have lived for three centuries (Skirry, n.d). As family beings, we are intimately connected to the functioning of other family members. As social beings, we are part of the interlocking webs that describe our various communities and demographics. In an exciting way, our small interdependencies mirror the essential conditions of the universe. Discovering these interdependencies and what they mean is one way to define the role of scientific inquiry. How do atoms combine? How do diverse elements of ecosystems fit together into interdependent wholes? How do trees exhibit intelligence by self-regulating their growth according to which others are growing nearby? It's literally impossible to think of any element of the natural world that stands absolutely alone. Life is not made that way.

Imago's emphasis on connecting as fundamental reality has implications for how we see the phenomena we tend to call the Self. In conventional religion and psychoanalysis, the self has been almost like an object, a separate and distinct "thing" with characteristics and needs, a definable entity that has an identity. Imago posits that the self is an "experience" that is cocreated by the continuous vibration between the outer world and the inner world and that participates in the cosmic oscillation between field and form. The self is always oscillating between form and flow in interactions with internal and external forces, which include actual material circumstances as well as the field of abstract cultural values, and their actions on the inner world of feelings and memory.

This is a shift in emphasis from the primacy of the inner life of the individual to the primacy of interacting between inner and outer experiences that form the inner world of the individual. The most significant influence on any one person is the intimate interaction between that person and those close to them.

This has big implications for conventional psychotherapy, as you will see as you go through the book. It means that the therapeutic techniques of psychoanalysis, behaviorism, and cognitive therapy, and all forms of couple's therapy derived from them, can be helpful, but they are not complete. We contend that **what transforms individuals is, ultimately, being present to the other and experiencing connecting in relationship, not attempting to change yourself or the other as individual persons.**

Connecting is not merely our primary characteristic; it is also our essential ingredient. Just as cells make up the connective tissue of the human body, connecting is the connective tissue of the human mind. Connecting is not what one does; it is what we all "are." Imago theory is an expression of this newly evolving paradigm that goes beyond psychology and that roots human experience in an ontology of connecting, which names connecting as a descriptor of the human being.

This leads to six meta-assumptions:

1. Since consciousness connects everything, we are interdependent and interconnected not only as a state but also as a process.
2. Since the basic composition of human nature is connectivity, we are interconnecting both internally and externally within ourselves, with others, and with our physical environment and the cosmos.
3. Since connecting describes our natural internal state, our body, its organs, and the human brain all operate interdependently

and reciprocally with each other, following the principle known as mind–body unity.

4. Since connecting is our nature, connecting also refers to our external interrelatedness with other human beings, with nature, and with the cosmos.

5. Since the quantum theory of nonlocality states that if any two particles that have been in contact are separated, and the spin of one particle is altered locally, the spin of the other particle will be altered simultaneously, non-locally, no matter the distance. This means that any event that occurs anywhere affects everything everywhere simultaneously, therefore proximity is not a requirement for connecting, including communicating and emotional-cognitive impact. When the effect of one thing upon another occurs when those things are an infinity apart, this is not viewed as a transfer of information but rather as evidence of the intricacy of the connection; evidence of the universe as a tapestry.

6. Since the density of everything before the Big Bang means that originally everything was entangled, the conditions for nonlocal effect were in place at the beginning of creation and take place everywhere at all times whether we know it or not (or believe it).

In essence, all local events have global and cosmic effects. There is no such thing as an isolated event or an isolated individual or an isolated particle. Everything is part of the web of being. Therefore, what we do locally in any given moment impacts, at varying levels of intensity, everything everywhere. While this is counterintuitive and essentially incomprehensible to logic and serial thinking, nonlocality has been definitively established.

THE SPACE-BETWEEN

Identifying energy, consciousness, and connecting as the driving principles of life focuses our attention on the central therapeutic concept of Imago. If we are saying that human beings are essentially made of conscious energy and this is the basis that connects us all, what does this tell us about therapy? Or, how shall we reframe the therapy process? It tells us that the place where these powerful but unseen forces reside is of crucial importance. It tells us that paying attention to the emotional force field that partners generate together is where we should start our work and where change happens.

We call that force field the Space-Between, a term we inherited from Martin Buber, the Austrian Jewish philosopher born in 1878. We have developed his concept of the I–Thou relationship (Buber, 1958) and made it central to both Imago theory and Imago therapy. The hyphen, which was central to Buber's concept, represents our Space-Between. This is the reality that we work with when we are helping couples. Before this clarification, our use of the term *Space-Between* was a substitute for *relationship* and served as metaphor to emphasize, for couples, the importance of prioritizing their relationship over their separate selves so they could learn the paradoxical and counterintuitive fact that creating a healthy relationship was the best thing they could do for their individual lives—an achievement called love!

What it means to us now is that the couple really consists of three entities, not just two. There is an "I" and a "Thou," but there is also what they have created together in the Space-Between that unites them or separates them. The Space-Between is not empty; it can be filled with appreciation, admiration, joy and confidence—positive energies that are cohesive. Conversely, it also be filled with behavioral realities like criticism, anxiety, mutual blaming, disappointment, secrets, shadowy feelings, and memories that are hidden from awareness—negative energies that are chaotic, and usually overpowering. According to George Wald, in a conversation, Einstein seemed to locate the source of negative energy in nature, although it could be interpreted as humor:

> *I used to wonder how it comes about that the electron is negative. Negative-positive—these are perfectly symmetric in physics. There is no reason whatever to prefer one to the other. Then why is the electron negative? I thought about it a long time and at last all I could think was "It won the fight!" (Wald, 1957)*

These are abstract ideas in the sense that they don't have corporeal manifestations, but their existence is real, and their effects are impactful and important. Physics has schooled us to accept the reality of things we know are there but cannot yet see (like black holes, dark matter, nanoparticles, etc.) and this has served our work with couples. We are more than the dynamics readily visible on the surface. Our connections go immeasurably beyond that which we can readily comprehend.

Therefore, the Space-Between is not a metaphor or a psychological construct, but a local instance of the quantum field that exists between everything, is in everything, and holds everything together. The important point here is: the field that constitutes the Space-Between, the hyphen, is not generated by the partners; it generates them and is the bond in the "between" that holds the polarities in tension. But partners can influence the quality of the field—chaotic or coherent, positive or negative—by what they think and do, and the effect of willful action becomes resident as memory in their inner world.

From this perspective, **the problems couples bring to our offices are not located inside themselves, in their intrapsychic spaces. The problems are located in their interactions with each other, in the Space-Between them**. If it is true that problems are precipitated by interactions with others, then change has to be initiated from the same place—from the interactive rather than the intrapsychic space. Change in the interactive space produces new experiences that are recorded as configurations of memory. Ruptures occur in our interactions with others, producing chaos, and when those interactions are regulated and become coherent, the interior self simultaneously becomes coherent.

Life is lived in the Space-Between and remembered in the Space-Within. There is an ongoing oscillation between the outside and the inside, but the initiation comes from the outside. Changing our inside world is dependent on, and a function of, changing the quality and content of our interactions with the outside world. Change in the inside world interacts with the outside world in a never-ending oscillation of influence. But the flow is from the outside in . . . and then from the inside out.

We have identified processes, not entities or objects, as the fundamental reality of the universe, which includes human beings and their complex behavior. Our job as therapists is to understand the implications of this idea and employ these processes for the purpose of rewiring the connections that have broken, thereby participating in the great ongoing work of the universe, which is to create coherence; which is turn is the source of our resonance with others and thus of our relaxed joyfulness and aliveness.

THE QUANTUM FEATURES OF THE SELF

Most theories falling within the individual paradigm are organized around the notion of a "self" as a self-contained and distinct unit that distinguishes the "me" from the "not me" (Sullivan, 1953), but does not include a "we." While varying in how they depict the self, these perspectives define the self as a more or less consistent and enduring entity that guides the person's perceptions of and responses to the environment. As we have seen, certain theories, such as those in the object relations school, point to a self that gets constructed out of our experiences of relating to significant others—our so-called "objects"—especially our parents. Other systems equate the self with the personality, or character. In any case, virtually all theories affiliated with the individual paradigm see the personality or selfhood as permanently shaped, enduring, and operating more or less independently from others—as a Newtonian atom, as billiard balls on a pool table, or, from a quantum physics perspective, particle-like.

In the quantum sciences, there is no such a thing as a "self" or any other separate psychological entity, because in the quantum world there are no "things." Instead, in the quantum world, we can think of the quantum self as the particle–wave duality, which is an interacting field of energy known as the wavicle.

This means that the quantum self, as wavicle:

1. is essentially energy—specifically, each of us is a point or node in the limitless web of universal energy. Therefore, our psyche is no more stable or unchangeable than are any other manifestations of universal energy;
2. is an instance of quantum consciousness. The quantum self, as wavicle, operates in the same way as the cosmos, everything ranging from the largest objects to the smallest particles. This means that the human psyche is neither fixed nor absolute, but rather is in constant oscillation with its context and undergoing constant change with each oscillation;
3. is constantly interacting with context. The interconnectivity of the quantum self connects mind and body, senses and emotions, and self and others;
4. responds to its interpersonal context and shifts with changes in context, which in turn changes the context, in a constant process of focus and flow;
5. is an oscillating process in constant movement between its particle and wavelike qualities; and
6. is devoid of all characteristics like autonomy, independence, self-love, self-soothing, and self-care, which are viewed as desirable by the individual paradigm.

THE QUANTUM FEATURES OF COUPLEHOOD

We did not begin our reflection on the nature and fate of couplehood deductively, but inductively. Clinical experience led us to the conclusion that the human yearning for connecting and the anxiety about connectional vulnerability appeared congruent enough with the quantum theory of connecting to posit a continuous oscillation from the cosmic to the personal and from the personal to the cosmic. When we began to look at couplehood through the quantum lens and saw that each quantum is both particle-like and wavelike and that particle creation is dyadic—i.e., each particle that jumps into space from the void is paired with another particle, and that the particle itself is an oscillation between matter and energy—we posited that couplehood is not only a social structure with psychological entities, it is also a quantum phenomenon. Each and every couple we work with is a wavicle interacting with a wavicle.

What does this mean for you as an individual? Or, as a part of a couple? What are the implications of this radical view of the self (or, more accurately, no-self) for human relationships? Specifically, if there is no such thing as a separate self, when we are in a relationship, who is it that we are relating to? How can we have a relationship with a "no-self"? Again, quantum findings provide a handy parallel for this discussion.

Let us assume, as do a number of contemporary quantum thinkers (Krauss, 2012; Cox & Forshaw, 2012), that since human beings are composed of the same stuff that make up quantum objects, we therefore operate according to the same rules. Following this reasoning, this means that a couple:

- is two wavicles interacting in the Space-Between, which is itself a wavicle;
- is a bundle of consciousness–energy–information oscillating between its particle-like and wavelike forms;
- is the outcome of the quality of its interactions;
- has open and fluid boundaries; and
- constantly cocreates each other with every oscillation.

Suffering in a Quantum Universe

But, for all human beings, something tragic has happened: disconnecting from a significant other causes suffering at the local *and* cosmic level. Although disconnection from the personal cannot disconnect from the quantum field, since that is an ontological state, the pain of personal disconnection can replace the "experience" of connecting to the field, in which case the disconnect is experientially real, although not actually. If connecting is of paramount importance, then it stands to reason that the suffering of disconnecting is equally important. This is the central narrative of Imago therapy.

As we shall see, ruptured connecting has fundamental consequences for individuals, couples, families, and, not least, for the whole of society.

While we cannot be expelled from a connecting universe, since we are a part of the tapestry of Being, when we experience a negative interaction, we can lose awareness that we are in it. What happens when connecting is ruptured by negativity? Any negative exchange activates the survival directive in the lower brain. That triggers anxiety, which forces us into a protective absorption with ourselves, which simultaneously causes us to lose our experience of connecting to our personal and social context, and simultaneously to the universe.

When couples come to us, that is their existential condition, no matter their psychological diagnosis. They want us to help them recover their original state, their true condition, which is the sensation of full aliveness, joy, and wonder. When we, as therapists, assist in the process of restoring connecting, we are in harmony with the fundamental forces of nature that drive all that exists, and, in the process of facilitating reconnecting for our clients, we experience our participation in the same energy field. For humans, the process of transformation is the process of conscious connecting. In this sense then, we are midwives to birthing consciousness, and we are also its beneficiaries.

Transformation in Imago is a journey to the place where it all started: experiencing connecting and the sensation of joyful relaxation, full aliveness, and wonder with which life began by creating the conditions for its restoration which include:

1. creating and sustaining a safe environment;
2. identifying earlier life challenges and becoming empathic;
3. learning how defenses developed as a result of negative exchanges;
4. removing all negativity from all interactions;
5. reconnecting to the person who both embodies one's challenges and has the power to help transform them;
6. connecting with each other in safety and nonjudgment through Imago Dialogue;
7. stretching to transform frustrations into requests for changed behaviors;
8. exchanging positive energy through giving and receiving appreciation and humor several times daily;
9. becoming an advocate for and celebrating each other's differences; and
10. practicing presence and resonance whenever engaged with each other.

This journey cannot be undertaken in darkness. One must be willing to walk into the light. If partners remain unconscious, they remain the victims of their own hidden suffering; narrow and closed. They interact with their partners through overly intense or minimized emotion. They are triggered to react rather than stimulated to respond. They react with no awareness of what is going on, continuing the legacy of pain that they have inherited.

Fortunately, we know that the past does not have to be a prison sentence. It is possible to open the bars and breathe deeply the fresh air of other possibilities. A new and different energy can create a new and different consciousness. A volatile partner who is under pressure can, over time, learn to calm down and become thoughtful and caring.

This is the purpose of Imago therapy: to free people from the prison of their reactive brains and regain their natural state of open collaboration with each other. If they cannot connect to their capacity for knowing their chosen other, they have no conduit for self-knowing and therefore they find themselves disconnected from feeling a broader communion with everything else in life—spiders, hedgehogs, clouds, rocks . . . all of it!

When Imago therapists sit with a couple, they see themselves and the couple as citizens in a conscious universe in which everything—including the partners to each other and the couple to the therapist—are connecting. But, the couple is not experiencing that, and that is why they are there, although they may not know that explicitly.

But, the Imago therapist knows that when they lost their connecting with each other, they lost this awareness of connecting to the larger whole. They intuitively know it is available in their relationship, and that they want it back. This intuitive knowing is why they came to therapy together. Now it is the job of the therapist to facilitate the restoration of connecting. The therapist knows their relationship will be mutually impactful and that everything they do will enhance or diminish their awareness of their connection to each other, and thus to the quantum field. The couple's connecting to each other is the conduit to sustaining their connecting to the cosmos. (When we discuss the therapy process in later chapters, we will describe and illustrate the process of helping couples restore connecting.)

What this means for Imago metatheory is that any sense of disconnection we might feel in our relationship with our partner—or with other human beings, for that matter—is fundamentally illusory. We are connecting so intrinsically that we know each other and impact each other beyond our conscious awareness, even when we are not physically proximate to each other. As we said earlier, we can lose awareness of connecting but not lose connecting itself. Awareness of connecting is usually lost locally, in early unattuned and intimate relationships, but its effect is felt cosmically. Our feelings of personal alienation tend to make the whole universe unfriendly. In reality, our mutual interconnectedness with all human beings and all other existence is as fundamental as the relationship between a nucleus and its electrons, between the human brain and body, and between the planets and the sun.

THE IMPLICATIONS OF THE QUANTUM
FIELD FOR SOCIAL TRANSFORMATION

Given the thesis that our consciousness, expressed in our behaviors, is not an epiphenomenon of our brains, but a derivative of the field *of* consciousness with which it interacts, it makes sense that such a shift would have a subtle, or perhaps dramatic, impact on our collective experience, rather than just something of personal or academic interest. For instance, a shift in the conscious quantum field toward a state of greater coherence may be experienced in personal consciousness as a feeling of congruence with the direction of the collective, and those persons may become enthusiastic advocates. On the other hand, that same congruence may disturb the personal consciousness of others, causing them to react against the forward movement of the collective and they may become enthusiastic opponents. In either case, this can be seen as an expression of complementarity that shows up as tension between the particle-like and wavelike human configurations.

For instance, in our current situation, we can posit that this tension of opposites seems to be occurring in the mental health field. For instance, psychological systems and therapy models based on the centrality of the individual are delving deeper into the self—with new brain and body sciences and with a proliferation of new models of psychotherapy and several hundred diagnoses. On the other hand, some psychological and therapy systems are emphasizing the centrality of relationships and developing new models of interpersonal engagement that includes individuals, couples, organizations, and culture itself.

The tension between the pull toward greater connection and cohesion and the pull back toward more individuality and separateness creates the tension of opposites, which expresses itself as conflict between disciplines and cultural conflict. The chaos and polarization in civilization can be viewed (and we do) as the birth pangs of the emergence of the next step in our social evolution. All forms—from particles to molecules to humans to social and economic systems to therapy systems and forms of intimate relationships—are constellated in the quantum field, and when any become irrelevant to the evolutionary process, they dissolve back into the field and the energy seems to be re-constellated as new forms in the next evolutionary step.

But social institutions, as well as the persons who inhabit them, do not know that these transitions are orchestrated in the quantum field, so when the dissolution occurs, they fight for survival, just as an animal does; they fight to preserve the status quo. We posit that the next step in our social evolution is expressed in the appearance of amazing technologies for connecting and rapid forms of travel; in economic globalism; and in the cries for the acceptance of diversity, universal equality, total inclusiveness, and the celebration of difference. It is this tension between the individual and the collective that moves the human race forward to its telos, which we posit is mirroring the organization and relations in the universe itself, in which we not only live but are an intrinsic part.

We look through the quantum lens of the wavicle to offer an interpretation of the transition to the next stage in our social evolution as well as assign that direction to the quantum process itself. Through the lens of the wavicle, classical physics, upon which our civilization was based and which gave us the individual as a primary cultural value and the separate self as the client in the mental health professions, can be seen as an instance of the particle aspect of the particle–wave duality. Given that, it makes sense that after the particle-like character of culture has achieved its purpose (in this case all the way from freeing persons from the serfdom of the Middle Ages to endowing some social groups with personal freedom and equal opportunity in the democratic revolutions), the shift to a wavelike culture would evolve to provide a vision of the larger reality of our intrinsic connection as humans that would achieve a higher level of cultural cohesion and conscious participation in our collective consciousness and at the same time create a culture that would serve the best interests of the individual, who is now understood to be a derivative of the collective rather than its center. This reflects paradigm science that states that paradigm change always includes and transforms the paradigm it replaces. In the shift from the individual to the relational paradigm in psychotherapy, the individual is not negated but is relocated to its relational context from which it is derived and upon which it is dependent.

Since the wavicle is the foundational feature of all forms, subatomic or classic, it can be used as a lens to observe how the tension between particle-like and wavelike features in any system—social and community organization, social movement, business, educational, or religious—are being managed and could be used as a diagnostic that would encourage whatever adjustment is needed for the system to achieve its optimal potential.

THE IMPLICATIONS OF THE QUANTUM FIELD FOR THE NEXT STAGE OF HUMAN SOCIAL EVOLUTION

It seems to us, from a cursory overview of the impact of physics on culture, that shifts in physics precede shifts in the human sciences, social structures, and personal values.

Just as Newtonian atomism offered the source and model of the autonomous and separate self for our current individualistic civilization, quantum field theory offers the source and model of the quantum self as the foundation of a relational civilization. Just as a new model of the self, based on the atom in classical physics, was the source of all our current cultural institutions, the adoption of the quantum self will transform our cultural institutions and create new institutions that will contain and express our as yet undiscovered potentials. Just as the features of our individualistic civilization valued competition, control, domination, and winning, the values of the coming relational civilization will be universal equality, total inclusiveness, and celebration of differences.

This evolutionary step constituted by quantum discoveries portrays the universe as an interconnecting organism and subsumes within it, but it does not negate the Newtonian universe of ontologically separate and independent objects. In addition, in the quantum universe, the phenomena we refer to as the basis of the "self," is a constantly changing field of information–energy–consciousness that alternates between focus and flow—mirroring the particle–wave duality, or wavicle—which quantum theory claims characterizes all phenomena in the quantum universe. This concept of the quantum self is also subsuming, as quantum physics subsumes classical physics—the concept of the separate, autonomous, and substantive "self" of Newtonian atomism—into itself as the point of focus in the flow. We are ontologically connecting beings rather than intrinsically separate and disconnected beings.

Therefore, we posit that the emergence of quantum physics in human consciousness in the twentieth century is primary evidence that this next evolutionary step is emerging from collective consciousness in the form of scientific discovery. We also believe that quantum theory replaces, as a worldview, the vision of the "human" bequeathed to us by classical physics. In the Newtonian universe, ontological separation and autonomy were not just features, they were the essence of everything, including human beings; so in the quantum universe, interconnectivity is not a feature of nature, it is its essence, and thus it describes us.

Given these shifts, we intuit that our collective humanity, and each of its members individually, is on the verge of something big, something beyond our imagination, which we can dimly intuit but not yet see. Here is what we think that is: *We believe there is evidence that we human beings, collectively and individually, are in transition to our **next stage of human social evolution.*** We invite you to join us in the exploration of what is coming.

Implications of the Quantum Field for Research

The practice of science since its inception around 1,000 years ago has been to break things apart to see what they are made of with the assumption that we will eventually find that of which all things are made. The last such experiment was the search in the Higgs field for Boson particle, the elementary particle that would yield its secret about how particles acquire mass. The lack of certainty about its discovery raised questions about whether it exists, and thus whether mass may be a function of relationship rather than a feature of an object. The outcomes of this research method and process have been that every breakdown, of even the smallest particle, only yields other, smaller particles. The implication for the quantum field is that at the very base, there is no "thing" that can be discovered; reality is an energy field of consciousness that exists between things and holds them together, and that is where they acquire mass.

This has many important implications for therapy and is a vast area for new research. From the quantum perspective, since reality is the Space-Between partners, change is constantly occurring as unceasing interactions *between* persons, of which therapy is a specialized instance, the quality of that change is determined by the way partners observe each other. Effective intervention in the Space-Between creates the cohesion that bonds partners, and that bond transforms what is inside them. This calls for a shift in the focus of research, from the impact of therapy on the internal world of each partner to research on the interactions in the Space-Between that transform their inner world by populating it with memories and dreams, and it portends a shift in therapy to intervening in the interactive rather than in the intrapsychic space.

Toward a Relational Value System as the Foundation of Civilization

Since this shift toward a relational value system is so tectonic, we propose a new field which we call "Relationology," the subject of which is the art and science of relationship collaboratively and creatively designed, grounded in research, and robustly conveyed through all educational institutions to all future generations. This will provide a relational foundation for the human sciences and the practice of therapy in all its forms, which on the one hand will be a benefactor and on the other, a contributor.

IMAGO
CLINICAL THEORY

INTRODUCTION TO CLINICAL THEORY

Metatheory has no objects but is the holder of all possible objects. It is the holder of the visible, but it itself is invisible. It is a construct that can be put into words that might evoke an image, but the object is not available to anything but our imagination. You might think of metatheory as a vision of reality, but not its particulars.

Also, you cannot see the object of clinical theory, because it is one measure less abstract and more concrete than metatheory. It is not yet about seeing or doing, but thinking about the particulars of clinical practice. And the content of the thought has to do with goals, not outcomes.

Part II is about Imago Clinical Theory which is a perspective about the human situation in a quantum universe.

In Chapter 3, Part II, we begin with an overview of our multifaceted and deeply complex brain, focusing on aspects of Paul MacLean's triune brain, Stephen Porges polyvagal theory, and Dan Siegel's neuroplasticity all of which contribute to the understanding of couples interactions and the ability to change what was once considered unchangeable. In Chapter 4, we elaborate on our thesis that connecting is the nature of human nature, and that we cannot think of human beings otherwise. We humans come into the world experiencing ourselves as a point in the tapestry of being, and our originating experience is full aliveness, joy, and wonder. Given that it is our nature to experience belonging to the universe, it makes sense that our goal as humans would be to sustain our original experiencing.

However, because we have not yet evolved to the level that our caretakers can hold us in our true being by staying resonant with us when we are infants, our experience of connecting is ruptured, which for all practical purposes is experienced as the loss of connecting because it is lost from awareness. In Chapter 5, we designate the loss of connecting as our deepest trauma, the trauma behind all traumas; and our life agenda is to restore connecting. In Chapter 6, we posit an organic, biopsychological process that is activated when connecting is ruptured in childhood. The memory of our original condition is stored in our DNA, which also stores the experience of the loss of connecting and the caretakers with whom it occurred. Waiting all throughout childhood, somewhat like a caterpillar in its cocoon, the memories emerge from the chrysalis in search of a partner who is similar to the caretaker with whom the rupture occurred. Upon sight of such a person, the neurochemistry of the body is activated, and a bond is created. But soon the bond is ruptured, and the butterfly goes on a never-ending search for the pupate stage—and winds up in your office looking for it.

The butterfly seems to organically inhabit its true nature without rupture. As far as we know, we humans do not know how to do that. We have to learn, and we can learn because it is our passion, and being cut off from it is our deepest suffering. In Chapter 7, we describe the processes that must take place to create the conditions for our natural experience of being to be restored and sustained. We call it conscious partnership. In some ways it is like a constructed cocoon, which we call the Space-Between, in that it contains the conditions that are just right to sustain the beauty of our original, natural state. And we end this section of the book with Chapter 8, exploring the developmental challenges in the couple's relationship.

3

Our Connecting Brain

To fully understand the drama of couplehood, we think it is very useful to have a cursory understanding of our brain, and especially what happened to it in childhood (see Chapters 4 and 5). And we think a rudimentary knowledge of the three-pound ball on their shoulders will help couples create and sustain a more conscious and better relationship.

Preemptively, we can say that our brains were shaped by our interaction with our caretakers; that environmentally shaped brain shows up in adulthood and determines the quality of all relationships, but especially intimate ones. Our relationships will sustain or change the operations of our brains, for better or worse, and since our brains are plastic (i.e., changeable) we can use our relationships to change our brains.

Before we present our understanding of the current views of the structure and function of the brain, how it was shaped, how it functions in relationships, and how it can be changed, let's take a brief look at how our brain has been viewed in the past.

Our first observation is that the brain has been of interest to us humans for a long time, about 2,500 years, at least, and its value and function have been interpreted through a cultural lens for nearly three centuries. Since we are all—including science—embedded in a cultural context that shapes our world view, current brain theory is what current brain researchers think. The achievements of neuroscience are immensely impressive, and dictate our current understandings. In some distant future, we will have new data and new theories with new potential.

While there is a scientific consensus that thought is produced, in some mysterious way, by the activity of billions of cells in the most complex structure in the universe, the brain has not always been perceived as the location of thought. Until around 600–300 BCE, the location of thought was the heart. That changed when Hippocrates, the most well-known ancient physician, located disease, madness, and pleasure in the brain (Cobb, 2020, pp. 15–19). Over the centuries, the brain was assigned the location of everything from spirits by religious leaders, to reason by Descartes (the first modern western philosopher) and our evolutionary adaptive survival instinct by Charles Darwin (the founder of evolutionary biology).

Consistent with the impact of culture on brain science, modern and scientific interest in how the brain works has produced a sequence of metaphors to understand our brains. In the sixteenth century, the brain was viewed as a machine; in the eighteenth century it was like a telegraph network and in the nineteenth a telephone exchange; and logically, in the twentieth century, it was like a computer. While its function was computing, its primary concern (inspired by Darwin's survival instinct theory) was survival. One of the most well-known metaphors, the triune brain, was presented by psychiatrist Paul MacLean in the 1960s. His evolutionary biological model had a hierarchy of three lobes: the reptilian brain inherited from lower mammals that is responsible for motor activity; the limbic system as the seat of our emotions; and the neocortex, where thinking, reflection, and computation occur. For MacLean, these functions were dedicated to specific regions with little if any crossover. That was his downfall, and criticism has been rather severe. Some writers, especially in the fields of psychology, psychiatry, and social science, rose to defend MacLean's construct (Cory & Gardner, 2002; Panksepp, 2002). A recurring theme in the defense of MacLean's triune brain concept, although accepting its limits, is that it nonetheless has explanatory and guiding power in social science, neuropsychiatry, and psychiatry (Cory & Gardner, 2002; Price, 2002; Ploog, 2003).

Contemporary neuroscience however has relegated his view to "neuromythology" and replaced it with a new model called the "network" which removes the dedication of specific regions to specific functions and replaces it with distribution of functions throughout the brain, both recognizing the brain's complexity and its capacity to change (neuroplasticity). A major shift in this direction was offered by LeDoux (1996, pp. 98–103) in a concept that replaced the image of hierarchal lobes with the concept of lateral functioning in which he argued that emotions may not be region-dependent, but rather spread over the whole brain. The idea of distribution of functions is consistent with many post-modern views of diversity versus singularity. It is interesting that in the latter part of the twentieth century, a shift from a static brain, a fixed DNA, and a separate self, to brain neuroplasticity, an experience-dependent DNA, and a self that is shaped in its social environment have appeared practically at the same time that quantum field theory spilled out of the physics labs into the domain of the human sciences and the public.

Even with all the progress that has been made in the neurosciences, most neuroscientists say: we know that the brain has billions of neurons working together, but we have no idea how all those billions work together to produce what we experience as the brain's activity. And, even further, we have no idea how the interactions of those neurons account for our subjective experience of say, a flower, the smell of bacon, or the touch of the skin of two lovers in an embrace—which is to say, consciousness. Some have hinted at a professional depression triggered by the mountains of data that has been collected with no organizing clue or theme about what it all means about the brain. Nor does the data provide clear insight into how we experience the world. In fact, the boundaries of the brain are now being extended energetically beyond the skull into the space of other brains with whom it interacts without the medium of language.

Since no one in the neurosciences, by their own admission, can account for the brain's activity or subjectivity, it is certainly not our intent to provide anything more than an introduction to those features of the brain that might be interesting to you and useful in your work with couples. That being said, the neurosciences, by meticulous observation and experiment, have learned an amazing amount about the structure of the brain, what those structures do, how they interact with each other and the world, and how we can consciously and intentionally interact with them.

While the perspective and conclusions of MacLean, and his hierarchal model, have been criticized, refuted, and replaced by other models, the case can be made, and most neuroscientists seem to agree, that the brain does have two hemispheres that consist of three discrete structures. Those structures and hemispheres have functions native to them. As they interact with each other, those functions are distributed across the brain regions and that, if needed, can acquire abilities to replace the loss of a function in another region. For instance, although speech appears to be located in the left brain, the right brain can learn to speak, and the occipital lobe can learn to smell. This means that the brain is not a static machine but a dynamic, living, adapting, growing, organism in constant interaction with its environment. The environment is changed by those interactions and, in turn, those interactions change the structure and function of the brain in ways that cannot be predicted, or in some cases, imagined.

Although hierarchal language is retained, the general trend, emphasized by LeDoux, is toward lateral or network functioning, which interestingly mirrors the network metaphor in the social and corporate worlds which reflects the operating view of the quantum world. These structures include: 1) lower brain, 2) central brain, and 3) upper brain structures (Siegel, 2020, pp. 32–34).

Our Three-Part Embodied Brain

The first point that needs to be made about the brain is that, although in conversation the brain and our body are often referred to as separate entities, by the deep well of knowledge accumulated by the biological, neurobiological, and related sciences, we know that they are, in fact, one and the same "thing." The brain and the body are as interconnected and interdependent as our fingers are with our hands and as we are with the universe. As Dan Siegel says (2020; personal communication, July 23, 2020), we have a "brain that is fully embodied and fully social." What that means is . . .

> . . . that the energy and information flow that streams through the interconnected connectome up in the head is influenced by streams of energy throughout the body. . . . We can also use the term "social brain" for how the electrochemical energy patterns in the head-brain are profoundly shaped by, and also shape, our interpersonal relationships . . . This is also why we can sense that the mind—who we are—is fully embodied and relational. (Siegel, 2020, p. 31)

Nothing inside or outside of the human organism exists independently, as we know from quantum theory's understanding of the relationship between energy and matter. Since what happens in one part of the universe has repercussions for all other parts, the same applies to every cell, organ, and organismic system that composes the human being as a whole and our brains in particular. So when, for example, a man hears his wife announce to him that she no longer loves him and wants a divorce, what happens inside the man's body—in his nervous, endocrine, cardiac, hormonal, and other systems—is comparable to how he might describe his emotional experience; it felt as though he had been kicked in the stomach. At that moment, biologically speaking, that is indeed what happened to him.

The brain and body are in constant communication, sending messages back and forth to adjust and readjust the feedback they produce, and upon which both are dependent for their balanced homeostatic functioning. Thus, for example, the body "knows," even before the higher brain processes it, whether someone who is walking a little too closely behind us is dangerous. This inner knowing or intuiting is hardly coincidental or imaginary. Quite the contrary—it is a byproduct of the sensitivity and complexity of the human nervous system, which operates like a massive homing device, scanning the environment, registering signs of safety or danger, and processing information from sensory and motor areas that are strategically placed throughout the brain and body.

Lower Brain Structures

The lower, primal brain contains the brain stem, which includes structures that direct respiration, blood pressure, heart rate, and other functions vital to preserving life. In effect, the primal brain is hard-wired for survival and is programmed to ensure the organism's safety. It operates automatically, as if on autopilot, requiring no conscious input from the upper brain to maintain our body in a homeostatic, steady-state condition. The survival value of primitive brain structures is suggested by the brain stem's protected location, deep within the lowest recesses of the brain, just above the spinal cord.

What drives the lower brain, first and foremost, is the irresistible power of the survival directive—that is, the compulsion to stay alive. To carry out that directive, the brain is equipped with a bundle of neurons called the reticular activating system (RAS) that starts close to the top of the spinal column and extends upwards about two inches. The RAS plays a big role in the sensory information we perceive daily. It is the gatekeeper of the information that is let into our conscious minds and filters out from the enormous amount of information available that which is relevant. In fact, all our senses, except the sense of smell, seem to come through that door, especially signals like the sound of our name being called, anything that threatens our safety or that of our loved ones or an indication from our partner concerning sex.

The lower brain, therefore, is in constant communication with the other parts of the brain. Here is how this mental trip wire dominates our thoughts and feelings once it has been activated. All the incoming information passes through the RAS to the thalamus to two receptors. If the RAS receives a danger signal, the first to receive it is the amygdala (located in the limbic system) which processes it instantaneously, and outside of conscious awareness, and if it is perceived as dangerous whether it is dangerous or not, the amygdala sounds the alarm, evoking anxiety, and a defensive reaction. While this is happening, the signal is also on its way from the thalamus to the cerebral cortex, which takes time, and where processing is slower, and if the situation is really dangerous, the cortex also activates anxiety and appropriate defensive reactions. Since the sensation of anxiety has two sources, the amygdala and the cortex, anxiety is our most important sensation because it alerts us to danger and our potential demise. On the other hand, if the situation is overwhelming (or the anxiety is overwhelming, but the situation is not) we are living in the nightmare of existence, which we call the essence of suffering.

The lower brain, also referred to as the primal or primitive brain, carries the heavy burden of ensuring our physical survival. This is the brain's most primitive area. It has features in common with the brains of all vertebrates, from reptiles to mammals (earning these structures the moniker of "reptilian brain").

Central Brain Structures

Located on top of the brain stem and under the forebrain, the mid-brain is the classically known mammalian or limbic brain. This newer portion, which emerged in later-evolved mammals, contains the hippocampus, the storehouse where new, short term relational memories are turned into long term memories, and its complementary partner, the amygdala, which, as mentioned, interprets the emotional meaning of all information that arrives from the senses via the thalamus. The amygdala and other limbic brain and cortical regions, structures that are thought to be present from birth, were thought to be the location of implicit memory (memories of the past that are experienced as events in the present) and are a foundation for our sense of ourselves. Somatosensory, or body memory, is also a part of the implicit process (Siegel, 2020, p. 127). It is now generally accepted that implicit memory is distributed throughout the brain. Of these two structures, the amygdala is the major culprit as far as triggering the emotional heat (as opposed to light) that gets generated when our brain senses something amiss in our partnership.

Expanding on MacLean's earlier work, brain researchers like LeDoux (1996) have identified the emotional circuitry of the amygdala as an evolutionary adaptation that arose to protect the organism from danger. This finding is supported by the amygdala's knee-jerk response to stimuli it interprets as life-threatening. Regardless of whether this interpretation is accurate, threatening information prompts the brain to discharge the survival-based chemical cortisol that evokes a defensive behavioral and emotional reaction.

The central and lower brain (together popularized as the "old brain") classifies incoming stimuli—something perceivable from the environment, whether the sound of a police car's siren or of the phone ringing when our child or spouse calls—in its typical dichotomous fashion: as something that is either safe or dangerous. "Safe" simply means something that will not hurt, harm, or kill us; dangerous, of course, means precisely the opposite. Note that the threat of "hurt," "harm," or "kill" may be conveyed to the primitive brain even when the harm is only emotional, not physical.

When safety reigns, the ventral vagal system is activated, the old brain lets down its guard and returns to its pre-set state of relaxed joyfulness. When danger appears, however, the sympathetic system goes on alert, and the primal brain sends out a distress signal. In response, the psyche immediately sounds the alarm, prompting the person to either minimize, by constricting energy (through freezing, hiding, or submitting by activating the dorsal vagal system), or maximize, by escalating (through fighting or fleeing). Keep in mind that these self-defenses are evolutionary and finely honed to work in the wild, yet they tend to be just as operative in our civilized world, even when there is no objective danger. But perception is everything, and if the primal brain perceives something as dangerous, no matter what it really is, it is dangerous. The imagination is as powerful as, if not more powerful than, experience.

Upper Brain Structures
The structures of the upper brain, usually called the neocortex, recently emerged in our evolutionary trajectory. Far more sophisticated than the other two regions, the new brain is sometimes also referred to as the "cortical brain," signifying its location in the cerebral cortex, and/or the "cognitive brain" indicating its mediation of complex information processing like perception, thinking and reasoning. While these functions are considered primary, it is important to recall that "the networks of the brain function as a whole to create global brain states" (Siegel, 2020, p. 33). Taking up five times more room as does the primal brain, the cerebral cortex is the precious crown jewels of the human species. Herein lie our uniquely human capacities for complex reasoning, speech, logical thought, judgment, planning ahead, self-reflection, and for moderating the raw emotion that gets triggered, willy-nilly, by the primitive brain. The capacity for this moderation depends on how well the lobes are integrated versus whether one lobe is undeveloped or another dominant. When thoughts, feelings, and action are coordinated in response to threat or pleasure, not only do we experience a sense of well-being, we can also create and sustain the conscious partnership we will describe and discuss later.

Imago theory posits that beneath the psychological presentation of a couple's problematic is an imbalanced and unintegrated brain. This accounts in part for the effective and rapid-fire survival reaction that comes along with the tendency to shoot first and then "ask questions." When feelings and action preside over thinking, we become reactive rather than reflectively responsive. Reactivity—acting on feelings without thinking or thinking and acting without feeling—is our universal human problem. The universal becomes local in our personal relationship when our acutely sensitive danger-meter interprets our partner's bad mood as a sign of an impending connectional rupture. Since anxiety about connectional rupture is tantamount, unconsciously, to the possibility of our demise, the ubiquity and intensity of the survival directive makes sense. Unless we stay very conscious of what we are feeling and why we're feeling it, we're likely to imagine our partner as an enemy soldier whose bayonet is aimed straight at our heart. Because survival comes first, all lesser matters (such as speaking logically) take second place, even when, in fact, they are the only guarantor of survival. Given our vulnerability to death and potential nonbeing as the possible outcome of any negative transaction, it makes sense that all of us, at one time or another, have said something foolish, if not outrageous, to our partner when we were very upset.

In any event, when we experience a high level of negative emotional arousal, it is the lower, primal brain that leads the action. By reacting at gigabyte speed, before the slower and more deliberate cerebral cortex has had enough time to figure out what is really going on, our efficient, unconscious, reflexive, animal-like, instinctual primal brain charges into action—effectively hijacking, for better or for worse, how we will react in the moment. The primitive brain classifies experience in the same way a combat soldier classifies anyone else on the battlefield: friend or foe. To the old brain, everybody we encounter is one or the other—safe or dangerous. "Safe" simply means anything that will keep me alive, and course, anything that is "dangerous" will kill me (whether literally or figuratively is not of any consequence to the primitive brain). Although the new brain is able to see shades of gray (some things are only a little dangerous, and they won't kill me), in the recesses of the unconscious primal brain, you are either one or the other.

There is another feature of the lower brain that does not help matters: it can't tell the difference between the present and the past. Everything is happening here and now, no matter the actual date or address. Our limbic system is the mother lode of implicit memories suspended in the eternal now and here. When the stakes are high, unintegrated feelings from childhood are easily awakened and seamlessly merge with whatever we're feeling right now, creating timeline confusions and wreaking havoc in our love lives. Such is the timeless and, in a sense, mindless realm of the primal brain. In addition to being atemporal, the lower brain is nonspatial with no recognition of space, merging self and other in a symbiotic union.

But there is some good news. While we may have much in common with other animals and often find ourselves in painful and, from a logical perspective, senseless predicaments, we also have a tremendous capacity for love and greatness. Although bound by the force of instinct, we are also endowed with the power of transcendence because we can do what no other animal can do: we can think about our own thinking, and we can shift the focus of our attention. This ability to notice ourself and to choose alternate options opens the door to a range of positive outcomes. According to biologist Bruce Lipton, if we change our perception, we can even change our genes. It all has to do with the will. We have the ability to change what we're thinking about. We can remind ourselves to take a deep breath before we say what we really think. We can see a situation in a new way, reframe it from the perspective of the other. We can decide not to make a big deal about a small problem, and so forth.

Both our hardest human problems and their most effective solutions are actually living in the same house; they're just on different floors. When all the regions of the brain are not linking, they are often at war. Our brain is either our best friend or our worst enemy. Which one it is depends on the level of hemispheric balance and integration of the lobes. Balance and integration determine which part of the brain is in charge at the moment. In a later section, we will show how balance and integration are facilitated by the Imago Dialogue process.

The Relational Features of Our Brains

Deeply embedded within the structures comprising the lower primal brain are massive arrangements of nerve fibers that run upward, toward the cortex, and downward, into the cavity containing the heart and other vital organs, called the polyvagal system. These neuronal arrays interconnect with each other and run along pathways to vital organs, including the heart, contributing to our ability to engage in a collection of seemingly unrelated activities: first and foremost, keeping us alive by ensuring our heart is beating at the proper cadence, but also more subtle functions such as turning our head to look at an attractive passerby, smiling at someone we love, speaking in a hushed tone during lovemaking, chewing, smiling, and modifying our voice tone.

The two-sided polyvagal system detects and communicates in ways that produce a diverse array of human behaviors: interconnected nerve fibers that communicate in an ongoing reciprocal fashion with other brain areas, with the muscles in our face that make us smile, with nerves in the vocal chords that modify our vocal tone, and with heart cells that regulate its beat. This vagal system maintains homeostasis by relaying messages up to the brain and down through the body to keep vital processes going. In encountering the environment, including other people, this vagal system—a two-sided, complex, survival-oriented detection system homes in on a given situation to decide the answer to a single question: Is it safe or is it dangerous?

Only recently have neuroscientists come to uncover and articulate the strategic roles played by vagal processes that go beyond basic survival. In fact, the nervous system structures implanted in the human brain and organs that keep us alive are the very same ones implicated in those emotional and behavioral patterns that keep us emotionally alive, which in turn relies on the quality of our perceived connectivity with other members of our species. That is, our physical survival is tied in with the quality of our felt connection with others. We cannot know everything, but we can strive to know how the body's systems impact the way we react and integrate and communicate.

One of the two sides of the vagal system consist of unmyelinated neuronal pathways that, when activated, trigger the slowdown of physiological arousal that defines immobilization. If you have ever closely observed a member of the reptilian species, you probably saw the animal freeze in place, presumably in an attempt to blend in with the environment and avoid your gaze in order to stay alive. That is how the evolutionarily older half of the vagal system (the dorsal vagal system, or DVC) operates; once activated, its immediate and sole concern is to limit energy use to the minimum required for basic metabolic processes. Think of a lizard going into its own version of shutdown mode: that is what the DVC does to the human being. It is a very good system for maintaining safety and staying alive if you are a reptile; if you are a human, extreme activation of the DVC can slow your heart rate down enough to kill you.

But the second part of the polyvagal system, while also concerned with organismic survival, attends and responds to different, more subtle cues involved in engaging in social behavior. This myelinated ventral vagal complex, or VVC, is the mammalian counterpart to the reptilian derived VVC. The VVC monitors cardiac output, among other things, to match it to environmental demands. Under normal conditions, the VVC regulates the heart rate in ways that maintain a balance between internal requirements and external or environmental demands. Like the endocrine and other systems, VVC activity depends on feedback received from other nerve centers or organs, allowing the person to shift between the steady-state relaxation produced by the parasympathetic nervous system to an appropriate level of cardiac arousal should things get interesting—for example, when someone we find sexually attractive looks our way and smiles.

The VVC neuronal pathways that are responsible for keeping us alive—respiration, heart rate, sympathetic arousal—are the same ones that are sensitive to cues of attunement and non-attunement, registering as either safety or danger, coming from others. Some of these pathways are part of phylogenetically or evolutionarily older systems that enabled earlier, more primitive species to adapt to their environment and survive. Other parts, including the more recent limbic segment of the vagal system, permit attuned and caring-based transactions to occur between people. The same structures and underlying mechanisms that operate automatically and outside awareness (i.e., autonomically) are also in charge of some of the most central emotional and behavioral components of human mating and pair bonding: facial expression, heartbeat, vocal tone, relaxation, and safety. This is referred to as the *social engagement* function of the polyvagal system, and it operates along the same neural pathways as those used to keep us alive.

The very existence of a complex monitoring system that relies on environmental cues of safety or danger provides empirical support of what mind–body theorists have long referred to as the wisdom of the body. But this innate wisdom comes with a set condition: it can be activated, accessed, and utilized only when the human nervous system detects safety in the environment. Safety, which is created in relationship and only in relationship, is what enables the brain to engage in socialization, nurturing, and growth-related activities. Without safety, the fight/flight or freeze responses take over, mobilizing the brain and body to respond to danger—whether the danger is objectively real or is merely imagined.

Thus, only when the brain detects safety in the environment will our nervous system activate the vagal pathways that allow us to engage socially with other people without anxiety or fear. Otherwise, in knee-jerk fashion, the system reacts defensively to mobilize against threat, depleting its precious metabolic energy that otherwise could have been diverted toward growth and expansion, including interactions with the environment and, especially, with safe others.

There is nothing wrong with the sympathetic fight/flight or parasympathetic freeze reactions except, of course, they inhibit the brain from accessing the higher cortical functions that are critical to relaxed, safe relating between two human beings. One should not be surprised, then, when witnessing the habitual pattern some partners have of shutting down emotionally and even physically when under extreme emotional duress; after all, as the piece of clinical wisdom notes, when under prolonged stress, people will revert back to using their most primitive coping mechanisms. These are the ones that involve relatively immature strategies like projection and denial; however, even those with more mature defenses eventually experience a breakdown in adaptive coping (Seligman & Groves, 1970; Peterson, Maier, & Seligman, 1995; Kubala et al., 2012).

OUR BRAIN AS RELATIONSHIP

While the brain, containing countless numbers of neuronal connections, is similar to a muscle, the mind can be thought of as a place where energy interacts with information (Siegel, 2007, 2020). While the exchange of information and energy is the experience of consciousness, it does not explain the nature of consciousness nor posit whether the brain is the source of consciousness or whether consciousness is the source of the brain. Our operating assumption, as we stated in the previous chapter, is that the brain is a derivative of collective and cosmic consciousness, and thus a receiver as well as a microphone. The other way around, that consciousness evolves from the brain is the perspective of the paradigm.

But the model of the brain as a computer, while limited and possibly outdated, can be used to graphically convey how energy and information transfer back and forth across the hard drive and into cyberspace. Or, like an email that is read and automatically saved to our hard drive, our every exchange with the world around us downloads, so to speak, a few more bits of information to our brain, thus modifying the brain's structure and context. Through this iterative process, which has been found to persist across the lifespan (Doidge, 2007), the brain is constantly changing, continuously in flux, growing new connections across neuronal pathways and reinforcing those already in place.

Since what we learn from our interactions with the environment is laid down layer by layer, life experiences are layered into the brain in priority order. Life sustaining brain mechanisms come first, unfolding early, during the preverbal period. This is when attuned parenting is especially crucial because this is also when the child's interactions with the environment pack the most wallop. Among developmental researchers, it is well-known that a child's earliest experiences are also the most formative in terms of neuronal patterning and the person's emotional development (Tierney & Nelson, 2009).

What happens to us in the morning of our lives, especially those interactions that occur day in and day out with intimate others, is most responsible for the mental mold we carry around with us. This mold is formed out of our family's idiosyncratic definitions of what is means to love, to be committed, to feel safe, to be part of a family, and other emotionally charged themes (Sullivan et al., 2006). There is a large body of literature documenting the links between children's early experiences in relationships and their later capability in performing adulthood relational tasks—finding a suitable partner, sustaining a marriage, raising offspring to become healthy adults, among other tasks (McCarthy & Maughan, 2010). We can give away only what we ourselves have received. If a romantic partner never experienced feeling loved, valued, and cared for by others, they are unlikely to have much skill at providing those same things to another person, even if the other person is someone whom they love. Children do indeed learn what they live.

In many ways, we human beings are like other mammals. We emerged as a species in communion with others, as groups and tribes, rendering us social animals by nature, not by adaptation. Our deeply rooted natural instincts are toward cooperation and fellowship with others, not competition, control, domination and winning. Those are pathologies. We want to be with others because we are social by nature; sociality, relationality, and the yearning for connecting is in our genes: they are not merely functions of our survival directive. On all levels, our survival hangs on grasping what is "truth" and actualizing that as our culture. Yet despite all the evidence, our western culture denies the obvious: that nobody makes it on one's own or by one's own devices. We all required two biological parents to get here. We are not the mythical goddess, Athena, who sprang from the top of Zeus' head. Despite all the Hollywood movies glorifying the "great man" or "great woman" of history who saves the world solo through their own magnificent power, such stories are nothing more than an illusion, a myth of human hubris. Try staying alive without the farmer who grew what you ate for lunch! Or existing at all without the mother who birthed you. To not be with others is a tear in the fabric of being.

The notions of self-sufficiency, self-reliance, and even of a "self" are a misreading of the map of existence, which shows that at every level, from the cellular to the universal, everything is in relationship, not as an adaptive mechanism, but as an expression of our relational essence. The fact that we were born is due to relationship, and the fact that we are alive and writing this is due to relationships. The fact that you are reading this is, as well. We become the person we are in the context of a network of relationships, and so we can experience the fullness of life only in relationship. And, in the final analysis, we do not "have" relationships; we are relating and that is our essence.

The person we are right now is the product of the many countless interactions we have had with all of the people who were close enough to us to make an impression on the surface of our psyche. Our brain is like a ball of soft clay that always maintains some degree of softness such that it retains, at least potentially, every fingerprint of every hand that touched it. This feature is called *neuroplasticity*. Just as the psyche is slowly shaped and reshaped every time an individual interacts with the world, so too are partners, in the conjoined space of the shared reality that exists in the Space-Between, constantly changed in the oscillation between focus and flow, which is the source of the potential for continuous change.

Although the brain clearly develops and changes the fastest during the first few years of a person's life (Sullivan et al., 2006), it retains some of its malleability throughout adulthood. This is when we first learn what love means, what we can and cannot expect of those we love, and whether the people who love us are reliable, warm, and safe or the opposite. These perceptions, rooted in the more primitive layers of the fast-developing early childhood brain, set the mold as far as the child's impressions about love, empathy, and other relational traits (Decety, 2010).

As mentioned, there is a large body of literature documenting the contributions of children's experiences with their caretakers to their later relational functioning. Included are findings documenting the strong relationship between how we were raised by our parents and how we will parent our own children (Lange et al., 2018). We can give only what we have already received.

If the resonance with which most of us began life with our caretakers was sustained, the sensation of full aliveness has been our constant experience and joy our ever present emotion, and our life has been a state of wonder. If they did not sustain "presence" with us, resonance was ruptured and anxiety has been our common sensation, accompanied by the terror of possible loss of being, which is so horrifying that we cushion ourselves with anger and depression. This the common human story. The other which reflects our nature is our possibility.

In the pages that follow, we will explore the psychological aspects of our true nature and what we needed as children to sustain. Then we will describe our existential situation of anxiety about the potential loss of being and spend the rest of the book on its recovery.

We look at that literature on the developmental stages in the next chapter, the fate of which determines our relational choices, the outcome of our significant relationships and the potential of recovering our original condition of connecting.

4

The Human Agenda
Restoring Connecting

I n William Wordsworth's *Ode on Intimations of Immortality from Recollections of Early Childhood* (Quiller-Couch, 1919) he shares his poetic vision of birth that mirrors our view of an infant experiencing the sensations of connecting, full aliveness, joy and the state of wonder of the world from "whence they came:" the quantum field.

> Our birth is but a sleep and a forgetting:
> The Soul that rises with us, our life's Star,
> Hath had elsewhere its setting,
> And cometh from afar:
> Not in entire forgetfulness,
> And not in utter nakedness,
> But trailing clouds of glory do we come,
> From God, who is our home:
> Heaven lies about us in our infancy!
>> William Wordsworth, 1770–1850

We had all the physical and psychological equipment we needed to undergo the monumental journey of becoming a mature human being, but the one thing we needed to sustain our original condition was the steady and attuned nurturance in the Space-Between that only our caretakers could provide. Given our initially helpless condition, when we were at the utter mercy of our parents' largess, it made sense that our first and arguably most important developmental leap was to sustain connecting, at first to one or both of our caretakers and later to a widening circle of others.

Each of us is one of an infinite number of cells contained within the magnificent body of the universe. At the core of our existence, we are as intricately intertwined and interdependent with others as drops of water in the ocean. Our relational essence predisposes us to crave relationship with others, not so much because we need them, but because the experience of cosmic connecting is our essence; relating is our nature; it is what we ARE. All that is needed to reach maturation and sustain awareness of our interconnectedness are the basics—presence, resonance, consistent and warm support and structure—from our caretakers. As long as we get that, all should go well.

At the very beginning, both infant and caretaker experience the quantum field in their Space-Between. Their wavelike features are expressed in the fact that they look like two people, a caretaker and their child or, later, two adults falling deeply in love. That is precisely what occurs, and it happens for good reason. Like the blissful ecstasy we feel when we have fallen in love, as though we have drunk a cocktail that dramatically heightens our sense of well-being and turns the beloved into our major focus of attention, all that matters to a new mother are the needs and desires of her precious offspring.

Accordingly, as far as the infant is concerned, the caretaker is the only person who exists, at least for the first few months of childhood. One explanation of this quantum wave pattern is that the baby's experience of connecting, and the instinct to sustain it, serves as a trigger for that same tendency in caretakers and others concerned with the child. This early love affair between caretaker and child is a powerfully adaptive mechanism that ensures the caretaker's investment in the child for (at least) the duration of childhood. This is called resonance, an oscillating flow of energy and information that signals being present and in tune with each other, without fear. Where resonance happens, connecting with the universe shows up. This is the magic of infancy that is sought with an intimate partner in adulthood.

Sustaining connecting is a by-product of the safety, structure, and support that characterizes the context of the child–caretaker relationship. Like a painted picture that gradually emerges from the series of random strokes made by a painter's brush, connecting is sustained, or ruptured, by the countless repetitions of responsive exchanges between a child and the caretakers. This means that sustaining the sensation of connecting through the developmental stages hinges not only on the sensitivity of the caretaker's responses but also on whether, and how well, the child responds to the caretaker's nurturing gestures.

In the following pages, we describe life before the rupture, or ideally life without the rupture, and what is needed to sustain the original condition or to restore it if it is lost.

BECOMING WHO WE ARE:
OUR RELATIONAL JOURNEY

Why, you may ask, do we include the stages of childhood development in a book on couple's therapy?

Because, as we progress from birth to death, we travel through specific developmental stages, and our success in sustaining connecting and our cosmic identity depends on our sustaining the concreteness of our relational identity in the relational environment we inhabited as a child while on that developmental journey. The fate of those stages impacts whom we choose as an intimate partner in adulthood, and the quality of the relational environment in which we live as we traverse the developmental stages will influence the emotional and behavioral quality of our adult relationships. Since each stage has an agenda, which can be achieved only in an optimal relational environment, whatever is not achieved in childhood will stall the developmental process and, in adult intimate and significant relationships, will show up as a need to be met, exactly as it was needed in childhood.

The identification of the stage-specific agenda that was interrupted when the stage-specific need was not met by the appropriate caretaker response is required in order for the appropriate response to be made by the intimate partner when the need arises in their relationship. In whatever stage the rupture occurs, that unfinished developmental task will show up in the adult intimate relationship for completion. And progression of the couple's development as persons, and as partners through the stages of relationship, cannot proceed until it is done. The successful completion of this journey is necessary for the creation of a conscious partnership.

Definition of the Self in Imago Theory

Before we move to the stages themselves, we ask "who or what is it that is developing?" This calls for a definition of the self. As we indicated earlier, the foundation of contemporary psychology and its therapeutics define the self as a separate entity that was derived from using Newtonian atomism as a model of the self and that self was subsequently used by Freud as the foundational construct in his founding of psychotherapy. While the concept of the autonomous, independent, and separate self has evolved toward a relational self, the self as an entity with features, called the substantial self, is still the centerpiece of the field of therapy, especially in western civilization.

We offer an alternate view of the self that is derived from quantum theory, which states that all features in nature, from the smallest quanta to the entire universe, have two features: one is particle–wave duality, and the other is the observer effect. This has radical implications for the field of therapy, which we will develop later.

Using the wavicle as a model of the self, as Freud used the particle, Imago replaces the "substantial self" of the individual paradigm and the "self in relationship" of interpersonal and intersubjectivity theories (see Chapter 1) with the Imago theoretical concept of "self-*as*-relationship," which we designate as the quantum self. The quantum self is not an entity that can be observed and described. It is a field of conscious–energy–information that oscillates between the poles of the Space-Between. Rather than a static entity that can be located and described, it is a quantum process, a flow that has infinite potential forms prior to the focus of attention. Since a form is contextually selected and functional, when the context changes, the form changes, defining the self as a process, not a thing. This is what makes it possible for intimate partnerships to respond to unmet developmental needs and to restore original connecting and for therapy to work.

With this view of the self, change is inherent and continuous and requires only the right environmental conditions to happen. Rather than exploration of the inner world as a process of change, the quantum self is changed by the quality of the interactions in the Space-Between, namely, whether or not there is an observer and how the observer "looks." The shift from the substantial self of the individual paradigm to the quantum self of the relational paradigm, from the exploration of the inner world to transforming the quality of the interactive space, has tremendous implications, which we will indicate along the way, for rethinking all therapeutic disciplines and practices.

Much of Imago's metatheory falls outside the mainstream of modern psychological thought; it pushes the envelope in the new and exciting direction taken by the relational paradigm and its foundations in the quantum field. However, Imago theory's position on the process of psychosocial development—how we become the person we are and why we think, feel, and act the way we do—in many ways resonates with, yet differs from, theories that preceded it. From the relational–cosmic perspective, development is a relational process that is shaped by an essential environment, and the inner world is the internalization of that environment as the furniture of subjectivity. What is inside was outside.

This involves two important principles. The first is that from childhood on, self-development and self-knowledge arise out of our engagement with others, not out of the contemplation and preoccupation with the self. We are relational creatures who come to know ourselves and becomes ourselves only in a relational context. We do not and cannot exist in any other realm. For instance, at the neurological level, whether our brains fill up the cranial cavity depends on whether or not we interact with others right after birth, and how we are mirrored by our caretakers determines the degree to which the hemispheres of our brain become balanced and our lobes integrated.

At the psychological level, the observer effect is the mirroring of the other, without which the self could not come into being, and whether the self that comes into being is chaotic or rigid or oscillates between focus and flow of energy depends on the quality and consistency of that mirroring. If the observer is resonant and warm and consistent, neural, emotional, and relational integration will emerge.

This means that our view of ourselves depends on how we are reflected in the eyes of significant observers. Initially, we see ourselves as others see us and what they reflect back to us. If their mirror resonates with our experience of ourselves, then we are at peace with them and ourselves. *We experience connecting.* If the mirroring does not resonate with our experience of ourselves, in order to discover who we are, we tend to separate and isolate, not differentiate, ourselves from others and from their view of us by self-declaration: "I am not that!" Through the process of negation, we discover we are "not that," and through the opposite process of affirmation, we affirm that we "are that." But both are defenses, and neither is differentiation. If our attempt to separate is not supported, then we identify with our caretakers view of us and sacrifice our experience of ourselves, or we rebel against the caretaker and develop a view of ourselves that is the opposite of our caretakers—and spend most of our lives trying to defend it. In other words, self-declaration is a failure to differentiate. The trauma of this split becomes the drama of later intimate relationships.

The second principle is a derivative of the first. In contrast to the substantial self, the differentiated self is a wavicle, an oscillating process between the poles of knowing the other and being known by others by knowing how we are different from and similar to them and their view of us. The quantum self is neither being known nor knowing, but the oscillation between those poles. Connecting between partners requires differentiation of other from the self. We cannot fully experience a felt sense of connecting with another person until we experience them as "other," as "not-self." The other may be similar to us, but they are not the same, and they cannot ever be otherwise. In addition, they are not our view of them, not the ideal we wish they were or think they should be. They are "themselves." To truly experience connecting, we must know and accept our partner as they are, and for whom they are. Any experience of connecting prior to differentiation is illusory; it is a connection with our projected self. Real and sustainable connecting requires not only differentiation but acceptance and affirmation.

Core Developmental Needs of the Child that Sustain Connecting
While successful progress on the developmental journey requires stage-specific relational support from significant others at the optimal time, there are general Space-Between conditions that must exist for the specific developmental impulse to mature and become integrated.

What's required to help a fully alive infant grow into an equally fully alive adult is nothing more or less than having at least one (and preferably more) caretaker who is willing, ready, and able to devote a couple of decades of their life to providing comfort and sustenance, protection and guidance, and emotional resonance—in other words, structure, support, and resonance—to the growing person. What would enough structure, support, and resonance, neither too much nor too little, look like?

It is no surprise that what the child needs to experience connecting is identical to what a relationship needs for couples to experience connecting and joy. As you read each point below, imagine them as a feature of a thriving relationship, and you will see the seamless connection between the relational features of development and the relational features of an adult intimate relationship. In other words, we all need the same relational factors across the full developmental spectrum, and the primary experience we must have is resonance with the primary caretakers and, later, with our intimate other.

If or when resonance is ruptured, the impulse to restore it is immediate and intense. In the first developmental phase, and later ones, the caretaker's responsibilities are straightforward, although hardly a walk in the park: the caretaker must resonate with the infant and respond reliably and empathically to whatever form the child's needs take at any given developmental juncture. In short, the caretaker's job is to maintain connecting by resonating with the child's experience and then to socialize without rupturing connecting, and in that order. This fundamental reality is also the agenda of intimate partners in adulthood.

The specific ingredients caretakers must deliver in order to optimize their child's psychological maturation and healthy development tend to shift every few years; still, there are a core set of provisions children need for the duration, no matter what age they are. As a backdrop for our upcoming discussion of how Imago theory depicts our psychological growth curve, let's first look at those persistent and nonnegotiable requirements. This will set the stage for us to talk about exactly which psychosocial nutrients are required from a caretaker as the child moves from life stage to life stage, becoming older and, hopefully, wiser.

This is the bare bones of what children need until (and even after) they become full-fledged adults:

1. to experience safety;
2. to experience and express full aliveness;
3. to sustain connecting;
4. to have structure; and
5. to experience support.

1. They Need to Experience Safety

Safety is nonnegotiable for all mammals, including humans, to thrive, according to Stephen Porges, the developer of polyvagal theory (Porges, 2011). We may survive without safety, but we cannot thrive. Physical and emotional safety are the nonnegotiable ingredients of a life worth living, no matter how old we are. These essential ingredients (or their lack) determine to a large degree whether our childhood, or our marriage, is an epic or a tragedy. Especially when a child's home feels dangerous—for example, when their caretaker is kind to them on some days and cruel to them on others, or their caretaker may or may not come home drunk and abusive tonight—the child's energy gets diverted in the direction of fight or flight, or freeze, anything that will keep them alive.

Conversely, when caretakers help soothe the child when the child is distressed and consistently show concern and offer to help the child do what they cannot do alone, the child gradually forms the conviction that people are generally trustworthy, that the world is generally a safe place, and, therefore, that life is manageable. An adult who grew up with such a responsive caretaker will trust what they perceive, because their perceptions were consistently supported by those who nurtured them. They are, therefore, well-positioned to deal with whatever challenges life throws at them.

Maintaining emotional safety for a child is as important as ensuring the child is physically safe. For various reasons—their size and strength, unfinished cognitive development, and less powerful legal status—children are sitting ducks for emotional exploitation, whether by someone at home or a bullying schoolmate. A large body of research has documented the immediate and long-term harmful effects on children who have suffered or even just witnessed emotional maltreatment (Gavin, 2011; Hamerman & Ludwig, 2000). This research demonstrates that children need emotional protection just as much as they need physical protection. Threats to emotional safety are unlikely to be forgotten. For nurturing to be sufficient, it must include keeping watch over the child's emotional well-being and intervening when called for.

This may sound easier than it actually is; after all, safety is in the eye of the beholder. In other words, children experience whatever they experience, and they feel whatever they feel, regardless of (so-called) objective reality or how the caretaker perceives the situation. For example, in mid-life a woman decided to talk to her elderly parents about her memories from childhood. During the conversation, she stated that due to her father's alcoholism, she sometimes felt unsafe around him. Upon hearing this, her father was shocked; he claimed there was "no reason" for her to feel unsafe around him. This is an example of how subjectivity, a person's subjective experience, typically prevails over objectivity, what "really happened." In other words, as far as caretaking is concerned, all that really matters is a child's experience. (We will raise this issue about the importance of subjectivity again in later discussions.)

Like all other species, we come equipped with a prewired survival switch, whose default mode, so to speak, is set on autopilot. But even given that, until we are old enough to have reached a minimum threshold of physical and mental prowess, survival on our own is virtually impossible. Until the beginning of the preadolescent ("tween") years, parents are by and large their children's life support. The child's vulnerable dependence is counterbalanced by another adaptive mechanism that revolves around the interlocking needs of the child and their primary caretaker. From the very first hours of life, whenever a caretaker responds empathically to their child's screams and wails, whether at mid-day or midnight, a helpful bit of information gets added to a rudimentary map that is slowly forming somewhere in the hidden mental realms.

While physical survival is, of course, the primary goal, staying alive means more than simply breathing. From the time they leave the womb, children remain on alert not only for ways to get their needs met but also for signs of the trustworthiness of those on whom they rely to meet those needs; and when the needs are met and the caretakers are trustworthy, children go from surviving to thriving.

2. They Need to Experience and Express Full Aliveness

Newborn infants are the precise embodiment of full aliveness. Full aliveness is relational. It is not a feeling but a neural sensation, triggered by safe interactions, that emanate through their entire being, through their squalling at all hours, their incredibly smooth and fragrant skin, their mighty push to crawl and walk, their incessant cooing and babbling, and even their seemingly endless fussing. When you watch a child who is beyond infancy, you will find other irrepressible expressions of full aliveness in the toddler who bops-till-he-drops, in the insistent questions of a four- or five-year-old child; in the proud artwork of school-aged children. In a few moments of watching children, especially young ones, one can see how naturally and unabashedly children express their energy. As long as there is enough fuel, in the form of caretaker support, to feed the developmental engine and as long as there is a safe structure holding them, children will invest the totality of their being—senses, voices, muscles, nerves, thoughts, emotions—into what they do. Whatever they do, they will do it with all of the life energy they can muster. All the caretaker needs to do is structure the child's atmosphere so that it is both protective and permissive—and then step back, watch, and mirror their child.

3. They Need to Sustain Connecting

Having been born into the tapestry of Being-experienced-as-Connecting, the child's top priorities are to experience and to express connecting, since that is their nature. The connectional drive is the inborn mechanism that steers the child along the first steps of the developmental pathway. Assuming that connecting is the preeminent developmental impulse, maturational progress can be gauged by the extent to which the child becomes capable of establishing and maintaining connecting in an increasingly broad range of relational contexts. Therefore, the most critical lesson that caretakers must transmit to their child is how to connect, to sustain connecting, and to restore connecting when it ruptures. Caretakers teach connecting in a variety of ways, but most effectively by building and reinforcing the experience of connecting between themselves and their child.

The most precious resource caretakers can bring to the task of sustaining connecting with their child is emotional attunement—that is, the caretaker's orientation or tendency to respond in ways that optimally promote the child's expression of thoughts, feelings, needs, impulses, joys, and struggles. As the child moves along the developmental pathway, the quality and consistency of attunement provides clues from the caretakers that the child can use to respond in ways that will best meet the current developmental needs.

4. They Need Structure

Structure means setting boundaries, as needed, to protect a child from dangerous (in either the physical or the emotional sense) people, places, and situations. In gauging the appropriate dose of structure, a caretaker should follow the principle that doctors use when treating a person with a serious mental illness: restrict the person's freedom as much as is necessary, but no more. For structure to be growth-enhancing, it needs to include ample room for the child to experiment with and learn from their interactions with the world. In contrast with discipline, which relies on rewards and punishments and is often coercive, effective structure avoids inflicting a single iota of shame or humiliation upon its recipient. Instead, it focuses on using the child's own experiences to help the child learn from interacting with the world.

What does proper structure look like? Above all, it strikes a balance between allowing for freedom and independence and thoughtfully setting limits, physical or otherwise. Structure keeps one eye on the child's age and maturity level and the other on the potential risks of the situation at hand. For example, it is well-known that many children become afraid of certain things at various ages. Many one-year-olds go through a period where they become afraid, or even terrified, of strangers. Preschool-aged children tend to fear the dark and whatever seems to reside therein—monsters, the boogeyman, ghosts, and so forth. Grade school children tend to become fearful or anxious in strange or unfamiliar circumstances, like starting at a new school. And of course, older children, sometimes even during the teen-age years, are famously afraid of making mistakes in front of others, being seen as weird, or being criticized or ridiculed. To adults, these fears may seem irrational or even ridiculous. However, structure does not mean telling the child that the fear is silly or unjustified. This would not restore the child's sense of safety, nor would it help them to deal with their fears now or in the future.

Yet this is precisely how many of us respond to our children's fears and other negative emotions. Many of us were reared by parents who dismissed our feelings as unimportant. Having practiced dismissing our feelings for most of our lifetime, we are highly likely to respond, in reflexive fashion, in the same way to our own offspring. The dilemma here, of course, is that it is notoriously difficult to overcome feelings by simply dismissing them. This often leads children (as well as adults) to continue to feel exactly the same but to work harder to deny or avoid what we feel. Even worse, trying to talk a child out of feeling whatever they are feeling sends messages that hardly promote the child's growth and maturation: "Your perceptions aren't correct. You shouldn't feel what you're feeling. Listen to me, not yourself. I'm right, and you're wrong."

The caretaker who provides effective structure verbally acknowledges what their child is experiencing. Although they may not agree with the child's assessment of the situation, they validate the logic of the child's experience. In doing so, the child is far more likely to become more open to listening to the caretaker's perspective on the situation. The child is more willing to reevaluate how threatening the situation really is. They may become more open to the caretaker's opinions, but still feel free to draw their own. This kind of structure delivers a double benefit: the child has the opportunity to learn from their own experience, and they also take in empowering messages, such as: "Your perceptions are valid. Your feelings matter. Your experience is meaningful. You are capable of making sense of the world."

This is only one form of effectively nurturing a child. As most parents realize, striking that fine balance between limiting and allowing our children's freedom is a difficult art form, one that most of us do poorly before we learn to do it better. Obviously, since young children (e.g., toddlers) need a different level of structure than older children (e.g., tweens), caretakers will need to balance structure and support, shifting back and forth many times between these two growth-related priorities throughout the course of their child's development. This means focusing at one point on setting boundaries that will prevent harm, and at another, encouraging the child to take risks, to spread their wings and fly. Imposing structure in ways that are inappropriate to the child's maturational status is not structure; it is more like oppression. Withholding the structure a child needs is not giving them freedom; it constitutes neglect.

5. They Need to Experience Support

Like safety and structure, appropriate forms of support from caretakers will depend on the child's age, maturational requirements, and life circumstances. At any developmental point, however, support requires a particular attitude on the part of the caretaker: one of warmth and availability to the child. To communicate a supportive stance, caretakers' warmth and availability must be both unwavering and unconditional. And the caretakers must view the child's behavior separately from their humanness; in other words, separating the child from the behavior, the deed from the doer.

Supportive caretaking encourages the child to explore and decide who and what they want to be, regardless of the caretakers' own preference and how the child is like and unlike other members of the family. Mirroring, too, is an effective way to provide support to children across the age spectrum. Mirroring, in the broader sense of the term, acknowledges the importance of the child's presence in the world, affirms their normalcy and legitimacy, and honors their essential humanness. Even as a child is approaching the cusp of adulthood, such as while going to college, they may continue to need a good amount of support from the caretakers. In some instances, caretaker support may be called for long after the child has become an adult (e.g., recent college graduates moving back home to save money and get back on their own feet). Support may not be financially related at all, however; each human is unique in their desire and need for caretaker connectivity. Maturity is a process and emotional development takes time.

Only within a context characterized by safety, structure, and support can children retain the fullness of their humanity while traveling the long and sometimes arduous road toward maturity. Since what happens in the nursery is repeated later by couples in the bedroom, it is illuminating for couples to know that in their drama, they are not only repeating their childhood trauma, but the specific developmental issue that was left unresolved in childhood. Looking at a couple through a developmental lens helps the Imago therapist develop a diversity of responses to the challenges that couples experience.

When these conditions are met, the child proceeds successfully through the six developmental stages described below (Table 4.1). The fate of the child if the conditions are not present is the subject of the next chapter.

THE DEVELOPMENTAL JOURNEY

Each stage has a specific developmental impulse that needs stage-specific relational support to achieve the agenda of that stage, and there are specific environmental conditions that must exist for successful passage. These stage-related impulses arise in a hierarchical, "first-things-first" order that ensures a strong and resilient foundation for supporting each developmental

Table 4.1: Imago's Psychosocial Journey of Childhood Development						
Approximate Age	Birth–18 months	18–36 months	3–4 years	4–7 years	7–13 years	13 years–adulthood
Developmental Stage	CONNECTING	EXPLORATION	IDENTITY	COMPETENCE	SOCIAL	INTIMACY
Primary Parental Messages	The world is a safe, connecting place. You are seen by me.	It is safe to separate and explore. I'm here when you return.	It is okay to be you. It is okay to "try on" different character identifications and affective expressions.	It is okay to be powerful. I'm here to encourage. It's okay to make mistakes.	It is okay to move away from focus on family and care for others.	It is okay to explore sexual impulses. I respect your privacy. I trust your choices. I'm here to listen.
Primary Parental Role	Reliable availability and warmth.	Allow differentiation. Set protective limits.	Mirror. Be consistent. Affirm self-assertion.	Mirror. Instruct. Praise. Clear boundaries. Warm and consistent praise for efforts in mastering skills and new achievements.	Approving of best friends. Help navigate non-family relationships when guidance is sought.	Maintain open communication. Respect privacy. Gentle guidance on healthy and safe choices. Encouragement around outside interests.
Healthy Outcome	Emotional security; basic trust and coherence.	Sense of separateness and safety within the context of connection; retains sense of curiosity.	Secure, differentiated and integrated sense of self and healthy self-assertion.	Feelings of effectiveness & centered power while mastering tasks.	Develop secure, healthy, and trusting "chum"; care for non-family members.	Ability to love, interact sexually, and make healthy choices.

layer. The hierarchical nature of this unfolding means that whatever happens in an earlier stage will have an impact on what comes later. If stage-specific support is given in a timely manner, the developmental process will continue to the next stage.

When a safe, structured, and supportive context is created by the caretakers, the developmental impulses spring forth at the right time and unfold naturally. Little else is needed to bring a child to a healthy state of relational maturity and an integrated sense of self.

The Connecting Stage (Birth Through 18 Months of Age)

Like all of the other developmental impulses, the sensation of connecting is supported as the child's growing physical maturity combines with the age-related demands of an increasingly complex social environment to "pull for" the specific personality aspects of the developing individual. The initial compulsion to sustain the sensation of connecting (or, more accurately, to sustain connecting, as the connecting impulse is an external sign of the psyche's inherent interconnectedness) nicely serves our overarching survival directive. After all, at this early stage each of us literally needs our caretakers to keep us alive.

Every newborn baby is primed to sustain connecting because they are formed in the quantum field where connecting is being. Therefore, the connecting impulse is not to achieve connecting but to express and sustain it. From the very outset of life, after leaving the comfortable cocoon of the mother's womb, a newborn baby struggles to recreate, in the radically transformed extrauterine environment, the blissful state of oneness that characterized life before birth.

Now think about all of the different kinds of interactions that forge and strengthen the sensations of this original state of joyful connecting, like nursing at mother's breast, gazing into each other's eyes, feeling each other's skin, all conduits to the connecting field (Beier & Spelke, 2012; Ishikawa & Itakura, 2018). In fact, infants are highly effective at eliciting nurturing responses from others through phase-specific behaviors like cooing, gurgling, crying, and various forms of fussing. These and numerous other repeated exchanges make up the warp and weft of the psychic fabric that mediates and sustains the cosmic bond. In these interactions, the child's search for contact with the caretaker sends cues that alert and activate the connecting experience, which in turn elicits the kinds of responses that are congruent with what the child needs at present. Mirroring is an overt expression of empathy, which flows naturally from the caretaker's experience of connecting to the child. Holding is a nonverbal type of mirroring that uses touch to respond to the child's need for physical contact and emotional soothing. These interactions do more than assure the child that they will survive; they also reaffirm the child's primordial experience of its cosmic identity as a resident in a connecting universe.

The developmental impulse to explore becomes activated when the once-helpless infant becomes physically capable of breaking out of the prison of their crib or playpen and making their way through the immediate environment.

The Exploration Stage (Ages 18 Months Through 36 Months)

Having experienced reliable connecting with the primary caretaker, the child is equipped to explore more diverse and distant aspects of their environment. This is driven by the child's hunger for direct experience of other people, places, and things in their surroundings.

The role of the caretaker is to encourage the child's forays into the environment while assuring them that the safety of the home base will be there upon the child's return. Because of the child's still-primitive understanding of the nature of the world, caretakers must impose limits that do not impede the child's natural curiosity nor expose the child to physical harm, fear of abandonment, or challenges beyond the child's level of maturity.

To wrestle up the nerve to tackle this new task, children rely on a frankly brilliant mental trick: they develop object constancy, the ability to keep the caretaker with them, inside a mental carrying case. In theoretical terminology, for the child to feel safe enough to leave their caretaker's side, caretaker—the conduit to connecting—must somehow be maintained in the absence of the mother. Exploration will not go well unless the connection to the caregiver is secure enough to remain unbroken by the child's taking leave to explore.

The Identity Stage (Ages 3 Through 4)

Once object constancy is in place, there's no need for the child to make sure that their caretakers are in sight; the child knows they will be back. Now they are ready to begin to explore the most daunting of all questions: "Who am I?"

With the exploratory achievements behind them and the growing capabilities of the new brain, it begins to dawn on the child that not only are other people "not me," but they also are not exactly like me, either. Like all other personality tendencies, the impulse to develop an identity emerges organically when physical maturation intersects with the child's interpersonal and social context. In this larger context, the child begins to gather essential data about self versus others. They act out stories, plays, and movies that star the characters they saw in the latest Disney film or heard about in the book their father read to them. They may mimic the voices of their favorite cartoon characters or dress up in their mother's or sister's clothes. Playing dress-up, acting out stories, inventing imaginary friends, being an animal, a movie character, or a ghost, acting like mommy or daddy, pretending to be a teacher, an astronaut, a monster—all of these provide data to answer the question, "Who am I?"

At this stage, the most essential ingredient is an attentive and mirroring audience in the Space-Between. By audience, we mean the consistent presence of at least one person, typically the caretaker, who watches, affirms, and applauds the child's efforts, however halting, to grow into the "me" they are slowly becoming. However, it can be challenging for some parents to mirror their child's more radical experiments in identity without judging the child's choice of characters. Yet, the price we pay to help a child retain wholeness is similar to the one we pay for freedom of speech: we defend the other's right to express ideas that we, personally, may find unsavory. So, especially during the identity stage, a child needs full permission to explore all the potential facets of humanness, whether or not some of the facets match our ideal model.

Here, again, is an opportunity to put faith in the inherent wisdom of a child's humanness, allowing it to proceed undisturbed and trusting in its ability to guide the child's developmental progress now and in the years to come.

The Competence Stage (Ages 4 Through 7)

The impulse of the competence stage is to move from "Who am I?" to "What can I do?" The competence stage is aptly named, as it reflects the target of this particular quest: the development of competence. The child wants to influence the world and the people they have explored— caretakers and siblings, teachers and babysitters, scoutmaster and pastor, neighbors and friends. They especially want to check out the physical world, to see how things work or how they can make them work. And when they take action, they look for confirmation that what they do makes a difference.

The competence stage provides plenty of opportunities for the Space-Between to be filled with clashes between the child and authority figures. In their determination to find a way to make their mark on the world, children of competence age (and older) routinely test the limits; they push the envelope, and sometimes they make a big mess. If a caretaker reacts badly to these tendencies, they need to remember to stay conscious and practice vigilance to view the child separately from the mess they have made. One way to do this is to mirror what the child intends to achieve while acknowledging the child's frustration over their partial success.

The Social Stage (Ages 7 Through 13)

When the social stage looms, the child, already bonded with their caretakers and other intimates, faces the challenge of connecting with people who may be very different from their family members and, on top of it, within contexts, such as school, that are far less familiar. The lion's share of developmental progress hinges on what happens outside the home, and the consequences show up in intimate relationships.

This next stage is the age of "chum-ship." It takes the form of showing loyalty toward friends, making new friends, becoming someone's best friend, and dressing and acting like our peers. It is the time when a young person begins to notice and care about what people outside the family think of them. The challenge now is to find their place within the circle of their peers. Of equal importance, becoming adept at connecting with their peers is excellent preparation for the soon-to-arrive challenges of relating to the kinds of people who one day may become their romantic partner.

To some extent, this movement relegates the caretakers, at least occasionally, to the sidelines. Parents may feel that they are beginning to lose control (assuming they felt they had any) over what influences their child.

The Intimacy Stage (13 Years Through Adulthood)

After spending the last years of childhood learning how to understand ourselves and others as peers, we now are ready to learn how to become a partner. Obviously, much of development must be in place by this point; we need, especially, to have a good sense of who we are before we can select someone with whom we plan to share the rest of our life. Indeed, we are not ready for intimacy until the mental and emotional transformations of adolescence, in combination with the bodily metamorphosis of puberty, have given us the kind of social, emotional, and cognitive capacity required to handle the vicissitudes of relationship, such as introspection, self-reflection, and self-awareness. If our ride down the developmental roadway has been smooth enough so far, we will greet this final developmental phase with the basic training needed for taking on the challenges, mystery, and risks of falling in love already under our belt.

Once again, a Space-Between filled by the caretaker's provision of support and structure plays a key role in helping a young person navigate the often turbulent waters of this final phase (which, it should be noted, extends throughout the rest of the lifespan). Adequate nurturing means striking a balance between allowing the intimacy impulse to naturally unfold and limiting, to whatever extent is feasible, the potentially harmful outcomes of the child's intimacy experiments.

How We Interact With Each Other and the World

While traversing the stages to relational maturity and an integrated self, we constantly engage with our social environment with what we call the four functions of relating: *sensing, acting, feeling, and thinking.* Recall again our assumption that we—all of us—are points of consciousness connecting in the quantum field, Consciousness itself. This universal conscious energy is expressed primarily through the four human functions. We come into the world with the equivalent of an internal GPS device that moves our development in the right direction. Under the influence of this internal wisdom, or telos, the four functions emerge in just the right order to respond to signals from the environment encountered by the developing child.

The first function to emerge is sensing, the ability to optimally use and enjoy our five senses that comes on line during our earliest months of development when we encounter our first developmental task—to sustain connecting. When a baby sees, smells, and touches their mother's skin and hears her voice again and again, every night and day, week after week and month after month, they learn to associate her (and only her) with the pleasure of seeing her smile, touching her skin, hearing her voice, and tasting the warm milk of her breast.

The next function in line is acting that is activated in the exploration stage. This impulse propels the toddler out of their playpen so that they can learn how to maneuver their way beyond it. Third to arise is the feeling function, which enables a preschooler to emotionally identify (or not identify) with the assortment of character types they try on during the identity stage. Finally, the thinking function brings with it increasingly sophisticated cognitive abilities, which are precisely what the child needs to effectively respond with competence to his increasingly complex environment.

Figure 4.1 depicts how energy flows through the four functioning channels of sensing, acting, feeling, or thinking. Unless, or until, it is trained out of them, children have the natural capacity to access and use their energy fully, spontaneously, and effectively. For example, think about how a one-year-old baby tries to master walking by trying and failing, stumbling and falling over and over again until they take their first successful step. That's how the acting function shows up in its full capacity, before repressive messages of socialization, which typically begin with "do" or "don't" or "you must" or "don't you dare," lead to its gradual diminishment. Or for that matter, watch a two- or three- or four-year-old boy hugging and kissing his pet dog or cat with unabashed affection, and you will see the feeling function in action before the child learns that only a sissy expresses tender feelings that way.

If we happen to have been blessed with an idyllic childhood, by the time

Figure 4.1:
Expressions of the Four Human Functions

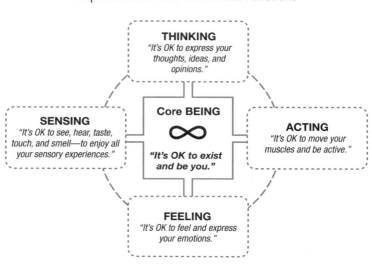

we are adults, we will be well-practiced in investing our entire storehouse of energy into whatever we do, whether it's learning a new language or starting a new job, throwing a party or getting married. We will feel free to use all of our senses and all of our capacities with confidence, which enables us to think things through, make good decisions, enjoy our bodies, and feel whatever emotions come up. We will be able, in other words, to live fully and to feel full aliveness.

But why do so few people live precisely that way? What happens along the way that gets us stuck, frozen at some long-defunct era from childhood, unable to keep moving forward, as we were meant to, toward psychosocial maturity?

SUMMARY

What we have described above is life in the connecting space before it is ruptured. The optimal condition for sustaining connecting is that, to a large extent, caretakers stay present to and connecting with the developing child as the child evolves and completes their developmental tasks. The degree to which the caretakers are not resonant with the child nor reliably and predictably present to them because of ruptured connecting in their childhood is the degree to which this drama will be carried into the adult life of the child. Integrated and connecting caretakers sustain original connecting. Ruptured caretakers rupture connecting at the developmental stage in which they experienced rupture. As they brought their rupture into their caretaker relationship, so their child will take their relational challenge into their adult intimate relationships. Responding to those challenges by helping couples restore connecting so that the developmental journey of each partner can be restarted is the intention of Imago Relationship Therapy.

5
The Human Problem
Ruptured Connecting

lthough we have a cosmic identity, we humans live out our lives
in the concreteness of lived experience at the macro-level of daily
interactions with others. The fateful consequence, as Wordsworth
says later in his poem, is that the light fades for us all as we are shaped by
our social environment.

> Heaven lies about us in our infancy!
> Shades of the prison-house begin to close
> Upon the growing Boy,
> But he beholds the light and when it flows,
> He sees it in his joy
> and. . .
> At length the Man perceives it die away
> And fade into the light of common day.
>
> *Ode: Intimations of Immortality from*
> *Recollections of Early Childhood*
> (Quiller-Couch, 1919)

As a therapist, you have certainly seen how fragile this connection can be as
you guide individuals and couples through their human perceptions, pain,
and offenses. A small offense may impact one human on a deeper level than
it might another, wreaking emotional havoc. Why is the human connection
with others so critical? The answer lies in our need for relationship.

Each of us is one of a limitless number of cells contained within the magnificent body of the universe. We believe our relational essence predisposes
us to crave relationship with others, not so much because we need them, but
because the experience of cosmic connecting is our essence; relating is our
nature. At the core of our existence, we are as intricately intertwined and
interdependent with others as drops of water in the ocean are with each
other. All we need to realize this human reality, to reach maturation still
aware of our interconnectedness, are the basics—resonance, consistent and
sensitive support and structure—from our caretakers. As long as we get

that, all should go well. But it does not for all of us, for all of human history, as Wordsworth so elegantly recognized.

What happens?

A DISCONNECTING EVENT OCCURS

We posit that for all human beings, a threatening event occurs in the child–caretaker Space-Between. An intrusive or neglectful caretaker, or both, ruptures the child's resonance which, in turn, fractures our cosmic connecting, and the sensation of full aliveness, joyful relaxation and wonder is replaced with anxiety, initiating the human problem.

Suffering in a quantum universe is defined as the anxiety driven imagination that our loss of the sensation of connecting with significant others may portend the loss of the experience of Being, and that we may disappear from the universe, entirely. This possibility is so unendurable that we convert anxiety into anger and depression, which become the source of all sorts of emotional and mental symptoms. Since this is a primal, universal human experience, the sequence recurs in adult intimate relationships and all significant relationships.

In the following pages we describe the experience of original rupturing. In later chapters we will describe its replication in adult intimate relationships and how the transformation that can occur in significant relationships restores the original condition.

THE CONSEQUENCES OF
CONNECTIONAL RUPTURE

Imago theory points to connectional rupture as the root cause of all dysfunction. Relational rupture is the outcome of a variety of factors that send development reeling. These factors diminish our wholeness, decrease our interconnectedness and distort our view of ourselves and others. They include negativity (in some form) that ruptures connecting, resulting in the sensation of anxiety that is so painful and self-absorbing that we lose awareness of other people. This loss of capacity for social engagement produces the feeling of a separate self that is so emotionally isolated and defended that it mirrors the separate self of classical psychotherapy. In fact, they may be the same. Loss of the capacity for positive social engagement erodes our natural capacity for empathy and the consequence of that is the objectification of others—what Martin Buber calls the I–It relationship.

When we lose the experiencing of connecting, we lose our humanity. It is an Imago postulate that we, the human race—all of us—want our humanity back, in its original condition before the fall into negativity and anxiety, but we do not know how to get it. And, everything we do, whether wonderful or negative, is an attempt to reexperience connecting, but we do so in a way that paradoxically deepens the rupture. Until it is interrupted by a transformational intervention, this is a loop that never ends.

The Cause and Consequence of Ruptured Connecting

The source of connectional rupture is the absence, in childhood, of optimal nurturing, emotional resonance and repressive socialization. It also seems to be the case that these relational deficits in childhood show up as needs in adult intimate relationships, and the resources that would have mitigated the challenges of childhood are essentials in healthy relationships in adulthood.

Nurturing Deficits

What sustains connecting in childhood is the experience in the Space-Between of reliable and predictable resonance with our caretakers so that our relational needs for attuned presence are being consistently met. Each time we experience the caretaker as reliably and adequately and warmly present to our experiencing, whether physically or emotionally or cognitively, we experience a sense of relief and quiet, which is pleasurable and fulfilling. You could call it trust, yet it is much deeper than that.

What ruptures connecting in childhood is the failure of our caretakers to be present to our experiencing, to resonate with us by mirroring us accurately, and to be inconsistent with warmth and holding. Since the caretaker is the conduit to the connecting universe, disconnection from the caretaker is experienced cosmically, collapsing our wavelike quality, and that has repercussions in every relationship.

Resonance failure in childhood activates fear and protest and disconnection from the tapestry of being. As we indicated above, the loss of the cosmic connecting triggers anxiety—the anticipation of the possibility of nonbeing—and that sensation is so dreadful that we cannot bear it, so we convert it into anger and depression. These emotional states underly most emotional, physical, and relational symptoms. If the angry protest fails, we shift into depression and develop chronic patterns of defenses that become characterological. Unconscious anticipation that frustration might become consistent and ruptured connecting might become chronic transmutes fear into anxiety, activating the survival drive. When all this happens, as it does with most children, our caretakers—and, by extension, the world into which we were born—become dangerous, the joy of being disappears, and suffering begins.

In Imago theory, connectional rupture is the fundamental human tragedy because it includes not only a loss of connection with the caretaker but also with aspects of ourselves and with our social and cosmic context. It is the root cause of all human dysfunction, the source of all social problems, and its repair is the hope in all our dreams of a better tomorrow. The protest against disconnection and its consequences and the hope of the recovery of connection and its benefits are what couples bring to therapy.

Given our inherent human tendency toward connecting, rooted in our ontological condition and concretized in the powerful sway of the connecting impulse at birth, how does connectional rupture manage to break through such a powerful human inclination? The answer lies, at least in part, with the intergenerational nature of childhood challenges. We were all reared by caretakers who themselves were once children being raised by emotionally and relationally challenged parents who, despite doing their best, could not figure out how to nurture their children without depriving, denying, or otherwise failing them in ways that they, too, were once failed. Because it is hard to provide the kind of nurturing one never received; as caretakers, we become one more link in the chain of intergenerational nurturing failures. Specifically, caretakers who lacked adequate caretaker resonance and support during a given developmental stage will fail their child in the same (or similar) ways that their caretakers failed them. Being emotionally and relationally challenged and searching for healing is the human story, and it's as old as the human race.

We think it is possible to give the story a new ending: to finish childhood as it should have been, thus breaking the transgenerational cycle of nurturing failures by restoring and sustaining connecting. As a therapist implementing this therapy you will be part of the movement to restore the experience of connecting and bringing humans and humanity full circle back to themselves.

Repressive Socialization
Socialization is the process by which children learn to harness and invest their energy toward constructive and productive ends and to consider the welfare of others as well as their own. This serves the best interests of the child and the human community. And there is nothing harmful per se about teaching children to regulate their own needs for the sake of the greater good and to help them see that their own interests may be best served when they care for the interests of others. But it is inevitable that the goals of socialization will, sooner or later, pit society's needs against the desires and needs of the individual.

The socializing process becomes abusive when it is repressive, and it becomes repressive when it produces the less-than-optimal developmental outcome that we so often witness: a pseudo-mature, half-alive grown-up instead of a truly mature and fully alive adult. Repressive socialization splits the self, robs it of its original experience of connecting and the sense of joyful aliveness, joining nurturing deficits as a source of depression and anger. While this is a great tragedy for the person and the source of their future personal and relational problems, it is also a great cost to society. Since most social problems, including abuse and violence toward self and others, come from depression and anger about the loss of connecting, repressive socialization could be considered the human problematic, thus the basis for promoting healthy marriages/intimate partnerships and healthy parenting, and a transformation of cultural values.

Socialization relies on its agents—caretakers, especially, but also teachers and other parental proxies—to filter its message down to future generations. Since caretakers serve as the torch bearers of culture as well as of their own family lineage, they are the most powerful transmitters of the socialization message. In fact, socialization generally proceeds according to the same tried-and-true formula, in which caretakers (and other social agents) are induced to mold the younger generation into the shape and form that fits the predominant cultural mindset. Socialization is a psychic coup that takes over the moral district of the psyche, filling it with whatever serves the best interests of the societal status quo.

Further compounding the detrimental impacts of repressive socialization, once a person grows up and finds themselves faced with the task of socializing their own offspring, they're likely to do the job pretty much the same way their caretakers did. It's also likely that while engaging in this important task they will be burdened by the load of their emotional scars, by the remnants of the repressive socialization messages that repeat across generations.

Although the various cultures differ as far as content, repressive socialization messages are generally oriented toward restricting a person's expression of one or more of the four human functions (Figure 5.1). Essentially, socialization prohibits us from thinking, feeling, sensing, or doing certain things that come naturally to us. It does so by issuing edicts designed to inhibit the free flow of life energy through our brain, muscles, nerves, senses, and emotions. In effect, we grow up with the understanding that it is not acceptable to be who we are. This produces many painful feelings, especially shame—an intolerable emotion from which any person feels compelled to escape, often through whatever means necessary.

Remember that to stay alive (at first literally and later figuratively), children rely on their caretakers as much as a skydiver relies on the parachute. It is the reflexive, unconscious, primal brain that is charged with the mandate to make sure a child's survival net does not disappear, at least not before they can survive on their own. A surefire way to ensure this is to subvert, reject, or discard those parts of ourselves that, for whatever reason,

Figure 5.1:
Messages of Repressive Socialization

THINKING
Don't trust your own perceptions
You don't know what's best for you
Don't think that way
Listen to me, not yourself

SENSING
Don't touch yourself there
Don't have sexual feelings
Don't enjoy your body
Don't indulge your senses

Core ENERGY
∞

ACTING
You can't make good decisions
Don't be too confident of yourself
Don't act without my advice
Do only what I tell you to do

FEELING
Feelings aren't important
You shouldn't feel that way
Don't feel vulnerable
Don't exaggerate things

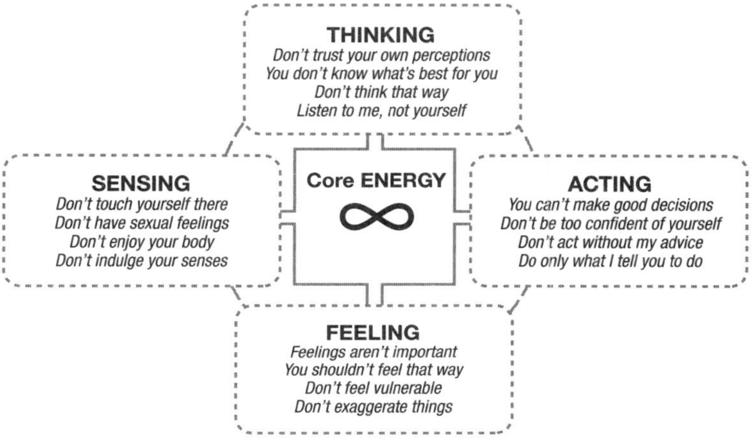

threaten the security of our lifeline—in other words, whatever threatens our survival. For example, the primal brain of a child who is told, repeatedly, to "stop being so bold" is likely to make a leap of (il)logic and conclude that there is something dangerous—even if they do not understand why—about expressing too much self-confidence. In this scenario, the most expeditious solution is to cut off the offensive part—to suppress, constrict, disguise, or deny its expression, like killing the village to save it.

Another reason the messages of repressive socialization have such a powerful sway is that they are adaptive; they serve a caretaker's primary mission—to keep the child alive and out of trouble. When push comes to shove, caretakers will do whatever they feel they must to keep their children alive all the way up to adulthood (and often beyond). Each caretaker has a unique socializing formula or parenting approach, but whatever the formula, it's sure to contain most, if not all, of the residue left by the caretaker's own earlier immersion into the depths of the socialization process. Like father (or mother), like son (or daughter): the intergenerational nature of socialization becomes apparent in the often close match between a child's character and that of the caretakers. We will explore this in greater detail in a few moments, when we discuss another manifestation of connectional rupture—defensive adaptations.

Repressive socialization, by the way, is not the same as authoritative parenting, in which caretakers hold the child responsible to rules and guidelines that are reasonable, in keeping with the child's maturity level and presented rationally to the child. In authoritative parenting, a parent and child collaborate in the service of the child's maturity (Baumrind, 1971). Not so with repressive socialization, which aims to tame and subvert the child's natural effervescence and to shape the child using authority and tradition above what is necessary to produce a socialized individual.

Typically, once a caretaker has invested a few years into socializing a child, the task gets considerably easier. If early socialization messages get set in stone, as intended, sooner or later the child takes the job on their own shoulders. They begin to practice self-censorship, a survival-driven self-inflicted ban on expressing all of their core energy. Self-censorship becomes a bad habit, eventually giving way to the formation of an internal split, a division between parts of ourselves we accept and those we reject. And splitting, of course, creates a rip down the fabric of our formerly whole and cohesive inner fabric.

The Consequences of Ruptured Connecting
Anxiety and the Development of Character Defenses
As children, we see danger looming whenever we experience 1) deficient (either neglectful or invasive) caretaker support for whatever maturational requirements we need at a given stage of childhood development, and 2) repressive messages that prohibit, limit, or discourage us from expressing our needs or our human functions. Danger triggers adaptive defenses.

Since anxiety is triggered by some sort of negativity, which is usually a negating observation, the quantum self collapses into its particle-like form, and shelters itself with its defenses, which gives it the character of the "separate self" it has replaced. It needs those defenses to deal with the imagination of the possibility of nonbeing or of not being at all. When the connecting link is broken, the quantum self as particle retreats inward and becomes totally self-absorbed in the pain of potential nonbeing. The anticipation of potential nonexistence is the ultimate disempowerment and devaluation. As we indicated earlier, this possibility is so intolerable that it is managed by two major symptoms: anger and depression. Anger is our protest against our potential demise, and depression is our submission to its possibility. Both numb the pain, but they use opposite neurochemical activations of the autonomic nervous system.

Anger is an amplification of psychic energy expressed by the sympathetic branch of the Autonomic Nervous System (ANS). The release of acetylcholine, adrenaline, and noradrenaline help manage the pain of our potential nonexistence by distracting us with activities like striving to succeed, taking on the system, active expression of prejudice, discrimination, and aggression, violence, or changing the world in some way.

Depression is an activation of the parasympathetic branch of the ANS, numbing the neural system by shutting down psychic energy. In contrast to anger, this is accomplished by the absence of chemical neurotransmitters. Norepinephrine, serotonin, and dopamine, chemicals of an elevated mood, are NOT found when a person is depressed. If the absence of specific neuro-chemicals is not sufficient to numb our neural system, we will supplement the numbing process with chemical additions or addictive behaviors that also produce emotional and physical fatigue, like work or strenuous play, or with fantasies of suicide. We will do anything NOT to experience the sensation of anxiety, and most psychological symptoms are an indication of the diversity of our response to this enervating cause. The pain of anger and depression causes us to retreat from the reception of signals from the social world and into ourselves.

Adaptive defenses include the particle-like *minimizing* style, which copes with anxiety by withdrawing from, divesting in, or dismissing anything that evokes vulnerable feelings. These exceedingly common strategies include withdrawing, staying silent, answering with as few words as possible, withholding emotions, reluctance to share feelings, dismissing the partner's feelings, etc. These are generally assumed to be more typical of males than females (a difference that seems to be getting narrower and narrower, as many Imago therapists report) although it is not gender based.

On the other end is the wavelike *maximizing* style, whose coping mechanisms all share an emphasis on making emotions bigger, louder, and stronger and behaviors more exaggerated. These include crying, running after the partner, incessant phone calls or text messages when unable to contact the partner, globalizing terminology ("you constantly," "you never," "you always"). While these traits and behaviors are typically assigned to women, they are not gendered, since they can also be found in men. These traits and behaviors are the consequences of nurturing deficits and repressive socialization, and their intent is adaptation to personal context.

Of course, both minimizing and maximizing maneuvers fall within the range of normal human behaviors because they are instances of the natural polarity of nature, the particle–wave duality. There is nothing wrong with doing either one. Because they are the foundational structure of nature, all of us do both, depending on the dynamics of our relationship and the requirements of other social contexts. We do whatever worked in childhood to regulate our anxiety. In adulthood intimate relationships, there obviously are times when one or the other style is not only appropriate but highly desirable; think of the salutatory role of the maximizing partner who lights a fire (so to speak) under the other whenever their relationship starts to go downhill, and you will see the value of maximizing. Likewise, for minimizing strategies, whose usefulness is reflected in *Don't*

Sweat the Small Stuff (Carlson, 1996), a book series that admonishes us to do just that.

But why does anyone end up developing one defensive style over the other? What turned one of us into a minimizer and the other into a maximizer? Imago theory identifies the following forces as casting the primary shape of our character structure: 1) the stage of childhood development during which repressive socialization and/or inadequate nurturing was first experienced; and 2) the specific content of the repressive messages that we received as children—the commands to "be this, not that," or "act this way, not that way." The character structure, then, becomes the wall behind which the rejected, thus missing, self with its disowned, denied, and hidden parts is kept out of our conscious awareness.

But the hidden costs of building a defensive pattern are, for the child, quite high. First, defense-building diverts energy away from the work of normal development; second, it tends to slow down, or even halt, our progress toward maturation, leaving us developmentally arrested.

The Birth of Desire

When anxiety is triggered by connectional rupture, *desire* is born, desire for the restoration of the wavicle nature we had in the original condition of connecting and the sensation of joyful aliveness that was lost with its rupture. We see this as the quest of "everyone." Some search inside, some search outside. Others search the above and still others search the below. But everyone searches, and few are finders, although the treasure is immediately present for anyone who discovers the access point.

Anxiety and desire are not indigenous to humans; they replace full aliveness, joy, and wonder, which are our natural condition. Both anxiety and deisre are derivatives of relational rupture, starting in childhood. Prior to the loss of our true nature as cosmic beings, nothing was needed. There was no lack. But when an unattuned caretaker, through no fault of their own, breaks the child's link to the cosmos, then joy is replaced with anxiety and the desire for the original state is activated.

Couples who come for therapy will share their complaints of each other. And if you listen carefully, you will hear their desire stated as a frustration about what they are not experiencing with their partner, a desire that would be fulfilled if their partner would change in specific ways. You may also be aware that they have responded to the lure of media information about how they can get it. Perhaps they have been customers, alone and together, of the personal growth industry with no success. Perhaps they have drugs socially or become addicted, gone on pilgrimages, meditated, prayed, exercised, changed their diet, experimented with affairs, focused on work, engaged in thrilling vacations—all in the service of experiencing a sensation that eludes them. All their efforts have provided some pleasure, but only transient happiness. Nothing has worked to make their relationship better, and they have brought the aftermath of their failure to you.

Self-Absorption

Ruptured connecting is so exquisitely painful that we cannot avoid turning in towards ourselves and becoming self-absorbed. Self-absorption is a necessary element of self-defense. In the self-absorbed state, energy is diverted away from engaging with others, causing us to focus instead on our pain, on our own subjective (and often distorted) reality. Self-absorption means being so absorbed in the self that nothing else is experienced or important. Here is an illustration that may help: Think of joyfully going to the beach barefoot and you suddenly stub your toe so hard on a rock that your toe breaks and bleeds. Abruptly, there is no beach nor sun nor memories of the preceding few moments. Pleasure and curiosity disappear. Your awareness has shrunk to only your hurting and bleeding toe. Imagine this scene happens over and over again. This is a metaphor of a self-absorbed life.

When the pain subsides and anxiety moves from the foreground into the background, we are able to turn our attention outward again, to increase our intellectual capacity, to develop our careers, and to create our families. But the background noise of anxiety is always there, the noise of negative possibility. We begin to protect ourselves from the repetition of such a trauma, closing our receptors to information about others. Without receiving pure, unfiltered data from the outside, the only information we have to process is from our memories and dreams, and with those we construct an inner world in which "our" world is the "only" world there is.

Symbiosis

The self-absorption that is operative in defending our selves leads to yet another barrier to intimacy: symbiosis, which is a lack of awareness of the separate, subjective reality of others. It is symbiosis that lies at the core of disconnection. It is symbiosis, therefore, that is responsible for the lion's share of human relationship problems, and because it is the disease of humanity, it needs extensive elaboration.

Symbiosis is the collapse of the wave function, restricting us to a particle-like, centric consciousness in which we place ourselves at the center of all experiences, while the experiences of others stay at the periphery or do not exist for us. To distinguish emotional symbiosis from biological symbiosis, the latter is a mutually beneficial relationship, like the cattle egret eating ticks off a cow's back. The egret gets a meal. The cow gets a back free of ticks.

In emotional symbiosis there is no reciprocity. The cow belongs to the heron, who experiences the event as a meal and assumes the cow had the same experience. This merger of self-experience with the experience of another is a consequence of self-absorption. It arises out of our woundedness, the pain of disconnection.

The basic operating premise of the symbiotic mind is that "my" world is "the" world. With emotional symbiosis, there is no room for two, or four, or a community, or a country, or for the human race. There is only one. This ego-absorption compartmentalizes others into "like me" (good/right) and "not like me" (bad/wrong). This produces the illusion that we are separate individuals and that others share our subjective states. (And if they don't, they should.) The individual "self" (i.e., form without energy) is essentially a defense mechanism threatened by the possibility of nonbeing.

Simply stated, symbiosis is the rejection of difference. In the symbiotic state, there may be an awareness of other perspectives, but to allow them any validity threatens my own, so they must be challenged and rejected. Difference activates the original anxiety, thus reinforcing the need for a defense against otherness. This cycle (difference → anxiety → defense) is considered to be the source of couple's conflict and the source of all human conflict. It is THE human disease. And nearly everyone has it. It is the most deeply entrenched and pervasive cause of relationship dysfunction, and its amelioration is the organizing principle behind all Imago therapeutic processes that facilitate differentiation.

Symbiosis is any interaction that is interpreted by the survival centers as negative. Such an interaction triggers anxiety. Anxiety shuts down our capacity for social engagement. This reduces our perceptual capacities to our own inner experience. The world outside is replaced with the world inside. The world inside takes on the character of objective reality and abolishes our capacity to imagine, much less accept, difference. Rejection, denial, negation, or judgment about difference is the source of the universal human problem. As evidenced in the absorption of human beings with their own personal and collective safety, symbiosis permeates both the microcosm and the macrocosm, manifesting at individual and global levels.

At the societal or national level, for example, a symbiotic consciousness claims that one's own religion, culture, or lifestyle is the "right" one. The way we see the world is the only way to see the world. Those who agree with us are part of the global "we," while those who see things differently, refusing to conform and insisting on imposing their own definition, become "them," "the other," and, in extreme cases, "the enemy." The collective survival impulse creates the mass delusion that "our world" is "the world." Just as the ancients fended off their fear of a mysterious and unpredictable universe by insisting that the Earth was at the center, human beings use symbiosis as a strategy to defend against the mystery, unpredictability, and dangerousness of the "other."

Creating reality fuels the false perception of controlling reality. For the symbiotic mindset, control is a spurious key to safety and, ultimately, to survival. For the sake of survival, symbiosis becomes the substitute for authentic connecting. Indeed, symbiosis—a virtual antidote to connecting— mitigates against human connection. *Symbiosis may be the most deeply entrenched and pervasive cause of relationship dysfunction.* It serves as the psycho-emotional icon of unconscious parenting that has been transmitted from one generation to the next.

Any force that invades the integrity of the personal psyche, as symbiosis does, is bound to emanate throughout the global psyche. On a grander scale, symbiosis is reflected in any framework, whether political, economic, or sociological, that wars against basic human strivings for differentiation, freedom, and self-actualization (which themselves are counter-symbiotic forces). Symbiotic mentality views human beings dimly, as a collection of aggressive instincts that require taming. Symbiosis operates from a dualistic perspective, deeming one side right and the other wrong, judging who is good and who is evil, determining whether something is true and false on the basis of certain truths espoused by one's own belief system. The formerly whole, interconnected self now lives within the symbiotic illusion of separateness and alienation from the true self, from others, from nature, and from the cosmos.

Manifestations of Symbiosis

Contrary to the arguments of some developmental theorists, Imago theory maintains that empathy, rather than symbiosis, describes our predominant mindset at birth. In fact, developmental researchers have discovered behavior in newborns that appears to be empathic (referred to as protoempathy); truly empathic responses have been observed at 3 months, with clearly empathic responses occurring at 8 months (Roth-Hanania et al., 2011). Symbiosis is, therefore, an unnatural state that is created after birth; it is the tragic byproduct of connectional rupture. In the absence of connectional rupture, we—and those around us—would interact far differently, far more empathically, and far more effectively.

Childhood Manifestations

Starting at the maturational point at which symbiosis becomes entrenched within the child's psyche, the elaboration of a distinct, integrated, and interconnected self becomes hindered. Both the depth of symbiosis and the manner in which symbiosis takes form in the character structure will depend on the developmental stage at which the child initially encounters connectional rupture.

Adulthood Manifestations

Romantic relationship is the arena in which the adulthood forms of symbiosis are most compellingly demonstrated. In couple relationships, symbiosis manifests as the belief that one's own reality must also be the reality of one's partner. Thus, criticizing one's partner indicates symbiotic thinking, because criticism inflicts verbal and emotional pain in an attempt to force or encourage the other partner to surrender his or her own subjectivity (or internal reality) and to conform to the image of "someone who meets my needs."

Symbiosis is the prime mover of the power struggle, the second relationship stage that marks the inevitable devolution from a brief glimpse of heaven in the first stage to one of eternal damnation (or so it seems) in the second. We will explain the intricacies later on, but we think it bears mentioning here that intimate relationships are not the only ones haunted by the problems spawned by symbiosis. Symbiotic thinking shows up in all types of relationships. Because of quantum entanglements, the more two people are invested in their relationship, the more their tendency to think symbiotically, especially when one or both are under stress. For example, have you ever worked for a harried boss who kept assigning you more and more work, to the extent that it was having bad effects on your health, your family, and other parts of your life? In this instance, it is a safe guess that your boss is concentrating on their priorities only; they have thought little, if at all, about the impact of their demands on you. That's just one of the many ways that symbiotic thinking shows up in our daily lives.

Truth be told, all of us, at one time or another, engage in symbiotic thinking. Although our primary interest here is on how symbiosis looks in intimate partnerships, let us take a quick look at the ways we can detect symbiosis in any type of human relationship. To demonstrate, it is a sign of symbiosis when:

1. We immediately dismiss another person's point of view because it happens to conflict with our own (sometimes called psychic annihilation).
2. We assume other people know what we expect of them and react negatively when they don't.
3. We guilt other people when they do not comply with our wishes.
4. We interrupt another person who is saying something we disagree with or don't want to hear.
5. We repeatedly point out what other people are doing wrong.
6. We refuse to listen to information that another genuinely wishes to share with us.

7. We seldom ask for feedback, but we give a lot of feedback to others.
8. We assume, without checking, that when we are talking, others agree with what we are saying.
9. We interrupt another person, not letting them finish, to express a different opinion.
10. We assume that other people like what we like and that they have bad taste if they don't.

Loss of Empathy

While symbiosis may be the universal human disease, the tragic consequence of the emotional/cognitive isolation is the loss of empathy, the capacity to experience the inner states of other human beings and distinguish them from our own.

Although controversial, prolific research tends to concur that empathy is an innate human capacity that is built into the hardware of the human brain, called mirror neurons. The presence of mirror neurons supports the idea that we have a natural capacity to experience others as they experience themselves in moment-to-moment interactions. We have not only the capacity to experience the inner world of others, but also the power to heal with empathic expressions, as has been promoted by the therapy literature since the 1950s (Rogers, 1951; Kohut, 1970).

But the capacity to feel empathic is another victim of the anxiety caused by ruptured connecting. When we are preoccupied with living with the threat of nonbeing, it is too challenging, nearly impossible, to be a receiver of other persons experiencing, or even to care.

When anxiety triggers the defenses and we become self-absorbed, the flow of the lifeblood of a relationship—empathy—becomes blocked. Here is why: First, to foster intimacy, partners must exercise awareness and understanding of one another's internal world and subjective reality; only by doing so are they able to genuinely relate to one another in the here-and-now. When defensive adaptations get activated by an implicit memory, our primal brain merges our past with our present.

In these circumstances, partners are likely to misconstrue each other's motivations and behaviors, because they are confusing what happened to them during childhood with what is happening to them right now, with their partner. Whenever we relate from a defensive posture, we are interacting with our partner not only in the present but also through the distorted lens of the past. Second, by definition, defensive adaptations protect us from fully experiencing our "softer" feelings, such as hurt or fear. As we pointed out earlier, emotional vulnerability—and the willingness to share it—are essential components of intimacy between romantic partners.

In truth, romantic partnership requires more than many of us are able to produce, especially if we experienced early relational challenges. Intimate partnership touches not only upon our greatest hopes for the future and our deepest fears about ourselves but also upon the earliest nurturing deficits we experienced. On top of this, relationship comes with heavy, adult-like demands, including the demand to be open to our own and our partner's emotions. It requires us, in other words, to be vulnerable. However, the sense of invulnerability that defenses provide us, actually block our feelings of vulnerability toward our partner. Without being vulnerable, we cannot experience true intimacy.

Objectification
Objectification erases the "human" from human race and transforms the "other" into an object that is useful, but only to me. "Others" become a utility of the self, as Martin Buber declared in his description of the I–It relationship. Self-absorption, emotional symbiosis, and loss of empathy contribute to our inability to see others as humans, so we objectify them. When they become "objects" to us, they are no longer human, and we can treat them as we wish. This is the source of our most grievous sins, prejudice, racism, manipulation, devaluation, inequality—you name it! Paradoxically, the dehumanization of another person dehumanizes oneself.

In this next and final section of the chapter, we discuss, for each developmental phase, how deficient nurturing experiences cause defensive patterns that show up first during childhood and then later on, in adulthood, especially around the time a romantic relationship begins to move into the inevitable power struggle.

DEFENSIVE STYLES ACROSS
THE DEVELOPMENTAL SPECTRUM

Under optimal conditions, humans evolve through six childhood development stages, and corresponding challenges are incurred if deficits in nurturing are experienced at any given stage. Table 5.1 shows the minimizing (top rows) and maximizing (bottom rows) strategies developed by children to defend against a specific challenge. While reading through this section, keep referring to this table.

Deficit nurturing and repressive socialization occur all along the developmental journey and take specific forms matched by a defensive style in each developmental stage, as you will see below in the description of the challenges and adaptions of each developmental stage.

Table 5.1: Childhood Challenges and Defensive Character Adaptations						

Ruptured connection caused by childhood wounding may manifest in childhood as *minimizing defenses*, such as constriction of energy, diminishment of affect, withholding, rigidity, self-centeredness, exclusiveness, and dominance

Childhood Character Adaptation	Avoiding	Distancing	Rigidly Controlling	Completing	Withdrawing	Rebelling
Childhood Challenges	Rejection	Smothering	Used/ Dominated	Punished/ Guilted	Ostracism/ Disapproval	Over-Controlled
Developmental Stage/Impulse	CONNECTING	EXPLORATION	IDENTITY	COMPETENCE	SOCIAL	INTIMACY
Childhood Challenges	Abandonment	Neglect/ Abandonment	Ignored/ Invisible	Competence Devalued	Needs Ignored	Uniqueness Suppressed
Childhood Character Adaptation	Clinging	Pursuing	Diffusing	Manipulating	Complying	Adapting/ Conforming

Ruptured connection caused by childhood wounding may manifest in symbiotic maximizing defenses, such as explosion of energy, exaggeration of affect, invasiveness, diffuseness, other-dependence, over-inclusiveness, and submissiveness

The fate of the stages of childhood becomes the template of the stages of intimate relationship. While everyone goes through the same stages of development, their challenges tend to be stage specific and their defenses may be opposite. In other words, partners tend to choose mates whose childhood challenge was in the same developmental stage but whose adaptation to the challenge was opposite to theirs. As we describe the stage progression, the challenge, and the defense, we will indicate how these are replicated in the developmental stages of intimate relationships.

The Connecting Stage

As pointed out in last chapter's discussion of childhood development, the connecting-aged child is focused on maintaining and strengthening their inborn cosmic connective bond with a primary caretaker. In Imago, rather than an attachment impulse, the child comes connecting, or already attached. What is required from the caretaker, therefore, is to be consistently resonant with, warm with, and available to the child to maintain the cosmic connecting with which the child came into the world which can only be maintained through resonance with the caretaker. Cosmic connecting is dependent upon the interpersonal.

Minimizing Adaptation to the Connecting Challenge:
Should the caretaker respond inconsistently, by being cold and only sporadically available or warm, the child may shut down their feelings and draw the conclusion that they are unlovable and unwanted. This very early, and therefore severe, childhood challenge cuts into a child's core need not only to be wanted but also to be protected and embraced by others and ruptures the sense of cosmic belonging.

If the caretaker is not available, or is inconsistently available, and alternates, being sometimes warm and sometimes cold, the child will minimize their attachment: the child deflects the terror of not receiving warm and consistent caretaker-contact by deciding that they do not need contact after all. We call these persons minimizers when they are children, and they are called avoiders in adult intimate relationships. And they also lose their cosmic connection.

Maximizing Adaptation to the Connecting Challenge:
In response to warm but inconsistently available nurturing at the connecting stage, a child may develop an unquenchable longing for more contact with the caretaker. The inconsistent availability of the child's lifeline creates the fear of abandonment, and unlike the minimizer who withdraws, the maximizing child clings to their prized caretaker in an ongoing campaign to ensure that the caretaker never abandons them. In their adult intimate relationship, this person will be a clinger.

The Exploration Stage
Some children succeed in sustaining connecting and experience a challenge at the exploration stage, when they encounter impediments to exploring regions beyond their caretaker's reach.

Minimizing Adaptation to the Exploration Challenge:
Children who experienced an overprotective and possessive caretaker learned to associate the return to the caretaker—one of the two essential components of the repetitive leave-and-return cycle—with being smothered; that is, any attempts to further explore were discouraged. These children adapt by isolating and distancing; that is, by going back to their caretaker reluctantly or, in some cases, not at all (e.g., by temporarily "disappearing" from the caretaker's sight). This reaction stems from the fear that once they

return, they might never again be allowed to leave their caretaker's side. In adult relationships, they become distancers.

Maximizing Adaptation to the Exploration Challenge:
Upon returning from their developmentally appropriate exploration of the environment, maximizing children discovered that their caretaker, rather than welcoming the child back, had not even noticed that the child had left. Such experiences of being neglected left these children with a bad feeling about separating from their caretaker. The safer alternative, these children seem to reason, is to pursue the caretaker, hoping for any tidbits of reassurance, guidance, and protection from the dangers that may lurk beyond the homestead. These children become pursuers in their adult relationships.

The Identity Stage
Mirroring is essential for all children across the developmental spectrum, and it has special importance for an identity-aged child. Since they do not yet have an identity, the caretaker becomes the perfect conduit, and mirroring becomes the perfect method, for encouraging children to explore the many permutations of humanness. How then can we as therapists promote transformation and wholeness?

Minimizing Adaptation to the Identity Challenge:
Some children receive only selective mirroring, which is far inferior to flat (or accurate) mirroring. Here the caretaker, instead of indiscriminately mirroring all of the child's experiments with identity, mirrors only the ones with which they feel comfortable. Feeling used and dominated by the same adult whose validation they crave, this child is likely to leave this stage with the challenge of consolidating an identity. Perhaps the parent or caretaker has their own subconscious reasons or fears that prevent mirroring their child's identity as a whole. But this is yet another cycle of unconscious relating.

To cope with this absence of mirroring, these children develop rigidity, an under porous, inflexible boundary around them. So-called rigid children interpret and then dismiss any feedback about themselves that doesn't match what they already believe. As a consequence, in the act of staving off information about themselves, they also keep out the very information that would help them solidify their sense of identity. In adult relationships they are called the rigid controller.

Maximizing Adaptation to the Identity Challenge:
Children who develop the maximizing adaptation to their identity challenge also have experienced deficient mirroring; however, in contrast to the overly

rigid minimizer, who has rigid boundaries, maximizing children defend themselves by forming no boundaries at all; that is, they take on a diffuse identity. Subjected to their caretaker's inaccurate or painful mirroring, diffuse children carry with them an invisibility challenge: in order to stay psychically alive in the face of onslaught (e.g., shaming) to their identity, diffuse children learned to lay low, remain invisible, and disown any definition that might be greeted with invalidation or scorn from others. In adulthood, they become a compliant diffuser.

This may go unnoticed by many, who admire the compliant diffuser for being a peacemaker, until it's not. It is sometimes revealed in family situations or personal intimacy scenarios in which a disgruntled spouse may require the adult to be less compliant, stand up, and become a more outspoken leader, for instance. As we travel through these stages of development, we can then see how the past affects the future.

The Competence Stage
In the competence stage, children who adopt the minimizing competitive adaptation don't just look good; they look extremely good. Often high achievers, they appear utterly self-confident and seem to be internally, as opposed to externally, driven.

Minimizing Adaptation to the Competence Challenge:
Their relational challenges, in fact, are invisible to casual observers because these children shine on the outside while suffering on the inside. At the same time that they are denying that anything is amiss, competitive children secretly suspect that, contrary to the evidence, they actually are inferior to others and that their successful young lives are nothing but a sham. Having been punished for their mistakes while receiving selective praise for their achievements, competitive children feel like they are running in a race they cannot win. The accolades of the world do not touch, and therefore cannot heal, the wounds of the competitive child. Therefore, in adulthood they become the compulsive competitor.

Maximizing Adaptation to the Competence Challenge:
Having experienced little or no praise for their achievements or, even worse, having had these achievements devalued, the competitive maximizer learns to manipulate others in order to capitalize on their inability, to "cash in" on their (pseudo) incompetence. While the fear of losing their caretaker's approval may lead the manipulative child to exaggerate their accomplishments, that very same fear causes them to downplay and devalue their achievements. By rejecting the impulse toward competence by giving up before they start, the competitive maximizer child expects to

lose, and they are usually not disappointed. Some might refer to this person as having a victim-mindset, however most will go undetected in adulthood as those around them attempt to make them feel better. In adulthood this child becomes a manipulative compromiser.

The Social Stage
In the social stage, a child begins the journey into their future social world by extending their exploratory impulse to social relationships outside the home. The energy these children invest in their forays outside the home depends on how solid they feel in their identity. If their sense of self has been validated by their parents and they have a secure identity, like the exploration stage when their curiosity led them to explore their home environment, they begin to explore the social world outside the family.

In this intermediate stage between childhood and adulthood, which H. S. Sullivan called "chumship," the child's primary concern is to find their place among their peers and to find and keep a best friend. The discovery of a best friend is attended with joy and excitement similar to romantic love, and so is the grief evoked by the loss of this emotionally charged relationship. The best friend tends to be of the same sex and their importance matches or exceeds the emotional importance of the caretakers or siblings. The similarity of this middle stage of childhood to adolescent and adult romantic love has led some students of this developmental stage to posit that chumship is not only the first step outside the family, but a preparatory stage for adolescent love in the same way that adolescent love affairs are the psychic preparation for adult love relationships. Therefore, this movement tends to relegate caretakers, at least occasionally, to the sidelines. Parents may feel that they are beginning to lose control (assuming they felt they had any) over what influences their child and how they handle this differentiation process will influence how their child succeeds in their future love relationships.

Minimizing Adaptation to the Social Challenge:
If the child with a solid identity experiences a social challenge, when they socialize with their peers, they assume leadership (or not) as seems appropriate, and they have no issues in either case. If they developed a rigid identity in order to survive in their family, they tend to become somewhat of an autocratic leader with their peers, maximizing their energy toward becoming popular and being a hero. In adulthood, they are called loners.

Maximizing Adaptation to the Social Challenge:
If the child's attempt to consolidate identity resulted in a diffuse identity, they will tend to engage with others, become dependent, and follow the crowd. Since they are not sure who they are or what to think, they leave

the decision-making to other people. To be accepted by the peer group and included in social events in and after school, they show a lot of interest in others to aggrandize their reputation and they take on lots of tasks to make themselves indispensable. In adulthood they become the sacrificial caregiver.

The Intimacy Stage

Anyone who has been the caretaker of a teenager knows all about the massive powder keg that lies beneath adolescent romances. Parents vary widely in their approaches to providing structure and support to their older children; what most parents seem to have in common, though, is how often they make mistakes—and big ones.

Minimizing Adaptation to the Intimacy Challenge:
In western culture, the last people an intimacy-challenged young male tends to turn to for advice about his relationship are his parents. Of course, an intimacy-challenged female might respond in exactly the same way. Therefore, parents who lean in the direction of overcontrolling are liable to find their teenaged child unresponsive, if not outright hostile, to any suggestions they may make about their child's romantic life. The minimizer's hypersensitive reactions to feelings of being controlled or dominated are likely to surface and lock the child into conflict with caretakers.

An adult who was intimacy-challenged as a child is likely to withdraw from their partner and resist their partner's entreaties for greater contact, just as they did with caretakers in earlier years. In adulthood, the rebellious teenager is referred to as the rebel.

Maximizing Adaptation to the Intimacy Challenge:
In nurturing their offspring in the dating stage, caretakers may err on the side of providing their teen with too little structure and support for the child's intimacy impulse. Having little, if any, idea how to function in a romantic relationship, the naïve teenager may adapt to their situation by maximizing. They are likely to take the safe and narrow road, for example, by latching on to the first potential partner who shows an interest in them. Using the maximizing defense, they, when interacting with a partner, are likely to suppress their needs and desires and subvert their growing sense of who they are and what they want to avoid, losing the degree of intimacy they have managed to obtain thus far. They may, in effect, lose themselves in their quest for intimacy with another person. As they replicate this in adult intimate relationships, they earn the title of the conformist.

SUMMARY: THE SEQUENCE
OF RUPTURED CONNECTING

We close this chapter with a summary of the sequence of events and their consequent experiences when connecting is ruptured in childhood (Figure 5.2). We have discovered that the sequence occurs when connecting is ruptured in adult intimate relationships and in other significant relationships.

This sequence comprises how we interact with the world when connecting is ruptured:

1. Our original state as a wavicle is connecting with our caretakers, through whom we connect with our cosmic identity as a participant in an interconnecting universe. The felt sense of connecting is the neural sensation of full aliveness, relaxed joyfulness, and wonder.

Figure 5.2:
The Sequence and Consequence of Ruptured Connecting

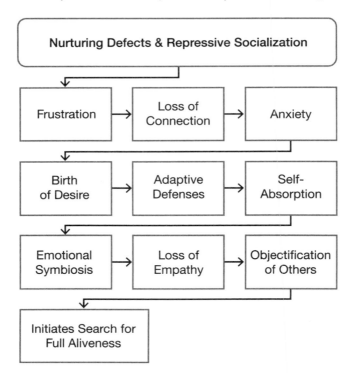

2. Our original connecting is ruptured by a negative interaction that triggers anxiety and collapses our wave functions, activating our particle-like defenses.
3. Anxiety raises the possibility of our nonbeing. In our particle-like state, we defend against the pain of that sensation by converting the energy into anger and depression and by adopting minimizing or maximizing strategies to protect ourselves.
4. The pain of the rupture creates such an intense internal focus that self-absorption replaces engagement with others, much less the cosmos of which we are a citizen.
5. Consciousness of the reality of others is replaced with a symbiotic state that assumes that others are extensions of oneself. The basic premise of the symbiotic mind is that "my" world is "the" world. Simply stated, symbiosis is the rejection of difference, the merger of the other into the self, and that is the disease of humanity.
6. The tragedy of symbiosis is the loss of empathy, the capacity to experience the inner states of other human beings and to distinguish them from your own. It is the ultimate loneliness.
7. When others cannot be experienced as they experience themselves, they have no inherent value, so we turn them into objects and do what we wish with them and to them. Paradoxically, the dehumanization of the other dehumanizes oneself.

Simultaneously, desire for the recovery of the sensation of connecting is born with the loss of connecting, and the drive to recover connecting permeates everything we do. What makes it possible for us to recover the original condition is that we have a memory of it from childhood, so we recognize it when we experience it.

Given we have experienced what we want to reexperience, it may come as no surprise that the drive to recover connecting is built into us. While this drive has a desired outcome, it has no map and no sense of direction or the skill to take the journey. It is driven by the lower brain, which has no technology to achieve its intention. But, over the centuries we have developed the capacity to discover and apply a technology that creates the conditions in which connecting can be restored. That comes from the upper brain, the prefrontal cortex, which has the capacity but not the information about how to restore the original condition.

In the next chapter, we turn to the function of memory in the restoration of connecting. Not only do we have a memory of the original condition, we also have a memory of the people and circumstances responsible for our loss of it. Since having it and the loss of it are connected to the same cast of characters in our childhood, it makes sense that our unconscious would look for them or a reasonable facsimile. That brings us to the Imago, the central aspect of our clinical theory, and the hope for the recovery of joy, wonder, and full aliveness.

6

The Imago

The Search for Original Connecting

That the past influences the present is an axiom in the psychological sciences and collective wisdom. That the past, whatever its quality and emotional tone, *repeats* itself in the present tends not to be believed by many, but it has been documented by extensive research. Since the brain has no template nor content but the past, our experience of living in the present is an illusion. Each time we reflect on a moment, it is gone. The bridge from the experienced past to the experienced present is memory, which is existentially, but unconsciously, uploaded into the present as "reality." Thus the present is the past reporting on itself.

This all has to do with how the Imago Process works.

What is the Imago?

As a word, *imago* is just one letter away from the word *image*, which is what *imago* means in Latin: an image. In Imago Relationship Therapy, Imago is capitalized to represent both a construct about a configuration of memory and because it refers to an intellectual system developed to explain the meaning and function of that memory configuration.

As a memory configuration, the Imago is more-or-less an internal photo chronology of the years of our childhood, featuring a collage of pictures of our younger self as we were being held, guided, loved, scolded, ignored, rejected, or in other ways powerfully affected by the most important people who will ever enter our life. Collectively, these pictures tell a detailed story about the people who reared us, how they made us feel, and what we felt about them as we progressed through the developmental stages. If the story is positive and exciting, it will repeat itself in the future with no need for editing, because it serves the survival directive. If it is stressful, painful, or traumatic, it will offer itself to the present for revision, because survival is at stake. This constellation of memories propounds itself to the present in search of an alternative future.

The facts that the past is in the present and that the past creates the present in the image of itself are the foundational experiences that constitute the concept of the Imago. The aim of the repetitive cycle is not to repeat the past, as Freud hypothesized, but to change it in the service a new future.

Creating the conditions for sustaining connecting and experiencing joy make the Imago the single most important of human projects, because its intention is to restore our original condition and true nature. And the success or failure of the project depends on how the first love affair turns out, because that is a precursor to the fate of the second.

To be aware of all this in the present and to move from repetition to reflection and from there to novelty is inventing the future, which is a function of the imagination. But as soon as it is invented, it becomes our past. However, it can then be a better past to be uploaded as a better future through the bridge of the present. The future comes from the past repeating itself, and a new future comes from intentionality and the creativity and imagination that are inherent in our nature as cosmic beings.

Since we did not and cannot get our needs met by our caretakers, because they were unavailable or circumstances did not permit, our unconscious is willing to finish our developmental tasks with someone who is *a reasonable facsimile of them.* When we find that person in adult life, we experience the phenomenon of falling in love, and we assign to them the task of helping us complete our developmental agenda by meeting our relational needs from across the spectrum of our developmental processes. The need is generic and universal: to restore connecting. The fulfillment of that agenda is the intention and competence of Imago Relationship Therapy.

The form in which the need presents itself for a specific person is stage specific. Whenever the need of a specific developmental stage was not met, progression through that stage was stalled, and that impacted progress in all subsequent stages, and the resumption of the developmental flow requires the satisfaction, in adulthood, of the generic need in the stage specific form in which it presents itself. That is where the Imago gets activated. It is the filter that lets the right person into our lives, although that person is similar to the one who was not present at a distinct developmental stage in which a need was not met. That is the conundrum of the selection process and the challenge of the Imago therapist.

Since our Imago consists of our own highly idiosyncratic definition of what love means, given the particularities of our relationship with our caretaker(s), the person our unconscious selects to satisfy that need will fail us, as our caretakers did. In our anxiety about survival, triggered by the failure of our caretakers to be present and the origin of our need, we will respond the same way we learned to respond with our caretakers. We will maximize or minimize our energy in a protest. If the protest fails to elicit need-satisfying responses from our partner, as it did with our caretakers, we will adapt by escalation or confrontation or by withdrawal or some other exit from the relationship—as we did in childhood.

Imago offers another option: *to transform the unconscious relationship into a conscious partnership* in which partners collaborate and cocreate a relationship that transforms the memories of the past with our caretakers into a dream relationship with our partner.

In your own practice you may have experienced the result of this scenario. If, when couples become our clients, we fail to help them get their unconscious agenda of need satisfaction, we will become a part of their drama. They will protest, withdraw, or leave therapy. So, we need to know why they are in our office and what we have to do to help them achieve what they came for!

To reiterate: Not only does this process of need satisfaction start from the first day of our lives, its impact will remain with us for the rest of our lives, because it is about survival. Since survival is our prime directive, that need never goes away. It is nonnegotiable, so the Imago dynamic has a greater impact on everyone than anything else in their lives.

The formation and agenda of the Imago has momentous implications for our relational future. It was present and active in early childhood in our selection of a best friend and emerged with intense energy in the early stages of adolescence, which launched our search for a romantic partner with whom we intended to complete the unfinished agenda of childhood. The significance of this appears personal, but its value extends beyond the personal to the collective, and it is an essential element for humans to move to our next developmental stage and for the human race to move to our next stage of social evolution.

To sum it up: Our Imago is an unconscious homing device that guides us toward the "right" kind of partner—that is, a partner who matches or fits our internalized image of our caretakers. When we find that person, we two become an Imago-Match, and we fall in love with the agenda of transforming the past, moving to our next stage of development, and ushering the human race forward to its next developmental stage, which from the Imago perspective, is considered to be a relational civilization.

The work of the Imago therapist serves the personal, the collective, and the cosmic, and since resolution of conflict constellates cohesion rather than chaos in personal relationships, that work impacts the quantum field. It is this cohesion that will encourage and multiply understanding and connection for humanity. Imagine then a future world where humans are far more relationally conscious.

CHARACTERISTICS OF THE IMAGO

Why does the Imago have such sway over our lives and, specifically, whom we love and how we love them? To get a handle on this elusive force operating outside our awareness and without our permission, let us review how it evolved and what it looks like.

1. Our Imago Comprises Our Childhood Experiences

The Imago is the storehouse of all our experiences with our childhood caretakers, whether remembered or forgotten. As far as Imago theory is concerned, the events of our childhood are not nearly as important as our internal take on those events, along with the powerful emotional residue they left behind. Most important of all are our impressions of how much our caretakers loved us, how available they were, how close and warm, and, especially, how safe or unsafe they made us feel. In Imago theory, these are the essential ingredients, and these feelings are what drive our romantic life. It is not the facts of our life with our caretakers; it is the emotional resonance between our internal Imago and the traits of our selected intimate other that leads us in the direction of an Imago-Match.

The subjective nature of the Imago becomes obvious when you ask, say, two brothers about their experiences growing up in the same household. One brother might recall his mother as warm and loving and his father as more distant and judgmental; the second brother, despite being reared by the same parents during the same period, may have similar memories of his mother but recalls his father differently—as being warm and accepting rather than cold and distant. This phenomenon is similar to what occurs when two people go to see the same movie and come out afterward with entirely different reactions—so different, perhaps, that it seems they had not even seen the same movie, or in the case of the brothers, they had had different parents.

As you will soon learn from our discussion of the romantic phase, whatever feelings we were left with from our experiences of being loved and cared for during childhood are the same ones that echo back to us when we begin our search for a partner. It is these same feelings, and emotional resonance, that fuel our attraction to *this* as opposed to *that* partner. Not just anyone will do!

2. Our Imago Changes with New Experiences

The neural network of memories that constitute the Imago is foundational and compelling, but permeable if there have been positive mitigating circumstances in later childhood. Since the brain is plastic, changes in the social environment, especially the caretaker's emotional health or the presence of another more available caretaker, creates new memories that alter the original template.

Therefore, our Imago is not like a handprint made in freshly poured concrete that, once dried, remains as a permanent fixture. The Imago can change if/when the child experiences *new and constructive experiences* in their social environment. Nevertheless, given that the beginning point of the Imago is very early—beginning in the womb (see Annie Murphy Paul's *Origins*, 2010) and expanding with the increased stimuli right after birth—it is likely that most people's "first draft" of the Imago—their perceptions of being loved and nurtured, or not, as an infant—establishes a tendency to perceive future partners as either available or unavailable, safe or unsafe (Asch, 1946). These perceptions may or may not be accurate, and therefore they are just our perceptions.

3. Our Imago Affects Us in the Present

When couples walk down the aisle, virtually none of them believe that they will be one of nearly 50% or so who end up divorcing. Nor do most of those divorcing know that their divorce is, in many ways, a replication of their emotional and behavioral solution in childhood. What makes so many people believe that, despite all the evidence to the contrary, their relationship will be different? Why do we keep trying again and again to make love work, no matter how many times we have failed at it?

Many partners find it difficult, at least initially, to identify and then connect the dots between the contents of their Imago and their experiences in their current romantic relationship (or those of their past). As an Imago therapist, sometimes you may have clients who claim to see little if any overlap between what they experienced as a child and the problems they are having in their romantic relationship now.[1] Other clients will report no recollection of turmoil, deprivation, or any other type of deficit during their childhood years. Some will state that both their caretakers and their childhood were ideal. Ironically, these are the same clients who now find their relationship markedly troubled and themselves deeply enmeshed in a power struggle with their partner—which is why they have come to you for therapy.

To shed some light on this difficulty let us briefly review the discussion of the nature of ruptured connecting in childhood. Although uncommon, it certainly is possible to get through childhood without significant rupture and intense suffering. As mentioned, frequently you will encounter partners who got far into later developmental phases, say 6 to 12 years old, before incurring any disturbing deficits in nurturing.[2] But when you encounter clients who deny experiencing any painful repercussions from their childhood, it's more likely that they are among those whose early life experiences were so painful that those experiences are deeply buried in their unconscious and to engage those memories would be too threatening for them to consider. It seems that the more intense the denial, the greater the defense against the anxiety of remembering the challenges of child-hood, the more severe the need deprivation. Given the pain of the trauma, which is often accompanied by shame about portraying their parents in a negative way, a client may say it is better, sometimes, to let sleeping dogs lie! But this avoidance does not prevent the problem from constraining a thriving relationship.

Recall, too, that these mechanisms operate outside of conscious aware-ness. This means that when partners become defensive toward each other, as is typical during a power struggle, they are not even aware of what they are defending themselves from, or even that they are defending themselves. They are just telling the truth, as they know it. Humans have this tendency to "forget" or repress the painful memories stored in our Imago and to be blind to their reappearance in their adult relationships.

Humans are likely drawn to a partner who arouses not only feelings of bliss but also of devastation. For better or for worse, it is our destiny to pick, as our ideal partner, an Imago-Match who will eventually do what our care-takers did: loved us the best they knew how but not perfectly enough to restore original connecting. Further, we are also bound to discover in our partner the same deficits and limits that our caretakers had. When we dis-cover that, as we inevitably do, we tend to consider the possibility that we married the "wrong person."

AN IMAGO-MATCH

Although over the centuries poets, philosophers, and psychologists have mused about the mystery of choice and suffering in matters of love, none had access to the scope of knowledge available to Imago theory and therapy that helps us with the question: what leads us to choose that one person (or maybe two or three or four) to spend our lives with out of the countless oth-ers we could have chosen? Why does your best friend Sally keep choosing the same man—the only difference being his name—always ending up with the same final outcome? Why does the same thing keep happening to us, over and over again, in our quest to love and be loved?

In Imago theory, we posit that the major reason we seek out this kind of partner is because of the assumption that lies at the very center of what Imago theory and therapy are all about: *An Imago-Match gives us a golden opportunity to restore the original experience of connecting we lost during childhood.* Behind the memory of a deficit in nurturing that produced the content of the Imago is a primal memory of our original nature—cosmic connecting experienced through resonance with our caretakers—which was lost with the original disconnect, and the desire for a return to that original nature is the intention of the unconscious presentation of the memory of its loss. Because the original connecting we seek is also in our memory, behind the memory of rupture, the yearned for future is available for the couple. In other words, the Imago can be seen as the memory of the context in which the survival directive was activated because of a caretaker's failure to be present and supportive of our developmental needs, and it is an attempt to recreate that context with a similar person (an Imago-Match) to try to turn off the survival signal that was activated in childhood. The Imago therapist is the midwife to the recovery of the original state, and only its recovery will turn off the survival switch.

Before we discuss the transformation of memory in the service of a new future, let us look more specifically at the person with whom our unconscious paired us to do that: our Imago-Match.

Specifically, in an Imago-Match both partners:

1. trigger each other's feelings and memories, good or bad, that are associated with their childhood caretakers;
2. encountered deficient nurturing during the same (or sometimes adjacent) developmental stage in childhood, leaving them with wounds that are similar in type and severity we call parallel wounding;
3. use complementary defensive styles (defensive adaptations), or opposite ways of defending against pain and frustration (minimizing versus maximizing);
4. became emotionally arrested around the same milepost on the highway of development, leaving them with equal levels of maturity (or immaturity); and
5. have complementary (opposite) deficits or blocked functioning in the areas of thinking, feeling, sensing, and acting.

This may strike you as a risky position for anyone to be in charge of choosing someone with whom to reconstruct the experiences of a challenging and often traumatic childhood, but the fact is that our brains have no other resources than the past, and the imagination of a different outcome in the future with a person similar to those with whom the past was experienced. Such is the paradoxical nature of our unconscious. As we drill down with curiosity, we will discover its brilliance, if only we will consciously cooperate with it.

Now, let us take a closer look at these five factors that contribute to an Imago-Match.

1. Our Partner Reminds Us of Our Caretakers

This idea, that we marry our caretakers (meaning whoever was primary in our childhood), is nothing original or earth-shattering, per the old song, "I want a girl just like the girl that married dear old dad." But Imago theory adds a unique twist to the conventional wisdom that suggests men go for women who resemble their mother and women are attracted to men who remind them of their father. The addition is that the Imago-Matching process is gender neutral. The primary attractor of a male could be their father and of a female, their mother. Ironically, it depends on the one with whom they have the worst memories.

The Imago lives outside the realm of logic and reality, so it does not split hairs over whether our caretakers were male or female. Anyone who did their part in keeping us alive when we could not do so by ourselves was incorporated into the Imago. So, regardless of which caretakers our Imago resonates with—mommy or daddy, grandma or granddad, a cool aunt, a mean nanny, or a creepy uncle—the alarm bell goes off when it picks up signals like those of our Imago's cast of characters.[3]

Because the Imago is based on our subjective, emotionally charged impressions of our caretakers as we perceived them during childhood, not as they actually were, even persons who are not a precise match can come close enough to hitting the bull's eye, which means we could end up falling in love with them. But, they have to be a reasonable facsimile.

2. Our Partners Have Parallel and Equal Challenges

Imagine you are working with a couple who have gotten themselves mired in the power struggle, which will probably be most of them. The wife complains about her husband's "stubbornness," "close-mindedness," and "sense of superiority," while he views his wife as "disorganized," "unsure of herself," and "indecisive." As you listen in on their exchanges—listening, especially, for primitive (or infantile) emotions such as fear of being abandoned or resentment over being smothered by the other or the sense of being disrespected or overlooked or invisible—you eventually detect a theme, or two, that unites just about everything they say to each other. These are the themes that point you toward their childhood challenges, which they are likely to have in common.

You can learn other things from listening to a couple's language, including that, despite the fact the partners seem to be coming from opposite sides of the planet, they actually sound quite alike; they may use different words, but they often are describing the same kind of pain. Partner A might say, "You never listen to me." Partner B answers, "Well, you never talk to me." Or one says, "Why don't you ever want to get close to me?" while the other responds "Why can't you ever just leave me alone?" These are signs of parallel challenges of equal severity and of the common universal theme that relational stress is behind every individual complaint.

3. Our Partners Use Complementary Defensive Styles

Let us go back to the distinction made earlier between minimizing and maximizing defenses. If you recall, minimizers constrict their energy when feeling threatened or unsafe, pulling it inward, shutting it down, downplaying its importance, or denying its existence. Maximizers use the opposite strategy: when upset, they expand their energy, discharging it outward by talking, exaggerating, yelling, crying, or other similar tactics. Note that neither defensive style is desirable nor undesirable; neither is superior to the other. They are the polar reactions of our autonomic nervous system: the sympathetic branch, which escalates emotion, and the parasympathetic branch, which de-escalates. Thus, both are typical human defensive tactics, knee-jerk behaviors, which we use when feelings of safety and disconnection begin to loom large.

Here is an image that might help describe the minimizer–maximizer dynamic: the turtle and the hailstorm. Think of the minimizer as a turtle; it sticks its head inside its shell at will; it moves slowly if at all; it hunkers down. The hailstorm, of course, represents the maximizer, who blows up conflict, then explodes it at their turtle partner, like a thunderstorm flinging golf ball-sized hail toward the Earth. The bigger the hail, the more tightly the turtle retracts into its shell. Likewise, the louder the maximizer gets, the quieter the minimizer becomes, and vice versa, like the call-and-response of an unending song and dance routine.

So why do partners behave like this with each other? When partners negatively react (are reactive) toward one other, it is usually for one and the same reason: they have, wittingly or unwittingly, triggered each other's deepest anxiety by behaving in some way that is similar to a caretaker behavior. Once again, it feels as though their emotional oxygen is about to get cut off, and once again, both partners do whatever they learned to do in order to stave off this survival threat. And so they react toward their partner—their one and only parent-proxy—in the same way they reacted toward their unattuned caretakers: defensively, but with the unconscious intention of a positive outcome that will satisfy a developmental need. One partner's most infantile behavior is met by the other's; the maximizer goes ballistic and confronts, and the minimizer goes mute and withdraws. That is what complementary defenses look like.

Yet, as powerfully as the past pulls on us at such times, our unconscious striving to finish the maturational process is as powerful as the connective drive implanted in our psychological DNA. In fact, as we indicated earlier, this striving to reactivate the developmental process is part and parcel of our unquenchable thirst for connecting, our primal memory behind the memory of ruptured connecting. And this is why people are drawn to their Imago-Match.

To reiterate these important points: the connectional rupture that couples bring into our office is rooted in, and recapitulates, the first connectional rupture that took place during childhood. Just as that earlier rupture came from our painful experiences with imperfectly attuned caretakers in the past, the current rupture is triggered by imperfect attunement with one's partner in the present. Caretakers' imperfections show up in different ways, but they all involve either *intrusion* (also called invasion) or *neglect*; in short, intrusive caretaking involves too much structure while neglectful caretaking involves too little. As we've already seen, to stave off further wounding, to cope with the pain of wounds they already have, and to combat emotional danger, children develop one of two defensive styles: minimizing or maximizing, withdrawal or pursuit, deceleration or escalation. The defensive style we choose is a mirror image of the kind of caretaking— neglectful or intrusive—that wounded us.

This defensive pattern, this same dynamic, is precisely what you will see, in one form or another, when a couple brings their power struggle into your office. We must help each couple differently once we've identified their patterns of interaction. (Identifying the intrusive or neglectful caretaking experiences and corresponding minimizing or maximizing defenses are a part of the clinical practice that we will explore in Chapter 14 with worksheets in Appendices 13–17.)

4. Our Partners Have Similar Maturity Levels

When minimizers are feeling defensive, they retreat or withdraw, essentially abandoning ship; they appear saner and better contained than the more maximizing partner, who seems overly emotional, aggressive, and chaotic. This is especially the case with couples with early wounds, who at times act like two toddlers pushing and pulling, attacking and withdrawing. Yet neither partner is living in the present. Both are reenacting the scenarios of ruptured connecting in their pasts. At this moment, each sees the other as their always absent, never reliable, or cruelly rejecting caretaker. Whether they cope with their temporary state of insanity by exploding or imploding, partners are usually operating at approximately the same maturity level, meaning they were arrested around roughly the same developmental stage.

5. Our Partners Have Opposite or Complementary
Blocks in the Four Human Functions

This final "matching" factor brings up a related axiom of Imago theory: What is dominant in one partner is recessive in the other.

This statement has to do with our four human functions—thinking, feeling, sensing, and acting. These are the four ways we express ourselves relationally: how we discharge energy in our social contexts. We do it with our minds by thinking, with our feelings by expressing them, with our five senses by receiving and responding to environmental signals, and by acting when we use our muscles to move.

Among the many valuable lessons we learn during childhood is whether to express or repress a certain function, such as thinking or expressing feelings. What we learn depends on how our caretaker responded to us when we made our choices in childhood. In other words, our relational interactions with others—how we discharge our life energy—is a function of our interaction with our caretakers. What our caretakers did when we engaged in a conversation, expressed a feeling about an event, responded to how something smelled or looked or sounded, or flexed our muscles to move toward or away from someone is embedded in memory images that regulate our interactive behavior in adulthood with everyone, not just our intimate others. If our caretakers approved of all the ways we used our functions, then we integrated them into a network of behaviors with which we interacted with the world of others or nature. If however, we expressed a function and afterwards received multiple judgments of its inappropriateness or were punished for expressing that function, that function took on the character of being so dangerous that we constrain the energy needed to express it, effectively repressing an organic part of ourselves. However, the function does not disappear, just its expression; but for all practical purposes it is missing or lost.

To our childish minds, the handiest way to deal with this dilemma was to get rid of the offending members, that is, to consign to the darkness of the unconscious whatever tendencies we have that are causing us trouble. Then, after years or decades of shunning these dangerous aspects, sooner or later we forget all about them and all about the fullness of life we once enjoyed. It eventually seems natural to us to be paralyzed by doubt when we try to make decisions, to second guess the decisions we do make, or to feel ashamed of our body. We come to believe that it's normal to hide our vulnerable feelings, such as sadness or hurt; we believe it's appropriate to control ourselves and the people around us. Of course, even with this, our four functions are still humming away; we can't get through a single day without tapping into our thinking, feeling, sensing, and acting abilities. But, like the star athlete who has not worked out in 10 years and is now carrying around 30 extra pounds, once we have lost full access to our core energy—once there is a disconnect between that energy source and the expression—it's as though part of us is in a coma. These comatose parts are what Imago refers to as the lost self. This lost self is worthy of identification, discussion, and reclamation.

In our experience of observing complementarity in couples, we have discovered that most partners have shut down two of their functions, say thinking and feeling, but they give full expression to their other two functions, sensing and acting. So, the partner whose sensing function is intact might be an artist, sensing the contours of their environment for their creative expressions, or an athlete, using their muscles to compete with others for the prize, or both—perhaps becoming an athlete with musical talent. Unconsciously, however, this artist—whose thinking function was shut down—may harbor yearnings to be a college professor, especially if someone they admired was a college professor, or a scientist who also loved music, and was able to cry in movie theaters, thus displaying those thinking and feeling functions. The partner whose sensing and acting functions were left intact was not good at expressing feelings or thinking about things logically. And the reverse also seems to be true.

What is interesting about all this is that partners criticize the functions in the other that are shut down in themselves. Because they were not able to express that function without criticism and so shut it down, if their partner expresses the function, they criticize the partner for expressing it, as their caretakers criticized them. It's as though they are saying: the exercise of that function is dangerous, and you should not do it. Or, they might be saying, if I can't have it, neither can you. But the paradoxical side of this is that it takes two people to have the four functions in the relationship, and since all four are needed to navigate life successfully, nature has paired us with someone we desperately need to provide those that are missing although we criticize them for having what is missing in ourselves.

THE THREE STAGES OF RELATIONSHIPS

All relationships, like life, go through stages. Intimate relationships and other significant relationships go through three. These stages have to do with the brain's interest in the neurochemistry of novelty, its disinterest in the loss of those chemicals when the novel becomes familiar, and its attempt to recover those neurochemicals by recreating the preexisting state of pleasure. Our biology is far more involved in our choices than we understand.

The first stage in all relationships is idealization and excitement, the second stage is boredom with routine and disappointment when the source of pleasure leads to frustration and disillusionment and we end up in the power struggle and the third stage is an attempt to return to the first stage with re-enchantment.

In intimate relationships, we call these stages romantic love, the power struggle, and adaptation/resolution. The first stage is usually short, the middle can be short as well or can last a lifetime, and the third stage is an adaptation to a hot or parallel relationship, the resolution of divorce, or the creation of a conscious partnership wherein real love resides. Because of the special meaning of the intimate partner as the source of need satisfaction, the stages tend to be more intensely positive at the start and more painful in the middle when the disappointment comes, and if the resolution is ending the relationship, more painful at the end. If the resolution is positive, the outcome is deeper satisfaction and joyful aliveness.

The Not-So-Lasting Power of Romantic Love
Two people can be sure they are an Imago-Match if they fell in love.

Romantic love is among the most sought after of all human experiences, the most intense and powerful, and perhaps the most important. And perhaps among the shortest. As we indicated earlier, the sensations that constitute romantic love are so desirable and intense because they are a transient reexperiencing of original connecting, the sensation of which is full aliveness, joy, and wonder. When we fall in love, connecting with the cosmos is temporarily restored through the relationship with our romantic partner, who is similar to the caretaker with whom we experienced it originally, and our experience of our cosmic identity is reexperienced—temporarily. No wonder the partner becomes so significant—even essential! When they respond to the unmet childhood need, they restore the experience of cosmic connecting.

The Biochemistry Behind Romantic Love
Neurochemically, the experience of romantic love is a cocktail made up of biochemical substances—pheromones, endorphins, phenylethylamines (PEA), dopamine, and adrenaline—all mixed together to create a potent cocktail that literally alters our perceptions, transforming the way we see ourselves and the world around us in immensely positive ways. In many of us, these alterations in brain chemistry show up in physiological changes, like a surge in our energy level and a decreased need for sleep, not to mention the infamous explosion in our sex drive. These biological changes, which show up cognitively as obsessive thinking and rumination over our partner and difficulty paying attention to or concentrating on anything but our beloved, make us even look a little like we're coming down with hypomania, a milder version of the mania of bipolar disorder. That is the amount of power romantic love wields over us.

The Psychology of Romantic Love

As we intimated above, essentially what is going on is a replay of our child–caretaker dance, with all its exquisite emotional acrobatics, that kept going and going until the curtains finally came down on our childhood. Anyone who has ever been in love knows what we're talking about here. Let us go through some of the most common signs, which not only your clients but you, yourself, are likely to have experienced a sense of:

- having known your partner forever
- timelessness; there is no past or future, there is only now
- belonging and oneness with each other
- certainty that this person is essential for our survival

This may strike you as a risky position for anyone to be in, but at least it does not last too long. One reason the romantic stage tends to be short-lived is simply because of how our brain works: it habituates to, or gets used to, the ebb and flow of brain chemicals thought to be responsible for the blissful emotions that accompany the romantic phase. Then there is the fact that the person we have chosen to give ourselves to, mind, body, and soul, is not the person we thought they were. Like any illusion, this one has to come to an end sooner or later.

This transient and highly pleasant fantasy called romantic love actually has a much loftier purpose than first meets the eye: *it is to cement a bond between two incompatible people that will last long enough for both of them to complete their unfinished childhood development, to fulfill their biological and evolutionary purpose through the propagation of the human race and to re-experience their cosmic identity by restoring the original sensations of full aliveness and wonder and the emotion of joy.*

Now that we have identified all of the pieces of the Imago-Match, let us see what happens to this Imago-Matched couple after they have launched the first phase of their relationship—the romantic stage.

1. Since one partner expresses what the other represses, each one embodies what is missing in the other. If we were asked to describe the model couple, we'd say one partner wants the windows open at night while the other wants them closed. Or one partner is quiet and reserved while the other is loud and outgoing. You see this with a lot of couples: she's cheerful and warm, and he is cerebral and sullen; he's an eccentric ascetic, and she's impeccably dressed and fashionable; she's a mess, and he's obsessive–compulsive; and so forth.

   Nature does its best to restore not only our experience of

original connecting but also our original wholeness, before repression. It does this by drawing us toward someone who expresses the functions we repress and whose missing aspects are a compliment to ours. Once we felt as though a part of ourselves was missing, but with our partner, we now feel connected to that part again.

2. We will do whatever it takes to make sure that this relationship, with this partner, lasts forever. Our best bet, then, is to keep our sunny side up, to be the kind of person, for our partner, that we ourselves would love to have as a partner. And we actually pull this performance off quite well—until we can't any longer. (More about this in the next section of this chapter, which is on the power struggle.)

3. We are blind to seeing anything negative in our partner. We not only see no downside, but we also find adorable and endearing the quirks that will one day drive us up the wall and out the front door. Have no doubt: the cheerful-laid-back-easygoing man his wife adores will turn into a shiftless-non ambitious-deficient slacker once the power struggle has emerged.

While partners are still in the romantic stage, their complementary defensive styles, minimizing and maximizing, have not caused any problems—yet. That is because while two people are in love, they feel little need to get defensive with each other (so far), so their complementary defensive styles haven't had much opportunity to clash (yet). In fact, the very nature of romantic love includes feeling utterly open and free, safe and undefended with one's beloved. At this point, then, it does not seem to matter that these two deeply challenged partners protect themselves in vastly different ways. For the interim, then, the polar natures of their defensive styles, where he pulls and she pushes or she attacks and he withdraws, is not relevant—yet. But as a therapist, it is certainly essential to understand this as you endeavor to see the whole picture.

The Purpose and Function of the Power Struggle

Getting past the romantic stage represents a critical leap forward in the development of a relationship. As we have seen, romantic love, with all its headiness and profundity and ecstasies, is purposeful; it is meant to burgeon to the point of full bloom. *It is also meant to end,* and *it always does.* But why? Why should two people who once fell madly in love end up in the power struggle? Why does the dream become a nightmare? There are three reasons.

1. **The objection to difference.** Why the dream becomes a nightmare is the question that began our intellectual and clinical
   journey to the construction of the Imago system and the clinical
   practice as a derivative. This question was raised by students in
   a graduate classroom and became an intense discussion between
   us and early adopters of Imago. After many hypotheses, we finally
   settled on the one that matched our repeated observations, and
   that of other Imago therapists, that the dream ends when one or
   the other partner discovers "difference" to which they object qui-
   etly or vehemently, depending upon their adaptive style. In other
   words, when we are in love, everything is the "same" and the few
   small discrepancies don't seem to matter (much). While we are
   high on our own neurochemistry, our symbiotic consciousness
   masks difference, but when frustration comes along, and keeps
   recurring, long enough and often enough, we begin to suspect
   that the person in our mind and memory is not the one in our
   experience; that they fooled us, or we made a mistake.

   In any case, difference ruptures our symbiotic illusion, and we
   are faced with a stark reality that has no place in our memory. Our
   attempt to annihilate difference begins the fight and sustains it
   until we give up and leave emotionally or actually. Otherwise, we
   keep trying, in every way we can, to get our partner to annihilate
   themselves and become the person we thought they were and to
   fulfill the agenda they signed up for, in our minds, and we thought,
   in theirs. But they do not, because they cannot, and their own survival directive launches counter measures in their defense, which
   strengthens our resolve. Thus, a struggle for power to reset the
   relationship to its former illusory status becomes chronic, until
   we shift to wonder and celebrate difference. Later, we will describe
   the options that may be taken to get to that exalted status.

   Because symbiosis is the mental condition created by deficits in nurturing and because it is the illusion of uniformity of
   thought and feelings, an encounter with an exception triggers
   anxiety about the status of our experience of reality. Our anxiety triggers our defenses, and that negative energy becomes the
   source of personal, group, and global objection to difference,
   and as we have said in our perspective, objection to difference is
   the source of all human conflict. This posits that the core problems of couples and humanity are the same: negativity, exclusion, and inequality. And the solutions are the same: affirmation
   of the other, celebration of difference, universal inclusion, and

equality. This makes healthy caretaking the incubator of healthy marriages, healthy marriages the incubator of a healthy society which, in turn, is the incubator of healthy families whose children produce healthy marriage whose inhabitants, in turn, occupy all institutions in our social space.

2. **Brain habituation:** The brain habituates to the enhanced bio-chemistry of romance. Just as a brain that has been on drugs for a while habituates to the drugs, a brain that has been in love gradually gets used to the surges of feel-good chemicals that circulate early on. Habituation can set in quickly or slowly; it can take weeks, months, or years (a joke among Imago clinicians is that this process takes somewhere between 9 minutes and 9 months). But however long it takes for our brain chemistry to settle down, sooner or later it does—often to the astonishment of the partners, who begin to wonder if they have fallen out of love or, even worse, fallen in love with the wrong person. They have done neither; they've simply stumbled unaware across the finish line of the romantic phase and their brains will soon habituate on negativity.

3. **Relationship habituation:** As a relationship lengthens and the partners' commitment to each other deepens, some subtle shifts begin to occur. Partners begin to:
   a. show more of their adaptive, that is, less than perfect, selves;
   b. become a bit lazy about pleasing one another;
   c. get careless about how they say what they say;
   d. act like the wounded human beings they are;
   e. realize that the rare and wondrous creature they are with is a wounded human being, too;
   f. suspect that their partner could meet all their needs but, for some unfathomable reason, is unwilling to do so; and
   g. move away from believing that their partner will meet all their unfulfilled needs.

As all these shifts begin to occur, partners begin viewing each other in a whole new light, and not a terribly flattering one at that. It used to be that when we looked into our partner's eyes, we'd see the best in ourselves reflected back; now when we look, we tend to see the worst in our partner, or at least what we imagine the worst to be. Instead of wanting to grab any available minute to be together, we sometimes find ourselves scanning our daily calendar, figuring out ways to avoid being available to the other.

What has happened? All that's happened is that our relationship is becoming real. The scales have fallen off, and the blinders have been removed. With our improved vision, we can clearly see our predicament: we are with a real person. And they are different from what we presupposed, and they live in a different cognitive–emotional world. Our symbiotic conscious is being ruptured by a differentiation process, and that scares us.

Our neurochemistry changes from endorphins to cortisol and adrenalin and that triggers the survival directive. At the unconscious level this person, as originally perceived, was supposed to be the source of my survival. If they are not that person, or if they have changed—so the unconscious narrative goes—then my survival needs will not be met.

To the couple who is going through all this, it is the end of their world as they know it or as they wanted it to be.

For Imago, this is the on-ramp from the romantic stage to the power struggle—from connecting to conflict.

Imago defines conflict as "growth trying to happen." It may feel awful, and it is experienced as a foundational threat: *but the tension of the opposites is a necessary and purposeful step in the right direction.* Conflict is supposed to happen, and it happens to everyone, i.e., *everyone who fell in love with an Imago-Match.*

And it happens, at some level, to everyone in all relationships. The meaning of our romantic partner, in our unconscious, makes it more intense and painful, but this is how the brain works in all relationships: things start off exciting—partner, job, new experience, new object—and then become disappointing, and we are challenged to give up our fantasy for reality.

The power struggle—the stage of disillusionment—is nature's savage gift, the opportunity hidden within every crisis, our rare chance to achieve transformation, if only we are willing to accept it. Since this is a universal process, our agenda as therapists is to help couples dialogue about this in their relationship and to cocreate the next step—conscious partnership.

But first, let us look at the mechanics of the power struggle.

The Mechanics of the Power Struggle

To understand what goes on between partners during this period, let's recall our earlier discussion on the brain. We know that the old brain is primed and ready to ensure our survival; it keeps a close eye on our breathing, heartbeat, body temperature, and so forth to keep us physically viable. When a couple is going through the power struggle, their life-preserving, hair-triggering, unconscious primal brains react as though the "threat" posed by their "dangerous" partner is no different than if each had a gun pointed at the other's head or they were in the forest millions of years ago and were approached by a tiger. Called the *negativity bias,* the first response of the brain to a new signal is: "Is this dangerous or safe?" Until proven safe, it is dangerous!

When a signal is read as dangerous, whether it is or not, the brain selects from three major options of the autonomic nervous system: 1) fight, 2) flee, or 3) freeze (shut down). Usually the first selection is some form of avoidance, similar to fleeing. If that does not work, the sympathetic system will become aggressive and fight. If fighting seems not to be the right choice—the enemy is too powerful—the dorsal vagal nerve in the parasympathetic system clicks in and we shut down, withdraw, or go numb, like playing dead.

The favorite choice of the maximizer is the activation of the sympathetic side of the autonomic nervous system. This includes any number of behaviors of displeasure that create fights: verbal harangues, shouting, swearing, threatening, stomping feet, throwing objects, breaking things, waking or keeping one's partner up at night to "talk," and a host of other misbehaviors. Of course, anyone who is confronted with such gestures is bound to respond with similar intensity. According to the quantum "observer effect," *What we do to others constellates how they respond to us.*

If that does not work for the maximizer, the second option of the sympathetic side of the autonomic nervous system includes: leaving the scene, slamming the door, finding someone else to off load emotions to. Whenever the maximizing partner explodes energy outward, the minimizer responds by fleeing inward, activating the parasympathetic side of the ANS by taking on a variety of behaviors: withdrawal, disappearing, silence, curtness, short answers to complicated questions, stonewalling,[4] and other tactics.

The third option happens when neither fighting nor fleeing is an option or both are ineffective. It is available to both maximizer and minimizer and comes, as we said, from the dorsal vagal system, but tends to be the favorite option of the minimizer. It involves simply shutting down, going numb, freezing, going dead. When that happens, the possibility of recovering becomes grim. The energy of life is now directed outside the relationship. Each partner goes their own way and invests their energy in other relationships. That may include another person, work, a new hobby, the children, or whatever is a source of pleasure and avoids the fear behind reconnecting: "If I connect, the disconnect will occur again, and that is too painful to bear."

To elaborate a bit on the psycho-neural components of the emotional reactivity that runs rampant during the power struggle: It seems to be an unavoidable remnant of our animal nature. The fight versus flight response we inherited from our mammalian ancestors certainly comes in handy when we find ourselves face-to-face with a dangerous animal in the jungle (or more likely, a dangerous human being on a city street), but it is downright counterproductive when given free rein in our relationship. In fact, the only thing our habitual fighting-or-fleeing-or-freezing accomplishes is to intensify the danger signals going off in our partner's primal brain. As far as

Imago theory is concerned, it's not crazy; it's purposeful. It's nothing more (or less) than nature's initiative to save us from what we couldn't—childhood connectional rupture.

Imago therapists remain aware that the key to a couple's dynamic—how they were relationally challenged and how they react to that challenge—isn't the content of their conflict; it's not *what* they are fighting about, but *how* they are fighting about it. As dysfunctional and immature as those methods may be, the couple is probably handling the chaos of the power struggle about as well as they can, given the developmental state in which they were arrested. When our partner fails (as they inevitably do) to give us what our caretakers didn't (and couldn't), we rally our defenses and use our best-practiced strategies to persuade our partner to hand over the goods. The unfortunate joke, however, is that our partner couldn't give us what we're demanding, even if they wanted to (which they probably do), because they don't have it to give. Nor do we.

Although contrary to all logic (as is much of our behavior), when this challenge recurs, we are geared toward responding in whatever ways that guarantee the worst possible response from our partner.

Stages of the Power Struggle
But the remarkable opportunity we are offered by the power struggle doesn't compensate for the disappearance of the pleasure we experienced in the romantic stage. The power struggle, in fact, is our response to an excruciating loss that activates the six stages of grief process. To help couples understand what they are going through, Imago borrows from the grief model devised by Elizabeth Kubler-Ross (1973). We've discovered that the painful evolution that couples experience during the power struggle has numerous parallels with the human response to grief and loss.

The six stages of the power struggle are:

1. **Shock:** Initially, partners go into a state of stunned disbelief; they utterly refuse to accept that anything is wrong in paradise.
2. **Denial:** Next, they try to ignore what's going on, assuring themselves that there's no "real" problem here or that perhaps they're imagining this.
3. **Anger:** Then they start to get angrier and angrier as the evidence mounts that the romantic stage is truly dead and gone.
4. **Bargaining:** Later, they come up with the brilliant idea of setting up tit-for-tat agreements—the "I'll do the dishes if you'll have sex with me" ploys would work just fine if they happened to be two business proprietors making a deal; but they are not, so it doesn't work.

5. **Despair:** Later still, they have reached the point of despair when they begin to feel there is no way forward, nothing will help, and they begin to fantasize about being with someone, anyone, else; or no one at all.
6. **Acceptance:** Finally, they come to the inevitable conclusion that, in this relationship anyway, they are not going to get the love they want. At this point, they have three options: they can leave the relationship, remain in a relationship, or get some help. The couple in your office, obviously, chose the third option.

Couples who have progressed to this point, the very height of the power struggle, but decide to stay together nevertheless, will end up looking something like those we'll describe in the next section.

Outcomes of the Power Struggle

Couples tend to adapt to the power struggle in four ways:

1. Those who use flight or fight to adapt to their pain tend to create a "hot" relationship—till death do we fight.
2. Those who adapt by shutting down their emotions and numbing themselves create a "parallel" relationship—we will never meet again.
3. Those who choose to give up and divorce—so long, it was good to know you (or not).
4. Those who decide to get some help and claim their potential to restore and sustain connecting and create a conscious partnership.

Before we describe the fourth option in the next chapter, let us briefly look at the outcomes of the first three. Each of the following adaptations to challenges are indications that the couple has not surrendered their symbiotic consciousness and differentiated. They live in the prison of self-absorption, unaware of the actual experiences of their partners. Instead of being curious about and engaging with each other, they try to change the other back into the dream person with whom they fell in love.

The Hot Relationship

Couples who settle into a hot relationship are the ones you hear arguing in the restaurant booth next to you. Hot-relationship couples are loudly and blatantly miserable, as evidenced by their high-volume verbal exchanges, some of which are liberally laced with pejorative terms, if not outright profanity.

As long as they remain together, neither gives up the fight, no matter what. Both believe they're right, and so neither is willing to give an inch, not even a millimeter. Work with them over the course of a few weeks and you will find they epitomize what insanity means, the repetition of the same behavior while thinking that somehow, this time, their partner will finally see the light and change.

But to be fair, hot relationships have a bit of the proverbial silver lining: these couples put a lot of energy into their relationship. The caveat, however, is that the high level of energy they invest in their relationship is predominantly negative, coming in the form of criticism, invalidation, and other types of negativity that are often worse than the childhood drama that is being replayed. They argue until the point of exhaustion, at which point something seems to break, and they then begin to talk things through more calmly and feel closer, temporarily. But their repetitive rounds of fighting and making up continue on and on, for years on end. Rather than divorce, "until death do they stop fighting," as some couples have said. Because of the intensity of the energy investment, they keep it in the relationship rather than having affairs and other exits, even if they do not change their tactics. We call this type of couple the "difficult couple." They can make us wonder: "Why did we become a couples therapist?"

The Parallel Marriage

Many couples who reach the pinnacle of the power struggle end up taking the path of least resistance: they remain together in a parallel marriage (or parallel relationship, for the unmarried). Think of a set of railroad tracks that has two parallel pieces running alongside one another, but no horizontal pieces connecting the tracks together. That is a good analogy for a parallel marriage: physically, the partners are still together, dwelling under the same roof and even having conversations. Although they may exchange information, they aren't sharing what's important to them, what they're experiencing in their day-to-day lives, or what is going on inside their heads. Like train tracks that lack cross beams, these partners act like colleagues who trade goods and services but little else. Because they have little if any shared reality, it's as though they live in two different worlds, existing side by side but with no interconnection.

Parallel marriages may look, to the casual observer, like perfectly normal relationships. Unless you lived under the same roof or were the couple's therapist, you probably would not notice their disconnection. There are, of course, a limitless variety of ways couples can manage to keep their lives from overlapping. They may work different shifts; they often work overtime, whether required to or not. They have their own circles of friends, different hobbies, opposite sleep–wake cycles. They communicate by e-mail or phone, but rarely face-to-face. They manage to find high-powered jobs on two opposite coasts.

Sometimes, a parallel marriage seems to "work," at least according to some couples. What they mean by their relationship "working," though, is the operative question. For example, a couple who have children together might decide to stay together "for the sake of the kids," despite the emptiness of their marriage. In such cases, the partners might go through all the motions of child rearing together, showing up for parent–teacher meetings as a unit and going on vacations with the kids as if they were just like any other happy family. They may remain in the same household until their children leave for college or get married or even, in some instances, they, like the hot couple, stay till death do they part. But all along, their relationship, and the impression it leaves on their offspring, is missing something vital, like a three-course meal that includes appetizers and dessert but lacks a main course.

One of the more troubling by-products of parallel relationships, especially those that go on for many years, is infidelity. In some couples, the partners take turns having affairs while the other pretends not to notice. Other partners agree (begrudgingly or not) to try having an "open" marriage, in which each has explicit permission to engage in outside relationships.[5] Imago's term for relationships characterized by infidelity and other serious types of relationship exits—behavior patterns that dissipate the energy needed to keep a couple's relationship alive—is the "invisible divorce." They remain in their relationship and continue inflicting tremendous pain on each other in the process.[6] It is the last option that we will now turn our attention.

The Invisible Divorce
We know couples who have officially broken up (in some cases, repeatedly) but never actually terminated their romantic involvement with each other. Instead, they go back and forth between hope and despair, loving and hating each other, being together and not being together, in an arrangement that is effectively a "separation that isn't a separation." This type of scenario can grow particularly painful because the partners receive neither the comfort and satisfaction of being in a long-term committed partnership nor the relief they might experience if they were to actually put an end to their tumultuous relationship.

Over the years we have asked: why do couples adapt in these ways? What we have discovered is fascinating. The primary reason couples adapt to their relationship with such negative interaction is the prime driver of the power struggle itself: the hope for need satisfaction paired with the fear of intimacy. It is paradoxical that the primary complaint of these couples is the lack of intimacy and that their primary defense works against the experience of intimacy which the above list outlines in such an elegant and gruesome way. It makes no obvious or logical sense, but it serves a profound unconscious purpose. We recall that the anxiety caused by the rupture of connecting in infancy is so dreadful that we defend against it with anger and depression, it does make sense that the act of experiencing intimacy and restoring connecting raises the prospect, in the unconscious, that connecting could be ruptured again and the intolerable sensation of anxiety could be reexperienced. The experience of connecting and the anxiety caused by ruptured connecting is, we posit, the primal memory of the human race. It makes sense, then, that to experience the prospect of reconnecting exposes us to the repetition of that original pain, located in the fibers of memory. It seems, therefore, that it is better for some couples to complain about the absence of intimacy and to be sure that they do not experience it again than to get it back and lose it again.

Here is a summary of intentions and behaviors in which unconscious couples engage to keep them interactive and defended at the same time. Let's look at the features of the unconscious relationship in preparation for the features of a conscious partnership in the next chapter. It will be obvious that these are the features of a symbiotic consciousness.

FEATURES OF AN UNCONSCIOUS RELATIONSHIP

1. Partners in an unconscious relationship alternate between merger and polarization. Merger happens when both are in agreement. Polarization happens with one of them offers an alternative perspective.
2. The primary energy of unconscious partners is anxiety masked as anger or depression. Any engagement with the experience of another activates defenses to attack, flee, or freeze.
3. Each partner in an unconscious relationship assumes their "world" is "the world" and is objectively true.
4. When a partner in an unconscious relationship expresses difference of any sort, it is experienced as a threat and immediately countered and invalidated.
5. In an unconscious relationship, each person is the center and the other is at the periphery.
6. Partners in an unconscious relationship exist for themselves and others exist for them.
7. Unconscious partners see their relationship as a resource for themselves rather than as an entity in itself that needs their care.
8. Engagement between partners in an unconscious relationship is chronic and polarized. They alternate between opposition and

competition, escalation and avoidance. The move from highly reactive to stoic.

9. The other is an object to be used for their own needs or emotionally annihilated to remove the threat.

10. Unconscious partners cannot experience, feel or imagine the experience of the other as distinct from their own experience.

11. Unconscious partners engage in transactions or quid pro quo: you do this for me and I do that for you.

12. Unconscious partners hold expectations without communicating their wishes and have anticipations that are not connected to a promise. They assume their inner world is known by the other and the inner world of the other is identical to theirs. "You know what I want because you want it too."

13. Unconscious partners complain about a lack of intimacy but engage in intimacy avoidance.

14. They have no awareness of their impact on others and when others report discomfort, they increase their position, often to the point of revenge.

15. Unconscious partners have no vision or goals for their relationship but live in a reactive mode that oscillates between war and peace.

16. Unconscious partners use negativity—put-downs, shame, blame, criticism, devaluation and contempt—to emotionally annihilate their partner and maintain their illusion of being the center of the relationship.

17. Not knowing that their partner is real and does not mirror their fantasy, unconscious partners react negatively anytime their partner does not match their expectations.

18. Whenever one partner, in an unconscious relationship, is talking, and what they are saying does not match the perspective of the listener, the listener objects, corrects and attempts to replace the subjectivity of their partner with their own thoughts and feelings.

If you would like to see how this compares with conscious partners, you may want to look ahead to the next chapter, page 167.

SUMMARY AND TRANSITION

The problem in childhood, and in all subsequent relationships, is ruptured connecting, and the desire for reconnecting, triggered by the loss of original connecting, is attached to our survival drive, which unconsciously selects *that* someone in adulthood with whom the chemistry is just right. We say that the child–caretaker drama replays itself in adult intimate partnerships because the relational awareness and competence necessary to optimize that opportunity to restore and sustain the sensation of full aliveness and joy and the state of wonder is not built into nature's program. Only our capacities to become conscious and to acquire such skills are innate.

Adult intimate relationships, and all significant relationships, go through three natural stages—romantic attachment, the power struggle, and resolution. The unconscious agenda of those stages is to recreate the conditions of childhood with a person similar, in general details, to the caretaker with whom they had the deepest unmet need and to get the need satisfied so that the developmental journey toward adulthood can be resumed.

In addition to the hot, parallel, or invisible divorce relationship options couples may take to resolve the power struggle, we pose a fourth option as an alternative to the unconscious, conflicted relationship in which they have been mired. We call it the conscious partnership. Let's take a look at its features, how they are acquired, and the contrast between unconscious and conscious couples.

7
Conscious Partnership
Sustaining Connecting

conscious partnership is a dynamic energetic pattern characterized by relaxed aliveness, positive affect, and joyful exchanges. Through the transformation that occurs in the safety of a conscious relationship, conscious partners reap individual and relational benefits that optimize their physical, emotional, cognitive, and spiritual well-being, and connecting is their daily experience. In back-to-the-future fashion, it looks like two people wallowing in the bliss of romantic love, but this time, it is real love, and the bliss has durability because they are participating in the energy of the quantum field.

Once partners are no longer reacting as though they were each other's neglectful or invasive parent—in other words, once they are able to be present to each other in the here-and-now—the entire basis for their attraction—the transformative power of an Imago-Match gets unearthed and springs into action. But there is one central distinction between the first stage and the third, between romantic love and real love: the intentions of the first stage are shrouded in the unconscious, while the third stage is a construction of consciousness, a cohesive cocreation of partners in collaboration and cooperation that resonates with Consciousness Itself. In a nutshell, it is consciousness that makes all the difference; it is consciousness that brings a relationship from reactivity to intentionality, from pain to pleasure, and from the hell of the power struggle to the paradise of real love (Figure 7.1).

THE FOURTH STAGE OF COUPLEHOOD

History has been populated with three forms of couplehood: the pair-bond of the hunter–gatherer societies that existed for millions of years; the arranged marriage that evolved over the last 11,000 years with the rise of agriculture, animal husbandry, and civilization itself; and the democratic-romantic marriage/intimate relationship that appeared with the end of monarchy and the rise of democracy in the seventeenth and eighteenth centuries. Just as the pair-bond was replaced by the arranged marriage, the arranged marriage was replaced by the romantic marriage—the foundation of contemporary marriage—which is the client of couples therapists. In our

Figure 7.1:
Journey to a Conscious Partnership

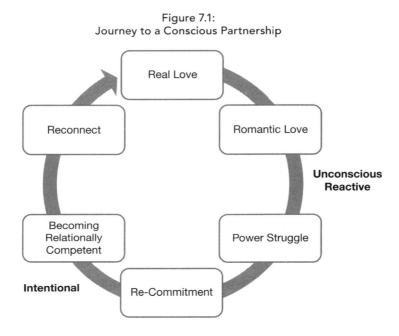

view, the democratic-romantic marriage is dying, because it is no longer a participant in the evolutionary process, and it is being replaced by the collective consciousness with conscious partnership, which is a step forward, toward real love and an evolving relational civilization.

We call the conscious partnership the fourth stage of couplehood in human history.

The idea of the conscious partnership is so recent and radical in human history that most people do not know about it, and if couples did know about it, they would know they have an option to move from the power struggle impasse to the relationship of their dreams. On the other hand, some couples might choose not to take the challenge because reaching that state of being—conscious relating—requires a new way of thinking and interacting that is largely unfamiliar. What is unfamiliar is scary, thus our primitive brain activates its defenses, until the unfamiliar become safe and perhaps discovers a better way to survive.

Unlike the unconscious processes in our lower brain that created our current form of marriage and other intimate and significant relationships, a conscious partnership requires discovering and using new knowledge and skills that activate the upper brain, the prefrontal cortex. If the knowledge is used and the skills are practiced, they invariably work towards conscious relating and authentic loving.

From the quantum perspective and a relational brain perspective—that all forms arise in the quantum field and dissolve back into field—it is possible to view (and we do) the cycle of the birth and death of different forms of couplehood as a quantum process, and the next stage in our social evolution toward embodying the love we want. It is also the case that culture, as a form, arises out of the quantum field and gives birth to the institutions, including marriage, that comprise it, which in turn shapes the culture that gave them birth—just as children shape their parents as their parents shape them. Therefore, as the culture of individualism evolves into a relational culture, it makes sense that a relational culture would give birth to a new, relational-centered form of couplehood whose agenda is the furtherance of a relational civilization. It appears that the shifts in the forms of couplehood over historical time, including the present, are not a function of individual human choice or will, but of a world historical process with a telos we cannot yet discern but can dimly surmise is moving toward social coherence and love. Our choice is to ride the wave toward what is unfolding or stay anchored in the present, which is no longer relevant. Given all that, it makes sense that "marriage by choice," birthed by the rise of democracies in the eighteenth century and with a focus on two individuals in a competitive marriage, is dying the death of divorce and delayed partnering to make room for the emergence of another form of couplehood, from the quantum field, that is given concrete shape by collective consciousness. It appears that the oscillation between the creation and destruction of forms is the essence of the evolutionary process, in humanity, and in the cosmos.

Because, in the quantum view, this oscillation is both cosmic and personal, the current oscillation is couples transforming their relationship from defensive strategies to open and spontaneous engagement. It makes sense that all this would be so because the cultural and the personal are derivates of collective consciousness, which itself is a derivative of the conscious quantum field. In other words, the cosmic access to the personal as the conduit is showing up as a cultural transformation, within which the personal is being transformed, making conscious partnership a quantum process.

What Does a Conscious Partnership Look Like?
Given that its appearance is recent and its adoption by couples is just beginning, there are few descriptors of its essence and process. However, there is enough data from couples who have helped to move from unconscious relating toward conscious relating that we can conceive of many of its features. There are enough clues to imaginatively construct a model. It is sort of like having a DNA fragment from which we can reconstruct the organism from which it came. In this chapter and the next, we will explore how a conscious partnership as the school of real love can be developed by willing couples with the facilitation of an Imago therapist.

Before we proceed to constructing the model of conscious partnership, let us take another look at the brain sciences and the theory of the quantum field.

According to the brain sciences, our brains become more efficient when we imagine or picture an outcome than when we just use words to describe something. Some brains adapt and survive by using words for all their mental processes and relational interactions. Although brain scientists now view the brain as a network rather than delineated structures with special functions, they still assert that the brain does have specific structures with specific functions, the expression of which is not limited to that structure. For instance, a brain adapted to its left side has difficulty accessing the imagination and creating pictures, which is a right brain function. Other brains adapt for survival by using images and pictures. A brain adapted to using the right side has difficulty accessing and finding words to express what they "see." Of course, a balanced and integrated brain does both, as needed. The interaction and interdependency of the left and right hemispheres is evident when words constitute a signal that lights up the visual cortex.

The concept in quantum physics that deals with this phenomenon is the particle–wave duality, which is considered by mainstream quantum physics to be inherent in every form, from the smallest particle to the universe, all of which emerge from the quantum field. For instance, words are particle-like and images are wavelike. Words come from the left hemisphere of the brain and images from the right hemisphere. According to the "observer effect," a core discovery of quantum science, if you focus or look, which is a left-brain function, the particle-like character of what you are looking at shows up. If you relax your focus, the wavelike quality of an image shows up. As asserted in quantum science, you cannot experience the wave and the particle at the same time. When you focus on words, you can see only words. If you relax your focus, an image will show up, but if you try to describe the image it will be replaced with your descriptive or judgmental words. You can shift your focus and describe the image you just saw or shift to creating a picture of the words you just used. You cannot experience the words and the image of a phenomenon at the same time. The importance of all this for you as a couples therapist is that you may want to deliberately engage this process with couples. Most importantly, when you convert words into images, the brain receives the image as a destination, translates it into words and then proceeds toward it. In other words, in the brain the collapse of the wave function into the particle function moves from imaging to creating, which is the primary feature of the quantum field. This is the process that happens when couples construct their future in the present by imagining their future as "now."

Let us delve more deeply into how this may be applied to conscious partnership. In this chapter we will use words to define conscious partnership, and we intend to describe enough of the thoughts and behaviors that you can image it—that is, create a picture out of the descriptive words and sentences. In other words, we invite you to oscillate back and forth between words (particles use left brain) and images (waves use right brain) until you have a generic "picture" of conscious partnership, the achievement of which is real love, which is the goal of therapy.

We invite you to do this clinical process, distinct from your clinical practice, to prepare you for your first session with a couple. We invite you to read the descriptions of conscious partnership and then transition to your right brain and exercise your own imagination and translate the words into images—hold them until you can "see" and "hear" and "feel" the generic conscious relationship described here. This will prep you for (Chapter 12) where you will learn to guide your couples to "revision" their dream relationship: you will invite your couples to describe their dream relationship and then to shift their imagination and inhabit it. While this chapter is specifically for you, it may be beneficial to share it with your couples so they can see a generic model as a guide for their cocreation of their conscious partnership—their dream relationship in which the fragrance of real love lives.

The Essence of a Conscious Partnership

Core clues to the essence of conscious partnership are embedded in the words themselves. Let us take a micro-look. As you read each of the paragraphs below, allow yourself to experience any images that may arise.

First, a conscious partnership is "conscious." That alone distinguishes it from the contemporary marriage, which is based on romantic love, a product of nature, driven unconsciously by the survival instinct of the lower brain. Its replacement, conscious partnership, emerges out of the same survival drive but with a different outcome because it is guided by the upper brain. The upper brain becomes intentional about survival; the lower brain reacts without reflection. That was okay when we lived in the forests and the savannahs, but it is dysfunctional in the bedroom. Our evolution as a society has skewed our basic survival needs, and this influence permeates all facets of our personage, both as a self and as a couple.

Second, it is a relational consciousness. This point is derived from analysis of the two Latin syllables that make it up: "con" and "scious." "Con" means "with" and "scious" means "to know," thus "conscious" means to "know with." We see this as an expression of quantum consciousness, the field in which all forms are connecting. Remember, consciousness is not a *feature* of the quantum field, it *is* the field; the field *is* Consciousness Itself. Consciousness, therefore, is "knowing with" on the personal and cosmic level; it is how we are connecting. Awareness of being in the field *with* others is a *feature* of quantum consciousness.

Consciousness, therefore, is not a feature of the mind. It is not something one has and or can develop, it is "knowing with" another. Conscious partners "know with" each other; this moves them from being figments of each other's imaginations to engagement with each other as they *are*, a real "other." They "know" each other's vulnerabilities and past and all the things that make them vulnerable and human. This "knowing with," not "knowing about" helps differentiate "self" from "other" and facilitates connecting around and beyond their differences, preparing the ground for real love which celebrates difference and holds it in a state of wonder.

Third, it is a partnership. "Conscious" is a new quality of intimate relationships. In the traditional marriage, the third form of couplehood, which has been around for around 300 years, couples built their marriage, unconsciously, on the hierarchal, vertical model of monarchy. One was the head of the household, and the roles and responsibilities of the others were to honor and support the breadwinner. In addition, most social, political, educational, religious, and economic institutions have inherited the same vertical structure. In these cultural institutions, one person is the leader and has an alpha role and ultimate authority, and everyone else takes direction from the leader, and their security depends on their relationship with that leader. Indigenous to ALL these institutions is inequality, usually economic and social, as in the middle ages. Competition, control, domination, and the necessity of being the best and winning at all costs is the value system that drives this social-cultural-personal structure. Hierarchy and inequality are indigenous features of most cultures and embodied in most marriages, and hierarchy and inequality are the source of conflict for all the institutions, including marriage.

The shift from hierarchy to partnership has been influenced, but not achieved, by the fight for political and economic equality by the women's movement. While measurable progress has been made, most households still have a vertical model of power distribution. As we indicated earlier, we believe that all this is changing. To repeat: we consider the agenda of the emergence of conscious partnership from the collective consciousness into the culture in general and into personal life, in particular, to be in the service of furthering the next stage in human social evolution, which we designate as a *relational* civilization. We see this as embodying universal equality, total inclusiveness, and the celebration of differences, and we see these as the embodiment of real love. In such a civilization, partnership will be a conscious choice, and competition will be replaced by collaboration, control by cooperation, and domination by mutual support and real love.

In the partnership marriage, couples become partners in the project of collaborating with each other to cocreate and evolve their relationship—to make it safe for each other, to grow each other into their full potential, and to restore the original condition of connecting, attended by the sensation of full aliveness and joyful relaxation and the state of wonder. They know that the agenda of their unconscious, in the selection process, was to create a context and a condition that would stimulate growth in the service of developing the capacity to restore connecting. They now consciously cooperate with that unconscious agenda and collaborate, cocreate, and cooperate in the project of recovering the connection lost in childhood. The mind is moving from the determinism of its unconscious processes in the individual paradigm and individualistic culture to consciously and intentionally cocreating a foundationally new relationship grounded in the quantum field which is embodied in a relational culture.

Practicing Conscious Partnership
The journey to a conscious partnership is by no means a straight line; no one progresses from one condition to the other without first going through many steps, with many stops and starts, sometimes over and over again. After all, that is the very nature of learning. But, because we ourselves have crossed this trajectory and have helped thousands of couples to do the same, we see ourselves and those thousands of couples as living witnesses to conscious partnership's potential.

Since the quantum field occupies the Space-Between partners, conscious partnership is an oscillation between "wave-like" qualities and "particle-like" qualities. In other words, it is more a process than a "thing." Like the wave–particle phenomenon, whose outcome depends solely on the observer, a conscious partnership is more context than content, more process than outcome. The condition of a conscious partnership might be compared to what a flower garden looks like over the entire course of the growing season. If you were to take a picture of it at any given point in time, it would of course look solid, and depending on the season, quite beautiful or not. However, when you image the whole garden without reference to a particular season, you see that every picture is one frame of constantly changing images. And like the complementarity of the particle–wave duality, you can't see the point of focus and the whole at the same time.

Like life itself, a garden is always in flux, through sun, rain, heat, and cold. A conscious partnership also remains in a constant state of becoming, changing from day to day and even moment to moment, depending on its context—that is, on the quality of the exchanges between partners who influence and are influenced by all of their other interactions. What both partners bring to a conscious partnership can be compared to the context in which plants are growing: the soil, air, water, and sunshine that together create something that goes far beyond what those components could create on their own, something that is seemingly miraculous and far more than the sum of its parts.

If we think of a conscious partnership as the occupant of the Space-Between, it consists of interactions between two people that support the thriving of both partners and their relationship by creating and sustaining reliable and predictable safety, the essential ingredients of real love. *Safety is the necessary and sufficient condition, the sine qua non, of a conscious partnership.*

If safety is the indispensable quality of the Space-Between, how is it achieved and sustained? While the texture of a conscious partnership is wavelike and essentially indescribable, achieving safety and keeping it stable is particle-like, consisting of specific skills that can be described, taught, and learned. Nothing esoteric about them! Like any skill, you do not have to know the science behind its effectiveness, but you have to practice until it is second nature in order to experience permanent results.

Safety is achieved and maintained by the three practices: Imago Dialogue, the Zero Negativity Process, and the Affirmations Process. In this chapter, we present only a brief description of each, since a full chapter is devoted to each of these skills later on, and each of which will include illustrations of specific exercises you can use with your couples that will empower them with the relational competence to be conscious partners embodying real love. As we will emphasize repeatedly, only relationally competent partners can create a conscious partnership in which real love lives. While real love is an affair of the heart, its realization is an affair of the mind and muscles. It is a choice that must be operationalized with intentional behaviors. The intent of the chapters to come is to provide specific and effective guidance through the therapy process in which couples become equipped to actualize their potential for unconditional loving. The inclusion of this overview of the three practices is to associate them, in your mind, with how conscious couples begin to live during therapy, how they live after therapy, and what they practice that sustains safety as the quality of the Space-Between. The Space-Between is the environment in which a conscious partnership is created and real love is born. It must be toxin-free and generously nurtured if its inhabitants are to not just survive, but thrive.

CONSCIOUS PARTNERS
PRACTICE IMAGO DIALOGUE

In a later chapter where we include an extensive presentation of Imago Dialogue, we will make the case that monologue, not dialogue, is the language of unconscious relationships, which includes intimate relationships and most other relationships on the planet, and has been the dominant form of communication for all of human history. Monologue is vertical and parallel; it demotes the other, making them unequal to the speaker and, therefore, unsafe in the relationship by triggering anxiety—the source of all our symptoms. For that reason, throughout human history talking has been among the most dangerous things human beings do and listening their most infrequent activity.

In Imago Dialogue, the unconscious power dynamic is inherently shifted. One person is talking without criticism, and the other person is listening without judgment, and both are connecting around and beyond their differences. This lateral form of conversation appeared only recently in our history (in the 1940s). Because it is lateral and consists of taking turns without competing for the stage, it creates equality and therefore a safe environment in which couples can talk without fear about anything that they are experiencing, from challenges to joys. We call it the language of the Space-Between and devote Chapter 9 to it.

The goal of any practice is to become competent in that skill. The outcome of practicing Imago Dialogue and the related practices is one that becomes "relationally competent" in intimate partnership, and all relationships. Practicing the particle-like skills creates the wavelike qualities of the relationship which are the qualities of "being-with" rather than "being-in-opposition-to." It is flow instead of push and pull.

With consistent practice, conscious partners integrate Imago Dialogue into their lives until it becomes second nature—and they become "dialogical." In the sacred crucible of the Space-Between, through their ongoing engagement with a specific set of principles and practices, couples gain access to the dimension we call "being-in-relationship."

As a preview of Imago Dialogue, which we present as *the* singular therapeutic process used in Imago therapy, here we introduce you to its structure and flow so you can begin to imagine the new way that couples talk to each other when they become conscious and then focus on learning the skill. What they learn in therapy with you is that Imago Dialogue transforms not only their conversations but also their lifestyle since it is the language of real lovers.

Operationally, Imago Dialogue is an intentional and structured conversation that conscious partners use when they want to discuss ANY topic. The core structure is three sequential steps: mirroring, validating, and empathizing, which proceed with the use of specific sentence stems that regulate the flow of energy and information that arises when two people are talking and listening. Conscious partners use Imago Dialogue in situations:

1. when they want to have a *structured conversation* about a specific topic with each other or someone else (a child, friend, colleague, etc.)
2. when they want to make *all* their informal verbal interactions with other people safe (like in the family or at a social event)

Some Observations and Explanations:

Observation 1: Imago Dialogue is a structured conversation that follows a specific sequence of step-specific sentence stems that create safety.

Explanation: The three-step structure creates safety, and the sentence stems regulate the sequential flow of the exchange of energy and information. It also creates safety by regulating our negatively biased brain, letting it know what to anticipate. With agreement to do this process, the brain knows that what is coming, after it becomes vulnerable and speaks its response to familiar sentence stems, is the experience of being mirrored and validated and of empathy. Paradoxically, the structure (a safe container) produces spontaneity, expressions of affect, and access to unlanguaged thoughts, all of which begin the process toward restored connecting—which cannot happen without safety. It is in safety that our conscious is free from the fears of our unconscious.

Observation 2: Conscious partners sometimes use only the mirroring process and its sub-steps.

Explanation: Some exchanges are short because a conscious partner just wants to be mirrored and does not need validation or empathy.

Observation 3: The consistent use of Imago Dialogue helps couples replace their symbiotic consciousness with a "differentiated" consciousness, and this is a precondition of real love of a real person that replaces the romantic love of a fantasied person.

Explanation: Everyone looks at the world and other people through a personal lens and believes that what they see is "there" and is "true." Seeing translates into believing. This is a symbiotic consciousness. Because symbiotic consciousness cannot imagine an alternative to its own worldview, difference is intolerable and thus the source of conflict between couples and between everyone else. Each sentence stem that comprises the flow in Imago Dialogue, whether sending or receiving, helps partners experience their partner's experience, thus replacing their symbiotic fantasy with their partner's reality. When the fantasied partner is replaced with the real one, the foundation is laid for authentic, real love, and until then, love cannot be born.

Conscious couples use the safety of the Dialogue process to deal with everything that constrains them from experiencing connecting, full aliveness, relaxed joyfulness and the state of wonder. In the sacred space of the Space-Between, they can use their new social engagement skills to talk about everything, since the Dialogue process is the container that holds the energy of any content. They share how their past has influenced their present as well as how they experience life and work and their relationship. It is the safe sharing of their fears and dreams without the anticipation of judgment and rejection that restores connecting, and without which connecting cannot be restored. Eventually, they realize that the way they used to speak with each other was, by comparison, little more than sounding brass and tinkling cymbals.

Eventually, they feel safe in the Space-Between; there is no anxiety, and change becomes easy. Once couples get a glimpse of this, they will never want to go back to their old ways of talking and interacting. Why would they? But to keep what they experience requires practicing skills that achieve relational competency.

CONSCIOUS PARTNERS
PRACTICE ZERO NEGATIVITY

In addition to the use of the structure of Imago Dialogue, conscious partners pledge to Zero Negativity to create safety and to make it predictable and reliable. They know that without making and honoring the pledge, safety will be episodic. Conscious couples get it that Zero Negativity is essential for reliable safety because they know that negativity is to an intimate relationship what cancer is to the human body, and that negativity is much more common than cancer. They know that if negativity is allowed to proliferate within the relational space, it can eventually degrade the emotional infrastructure of their relationship. They understand that just as serious, untreated cancer leads to death, uncontrolled expressions of negativity, in the form of verbal put-downs, criticism, sarcasm, threats, and a host of other relational anathemas, is a strong predictor of a relationship's deterioration and death, emotionally and physically.

The definition of negativity is to "negate" or to nullify. To negate in the interpersonal sense can be construed as engaging with another person in a manner that leaves them feeling diminished, made less, devalued, invisible: all variants of a "put-down." It is no wonder that negative exchanges leave both partners feeling exactly that: put-down, which of course is the exact opposite of what people are seeking in an intimate partnership—safety, intimacy, friendship, equality, and affirmation. The problem is, in the context of contemporary couple relationships, focusing on and expressing negativity seems to be standard operating procedure. Normative or not, Imago regards negativity as a universal relational toxin that is incompatible with a conscious relationship and cannot exist in an atmosphere of real, authentic love.

Zero Negativity is the essential ingredient in the formula for creating a conscious partnership. It is no less important to the formation of a conscious relationship than is the integrity of a cement foundation on which a home is built. By living according to its precepts, couples can ensure that the Space-Between achieves and maintains a high quality of safety.

When a couple expresses readiness to find their way to the rarified atmosphere of a conscious partnership and to give birth to real love, they must begin at the starting gate by committing to Zero Negativity. Non-negotiable. Before instructing them on how to do so, we suggest you share with them some of the very real benefits of their persisting, at least until they reach the finish line of a conscious partnership.

Among the many good rationales for working toward a negativity-free relationship is that, in the process of achieving it, the brain of each partner is constantly getting nudged in a healthier direction. When our brain is running on negative arousal, the higher cognitive functions—judgment, planning, reasoning, moderating impulsivity—become less accessible and more impaired (Clore & Huntsinger, 2007; Storbeck & Clore, 2008). Since the practice of Zero Negativity goes against the grain of the partners' usual thought patterns, an effortful shift is required to move mental energy from the negative to the positive direction, providing a form of vigorous exercise for the cognitive brain! In short, when it comes to optimal brain functioning, the less negativity, the better. In fact, the outcome of a practicing Zero Negativity is a healthier, integrated brain.

Another major benefit of engaging in a negativity-free relationship lies in the similarities shared by negativity and anxiety. By definition, a negativity-free relationship must also be one in which anxiety is low. Since anxiety and negativity are virtually biological twins and cocreate each other, they have similarly destructive effects on the quality of a relationship, especially its baseline level of safety. When negativity is kept at bay, there are far fewer opportunities for the reactive brain to sound the alarm for danger. There is no need for any anxious arousal to set off the body's rapid response system. Without having to combat the noxious neurochemical side effects of anxious exchanges, each partner's brain and body remains calm, more relaxed, and therefore healthier.

Sometimes, when clients really understand all this, they become vulnerable and share anecdotes of their own journey to consciousness. Consider this story reported to an Imago therapist:

My husband left an open bag of pretzels on the bedroom floor near the base of our bed and went to work. I was off work and cleaning the townhouse when I found the pretzels. I was incensed; who did [husband] think was supposed to pick up the bag of pretzels?? Was I his maid? I called a good friend to complain about [husband's] insensitivity and ask his advice. Rather than agreeing with me, my friend asked me, "Do you want him in your life?" I said, "Yes." He asked me, "Do you see the rest of your life with him?" I hesitated a bit, then confidently said "Yes." My friend then told me "Then you leave the bag of pretzels on the floor until it doesn't bother you. When the pretzel bag doesn't bother you, then you can choose what to do."

Creating a relationship free of negativity is not possible without possessing at least a baseline capacity for being present, in the moment, able to focus on one thing at a time. This characteristic is described by some traditions as *mindfulness*, or a mindfulness practice (Linehan & Dimeff, 2001; Parker et al., 2015; Atkinson, 2013). The description of this kind of mental stance has striking parallels to that of experienced meditators, whose meditation practices have been found to bestow profound benefits on the functioning of the brain (Iwamoto et al., 2020; Keng et al., 2011). We feel confident, then, that the exercise of brain matter required by the practice of Zero Negativity will have similarly salutary brain effects. The brain is like a muscle. Just like the muscles of the body, the brain must be honed and strengthened with exercises that keep it in peak condition.

The Zero Negativity Pledge

To remove the toxin of negativity from their relationship, conscious couples take a Zero Negativity pledge by which they commit to *do their best* to adhere to the mindset, attitudes, habits, and behavioral exchanges that establish relational safety. There are, however, specific antidotes for occasions when negativity erupts.

Conscious couples adhere to the basic requirements that fulfill the first part of the pledge. They agree to:

1. train their minds to stay focused on the present moment, relating in the here and now rather than through the filter of old negative memories. They know that to be conscious they need to be present while in the presence of each other, much like meditating with their eyes open;

2. avoid speaking or acting in ways that bring about negative feelings in the other;

3. communicate and behave with intention, eliminating from their behavioral repertoire anything that diminishes the ongoing

sense of safety, relaxation, joy, and wonder that are the aspired backdrop of a conscious partnership; and

4. use whatever tools are required to quickly and effectively restore connecting in their relationship when they are anxious or otherwise experiencing difficult emotions.

Since conscious partners accept that *negativity is anything a partner perceives as negative, and that negativity is a put-down,* they agree to signal to each other that one of them has experienced an "ouch," an emotional reaction to anything that feels hurtful, scary, or demeaning. They accept this as the case, *even if the partner who is the source of the upset did not intend it that way. And they move quickly to reconnecting.*

Conscious partners see the "put-down" as the enemy of their dream relationship. They know there is no way for them to feel good when they are in the presence of a person—especially their partner—with whom they feel badly. They know their brain learns to associate a given stimulus (like their partner) with a certain emotional valence, that is, with some degree of positivity or negativity (Pavlov, 1927; Jarius & Wildemann, 2015). Further, they know that put-downs themselves include a range of messages, all of them communicating that another person is somehow "less-than"—less caring, less intelligent, less attractive, less talented, etc.—which, taken to its logical extreme, makes the recipient of the message feel invisible, worthless, and less-than-human.

Regardless of its content, conscious partners know that a "put-down" of any kind is a guaranteed way to trigger the anxiety center in our brain. They know they simply cannot feel safe and put-down at the same time. When they are unsafe for their partner, they know their partner's brain has no other choice than to see them as an enemy and, naturally, to use everything they can to protect themselves, including countering with equal or greater negativity. At the same time, they know that negativity, in turn, is incompatible with real love; that negativity, in a nutshell, is the antithesis of love; and that Zero Negativity is looking at each other through the eyes of love, real love!

Conscious partners know that it is one thing to adopt safety as a motto; it is quite another to live up to it day after day, month after month, year after year. They understand that it was one thing to keep their relationship safe while they were floating down the gentle river of the romantic phase. And that it is another to restore safety to their relationship when it has been battered and bruised from years of fighting on the front lines of the power struggle.

Conscious couples also know that everyone's brain has a negativity bias, and that is the basis for some empathy when negativity erupts. Negativity bias means our brains have the natural tendency to react to any signal of approach by another human with suspicion and negative judgment and that only those who honored that tendency made it through the evolutionary process to be here now. While they know this is a residue from the millions of years our genetic ancestors lived in the forests and savannahs while evolving into *homo sapiens*, they also know it is not useful in a contemporary intimate relationship.

Given their evolutionary tendency toward negativity, conscious couples know that no matter how well-intended, some days will be better than others, as is true for virtually all realms of life. Conscious couples know that a relapse into negativity is neither the end of the world nor the end of their journey toward a safe and thriving relationship and that there is much they can do to restore connecting when their relationship is ruptured. To negate the power of a put-down, they use a reconnecting process when either of them experiences an "ouch" as a sign of a transgression.

Conscious Couples Practice the Reconnecting Process

Conscious couples have learned that the reason their conscious mind sends the signal that a put-down has been experienced is that it prevents them from saying something else that might be the equivalent of a verbal nuclear bomb. They know that if they work collaboratively to accomplish reconnecting, they will then be able to promptly resurrect, like a phoenix rising from the dust, the steady background of safety and connectivity.

The reconnecting process that conscious couples use is simple, direct, and effective. And as we say in our workshops, a sign of a conscious and thriving relationship is how quickly couples can restore connecting. And conscious partners know that removing negativity is not enough. It must be followed by engaging in a chronic process of expressing affirmations. We will explore this further in Chapter 15.

CONSCIOUS PARTNERS PRACTICE
THE AFFIRMATIONS PROCESS

Years ago, our (Harville and Helen) relationship was mired in negativity, nearly to the point of divorce. Later, after we discovered the Zero Negativity Process and personally experienced its effectiveness, we invited couples to practice it and, finally, made it a core part of Imago theory and a nonnegotiable practice.

It seemed logical that the removal of a toxin would facilitate the full recovery of the organism, but logic often fails. If we think of the relationship like our bodies, once both have been relieved of a malady, they have to recover, and that requires nurture. While the removal of negativity was essential for creating safety, by removing negative behaviors from interactions and cortisol from our neurochemistry, it left some confusion in the brain about how to proceed. To discover why Zero Negativity was not enough to transform a relationship, we discovered in brain research that, for our primitive brains, negative interactions are a defense triggered by the perception of potential danger. To remove that defense created some relief and relaxation, for a while, but it also created some anxiety—which was puzzling. In fact, the more we restrained our negativity, the more anxious we became. We finally figured out that going zero-negative ruptured the homeostasis of our brains, taking away a primary, evolutionary defense that left us feeling vulnerable. Not knowing what to do and having no replacement defense, our brains became chaotic, and we became more and more anxious, so much so that the temptation to reengage in negative behaviors was overwhelming since no alternatives were available.

Finally, it occurred to us that we had to fill that void with a behavior that would make our brains feel safe. In other words, provide our brains with a new behavior that would serve as a new defense. So, rather than a negative behavior, we used one that was positive and affirming. Using ourselves as guinea pigs and our couple's practice as a laboratory, we experimented with implementing a set of positive behaviors that we later called the Affirmations Process. It took a few weeks of consistent practice, with no sidebar negativity, for our anxiety to subside and for us to feel safe with each other. In other words, affirmation works better as a defense than negativity!! Using the principle of neuroplasticity, we had rewired some parts of our brains. We experienced a parallel process with the couples in our practice.

In our continuing experimentations, we eventually discovered that the most effective process for creating and sustaining safety was alternating an intense positive behavior with a quiet one—like an orgasm followed by quiet cuddling. In neurophysiological terms, this constitutes a shift from the sympathetic branch of the autonomic nervous system to the ventral vagal nerves in the parasympathetic side of the autonomic system.

Over time we have discovered several simple and easily repeatable behaviors—like flooding each other with verbal intensity and then hugging each other for at least 20 seconds—that can intensely impact these neural systems, producing a cocktail of pleasurable neurochemicals and waves of pleasurable sensations and emotions, including the experience of connecting attended by the sensation of full aliveness, joyful relaxation, and the state of wonder.

So, conscious couples have learned that heavy doses of the emotions falling on the positive side of the spectrum—such as excitement, enthusiasm, joy, amazement, even passion—are essential to counterbalance negativity. After an "ouch" occurs is prime time to initiate these pleasure inducing activities, or if necessary, plan to do so in the near future. The possibilities are nearly endless. Some couples like to spontaneously start dancing together; some like to wrestle or throw pillows, others prefer watching comedies, belly laughing, or making love (so-called "make-up sex"). Partners can verbally express appreciation, admiration, or gratitude to each other; together they might brainstorm better ways to cope with negativity that emerges in the future; or they might choose to simply relax, congratulate one another, hold hands, and place a happy face sticker on their negativity tracking chart.

Whatever conscious couples decide would effectively restore connecting, and quickly, they do it. The important point is that conscious couples understand that it is not how many ouches occur that matters, it's how quickly you restore connecting!

Once couples learn about the rigors of commitment to conscious partnership—living inside what Imago therapists refer to as "the Imago vortex"—they often make comments such as, "But a relationship shouldn't be so much work! If you really are meant for each other, it should be easy to be together; it shouldn't be like this." Their comments make sense because the creation of a conscious partnership is practicing specific skills until they become integrated into daily life. That requires commitment and discipline on a daily basis. We (Harville and Helen) know how hard that is, and we also know there is no positive outcome without consistent commitment and practice. So we sympathize and even agree with these couples complaints about why what should be natural is so difficult and needs so much attention. That is why we place emphasis on the construct of a conscious partnership as a cocreation of a new way of being with each other and cooperation in the implementation of its practices. It is the outcome of the dream of romantic lovers, but it is not possible if romantics wait for it to come to them; they have to learn that real love is only for those who commit and revel in creating it.

For this reason, in Imago therapy, couples are introduced to Imago Dialogue in the first session and guided through the sequential steps to help them create a conscious partnership as their dream relationship, and then proceed to deepen their sense of safety and connecting through the continuous use of the Dialogue process. This ultimately brings the couple to the wide and open playing field in which passion, fun, and pleasure can be given full reign.

Gradually, but inevitably, the steep uphill path levels off, and the couple's movement toward the promised land of real love becomes less strenuous, more doable, and, eventually, more pleasurable. The particle-like behaviors are then experienced as relaxed joyfulness, a wavelike flow of pleasure. Perhaps the most obvious reason this occurs is the fact that any pleasurable thing a person does repeatedly, day after day, year after year, and decade after decade, creates muscle memory that becomes, literally, etched into their brain matter. Thus, when a couple is trying to conform to the shape of a conscious partnership, they drop the old mental and behavioral patterns that kept them alienated, and they focus instead on and emphasize what they love and appreciate about each other. They are literally recreating how they view, think, and feel about each other and the memories they have together. In doing so, it is as though they are engaged in an act of creating new memories and, in most cases, the reconstruction of past memories, thus changing, enriching, and upgrading the furniture of the brain.

Eventually, all of the rigors and hard work entailed in the task of growing a conscious relationship begin, much to the couple's delight and astonishment, to yield a subtle but growing sense of effortless flow in the Space-Between. Zero Negativity, amplified by the Affirmations Process, make the couple's relationship "feel" easy! This leap in their progress toward the relationship of their dreams leaves the couple infused with a background of relaxation, punctuated by experiences of full aliveness, joyful relaxation and states of wonder. It is as though in arriving closer to their destination, they come back to the place where they started. Only this time, they experience a new, more conscious form of the spontaneous oscillation that is our default setting when we are born. On the sacred ground of conscious partnership, spontaneous oscillation, which lies at the root of our being and provides the fuel for our existence, can once again become our personal and relational norm.

WHAT DO CONSCIOUS PARTNERS KNOW

Based on the practices conscious couples engage in, we created a list of *what conscious couples know* and *what they do with what they know*. Here are 25 things that conscious partners know. You may find it interesting to compare these lists with the beliefs and behaviors of unconscious couples on page 147. Conscious partners know that:

1. Safety is nonnegotiable for thriving in their relationship.
2. Imago Dialogue creates equality and safety and facilitates connecting.
3. Negativity arouses anxiety and disconnects them from each other. They keep all negativity and judgment out of their transactions.
4. Both of them have an original innocence that was lost in their childhood challenges, which occurred at approximately the same developmental stage.
5. The conscious agenda of their relationship is to meet the unmet childhood needs they each brought into their relationship.

6. They have complimentary defenses that are natural, and they accept that fact about each other, without judgment.

7. They can reconstruct the memory their partner has of them by expressing new behaviors with intensity.

8. They are different from each other and will never be the same. Similarity is as good as it gets.

9. They came together to participate in the sometimes painful, sometimes joyful dance of romantic partnership, and they know why.

10. That anxiety gets aroused between them, and how to take steps to prevent negative emotions from taking hold.

11. They can assume that their partner's intentions are good, even if their behavior is not.

12. To prevent episodes of unnecessary pain, suffering, and damage to their relationship, they need to be intentional and think before they speak.

13. They need to differentiate so they can move from symbiosis to connecting.

14. They need to remove all forms of negativity that show up in the Space-Between; instead of picking a fight and using negativity to get what they want, they ask their partner for a Dialogue.

15. They need to do their best to meet the other's needs and desires, knowing that in doing so they are serving their partner's and their own best interests.

16. Being conscious means taking responsibility for (only) their own behavior and allowing room for their partner's flawed behaviors by not taking them personally, as indeed they are not personal.

17. They need to be sensitive to their different needs for space and togetherness.

18. Having a healthy relationship is the best thing they can do for their physical and emotional health.

19. The quality of their relationship shapes the relational, emotional, and cognitive future of their children, if they have any.

20. The energy in their relationship has a ripple effect in their social environment.

21. They know how to orient themselves toward maintaining connection with each other, while staying open to all parts of themselves, their personality, and their sense of individuality.

22. Connecting is sustained by intentionality, so they speak with a positive tone and use only appreciative or neutral words in all transactions, which helps them feel connected most of the time.

23. The sign of a thriving relationship is how quickly partners engage in curiosity rather than judgment.
24. They need to acknowledge each other's "otherness," accept each other's differences, affirm each other's reality, adore each other's traits, and advocate each other's reality and potential.
25. They must differentiate before they can connect, so they accept each other as an "other" and accept each other's differences.

WHAT DO CONSCIOUS PARTNERS DO

In addition to what they know, conscious partners engage in specific behaviors that create safety and connecting which is the precondition for the sensation full aliveness, relaxed joyfulness and the state of wonder. These behaviors tend to be so unusual, in non-conscious relationships, that they stand out. Conscious partners:

1. Look into each other's eyes with a gaze, rather than a glare, as an expression of relaxation, safety, and contentment in the other's presence.
2. Resonate with their partner's experience by saying things like: "Look at that!" "I see it too." "That must have been challenging." "Wow, I can feel your excitement while you were doing that!" Asking the other, after they went to the doctor, "How did it go? Is everything ok?"
3. Hug each other for a full minute in the morning and at night, and other times when desirable.
4. Stay together at public events and ask to be seated together.
5. Ask for an appointment when they want to talk about something.
6. Mirror back what they hear their partner saying and check for accuracy by saying: "Did I get that?"
7. Show curiosity in what their partner is saying, after mirroring, by asking: "Is there more about that?"
8. Validate their partner's point of view by saying: "You make sense," and "What makes sense about that is . . ."
9. Empathize with their partner's experience by saying, "I can imagine you might feel . . . about that. Is that your feeling?"
10. Give each other three appreciations each day by saying: "What I appreciate about you is . . ."
11. Acknowledge a caring behavior from their partner by saying, "I feel cared about and loved when you . . ."
12. Engage in spontaneous play and high energy fun on a regular basis.

13. Give each other a surprise once a month that is actually would *be* a surprise, thus showing they have been listening!

14. Flood each other with intense positive energy at least once a day by saying in a loud voice: "You are amazing" or "You are wonderful" or "I can't believe I am in a relationship with someone who . . ." (positive trait or behavior).

15. Say some form of "ouch," rather than criticizing or avoiding engagement, when they experience something that seems negative to them.

16. Reconnect quickly when there is a rupture by saying, "What can I do to restore connecting?" And they do it immediately.

17. Sign the Zero Negativity Pledge and practice Zero Negativity all the times.

18. Ask for what they want by converting their frustrations into a wish, such as saying, "While I was frustrated when you were late, what I want is for you to call and let me know when you will be home."

19. Express strong emotions when they celebrate each other's successes, such as by saying: "Wow! You did that!"

20. Empathize with each other's stresses by saying, "I can imagine that feels (awful, sad, painful, etc.)"

21. Close all exits and make their partnership their top priority.

22. Speak with a positive tone and use only appreciative or neutral words in all transactions.

23. Express appreciation for the mystery of their relationship, and its miracle and its wonder.

24. Express joyfulness, full aliveness, and wonder by playing and laughing a lot.

25. Make love all the time, and sometimes have sex!

There are additional essential ingredients of a conscious partnership. Perhaps the most crucial among these is that both partners sense that the relationship is based on a fair, even, and equitable playing field. This is in stark opposition to the still-mainstream patriarchal mindset where a woman, by virtue of being female, "owes" something to her male partner, which thus diminishes her relative status, making her "less than." In a conscious partnership, there is no hierarchy, no diagram of assigned authority with one person arbitrarily occupying the number one position. The conscious partnership is horizontal, eye-to-eye, between two equal lovers and friends operating on a level playing field. The deck is not stacked toward one partner or the other; there is no master or slave, no boss or underling. Common as they may be, unequal relationships are, in our view, a recipe for abuse, divorce, and, ultimately, societal disaster. Inequality in any form makes a conscious partnership impossible.

Just as the survival directive is deeply embedded in the brain and acts without any direction from the mind, conscious partnership reflects the survival directive nature embedded in our collective unconscious. *If nature's directive is to keep all of its creation alive and well, then a conscious partnership must be nature's ingenious invention to accomplish just that and real love its outcome.* The prospect of relinquishing old grudges, resentments, and reactive behaviors can, for many couples, seem overwhelming, even impossible. Asking people who were raised on criticism and judgment to eliminate negativity from their repertoire seems, on its face, absurd and impossible. However, counter to our own experiences, there is a large and growing body of neuroscience findings that support the idea that old dogs *can* learn new tricks and that couples—even long-married, deep in despair couples—can change, if they are willing, on the deepest levels of human experience.

The relief that comes after a person has decided to permanently relinquish their old anxiety-based defensive strategies cannot be overestimated. The true joy of leaving the power struggle behind and getting the first glimpses of a relationship that is far different and far better cannot be fully understood without direct experience. It is much like what first-time parents say about the experience of witnessing one's first child being born: you cannot fully appreciate it without going through it yourself.

But first, of course, as an Imago therapist, it is your role to teach couples about the prospect of conscious partnership, to describe what is required, and to engage them in the processes that can help them achieve, slowly and incrementally, the relationship of their dreams and the transition from the illusions in romantic love to the realities of authentic love while retaining the passion that brought them together in the first place.

FROM ROMANTIC LOVE TO REAL LOVE

Real love cannot develop during the romantic stage because of the unconscious and also because at that time, the old brain is engaged in the agenda of survival and the partner is a resource; an object, not a person. Nor can real love come forth during the power struggle, which also is unconscious and the intent is the same as romantic love, but the methods have shifted from courtship to coercion. Real love needs the light of consciousness that is reborn in the darkness of that struggle to survive. Thriving is not a priority when surviving is a struggle!

What consciousness brings to fruition is what we call real love. Unlike fantasy-based romantic love, real love is based on something far longer-lasting: a deep knowing of one partner by the other. Remarkably absent from this kind of love are reactivity and defensiveness. When love is real, there is no need for reactivity or defensiveness, because real love is safe, and with it there is no sense of lack, so no desire, because real love is the co-experiencing of being. We can relax and be ourselves in the Space-Between; there is no threat and no desire, so there is no tension and no threat, but a reexperiencing of the fullness and resonance with which it all began, which reappeared in romantic love and which now becomes the atmosphere in which we live together.

When partners can see each other clearly in the here-and-now as two people who are different from yet intricately connected to each other, real love replaces the power struggle as the driving force of a relationship. They transcend their symbiotic state.

This describes, in fact, a conscious partnership par excellence. It is based as much on separate knowing as on connected knowing, on objective knowledge as on subjective knowledge of the other. But something else happens in a conscious partnership that has unexpected side-benefits for the partners. Since consciousness, like a muscle, grows the more we use it, when we practice being conscious with our partner, we unavoidably become a more conscious human being. We are confident that you agree with us on one point: the world needs more conscious human beings.

When consciousness displaces unconsciousness, many powerful shifts occur, at the most basic and the most sublime levels. By design, the Imago Dialogue activates and exercises some of our higher (meaning more recently developed and sophisticated) brain (or cortical) structures. All of its steps— mirroring, validation, and empathizing—engage the brain in ways that promote better balance and integration among parts of the brain. Other Imago processes, especially those designed to build passion, enhance the release of feel-good hormones and neurotransmitters—endorphins, for example, which are released during pleasurable experiences (of both drug and non-drug varieties). This rejuvenation of the partners' neurochemistry enables them to better regulate anxiety—their own and their partner's—which in turn allows their defenses to relax. And with overall relational wellbeing improved, so does emotional, mental, and physical wellbeing.

With defenses gone, projections slowly vanish, allowing judgment to be replaced by curiosity. By definition, when defenses, projections, and judgment are removed, symbiosis vanishes and is replaced by differentiation. Without symbiosis, love for one's partner is based on who one's partner is, not on who one imagines their partner to be, and one does not love their partner because one's partner is (in our imagination, at least) like oneself.

When we no longer feel the need to defend ourselves against our partner, we come to realize that there is no need to defend ourselves against ourselves—that is, we no longer need to block or cut off any aspects of ourselves. We remember who we really are, which is a connecting human being with a cosmic identity. When we experience connecting, we are experiencing safety, and that allows us to experience our wholeness. It no longer seems like parts of our self are missing. We have everything we need, and we are everything we need. We no longer need our partner to be like us or to make up for something we lack. It's as though we are finally waking up from a very long nightmare to find that our partner isn't our parent after all and that we can, in fact, get the love we have always wanted and give the love they have always needed!

Some of the shifts that come out of the transformation to conscious partnership are more tangible and practical. We frequently notice that conscious partners appear to be healthier, both physically and mentally: they eat better, exercise more, go to the doctor less, and tend to be proactive, action-oriented people. Having experienced what it's like to be liberated from a self-imposed prison—which is exactly what the power struggle is— many couples find themselves drawn toward improving other aspects of the world, beyond their partnership. Some go so far as to become social activists, often for the first time in their lives.

"Sounds wonderful," we have heard couples say after hearing all of the above. Then they ask, "Who could possibly pull this off? Are you kidding me? You're telling us that we can do this?" Our answer, based on the research, our relational intuitions, and our own clinical and personal experiences, is YES, you can, because you have a brain designed and equipped to do just that. All you have to do is use it!

This is what you will be aiming to achieve with the couples who come to you for help. This is the bar you will be reaching for—to become a catalyst for the transformation of an unconscious relationship into a conscious partnership. You will guide the transfer of the passion of romantic love into the Space-Between, where real love lives. What you do, if you do it well enough, will go beyond facilitating healthier relationships. As an Imago therapist, you will be aiming a lot higher than that. Your ultimate goal is to bring couples into the kind of relationship that transforms each of them into the fully alive and interconnected human being they are in their essence, which they experienced at their birth and can experience again, and make it not just an episode but a way of living that contributes to the emergence of a relational civilization.

We turn now to identifying the developmental challenges to creating a conscious partnership a and how to respond to engage them at their developmental stage in their transformation process.

8
Developmental Challenges of Connecting

The journey from childhood to adulthood progresses organically through specific developmental stages, each of which has an agenda that, if achieved, eventuates in the evolution of the person to their full potential. It has become clear from developmental research that the achievement of this agenda requires a relational environment that includes the reliable presence and warmth of a nurturing caretaker. If the relational conditions are not optimal across all the developmental stages for the child to achieve the agenda of each stage, then the agenda becomes a need that is unconsciously brought to adult intimate relationship for fulfillment. While the rupture is universal and the desire for reconnecting is also cosmic, the special features of the rupture are determined by the developmental stage in which it occurred.

While Imago therapists tend not to use the diagnostic vocabulary of the *Diagnostic Statistical Manuals*, they are encouraged to think diagnostically about the developmental stage in which each partner was challenged and the adaptive defense they selected, since that will guide them to the specific developmental character of the Dialogical conversation the couple will have.

Couples tend to present their complaints about their rupture in the language of the unfinished agenda of the specific developmental stage in which it occurred. Since couples tend to be challenged in the same or adjacent developmental stage, their complaints will be presented in similar language. It is important that the therapist hears the complaint developmentally rather generically. For instance, if the rupture was early, in the connecting stage, the intensity of anxiety about abandonment for one partner will be matched by their partner's anxiety about feeling engulfed by clinginess. On the other hand, if the rupture did not occur until the identity stage, they will not complain about the security of the relationship but about the difficulties they have making decisions, since the rigid partner wants it one way and the diffuse partner cannot say what they want. The partner with a diffuse identity will complain about the rigid traits of their rigid identity partner, and the rigid partner who is "objectively clear" about everything will complain about their partners inability to be clear or make a decision. Their exchange will not be very intense because it is not driven by primal fears of abandonment or engulfment.

The Imago Dialogue process is the intervention of choice and the only one needed for all couples in all developmental stages, but the therapist needs to listen carefully to the language of the couple's frustrations and desires to assess the developmental-stage challenge with which this particular couple is dealing. Their conversations will have a developmentally specific theme, and while their underlying desire will be to connect, the constraints to connecting will be language related to the stage of their developmental challenge.

DEVELOPMENTAL STAGE SPECIFIC CHALLENGES AND DEFENSES

There are six developmental stages in childhood: connecting, exploration, identity, competence, social, and intimacy, in which developmental challenges and defenses occur that show up in adult intimate relationships. In our experience, the challenges and defenses in the social and intimacy stages tend not to show up in therapy because as children these adults were secure in the first 6 years of life. Whatever issues they may have, they are not severe enough to warrant therapy. Because of that, we limit our discussion to the first four developmental stages: connecting, exploration, identity, and competence. Of these, the earlier the challenge, the stronger the defense and the more compelling the need. If the challenge was early, say in the first months or 1st year of life, the challenge will be greater, and all the stages coming after that will be compromised by what came before.

The stage specific needs include the experience of connecting, success in exploration of the physical environment, achieving a clear identity and sense of self, and developing competence in the use of the four functions of thinking, feeling, acting, and sensing. Because our neural system is limited to polar defenses, maximizing and minimizing, these defenses will be used to manage anxiety at all stages, but their strength will be stage specific, which earns them a stage specific name. And because of the complementary balance of all couples, the challenge will be similar, but the defense will the opposite.

The Connecting Challenged Couple:
Clinger (Maximizer) and Avoider (Minimizer)
The core themes of connecting-challenged partners are related to the fear of being taken over or enmeshed, the fear of being rejected and abandoned,

and the longing for or aversion to intimate contact, whether through touch, attention, discussion, or nonverbal messages. Given the early hurts these partners suffered, their conflict may become extremely intense, even violent, AND they are desperate to stave off their worst fears, which typically involve being abandoned or annihilated by the other. You may hear connecting-challenged partners recount memories of being abused, severely neglected, or abandoned by their caretakers (Table 8.1).

In adulthood, we call maximizers clingers. The overriding impulse of a clinger is to be attached, which they demonstrate by "clinging." Their intimate bond with a partner becomes like life-saving water to someone dying of thirst. They cling to their partner for dear life, just as they did with their caretaker many years earlier. The clinging partner, with their early history of abandonment, has great difficulty tolerating normal amounts of separation from their partner. Their partner, whose developmental challenge is likely to be in the same early state of connecting, responds by avoiding, which triggers the clinger's greatest fear of being, once again, abandoned.

Table 8.1: Characteristics of the Connecting-Challenged Couple		
	Maximizer	Minimizer
Character adaptation	Clinging	Detaching, avoiding
Internalized Message	"I'll be safe if I hold onto you."	"I can't initiate contact because you'll destroy me."
Sees partner as:	Unavailable, unfeeling, cold	Demanding, all-consuming
Defensive behavior	Clinging, demanding, attempts to fuse	Detaches, avoids
Core issue	Partner's detachment and unavailability Too much separateness	Partner's demands and neediness Too much togetherness
Conflict management	Hyper-emotional, demanding, giving in, compromising	Hyper-rational, avoiding, passive aggressive withdrawing, cold
Growth challenges	Let go, self soothe, connect more to self, differentiate Listen to self, think things through	Assert own right to be Be more aware of the other Express feelings

They actualize the idea that "you and I are one, and I am *the* one" by viewing their partner as an extension of themselves.

In adulthood, minimizers are called avoiders. Avoiders face numerous handicaps in establishing a romantic partnership in the first place. Having never developed a connection with their caretaker, or a weak one at best, as adults they hold on to their deeply entrenched distrust of intimacy. It is no surprise that when their partner clings or gets upset with them, they react the only way they know how: by avoiding.

How to Identify the Connecting-Challenged Couple
- They often have a history of long, protracted, and volatile periods in which they alternate between fighting, separation, and reconciliation.
- One or both partners resist taking any responsibility for contributing to their relationship debacle. They resist engaging in self-reflection, as they experience it as too painful.
- They may have great difficulty following through with appointments.

How to Attune to the Connecting-Challenged Couple
- Go slowly, remembering that your number one goal is to create SAFETY in the interactive space between partners who often are fearful and reactive toward each other.
- Don't place office chairs too close to each other at the start.
- Use generous amounts of warmth and eye contact.
- Show consistent caring and be fully present to both partners.
- Model high levels of reliability, trustworthiness, and unconditional acceptance of the partners.
- Be prepared to do more mirroring and validating than the partners do, especially in the early stages of therapy.
- Take all of their questions and concerns seriously and respond to them thoroughly.
- Normalize their difficulties; reassure them that you will help them "get through the tunnel."
- Discover what you genuinely like about this couple, and then emphasize this to them.
- Consider a session successful if the partners succeed in making safe contact and connection with each other.
- Give homework sparingly, if at all.

The Exploration-Challenged Couple:
Pursuer (Maximizer) and Distancer (Minimizer)

We call the adult maximizer a pursuer. The maximizer child pursued the caretaker, looking for reassurance and guidance. The adult pursuer does all of the work of a relationship: they monitor its every aspect—physical, social, financial, emotional—and leap at a moment's notice to provide to the other the nurturing and protectiveness of which they themselves were deprived. This is well and good at the appropriate times, but by insistently pursuing the partner to make sure they stay close by, maximizers seem to be reenacting a childhood struggle to avoid the painful surprise of returning to an empty place (literally or figuratively; Table 8.2).

The minimizing partner, whom we call the distancer or isolator, has a habit of isolating themselves from their partner to avoid emotional suffocation. This isolation may take any variety of forms: they may, for example, stay emotionally "walled off"; they may make themself only sporadically available to their partner; they might be physically but not emotionally available; or they may engage in a revolving-door, leave-and-return-to-the-relationship cycle, repeatedly breaking up and then making up with their partner. Just when the romantic relationship is getting on solid ground, the isolator typically goes on high alert for signs that their partner might "take them over." To ward off any possibility of this transpiring, the distancer insists on "getting more space." Some distancers need so much "space" that their partner, and their relationship, ends up far away, on the periphery of their life.

Although their hurts are not quite as deep or severe as those originating at the first stage, exploration-challenged couples, like their connecting-challenged cohorts, are viewed as "early challenged." "Early" refers to both the chronological age of their challenges as well as the maturity level of their relational conflicts.

While painful memories around connecting leave partners terrified of either making or losing contact with each other, exploration-challenged partners feel anxious and ambivalent about how much time they spend together, whether they do things on their own or everything together, explore new ways to be a couple, to have sex, new vacation destinations or just stick with traditional models. As with other couple-types, you can recognize exploratory-challenged couples by the themes of their arguments and the language they use: you will probably hear them complain about their spending too much or too little time together, about feeling that the other is not reliable or trustworthy enough or is too needy or independent. The distancing stance of the minimizing partner sets limits on how much closeness there is, seeing the other as too insecure, fearful, and smothering.

Character Adaptation	*Maximizer* Pursuer	*Minimizer* Distancer
Internalized Message	"I'll be loved if I can get close to you."	"I can't get too close because you'll absorb me."
Sees partner as:	Distant, neglectful, having no needs	Insecure, too anxious, smothering
Behavior toward partner	Pursues and withdraws, ambivalent	Limits togetherness, distancing
Core issue	Partner's unreliability, neglect & lack of support	Personal freedom & autonomy, no space, partner's smothering
Conflict management	Blaming, demanding, pursuing, devaluing, chasing, complaining	Oppositional, distancing
Growth Challenges	Initiate separateness, develop outside interests, internalize the partner	Initiate closeness, share feelings

Table 8.2: Characteristics of the Exploration-Challenged Couple.

The minimizer's need for personal freedom and autonomy stands in tension to both of their needs for connection. How does the distancer cope with this conflict? By distancing—which leaves the maximizing partner feeling further neglected, unsafe, and insecure, and even more forgotten and insignificant in the eyes of the minimizing partner.

How to Identify the Exploration-Challenged Couple
- The defensive behaviors of exploration-challenged partners are relatively extreme—the minimizer strongly minimizes, and the maximizer strongly maximizes.
- Minimizers keep feelings in, downplay their own and their partner's emotions, deny having any needs (except for needing lots of "space"), have rigid boundaries, and are self- as opposed to other-directed.
- Maximizers stay on the defensive, let their feelings out, exaggerate their needs, act submissively and manipulatively, have unclear self-boundaries, and are other- as opposed to self-directed.
- Progress may seem slow, and the couple might continue to express ambivalence about their relationship.

How to Attune to the Exploration-Wounded Couple
- Maintain consistency in appointment times.
- Have the couple master mirroring and summarizing before introducing the more difficult step of validation (which they might find especially difficult, given that differentiation is a particular challenge for them).
- When teaching them to validate, keep the examples and sentence stems you use short and simple, such as, "I see what you're saying," "You make sense," and so forth.
- Invite them to be curious instead of judgmental.
- These partners probably lost touch with their own empathic ability due to the self-absorption that early wounding causes, so you can model empathy for them.
- Help the partners use the Behavior Change Request process (see Chapter 16 for details) to craft agreements and boundaries around spending time together and apart.
- These couples respond well to analogies, like the image of a turtle in a hailstorm depicting the minimizer and the maximizer.
- Use appreciations religiously at the beginning and end of every session.

The Identity-Challenged Couple: Diffuse (Maximizer) and Rigid (Minimizer)

The identity-challenged partners struggle with issues revolving around their identity, or their sense of self, and what or how to express it. The maximizing child with an unclear identity is, in adulthood, a diffuser. Diffuse partners are relatively easy to detect. They are overly accommodating, too easily persuaded, and too often confused over who they are and what they want. They tend to maintain a vague identity and hesitate to take strong positions vis-à-vis their partner, giving off a message amounting to, "You tell me who I am, and I'll be that." Although the diffuser views their partner as insensitive and controlling, they go along with what their partner wants, at least initially. But sooner or later, the diffuser begins to resent their partner for telling them who they ought to be and how they should feel, talk, and act. The rigid partner, in the meantime, sends the message, "In order for me to love you, you need to be the way I think you should be." The rigid minimizer tends to automatically criticize or disagree with his partner's statements, often responding with statements like: "You should . . ." or "You need to . . ." (Table 8.3).

As adults, identity-challenged minimizers have a rigid identity and are notorious for their tendency to remain unmoved by what their partner

Character Adaptation	Maximizer Diffuse Identity Compliant	Minimizer Rigid Identity Controlling
Internalized Message	"I'll be loved if I please you."	"I can't open myself to you because you'll try to take away my identity."
Sees partner as:	Domineering	Scatterbrained, vague
Behavior toward partner	Submissive, passive-aggressive	Domineering, critical
Core issue	Partner's dominance and rigidity	Partner's vagueness
Conflict management	Confused, compliant, makes few suggestions, masochistic	Imposes will, takes charge, sadistic
Growth Challenges	Establish boundaries, become more self-aware & expressive, be direct	Relax control, listen, mirror partner

Table 8.3: Characteristics of the Identity-Challenged Couple

(and sometimes their therapist) has to say. These rigid partners are quick to discern slights; they frequently misconstrue a partner's suggestion as an insult and interpret benign complaints as stinging criticism. Their determination to ward off any semblance of the domination they endured as children often manifests, ironically, in their tendency to maintain dominance over their partner.

As with the other couple-types, the defensive adaptations of these two couples fit together like hand in glove: the more diffuse the maximizer becomes, the more control the rigid partner takes. The more control taken by the rigid partner, the more compliant the diffuse partner becomes.

How to Identify the Identity-Challenged Couple
- One or the other partner complains about feeling used, not understood, not appreciated, or not listened to.
- Their perspectives—especially about their relationship—tend to be vastly different.
- They learn Imago Dialogue easily and respond well to homework assignments, reading, workshops, etc.

How to Attune to the Identity-Challenged Couple
- Emphasize the responsibility of the sender: teach them to use I-statements, to focus on their feelings rather than on their partner, to avoid mind-reading ("I know what you're thinking better than you do"), etc.
- Deepen empathy statements in the Dialogue by asking, "are there more feelings?"
- Normalize their struggles and conflict—for example, by sharing with them issues you might have in your own relationship that are similar to theirs.
- Encourage the diffuse partner to finish the sentence stem, "The point I really want you to understand is . . ."
- Encourage the rigid partner to use the sentence stem, "That's my perspective, and I'm open to hearing yours."
- During Dialogues about frustrations, include small behavior change requests as the couple becomes willing to stretch.
- Include educational pieces during sessions, as this couple usually enjoys learning about Imago theory.
- Have them use appreciations to repair negative exchanges.

The Competence-Challenged Couple:
The Manipulator (Maximizer) and the Competitor (Minimizer)
In adult relationships, we call the maximizing partner the manipulator. The manipulative partner can be described as "being competent at being incompetent." This, in turn, puts their partner at their service. In a commonly seen dynamic, a manipulative partner seems to force the other partner to "own" or "carry" the competence required for two people to function in the world. Laboring under an illusion of meager personal power, the manipulative partner habitually "borrows" from the other's competence, keeping in motion the characteristic "under functioning/over functioning" reactive pattern of the competence-challenged wounded couple (Table 8.4).

The manipulative partner needs to recognize that they do, indeed, matter and that they, too, have the power to make an impact on the world. The growth challenge of this partner is to shift away from a position of helpless withdrawal and to move toward a sense of empowered engagement with the world. In doing so, this partner not only gains valuable personal resource but also gives the nonmanipulative partner a much-needed break.

Like the competitive child, the competence-challenged minimizer adult, whom we named the competitor, usually looks good and often looks far better than their partner (who is likely to be a competence-challenged maximizer). Their defensive strategy of remaining in a one-up position vis-à-vis their partner of "reminding" their partner to do better and of "keeping it all together" is in concert with the values of many industrialized nations. Also similar to the competitive child, the competitive partner appears healthier on the outside than they feel on the inside. The childhood-based fear of inferiority drives the minimizer to greater heights, sometimes to the detriment of their personal well-being and often to the detriment of their relationship.

When they're arguing, competence-challenged partners sound like two kindergarteners fighting over who's right and who's wrong. They are both 100% certain; neither will give an inch. This makes perfect sense, since their wounds date back to the period when they were 5 or 6 years old, when they were first trying to get a sense of mastery in their interactions with other people and the world outside the home. The partner in the competitive (minimizing) stance strives for nothing less than perfection, often in the world of work as well as in intimate relationship. Having experienced deficient mirroring of competence early on, the minimizer's underlying longing is to be seen and admired by others but most of all by their partner, whose criticisms sting them deeply. At the same time, however, the competitor seems chronically dissatisfied with his partner, seeing the partner as

Table 8.4: Characteristics of the Competence-Challenged Couple		
Character Adaptation	Maximizer Strategizing Manipulating	Minimizer Compulsive Competing
Internalized Message	"I will be loved if I am good."	"I must be perfect."
Sees partner as:	Never satisfied, having to be in charge	Manipulative, incompetent
Behavior toward partner	Manipulative, compromising, and sabotaging	Pleasing, satisfying partner, being beyond reproach
Core issue	Partner's competitiveness	Partner's manipulative behavior
Conflict management	Compromises, manipulates	Competes for control
Growth Challenges	Develop competence, express power, praise partner's success	Accept self-competence, become cooperative, mirror and value partner's efforts

incompetent, as having little ambition, and as using manipulation to control things (especially the competitor).

The growth challenge for the manipulative partner is to be direct, to express their own power, to develop competence, and to stretch into praising their partner's successes. The competitive partner can grow by validating their partner's competence and becoming more egalitarian and cooperative with their partner, who longs, deep-down, for the competitor to mirror and value their efforts.

How to Identify the Competence-Challenged Couple
- They complain about feeling disconnected, with each blaming the other for the disconnect.
- Typically, one partner is an overachiever while the other tends to be critical and withholding.
- While they may be intelligent and sophisticated, they seem mystified over what is causing their relationship problems.
- They learn the Imago Dialogue easily.
- They make effective use of sentence stems (e.g., "And what hurts the most about that is . . .") and can tolerate deep emotions.
- They appreciate learning about the theory behind Imago therapy.
- They have strong intellectual defenses.

How to Attune to the Competence Stage Couple
- Normalize their dynamic.
- Model specific and sincere praise, for example, "Congratulations for taking time out of your schedule to do this important work for your relationship."
- Stay aware of the minimizer's need to be fully seen and appreciated.
- Stay aware of the maximizer's need to be in control.
- Encourage the maximizer to stretch into imagining the more vulnerable emotions beneath their partner's angry withdrawal.
- Encourage the minimizer to speak openly and honestly while validating their difficulties in doing so.
- Have the partners express their intentions regarding their relationship and what they wish to accomplish during sessions.
- Elicit and support emotional sharing between partners by using sentence stems and the Holding Exercise (see Chapter 14).

The Social and Intimacy Challenged Couples
If the child caretaker bond is secure through the first six years of life, the child has successfully negotiated the first four developmental stages. With connecting, exploration, identity and competence intact, most children succeed in

developing friends in the social and romantic partners in the intimacy stage. Therefore, they tend to have satisfactory to great marriages/ intimate partnerships and do not go to therapy. We can learn about their marriages from research on thriving relationships, but since the do not come to therapy, they do not provide us with therapeutic challenge to develop any processes except relationship enhancement skills. We have learned that the core skills challenged couples need will enhance a thriving relationship, so we offer those as relationship education. But we do not include those couples in this book. Before we turn to the clinical processes and practices of Imago therapy, here is a brief recap.

SUMMARY

Couples tend to be developmentally challenged at the same developmental stage and to engage in opposite defenses with an emotional intensity relative to that stage (Table 8.5). When they break their impasse by relaxing their defenses and responding to each other's developmental need, their relationship takes a developmental step. But then they will face a challenge:

Table 8.5: Relational Patterns in Adulthood

Ruptured connection caused by childhood wounding may manifest in adulthood as *minimizing defenses*, such as constriction of energy, diminishment of affect, withholding, rigidity, self-centeredness, exclusiveness, and dominance

Adulthood Relational Pattern	Detaching: Indifference to / denial of relational needs of self and partner	Isolating: Minimizes / resists need for contact with partner	Rigid: Domineering, constricted, unmoved by partner	Competitive: Judgmental of / feeling superior over partner	Withdrawing: Exclusion / rejection of others from ones relational life	Rebelling: Rejection of conventional relationship roles
Developmental Stage/Impulse	CONNECTING	EXPLORATION	IDENTITY	COMPETENCE	SOCIAL	INTIMACY
Adulthood Relational Pattern	Clinging: Terror of losing relationship; constant need for reassurance	Pursuing: Resistant to separations from partner; fear of autonomy	Diffuse: Acquiesces to and subjugates own needs to those of partner	Manipulative: Feigned incompetence reliance of partners achievements	Gregarious: Overly over-inclusive / caretaking of others	Conforming: Adhering to rigid gender bound roles

Ruptured connection caused by childhood wounding may manifest in adulthood maximizing defenses, such as explosion of energy, exaggeration of affect, invasiveness, diffuseness, other-dependence, over-inclusiveness, and submissiveness

Their frustrations and complaints will change because they are encountering the unfinished agenda of the next stage.

This happens because in childhood they did not engage the agenda of the next stage due to the challenge of the preceding stage. In adulthood, for instance, when the exploratory-challenged couple resolves their issues and organically moves toward the identity stage, they will encounter the challenges of the unfinished identity stage. Co-meeting those needs becomes the next agenda in therapy.

Now that you have a view of the primal challenges couples may face and the specific form they take in each developmental stage, we invite you to become acquainted with the six steps that lead to the conscious partnership we seek, in which the agenda of childhood, no matter the developmental state issue, will be fulfilled.

Part III

IMAGO CLINICAL PROCESSES

THREE COUPLES STARTING IMAGO RELATIONSHIP THERAPY

Clinical processes move us from the invisible to the visible. A process is a strategy that puts clinical theory into a plan. It is not yet an action. That comes next. But it is a description of the action that gives birth to the visible. The fact that it can be observed educates you for the next step into concreteness: clinical practice.

THREE COUPLES STARTING IMAGO RELATIONSHIP THERAPY

As we shift now into the clinical processes and, subsequently, clinical practice, we introduce three couples who will provide us with clinical vignettes for illustration. These three couples look something like the thousands of couples with whom we've walked down the road over the years. By learning how Imago therapy views these three couples and their problems, you will gain some insight on how Imago therapy views couples in general and what an Imago therapist focuses on. You will discover what the partners experienced while growing up in their childhood homes, the memories of their caretakers, both good and bad, that they carry around with them; the things they fight over, again and again; what they need now in order to restore connecting; and how one can become a source of the other's transformation. These composite couples, Diana and Mark, Len and Ping, and Fran and Alicia, will help us bring to life the theoretical framework and clinical techniques that make the Imago clinical approach so powerful.

DIANA AND MARK

Diana and Mark make a striking pair with their dark hair, dark eyes, and trendy clothing, giving them a faintly European flair. They obviously know each other very well; like couples married far longer than they, they often finish each other's sentences. They work together for the same Silicon Valley tech company, a surprisingly successful computer graphics design outfit that Mark started a few years before he met Diana.

Like virtually all well-matched couples, however, these two differ in several ways—most importantly, their chronological ages. Diana just turned 31; Mark is 46. They recently launched a new venture: raising a child. Jake was born just over a year ago. For Diana, motherhood is bliss, much as she had expected. Diana is the youngest in an Irish Catholic family of two girls, three boys, a hard-working father, and a stay-at-home mother. Having a child was a key step toward having it all—getting married, having a family, and being an artist, or at least something like one. She reminded Mark many times, both before and after they got married, that she would not want to give up any of these three things.

Having a 17-year-old daughter with his previous wife, Mark's exuberance over having a toddler at the age of age of 46 is decidedly more muted than Diana's. He insists that he loves Diana and Jake and that he would do anything for them. But at this point in his life, he's unsure of having additional children and bemoans putting "his life" on hold for another 18+ years. They are feeling less and less connected, which is what prompted them to come to therapy.

LEN AND PING

Len and Ping had been together barely 8 months, but they had already run into some problems in their relationship. Upon his sister's recommendation, Len grudgingly agreed to therapy with Ping. Len was 25; Ping was 22. They were just starting out, both in their relationship with each other and in their lives as full-fledged adults.

Until the age of 12, Ping was raised in mainland China, and her "exotic" background and her intense interest in him were features that Len found attractive about Ping. But while he thought she was different, much to Len's surprise, she was remarkably similar to the other women he'd dated.

Len and Ping had moved in together only a couple of months after they had met, mostly because Ping wanted to. He loved Ping, but she was always so needy and serious about everything—especially him. As for Ping, she just did not understand Len at all. For example, they were in love, and they were living together, right? So why didn't Len want to spend more time with her? For example, he has to have his regular nights out with the guys, twice a week. Although she had no aspirations to become a stay-at-home wife and mother, Ping said that she wanted a relationship that was as "tight" as the one her parents had.

Len clearly saw things differently. On hearing her perspective, he'd respond, "No, thanks. It's like the poem says: 'If you love someone, set them free, and if they don't come back, let it be.'" Len and Ping are a living example of a couple at an impasse—where the immoveable object meets the irresistible force—and their relationship has only just begun.

FRAN AND ALICIA

Fran and Alicia describe themselves as "battle-worn." Both were in their early forties and neither of them had children. Their 11 years living together were marked by long cycles of fighting and breaking up, followed by equally long cycles of reconciling and falling back into the same old rut. Fran, a few years older than Alicia, is a vice-president of a large local bank. In her tailored dark suit, high heels, and her neatly coiffed hair, she makes an impressive figure, looking every bit the successful executive she is. Alicia, about 6 inches shorter and 50 pounds lighter, wears a uniform of old blue jeans and a T-shirt emblazoned with the slogan of the day—usually something like "PEACE NOW."

During their first few years together, Fran took classes for her MBA on the weekends and worked in an entry-level position at the bank during the week. While Fran labored her way up the company ladder and pored over books for hours on end, running the household had fallen to Alicia. This, to Alicia, was a good plan. Having finished a bachelor's degree in psychology years before she and Fran met, Alicia found taking care of the home front economical and joyful. So, over the years, as Fran's bank responsibilities became more demanding, Alicia spent her days buying the groceries, paying the bills, doing the laundry, making meals, and setting up their social dates with their wide circle of friends.

As we dive into the processes and practices of Imago Relationship Therapy, we will learn more about these three couples all of which, from the very first session, are introduced to a new way of listening and talking. And now we turn to the core engine of Imago Relationship Therapy: Imago Dialogue.

9

Imago Dialogue
The Process of Connecting

Having an experience of a "casual conversation" exploding into a full-fledged argument is a common experience of couples and most people. But these are really not conversations; they are parallel monologues. A conversation is talking *with* (con=with, versa=talking) someone. A monologue is one (mono=one, logo=word) person talking *to* someone, and usually down to them. And that is the problem of people talking. Monologues are parallel because one person/partner just waits until the other is finished or attempts to talk at the same time. Neither is listening in either scenario. This is usually referred to as the problem of communication, and the solution is learning how to communicate. The problem, from our perspective, is not communication but the relative position of the speaker. In monologue, the exchange is vertical, from the top down, and one-way. The speaker owns the "truth" and claims implicitly, if not explicitly, authority and superiority, and annihilates the "truth" of the other. The other has few options and tends to take the ones most naturally available to the human defense system: turning away (rejecting), turning toward (confronting) or shutting down engagement entirely (leaving the scene). And there we have the human situation: the oppressive use of language.

Dialogue is not only a distinct use of language that is different from monologue, it is different from most forms of verbal interaction like ordinary discussion, daily conversation, decision making, debate negotiation, problem solving, conflict resolution and communication skills. All these tend to be forms of parallel monologues that are used in most human transactions where the transactors are trying to get something done. In contrast, as the quantum physicist David Bohm stated so eloquently, dialogue is not trying to get anything "done" but a process that creates a context in which two human beings become transparent to each other in a way that both are changed by the process (1996). Dialogue allows one person to share fully the domain of their interior world with another person without fear and for that person to reciprocate so that they fully understand how they are similar and different and to engage and embrace their mutual realities with acceptance, appreciation and wonder. While agreement is not necessary, the experience of shared interiorities without judgment is so profound and impactful that each is inevitably changed by it, so that something miraculous happens, and agreement occurs in the transformed state of genuine connecting.

Now let's distinguish dialogue from monologue as the foundation for discussing the Imago Dialogue Process.

FIRST THERE WAS MONOLOGUE

For eons, monologue and its vertical structure have predominated not only intimate partnerships but also in virtually every other kind of human relationship—king and subject, lord and servant, father and son, political leader and citizen, priest and penitent, physician and patient, teacher and student, boss and subordinate. A monologue is, plain and simple, a message transmitted from one person to another in one direction only—from up to down, that is, from speaker to listener (or sender to receiver). It follows the same order as a speech given to a group of listeners during which the speaker is proclaiming some "truth" that they know, and their audience does not, but should. This mode of talking operates on an unequal playing ground—with one person over the others—and creates personal and social anxiety. By design, the vertical, top-down, hierarchical structure of monologue elevates the speaker's priorities over the listener's priorities. This makes monologue incompatible with an egalitarian relationship, especially a romantic one, and from inefficient to oppressive in all relationships.

The reign of the vertical structure of talking faced opposition, however, during the twentieth century, when the ideals of traditional marriage came face-to-face with the converging movements for women's rights, racial equality, and gay liberation. Predictably, during the tumultuous period that immediately followed, the divorce rate shot up. It is no wonder, then, that around that time we saw the emergence of new marital therapies, but most of these approaches involved teaching couples new behaviors and skills for improving communication, especially negotiation, conflict resolution, fair fighting, and so forth. But even the best of these approaches did not modify or even acknowledge what amounted to their major barrier to intimacy: the implicit and explicit vertical arrangement in which the two persons operated like two individual entities negotiating a quid pro quo arrangement as in a business rather than as partners cocreating their lives together.

FROM MONOLOGUE TO IMAGO DIALOGUE

In the psychotherapy arena, the trance of monologue, especially in therapeutic circles, was broken in the 1950s by the writings of psychiatrist Harry Stack Sullivan, humanist psychologist Carl Rogers, and the Jewish theologian/philosopher Martin Buber. Sullivan is famous for his declaration that what matters most is what happens "between" people, Rogers for his view of argument as a mutual exchange of talking and empathic listening, and Buber for his attempt to awaken culture and therapy from this trance by positing that conversations require a horizontal plane where verbal exchanges occur among equals, where the "It" becomes a "Thou."

Genuine dialogue (Buber's I–Thou relationship) takes place when the speaker and the listener attempt to understand the otherness of the other (Buber, 1958) by putting aside their desire to change or control the other. It is in these very deep conversations, where judgment drops away and a genuine effort to understand the intersubjective views of the other, that both speaker and listener are made human. Each is changed by allowing the world of the other to occupy space in their mental and emotional universe. Whereas monologue is a remnant of the individual paradigm, and the monarchial culture which spawned it, Imago Dialogue is the language of the relational paradigm, spoken in the Space-Between (Table 9.1), and the vehicle for transforming personal relationships and all social institutions.

In couple's therapy, Imago Dialogue helps partners differentiate by achieving awareness of how they are different and similar, and ultimately leads to acceptance of our distinct and personal subjectivities and our contrasting ways of seeing the world. Differentiation is a transformational process that restores the original connecting, with which we all came into the world and lost in the primal disconnection of childhood, a rupture that produced, what in Imago we call the "disease of humanity—a universal symbiotic consciousness that resides in all our brains, and tends to be outside our awareness. Through the dialogue process, partners can create a safe-enough atmosphere for accessing and putting into language their unlanguaged experiences: their thoughts and feelings, memories and dreams. This allows all aspects of both partners to emerge and become fully integrated. As a result, each partner can more fully see the other, and each can be seen and mirrored more accurately, rather than perceived through the

Table 9.1: The Reactive Monologue versus the Imago Dialogue	
Reactive Monologue	**Imago Dialogue**
• Spur of the moment	• By appointment only
• Boundary violation	• Boundaries honored
• Driven by emotion	• Driven by intention
• Neither partner feels heard	• Both partners feel heard
• Partners end up feeling alienated	• Partners end up feeling connected
• Results in greater fusion	• Results in greater differentiation

filter of their memories and their partner's projections. And the extension of this differentiation-reconnecting process to a tipping point of the world's population is the path, we think, to the creation of a relational civilization, the next stage of human social evolution. We turn now to look at Imago Dialogue as both a process of connecting and a relational skill that connects.

THE ESSENTIAL SKILL: THE IMAGO DIALOGUE

Our most surprising discovery, working with couples, was that talking is the most dangerous thing they do, and listening is the most infrequent. We also found this to be true in our own relationship. In fact, the development of Imago Dialogue was the ultimate outcome of a monological melt down between us, early in our relationship. In the middle of a heated discussion, Helen became the de facto creator of Imago Dialogue by firmly insisting that we "stop, and one of us talk and the other listen, and take turns." Responding to her assertion, and taking turns listening, both us felt such a decrease in our emotional intensity that we took "taking turns talking and listening" to the clinic and experimented with couples where it proved so effective that it evolved into a complex, multilayered skill that eventually became the only Imago intervention used, and we think needed.

Another discovery is that while a conversation is always about a topic, whether the conversation creates connection or polarization depends on the nuances in the verbal exchange, such as tone of voice, facial expression, soft or hard eyes, and stiff or relaxed cheeks—not so much similar or different views about the topic. When a conversation is safe, partners can talk about *anything* without polarizing, no matter how challenging the topic may be. They can plan their lives, solve their problems, share decision making, and make love and laugh. When it is dangerous, they cannot talk about anything without some tension or polarization and they will instinctively defend themselves, emotionally injure each other, polarize over issues, and develop symptoms that can lead to catastrophic outcomes. That is how our social brain is wired. Its primary agenda is to stand against threat—which all negativity is—and to survive. Although connecting is its nature and offers the best chance of survival and Imago Dialogue is a conversational skill that, when practiced appropriately and consistently, creates the safety essential to restoring connecting in the service of survival, negativity overrides its social nature and it shows up as a separate entity seeking security in a dangerous context.

At the basic level, Imago Dialogue is two people taking turns talking without judging, listening without criticizing, and connecting around and beyond differences. It is the skill of using a series of specially designed sentence stems that ensures clear and congruent verbal exchanges that ultimately lead to relational competence and relational wellbeing which is a precondition for emotional and mental wellbeing, and we are now learning physical wellbeing as well.

At a deeper level, this alternating process of talking and listening and sequential process of specific sentence stems creates a safe emotional and physical environment which is essential for experiencing the sensation of connecting, full aliveness, joyful relaxation and the state of wonder.

Therapeutically, Imago Dialogue is an intervention that helps partners connect through resonance and communicate through language about and beyond their differences, thus *changing their interactive space*—the Space-Between—and *simultaneously changing their intrapsychic space*. Changing the space between them changes the space within them which, in turn, changes the space between them.

At the deepest level Imago Dialogue becomes *a transformational process* akin to a spiritual practice and social transformation. This transformational process creates a Space-Between in which communication about similarities and beyond differences takes place, polarization is overcome, and collaboration about options leads to cocreation of new ways to be together which partners cooperatively implement. Although Imago therapy includes a range of clinical processes and practices, all are variations on this central dialogical process. Given its power to transform the personal and the collective, Imago Dialogue is the *most important skill set a couple can possess*. It is the language of conscious partnerships.

Ultimately, when couples experience connecting to each other, they simultaneously reexperience the sensation of full aliveness, relaxed joyfulness and the state of wonder which attended the early days of their romance and, simultaneously with that, a reconnecting to the cosmos in which we are all residents. In doing so, they become more conscious in all other communications and relationships. Imagine if everyone could benefit from safe conversations instead of just the small percentage of humankind seeking therapy or other relational training and experiences.

The Basics of Imago Dialogue
Every Imago Dialogue has a sender (speaker) and a receiver (listener). Your role as the therapist is to facilitate the dialogical process in the office, guiding the couple so that they gain enough competence to take the process home. At its most fundamental level, Imago Dialogue is a three-step process:

1. Mirroring: accurately reflecting back what was heard without changing anything.
2. Validating: seeing the "truth" of another point of view and maintaining one's own.

3. Empathizing: feeling/imagining the emotions another person is experiencing in their world.

Each step also has sub steps that consists of sentence stems to be used in a specific sequence. Learning, teaching and practicing these sentence stems is essential to the Dialogue process. What is a sentence stem? A sentence stem is the first part of a sentence followed by a blank which is filled in by the speaker.[7] Careful and consistent use of specific sentence stems has become a trademark of Imago therapy. They have been honed from experience and should be used as close to their original form as possible, because they have passed the test of efficiency over a long period of time. We think the use of sentence stems is essential to creating safety in the dialogical exchange and in the environment of the therapy office because they regulate emotions and keep the focus on the topic. They are efficient because they regulate the on-ramp of exchanges between partners and that, in turn, regulates their brains, thus preventing negativity and polarization, and producing brain integration. Brain integration is achieved by the regular use of the sentence stems because they engage the prefrontal cortex in the regulation of emotional centers in the amygdala and this contributes to the integration of the upper and lower brain regions and the two hemispheres. With integration comes the capacity to replace reacting with intentional, focused responding, which are the features of a relational brain.

The Imago therapist uses a specific sentence stem to help the sender and receiver stay focused on the topic at hand, to regulate affect, and to contain the flow of the conversation. The sentence stem is offered to the sender who is asked to fill in the blank with what they want to say. For example: the sender might be prompted to say: "Is now a good time to talk about . . . (a topic)", and the receiver may be prompted to say: "If I got that, you wonder if now is a good time to talk about . . . ."

At the beginning of therapy, sentence stems need to be memorized and used by the therapist and the clients in every session so they can be integrated into *every* conversation by the couple. Integration includes using the three-step process for conversations about a specific topic *and* integrating the sentence stems into every conversation, casual or serious, so that every exchange is safe, eventually making all conversations dialogical, although all conversations need not be the structured three-step process. The process is from structure to spontaneity, like moving from the mastery of the skills of a sport to the creative flow of artistry.

As their therapist, you have to be patient until they discover that practicing and mastering Imago Dialogue *IS* the therapeutic process, not the topics they want to talk about. "How" couples speak with each other rather than "what" they say is the bridge to safety, which is the precondition to connecting. This makes successful therapy the achievement of safety so couples can restore original connecting; making all conversations safe IS the therapeutic process. You may have to see it yourself before you believe it.

Each sentence stem is designed to:

- create safety through predictability;
- create predictability by providing structure;
- create structure by providing a sequence of responses;
- keep the focus on the topic and avoid side bar comments;
- contribute to brain integration by regulating interaction between thinking, feeling, and acting;
- deepen access to unspoken feelings and thoughts, to implicit memory;
- deepen the connection between partners;
- allow the therapist to facilitate and sustain the dialogical process; and
- deepen the connection between the couple and the therapist.

A Homework Option: Practicing using sentence stems in the flow of a conversation makes a good homework assignment. Since the therapist's goal for the therapy is to help couples speak dialogically, the homework options could be: 1) Practice mirroring each day on a safe topic or 2) Practice using one sentence stem each day. "Let me see if I got it. If I did you said . . ." These options are most helpful for stopping partners from interrupting each other or deflecting each other. Practicing "Is now a good time to talk about . . ." (a safe topic) is very effective in establishing boundaries before engaging in the exchange of information. The ultimate goal is to use all the sentence stems, as appropriate, to facilitate and sustain the flow of a conversation in much the same way as the return of a ball by a tennis player depends on what comes over the net.

The Rules of Engagement
Below are some guidelines for setting couples up for a successful Imago Dialogue.

Decide on the Sender-Receiver Sequence
Before launching into the steps, it is important to decide who will be the first sender. Generally, it is up to the partners to decide who will start as the sender and who will be the receiver. One consideration, though, is to find out who tends to speak first in their daily conversations and ask them to reverse that in order to change the initiator/responder dynamic of their relationship. Even these small changes in patterns shift the relationship

toward more flexibility and exercises the other side of the autonomic nervous system.

Set Up the Appointment Making Process
To illustrate the sentence stem concept, you can ask the sender to say: "Is now a good time to have a Dialogue about _____?" This is "the appointment only rule," which insists conversations (whether sharing something simple, such as an appreciation, or something more complex, such as a frustration) be by appointment only.

Stating the topic should come with the request for an appointment, and is essential. Otherwise, because our brains have a negativity bias, our partner will automatically experience anxiety because their first thought will be that you have something negative to say. If the sender's topic will be challenging to their partner, you can help the receiver regulate by taking several deep breaths and clearing their minds of the fearful possibility.

The receiving partner should be coached to say: "Yes, I am available now." Or, if they are not—the receiver is free to decline momentarily, but they need to offer a time when they will be available within the next 24 hours. So, if they are not available now, the therapist coaches them to say: "I am not available now, but I will be at _____" (set a time within the next 24 hours).

NOTE: This process alone addresses the childhood issue of the deflecting caretaker, which most human beings on the planet have experienced. It begins to create safety, thus easing the way to the experience of connecting.

There are several reasons for making an appointment for an Imago Dialogue:

- **Honoring Boundaries**: Because of our ego-centric mindset, we assume the other is available 24/7 for "me." The appointment-only rule starts to break this symbiotic fusion.
- **Containing Energy:** Some partners, especially maximizers, tend to immediately launch into a monologue, with predictable results. But part of a conscious partnership involves regulating reactive emotions.
- **Being Emotionally Available:** We live in a modern culture where our attention is being pulled in many directions by TV, the internet, phones, kids, work, texting, and other everyday divergences. We are physically present but emotionally absent or mentally somewhere else. An appointment allows both partners to get ready and be fully available, to be present in the here and now, without competing distractions.

Coach Couples in the Onramp Sequence

After an appointment has been accepted, guide couples with the onramp to Imago Dialogue:

Engage in nonverbal communication: We guide couples to sit comfortably, face-to-face, with knees touching and arms uncrossed. Couples are then asked to do some long, deep breathing in unison while gazing into each other's eyes. This has the effect of inducing a more relaxed physiology and reducing anxiety. We ask partners to make eye contact for a reason, and it is not romantic. It is a precondition for safety and potential connecting. Here is the reason: When we are anxious or angry, our pupil's contract and become smaller. When we are relaxed and feeling safe, our pupils relax and get larger. Our brains, outside of our awareness, can detect the size of our partner's pupils. In polyvagal theory this is called neuro-ception. If their pupils are relaxed, the partners' brains will read each other as "open" and "safe." If they are contracted, their brains will read each other as "closed" and "dangerous," and that will determine the level of vulnerability they will have with each other. An amazing fact: three to five deep breaths in synch will relax the pupils. This practice helps partners feel safer with each other before they begin the Dialogue.[8]

Express a one-way appreciation: After they have gone through the setup process and the sender asks for an appointment, the sender does a one-way appreciation and the receiver mirrors it back and checks for accuracy. The receiver does NOT ask, "Is there more?" But they do say: "Thanks for your appreciation," and the sender responds with "Thanks for receiving it."

Step One: Mirroring

Now that the setup is complete, you can proceed to the first step of Dialogue—mirroring. Mirroring and paraphrasing have been a part of couples counseling for decades, dating back to early couples education workshops conducted by David Mace in the 1960s (Mace, 1960.) It has been used as a way to determine if the sending partner was heard accurately. Mirroring a partner's words creates an initial connection and assures that the listening partner, the receiver, is fully engaged and hearing what is being said. When couples are in a reactive conversation, they are not fully hearing the other, rather they are thinking about how to defend themselves. Precise sentence stems that optimize attuned listening between partners are unique to Imago.

Mirroring is an apt term for the act of reflecting back, with as much thoughtfulness and sensitivity as possible, what the receiver has just heard the partner say. Mirroring requires that the receiver act as though they were a mirror, reflecting only what the sender said—nothing more, nothing less.

There are three types of mirroring: flat, convex, and concave. To be accurate, mirroring must be flat; the mirrored message should follow the same contours as the sender's message. *Flat* mirroring (the goal of conscious partners) involves repeating or paraphrasing what the other person said without adding to or emphasizing anything. Our brains have mirror neurons that crave accurate and clear reflection. This is true listening and the type of mirroring that connects. *Convex* mirroring is reflecting back every word but distorting it with additions or interpretations. *Concave* mirroring is focusing on one thing that interests the receiver and omitting the rest. Flat mirroring requires not only that partners practice the skill of paraphrasing but also that both the sender (speaker) and the receiver (listener) take on a special attitude, one characterized by intentionality and good will. Flat mirroring is harder than it sounds: it requires mirroring back messages that might, to the receiver, seem unimportant, illogical, or otherwise at odds with the listener's perspective. It also requires accurately mirroring the sender's emotional tone and intensity.

Hearing your own message mirrored back to you accurately and completely, with all its emotional overtones included, cannot fail to give you the impression that the listener is, in fact, really listening to you and hearing what you're saying. And that makes your mirror neurons sing and satisfies your "mirror hunger" (Kohut, 1971). The attitude thus conveyed is that your thoughts and feelings, your way of seeing and being in the world, are logical and sane. Remarkably, this may be the first time that some partners have felt heard at all, much less completely heard, by their partner—or by another human being, for that matter. Feeling fully heard is precisely what the first step of the Dialogue is meant to provide.

Partners who have grown up with too little positive attention and too much criticism from caretakers especially need to receive mirroring. If we were rarely listened to as children—if we had little or no sense that our caretaker was fully present with us—we are bound to find it difficult if not impossible to give this to our partner, since we cannot give what we have not received. What many of us never received, and continue to long for, is to see our own deep-seated and inherent goodness reflected in the eyes of another. We needed mirroring when we were an infant and, all along the developmental continuum, when we were trying to discover who we are, how to connect with other people, and how to interact with the world inside of and outside of our home. With sufficient mirroring, we would have been able to fully meet and grow from the challenges awaiting us along the developmental pathway. We would have been able to accept and reconcile all parts of ourselves—our four functions, our strengths, our challenges, and our limitations—and thus see them coalesce into an integrated sense of who we are.

By mirroring one another, partners effectively reverse the nurturing deficits of their childhood; they are providing the very thing that attuned parents give to their children throughout the span of development: the message that you are inherently worthy, important, valuable, and lovable.

Mirroring: Responsibilities of the Receiver

When partners are in Dialogue, they alternate being sender and receiver, in a balanced to-and-fro that is both egalitarian (both have the opportunity to send and to receive) and generous (as reflected in what the listener says to the sender: "Is there more?")

Mirroring is simple, but it's not easy—especially when partners are discussing emotionally laden topics that tend to trigger each other's wounds. Here is an example of how a reactive monologue can get short-circuited by a single, brilliantly timed instance of mirroring.

Imagine the couple we met first, Mark and Diana, are in an import store looking at some merchandise. They are examining an exotic and brilliantly colored wall hanging from Mexico. Mark suggests that they purchase it; to him, it looks like one-of-a-kind. Diana disagrees; she thinks the wall hanging is overpriced.

> **DIANA:** *$500 for this? No way, Mark. It's not worth it, and we can't afford it.*
> **MARK:** *$500 is a steal for this, Diana. And what do you mean "we"? I'll pay for it if you don't want it.*
> **DIANA:** *But that's not the point, Mark. Whatever you buy affects both of us on the bottom line. I don't think we should get it.*

At this point, it is possible that one or the other partner will start to feel triggered. Perhaps this is what is going through Mark's mind:

> **MARK:** *(She's telling me how I should spend money—in fact, how to live my life. I can't let her get away with that, or she'll keep doing it whenever I want to make my own decision about something . . .)*

In the meantime, Diana may be thinking:

> **DIANA:** *(Typical Mark. Always spending lavishly on what he wants, but tight as a locked deadbolt when it comes to giving me something I want! He's thinking only of himself, as usual.)*

Next, imagine the kinds of comments that would come out of their mouths should either decide to put their thoughts into language without first going into Dialogue. Perhaps you would hear something like this:

> MARK: *I have the right to get it if I'm willing to pay for it. You're not my mother, Diana.*

How do you imagine Diana would reply? Would she take offense at Mark's reactive comments, leading her to reply with equal if not greater ire? What if, instead, she mirrored Mark's statements back to him:

> DIANA: *Mark, if I got what you're saying, you like the wall hanging enough to buy it, and you feel as though I'm acting like your mother when I say we shouldn't buy it.*

How do you think Mark would respond to Diana's mirroring (once you picked him up off the floor, because he fainted upon hearing it)? Most likely, Mark would immediately move into a less defensive response with something like this:

> MARK: *Yeah, that's exactly it, Diana. Wow, I'm glad you understand that. I'm sorry if I got too sharp with you about this. It's a sore spot of mine, I guess, being told I can't spend money the way I want . . .*

Mirroring is the soft response that turns away wrath, to paraphrase religious texts. Still, mirroring often is not easy; it requires a lot from the receiver, including:

- focused attention and concentration;
- emotional availability and attunement;
- the replacement of criticism and judgment with curiosity;
- the willingness to temporarily suspend our own perspective to fully consider the viewpoint of our partner;
- ending symbiosis by accepting the fact that our partner experiences some things—including our relationship—differently than we do; and
- the ability to regulate (contain) our own emotional reactions and responses, both verbal and nonverbal, until it's our turn to speak.

Although the receiver/listener/ does much of the heavy lifting in the Imago Dialogue process (and of course gets their own turn at being the sender), the sender also has their share of the hard work.

Mirroring: Responsibilities of the Sender

While the sender benefits from the relief of depositing their thoughts and feelings at the feet of the listening partner, the position of sender comes with its own set of guidelines. These include:

- talking about yourself, not your partner;
- using sender responsibility, that is, using I-statements ("I feel . . . ," "I need . . . ," "I wish . . . ," "I want . . .") rather than you-statements ("You never . . . ," "You won't . . . ," "You are . . .");
- avoiding all shaming, blaming, criticizing, belittling, or invalidating of the partner or their perspective;
- sending short-enough and to-the-point messages that do not overwhelm the receiver;
- talking about one topic, and one topic only, without bringing in other issues;
- avoiding repetition of the same point over and over again once your partner has accurately mirrored it back.

Being a responsible sender is just as essential as being a good receiver.

Imago Dialogue Step 1: Mirroring

After the sender speaks, the receiver:

1. Mirrors: *If I got that, you are saying . . .* or *You are saying that . . .*
2. Checks on the accuracy of the mirroring: *Did I get it?*
3. Expresses curiosity by asking: *Is there more about that?*
4. Summarizes, if there is no more, the sender's entire message: *If I got all of that, you said . . .* and check for accuracy: *Did I get it all?*

Fine-tuning the mirroring

Along with repeating the cycle of sending, receiving, and mirroring, Imago Dialogue includes more subtle substeps that help to enhance the impact of mirroring, which ultimately strengthens the dialogical atmosphere between partners. These include invitation statements made by the receiver after mirroring, such as:

- Did I get it?
- Did I hear you accurately?

This sentence stem is called an accuracy check. Since our brains so easily succumb to our own inner chatter, this accuracy check increases our ability to focus on the other.

After the accuracy check, another powerful fine-tuning is to become curious and use this sentence stem:

- Is there more about that?
- Tell me more about that.

This question conveys that you are not only listening, but also curious about what the other person is experiencing, and you want to hear more. Expressing curiosity shows that you are interested, and your interest deepens the sender's sense of safety in the conversation. With the increase of safety, the sending partner will express more and go deeper into themselves. This is the golden mean of Imago Dialogue. Curiosity facilitates connecting.

After there is "no more," and after the accuracy check, an Imago therapist facilitates the receiver to offer a summary of everything they have heard, but to paraphrase it. The sentence stem goes like this:

- Let me see if I got everything you said . . .
- Did I get it all?

Sentence Stems

Since sentence stems are so important, we will elaborate on them a little by demonstrating their use with the earlier scenario between Mark and Diana. Diana has just finished mirroring Mark, whose response reflects the power of mirroring to circumvent conflict.

Mark: *Yeah, that's exactly it, Diana. Wow, I'm glad you understand that. I'm sorry if I got too sharp with you about this. It's a sore spot of mine, I guess, being told I can't spend money the way I want.*

Diana: *Honestly, I've never heard you talk about this. Would you be willing to tell me more about it?*

(Assuming Mark agrees) Diana: *So this issue about buying things for yourself makes you feel _____?*

The sentence stem in Diana's last statement expresses her interest in what Mark is thinking and feeling, and in the same exchange, she uses a fill-in-the-blank format to encourage Mark to share more with her. (More on this later.) Be aware, however, that using sentence stems is another of the so-called high-level skills that couples are not likely to master right away. That's why the Imago therapist makes heavy use of sentence stems when first teaching and coaching a couple to use the Imago Dialogue. Until the couple has achieved a fairly high level of skill, especially when they are first learning Imago Dialogue, the best way to teach them to use sentence stems is to model it for them. For example, you might offer the sender sentence stems like:

> And that made me feel . . .
> And what that reminds me of from childhood is . . .
> And when that happens, I react by . . .
> When I am afraid that you . . . , I get angry and . . .

Enhancing the Power of Mirroring

Let couples practice mirroring (only) for a while before introducing them to the second and third steps (validation and empathy) of the Dialogue.

Note that different people like to be mirrored in different ways. Some prefer word-for-word mirroring, while others like paraphrasing. Coach the receiver to mirror in the way the sender feels most heard, not the way they do. Most partners have opposite preferences.

Monitor how much the receiver is capable of taking in at any one time, and teach the receiver (listener) to send a signal when they cannot hear any more and need to stop and mirror (for example, putting their hand up gently and saying, "Let me see if I got it thus far . . .").

If partners start to get reactive, take a time out; ask them to breathe, rest, and center themselves before getting back into the Dialogue. When they are ready, have the receiver mirror the last message the sender sent as accurately as possible or have the receiver mirror the sender's affect, for example, "I hear you're feeling really angry with me." Go into receiver role yourself and start to mirror, validate, and empathize, modeling the process and helping both to feel heard. Get the partners back into the Dialogue as soon as possible to stay in good connection with each other. Help partners practice mirroring to the point that it becomes overlearned.

The Challenges and Benefits of Mirroring

Although it may seem simple, hearing and repeating back accurately—without distortion or additions—can be very challenging for partners. It's a muscle that is weak for most of us and can be a mentally and emotionally demanding task. Remember, this is a training for quieting the inner mind (i.e., reactivity) in order to hear the pure voice of another without judgment.

Mirroring is also difficult because it is extremely hard—if not impossible—to give to another what we rarely received. Paul, for example, grew up as the last born in a large, chaotic family led by an alcoholic father and an overwhelmed mother. He was deprived of mirroring early in life, at the time when who "I" am is shaped and formed out of the experiences of being mirrored by others. When Paul tried to mirror his wife Julie, he had to repeatedly ask her to resend it because he could not focus on her message. Also, when he did mirror, he kept guessing what she was really saying (which, of course, only triggered Julie's own similar wound of never being heard). Unfortunately, we cannot give what we have not received. But we can learn how to.

Couples will also report that they feel like they are making fun of their partner by "parroting" them or that their partner is making fun of them. That makes it important to reframe the conversation as a connecting process that creates safety so partners can communicate about their similarities and differences. Having this experience with an empathic and skilled therapist helps couples learn the process and gets them through the awkward initial dialogues.

But having developed, refined, and practiced mirroring as part of our dialogical discussions over the past several decades, we have witnessed the profound impacts of the simple act of mirroring on both the sender and the receiver. We have seen partners, who have never experienced what it feels like to be listened to so closely and to have their own words said back to them, break down in tears because they felt so profoundly moved by the experience. Remarkably, this may be the first time some partners ever feel completely "heard" by their partner. Without an echo, the voice dies.

Research evidence indicates that humans have innate mirror hunger (Kohut, 1971). Mirroring is part of the human longing to experience connecting with others. At any age, when one person mirrors another, it sends the message: "You matter. I care enough to listen to you, to really get you." And it also says: "I am no longer the sole person in the universe. I am acknowledging your separate existence. Your thoughts are important to me." Mirroring effectively starts to reverse the nurturing deficits of childhood—a relational injury dissolved by a relational response.

Mirroring stops destructive patterns in its tracks. With practice, receivers learn to monitor the flow of their internal thoughts and emotional reactions and increase their ability to suspend judgment and replace it with curiosity. When we first introduce mirroring to couples, we ask them to practice it throughout their daily routine. "If I heard you correctly, you said pass the salt. Did I get that? Is there more about that?" That makes mirroring fun while building the listening muscle. We introduce mirroring in our very first session with couples as we guide them to share an appreciation for each other. Simple, positive tasks strengthen the atrophied listening muscle, calms the reactive stance, invites both partners to be present mindfully, and creates the safety necessary to continue the reconnecting process.

Step Two: Validation
One definition of *validate* is "to confirm or establish the truthfulness or soundness of something"; another is "to make somebody feel valued as a

person, or feel that his or her ideas or opinions are worthwhile." The latter definition is precisely what the second step of Imago Dialogue, validation, is meant to do. Very simply, it sends the message from the receiver to the sender, "You make sense, and what makes sense is . . ."

Validation requires the receiver to suspend their own personal truth for a moment and see the "truth" of the sender. This does not mean agreement or surrendering any of one's own "truth." It means that two "truths" can occupy the same space. In fact, no two truths can be the same because of the unique perceptual facilities of each of us. And, further, no one person can know the "Truth" because it cannot be contained by a single mind in a single location. Additionally, pure agreement isn't really possible given that "difference" is the defining feature of everything in the universe. Everyone makes sense from where they stand, and every location has a unique vantage point on the "truth." Both partners stand on what Buber calls "the narrow ridge" (Buber, 1947, p. 184), the space where one has to be both confident in the self and vulnerable to the other as they listen for the reality that both positions can peacefully coexist. Seeing clearly requires an awareness of the emotional filters that can cloud our perceptions of who we believe our partner to be or who we want them to be). It invites entrance into the mental sanctuary of another by looking at the world through their eyes.

Of course, validation may be more difficult to pull off than we're making it sound; in our experience, validation seems to be the most demanding step of the Dialogue for many couples. Yet, it may be the most important step of all, and here's why. Being validated—receiving the explicit message that what we are experiencing makes sense to another—is precisely the opposite of what many of us experience much of the time. Invalidation, unfortunately, is the norm in many kinds of relationships—between parents and children, between boss and employee, among siblings, and between romantic partners. How often have you heard one person say to another, "You're crazy!" or "You shouldn't feel that way," or "That makes no sense"? If you've ever been on the receiving end of an invalidating statement, how did it make you feel? What kind of impact did it have on your communication with the other person? Did it affect your receptivity to hearing the other's perspective? Did it encourage you to share more of your thoughts and feelings? Or did it cause you to withdraw, retreat, and shut down out of fear that, if you were to continue, you'd be greeted with more invalidation?

To reiterate, to validate a message our partner is sending us, we have to leave the comfortable confines of our own personal "truth" to view the world through a different pair of eyes—our partner's eyes. With validation, we enter into our partner's mental sanctum to see what lies within. Next, we try to make sense of our partner's experience, and once we have done that, we articulate to our partner: 1) that their experience make sense to us—*What you're saying makes sense*, and 2) why it makes sense to us—*And what makes sense about it is* _____.

Let us revisit Mark and Diana's conversation about purchasing the wall hanging to see how validation could impact the exchange between these two partners.

> MARK: *I have the right to get it if I'm willing to pay for it. You're not my mother, Diana.*
>
> DIANA: *Mark, what I'm hearing you say is that you like the wall hanging enough to buy it, and that you feel as though I'm acting like your mother when I say we shouldn't buy it.*
>
> MARK: *Yeah, that's exactly it, Diana. Wow, I'm glad you understand that. I'm sorry if I got too sharp with you about this. It's a sore spot of mine, I guess, being told I can't spend my own money the way I want . . .*
>
> DIANA: *If I got that, you have a sore spot about being told that you can't spend your own money. Did I get that?*
>
> MARK: *Yes, you got it.*
>
> DIANA: *Is there more about that?*

(Now, notice what Mark adds here.)

> MARK: *You know, my older brother Jack had a big problem with alcohol when he was a teenager. I was still in grade school, and once this started, it was as though I didn't exist. My parents were constantly worried about him, and it took up all their time and energy to deal with him and his problems. He got arrested a couple of times for underage drinking, and he got in a car accident while drinking when he was about 17. He ended up having to choose between going to jail or going into rehab. It must have cost my parents a fortune to bail him out and pay for his rehab. It took a while, maybe 5 or 6 years, but he finally ended up staying sober. In the meantime, as far as my parents were concerned, I didn't exist. My needs weren't important—only Jack's needs were.*

(Next, Diana *summarizes* Mark's message before moving into the validation step.)

> DIANA: *Let me see if I got everything you're saying. One reason this money issue is triggering to you is because of what happened during the period when your older brother took up all of your parents' time*

and resources. You felt invisible, as though you and your needs didn't exist, as far as your parents were concerned. Did I get that?
MARK: *Yeah, that's it; you got it.*

(Now Diana makes a validation statement.)

DIANA: *Well, that makes sense Mark, that you would react strongly if you perceived me as trying to stop you from buying something that you really want. I can see how that would bring up memories of your parents putting all of the financial resources into your brother while ignoring or overlooking what you felt you needed. Did I get that right?*
MARK: *Yeah, that really hits the bull's-eye!*

As is clear from its positive effects on Mark, validation truly is a gift from the listener to the speaker. The experience of validation begins the process of reversing the messages we received from our childhood caretakers and others who, whether wittingly or not, left us with the impression that we were wrong to feel what we felt or to want what we wanted. But validation is just as much a gift for the one giving it as it is for the receiver. Validation benefits the validating partner because it "pushes" or invites them to relinquish the symbiotic belief that there is only one right way to see thing. And, as symbiotic thinking lessens, differentiation increases.

Validation: Responsibilities of the Receiver (Validator)
- Listen to the speaker's perspective with openness and curiosity rather than judgment.
- Postpone validating the partner's message until you see they actually do make sense; everyone makes sense, but no one sees anything the same way.
- Acknowledge that there is more than one way to view reality.
- Accept that another's perspective is as valid as your own.
- Relinquish the privilege of making your partner wrong for disagreeing with you.
- View validation as an opportunity to grow beyond the limits posed by early life challenges.
- Check out the accuracy of the validation statement.

> **Imago Dialogue Step 2: Validation**
>
> After the sender confirms the accuracy of the receiver's summary, the receiver makes a validation statement:
> *What you're saying makes sense to me, and what makes sense is . . .*
> *You make sense to me. I can see that you think . . . because . . .*

As the therapist, you may find, with some couples, that just at the point where the receiver is ready to validate the sender's message, the receiver cannot come up with a validating statement. There are at least a couple of reasons why this might happen:

1. The receiver has not received enough information to understand the sender's perspective, and they cannot validate what they do not (yet) understand.
2. The receiver is having difficulty containing (putting aside) their own thoughts and feelings enough to make a clear space to understand the sender's message.

In either case, the solution is the same: the sender needs to say more, with the receiver continuing to mirror, until the sender's message makes sense to the receiver—enough sense that they can validate it, that is, see how it is the "truth" for the sender.

Validation: Responsibilities of the Sender
- Send a sufficient amount of information briefly and clearly enough to help the receiver understand your thoughts, feelings, and experience; and
- Accept the validation as a gift from your partner without insisting they give up their own perspective and agree with you or come to think and feel the same way you do.

After the receiver has made a validating statement—"That makes sense to me, and what makes sense is that given what you experienced, you would think . . ."—you, the therapist, should suggest the receiver ask the sender, "Did I get that? Does that feel validating to you?"

Remember, validation is in the ear of the receiver. If the validation statement does not feel validating, it is not. If this happens, as it often does, there's an easy solution; simply ask the validating partner to try again, and again, until the statement feels validating. If it feels validating, it is.

NOTE: Coach receivers who tend to use the word "right" when they are reflecting what they heard to drop that word and simply say, "Did I get it?" This helps facilitate positive dialogue and reduce misunderstandings.

Challenges and Benefits of Validating

Validating the other can be the most demanding step of Imago Dialogue. Most of us are so ingrained in the symbiotic belief that "the world is the way I see it!" that we cannot imagine, much less accept, that another point of view is as valid as our own. But again, validation is not agreement. The goal of an Imago therapist is to help couples discover what distinguishes them from each other and to accept difference without judgment, since difference is reality. Validation is essential to the process of differentiating the other from the self that makes connecting possible.

On occasion, especially when couples are first practicing Imago Dialogue in your office, you may discover a listener who states they are not ready or are unwilling to provide validation to the speaker. This might happen for several reasons, the most likely one being that it may be too soon in the process to expect this of the listening partner, especially if they are in strong disagreement with what is being said. This reason would indicate that the partner is isolated in their symbiotic consciousness. In such cases, we suggest you postpone asking the listener to validate until there have been more rounds of mirroring and, therefore, more information shared between partners. Several rounds of mirroring exchanges create an environment of safety that starts the differentiation process.

Validation pushes credibility by moving from acknowledging difference to assigning validity to difference. "I can see that you have a different point of view" becomes possible with repetitive rounds of mirroring, but accepting the "truth of your point of view" pushes the anxiety button for most people. It raises the specter of *their* invalidity. "How can two different things be 'true'?" is the question of the symbiotic mind. However, regardless of whether one partner can see or understand the perspective of the other, validation is essential if they are to experience sustained connecting. Differentiation is the precondition of connecting.

While some clients may worry that validating the partner may bring about enmeshment or sameness, quite the opposite is true. Validation begins to distinguish "you" from "me." Because the relational paradigm emphasizes healing at the place of meeting, validating is often that place where our being is confirmed and affirmed. As Kenneth Gergen says:

> *It is one thing to relate one's feelings or life experiences; however, it is quite another to gain a sense of the other's affirmation. Because meaning is born in relationship, an individual's expression doesn't*

acquire full significance until supplemented . . . To affirm is to grant worth, to honor the validity of my subjectivity. (Gergen, 2001, p. 704)

Validation is intended as a gift from the listener to the speaker. It is the ultimate affirmation, the negation of negation. The experience of validation reverses the messages we received from our childhood caretakers and others who, wittingly or not, left us with the impression that we were wrong to feel what we felt or to want what we want or to think what we think. On the other hand, validation is also a gift for the one who is providing it. It is the breaking of symbiotic fusion. The validator is freed from the symbiotic illusion of omniscience and is now open, with curiosity, to a world they have never before known.

Step Three: Empathy

While mirroring aims to accurately reflect the content of the sender's message—the what—empathy shifts the focus to how the sender feels, to the emotional experience behind the message. Validation is about thinking and understanding; empathy is about being attuned to the emotions the partner is experiencing.

This third step of the Imago Dialogue, empathy, is an exercise in "feeling with" the other, walking a mile in their moccasins, imagining what the world feels like in their experience. To express empathy, the receiver must first listen for the emotions the partner is experiencing or, if the emotions are not overt, they must listen for feelings that are lying between the lines of what the sender is saying. If the emotions are not visible, the receiver also tries to imagine or intuit how the sender must feel, given the content they just communicated. The receiver may or may not be accurate about what the sender is feeling. The most the receiver can do, as far as expressing accurate empathy, is to 1) listen and mirror carefully and thoroughly; 2) try to tune into the emotions the partner is expressing, whether verbally or nonverbally; 3) and check with the sender to see if the empathy statement was accurate.

Remember, though, that empathy is not the same as imagining how you would feel if you were in your partner's shoes. Rather, to paraphrase one definition, empathy is an imaginative projection into the subjectivity of the other. This differs from imagining what you would feel in that situation. The latter is called sympathy.

Let us clarify a bit what we mean by empathy, which we view at two distinct levels: cognitive empathy and participatory empathy (Staub, 1987). Empathy can be challenging to imagine, much less to experience, when one or both partners are feeling hurt and angry because of a transaction that touched a tender memory or challenged one's symbiotic views. In cases when the speaker's feelings about their experiences make no impact on the listener, it is important that the therapist regulate the energy between the partners with eye contact, deep breathing, and asking the resistant partner, whether they can feel it or not, to take a moment and use their imagination to create an image of what it must feel like to have had that experience. At the first level, cognitive empathy, the receiver imagines the affective world of the sender and articulates it to the sender. "And given all that, I can imagine you might feel _____ ." Most of the time, the cognitive shift from words to images, from the left brain to the right brain, can result in cognitive, if not affective, mirroring.

At the second level, participatory empathy, the receiver, while holding on to their own experience, also experiences the sender's feelings. This second level of empathy communicates, "I understand what you understand because I am experiencing what you are experiencing, although I remain myself." Ultimately, participatory empathy becomes a feature of the Space-Between, and the contents become secondary to the partners' contact. This is what we mean by an empathic acceptance of the other as delineated from the self.

Through empathic attunement, couples experience safety, which restores connecting. After engaging in this process for a while, many couples cannot recall the precipitating incident that ignited their conflict; when they do remember it, they typically discover that it involved an actual or threatened connectional rupture. Still, once they've engaged in Imago Dialogue, there is little need to rehash what happened because, through the Dialogue process, connecting has been restored.

Typically, empathy comes immediately after validation. To illustrate, let us briefly return, once again, to Mark and Diana.

> DIANA: *Well, it makes perfect sense to me, Mark, that you would react strongly if you perceived me as trying to stop you from buying something that you really want. I can see how that would bring up memories of your parents putting all of the financial resources into your brother while ignoring or overlooking what you felt you needed. Do I have that?*
> MARK: *Yeah, that really hits the bull's-eye!*

Next, Diana moves into the third step, empathy.

> DIANA: *I can imagine, then, that when we had that exchange, where you heard me placing unfair limits on you as far as buying the wall-hanging, you might have felt irritated, maybe angry.*

NOTE 1: It is important to help couples distinguish feelings from thoughts. For instance, in the above Dialogue, Diana might have said: *you felt insulted or patronized* rather than *angry about being insulted or patronized.*

NOTE 2: Note that Diana now checks on the accuracy of her empathy statement.

> DIANA: *Did I get that?*
> MARK: *Well, not exactly.*
> DIANA: *Will you send it again or send what I missed?*
> MARK: *Maybe it was more like feeling hurt and deprived, or over-looked, like you were telling me I didn't deserve to get something I wanted.*
> DIANA: *So when I said we shouldn't buy the wall-hanging, you felt deprived, as though I didn't want you to have something you wanted, and that made you feel unimportant, unworthy, or over-looked. Did I get those feelings?*
> MARK: *That's right.*

When all three steps are completed, the sender thanks the partner for listening and the receiver thanks the partner for sharing followed by a 1-minute hug. Then they switch roles. The sender now becomes the receiver and the receiver now becomes the sender. The new sender starts with expressing an appreciation for their partner's point of view and then moves into stating their view or experience of the subject matter. The new sender, however, cannot criticize or negate the just stated reality of their partner but rather focuses on their own perspective. To do otherwise would imme-diately dispel the safety created in the Space-Between. For example, Diana would not now accuse Mark of being frivolous, but she may share with him her perspective that spending $500 on some artwork triggers her concern around having enough money to pay the upcoming property taxes. Her need for financial security can stand side by side with his need for being seen. One reality does not negate the other.

At bottom, empathy's aims are the same as those for the entire Imago Dialogue. These goals are both uncommon and profound. Every step—mirroring, validation, and empathy—offers both sender and receiver a golden opportunity for something that cannot be bought with money: for the listener, differentiation and connecting; and for the sender, con-necting and differentiation. Expressing empathy elicits the same internal shift as the rest of the Imago Dialogue: a movement through the dialogi-cal dance toward restoring connecting and full aliveness. When you're in the dialogical stance, empathy becomes not only possible, but also relatively easy.

This dialogical stance entails:

- taking full responsibility for our feelings;
- maintaining a no-blame, no-shame position when talking about frustrations with our partner;
- reclaiming our lost-self aspects by learning to love in our partner what we hate in ourselves;
- embracing, rather than rejecting, the differences between ourselves and our partner; and
- distinguishing between the deed and the doer, between what our partner says or does and the person our partner inherently is.

Imago Dialogue Step 3: Empathy

After the sender confirms the accuracy of the validation statement, sentence stems partners can use to express empathy:

1. *Based on what you said, I imagine you might feel* . . . (use emotional terms: *hurt, frustrated, disappointed, lonely, relieved, relaxed, etc.*)
2. Checks on the accuracy of the empathy: *Did I get that? Or Did I get your feeling?*
3. If empathy was accurate: *Are there other feelings?*

Empathy: Responsibilities of the Receiver

Expressing accurate empathy (and if it is not accurate, it is not empathy) requires us to:

- reflect back what our partner said but also what they did not say about how they feel; in other words, we may need to read between the lines;
- increase our "feeling vocabulary" beyond the basics of mad, sad, glad, hurt, angry, and so forth so that we can better articulate our partner's emotions, as well as our own;
- check out the accuracy of our empathy statement: "Did I get your feelings?";
- give up the symbiotic notion that our partner feels the same way we would in that situation; and
- relinquish the certainty that we must be correct about what our partner is feeling.

Empathy: Responsibilities of the Sender
Receiving empathy requires us to:

- give honest feedback on the accuracy of the partner's empathy statement;
- suggest other, more accurate feeling words if the partner's empathy statement wasn't accurate; and
- open up to receiving the gift of empathy, not blocking nor rejecting the experience.

The Challenges and Benefits of Empathizing
Like validation, empathy can be harder to deliver than it might sound here. For example, you might find occasions where the sender message is virtually devoid of emotional overtones. In such cases, as the therapist, you can make suggestions to the sender by using sentence stems like, "And that made me feel . . ." Although senders may have difficulty expressing or confirming feelings, most of the challenges with empathizing revolve around the receiver. For example, the receiver may:

- be internally judging the sender for feeling the way they do;
- be reacting to feelings of guilt for having "caused" the partner's painful emotions;
- feel uncomfortable expressing strong emotions due to socialization experiences; and/or
- be afraid of getting absorbed into the partner's hurt and misery, especially if they had an upbringing with similarly painful characteristics.

But again, starting with positive messages, gentle guidance, practice, and time, your couples will overcome these challenges. The physical aspect of this process cannot be underestimated and is just as important as the emotional and verbal aspects of Imago therapy.

Research shows how empathy works neurologically. In short, when an observer encounters someone in pain, their body experiences the felt aspect and resonates with the observed. Quickly, the prefrontal cortex steps in to become aware of the situation, make sense of the information, and it recognizes the feelings are not localized and then cognitively understands that the feelings belong to someone else—a continual circuit from interoception (becoming aware of what you are feeling in your own body) to interpretation (understanding that the felt experience is not actually within the observer) to attribution (attributing the feelings to the observed (Siegel, 2007; Carr et al., 2003).

The mirror neurons are part of a larger resonance circuit that enables us to feel another's feelings and not get lost in their internal states. We can resonate and not become fused with another person. This resonance allows us to "feel felt" by the other person and that person can "feel felt" by us. This is quite different from *becoming* the other person—of excessive linkage without differentiation. Integration requires that we maintain both "linkage and differentiation." (Siegel, 2020).[9] Empathy furthers the differentiation process and is the doorway to our humanness. And finally, as you will see later, it is also the portal for change.

A Short History of Empathy
Empathy is a late comer to our capacity, as a species, to connect with others vicariously. It was not discussed as a human ability in the psychological literature until the late 1800s, when German artist and philosophers began experimenting with what they called *Einfühlung* or "feeling into" (Visher, 1873; Montag et al., 2008). Initially a way of looking at art aesthetically, philosopher Theodor Lipps used the term "inner imitation" to describe how we might feel when we watch someone do something dangerous, like a trapeze artist—our own bodies react as if it is precariously hanging from the ceiling. We had an *Einfühlung*, or empathic resonance, with the other in the dangerous situation. Lipps' work was eclipsed by the emerging behaviorism that became far more prevalent in that time period, but he did give us the basis of understanding that humans can understand viscerally what another may be feeling. As mentioned previously, humanist and dialogical psychotherapists began using empathy in their work, and in the 1980s, feminist psychologists began to understand the importance of empathy, especially in understanding women's development (Gilligan, 1982).

Most of us in this field know about empathy. We were taught it in our graduate programs and practice it daily with our clients, if not with our partners. Most therapists know that listening and empathy skills, combined with an active treatment plan that includes new skills, yield the best outcomes in treatment. However, while we can be great models of empathy ourselves, most of our treatment models seldom encourage that we teach empathy skills to our clients.

IMAGO DIALOGUE AS A CONNECTING PROCESS

Imago Dialogue's impact isn't confined to better communication. In fact, its most profound benefits don't show up so much in what couples discuss; the real power lies, rather, in restoring their connectional rupture and their unrestored rupture from childhood. When Imago Dialogue helps couples create safety so they can connect, it fixes the rupture that has occurred within the partnership as well as the original rupture that each of the partners suffered in childhood, long before the two ever laid eyes on each other, fell in love, and started the boxing match known as the power struggle.

But how, specifically, does Dialogue restore connecting, the original condition before the rupture? Part of the explanation lies in one of the theories we touched upon previously. Hans Kohut, founder of Self Psychology, discusses, like Imago theory, our human need to be seen, or mirrored, the absence of which leaves us with mirror hunger. Being mirrored gradually leaves an impression on children that contributes significantly to their healthy development: You are seen. Mirroring is an essential nutrient for a cohesive and integrated psyche and a connected relationship. When a child's perceptions are mirrored back to them, the child integrates the myriad and diverse self-aspects that emerge over the course of development.

In real life, though, good mirroring is in very short supply. Children that get it at all generally get it selectively, offered only on the condition that child's behavior meets the standards of the caretaker. At other times the mirroring may be deflective, missing the mark as far as affirming the child for who they are. In any case, when mirroring is insufficient, the child doesn't quite get the message that they are inherently valuable, and intrinsically worthy of love.

Here's one scenario that demonstrates the kind of impact that deficient mirroring can have on a child: a four-year-old boy, Chris, was lying in bed, unable to sleep, until very late one night. He could hear every word of the fight his parents were having in the bedroom next door to his. He also could hear them calling each other names and saying words like "hate" and "divorce." The little boy doesn't feel safe enough, out of the reasonable fear of disturbing a hornet's nest, to go to his parents for comfort or solace. He covers his head with his pillow and pretends that what he hears isn't happening. The next day, he summons up the courage to timidly ask his mother what the fight last night was about. His mother, feeling distressed and defensive over what is going on in her relationship, tells Chris that it's none of his business, and that he shouldn't worry about it. She adds that he shouldn't, in fact, be eavesdropping on his parents' "private conversations." At this point, not only will Chris continue to bear the burden of their childish imaginings about their parents' relational demise, but they also hears the message that what he heard and experienced the previous night was, in his mother's eyes, "wrong." Their perception was negated, his experience was dismissed.

It should be no surprise, then, that mirror-hungry children grow up with an internal ambiance of confusion, self-doubt, apprehension, and anxiety. In the absence of the self-confirming messages provided by mirroring—messages like, "You matter," "You can think for yourself," "You make sense," and so forth—the child grows up mistrusting their own perceptions and self-censoring their intuitive insights. These effects of mirroring deficiency are especially potent during the period when a child isn't old enough or cognitively sophisticated enough to make sense of their experiences.

This is why children have to come up with a fail-safe method for defending their tender psyches against the anxiety, or even the chaos, that can be fomented within the tender psyche of a child like Chris. That's where the defensive structure (or character structure), that collection of strategies we use to shield ourselves from the fallout of our caretaker's deficiencies, comes in. Whether we learned to protect ourselves by maximizing our energy—fighting back, attacking, getting scary, and so forth—or whether we preferred to minimize—by laying low and pretending all was well, dismissing or denying our feelings—we somehow manage to stay emotionally intact long enough to make it to the age when we're cognitively sophisticated enough to fashion more mature ways of handling disappointment, discouragement, and other normal human emotions. The problem is, though, that upon reaching the age of physical maturity, most of us make few if any modifications to our defensive strategies. We continue to rely on our old, tried and true childhood methods of coping with disappointment, fear, anxiety, anger, and other problematic emotions that invariably crop up, especially once we have gotten invested in a long-term, committed structure. *Childhood defenses, though, only go so far. They may diminish pain, and they may deny reality, but they rid us of neither.*

Defenses certainly do not ameliorate the long-term effects of childhood challenges, and in fact only exacerbate them: the more defensive we are, the greater the challenge's impact on us will be, leading to the need for greater defensiveness, and so on. When we get hurt, our integration and cohesiveness break down, slowly but surely. Then our challenges and our defenses against them become crystallized as a part of our character structure. It is those wounds and that structure that cast additional fuel on the flames of the power struggle.

There is, however, a solution, one that you very well may have already experienced with your own partner, or with another human being, for that matter. The antidote for symbioses, the cognitive–emotional consequence of connectional rupture, is empathy. So important is empathy to Imago Dialogue that it is embedded in its very structure, as the third and final step.

THE IMAGO DIALOGUE AS A
TRANSFORMATIONAL PROCESS

Having looked at the Imago Dialogue at its first two levels—as a communication technique and as a connecting process—we're ready to extend our perspective to include the deepest level of Imago Dialogue—where it has the impact of transforming the very structure of partnership. Imago Dialogue accomplishes this transformation by making the following shifts:

- from monologue to dialogue;
- from the past to the present;
- from the lower brain to the higher brain; and
- from the vertical to the horizontal.

Imago Dialogue, along with every other process in Imago therapy, throws off the vertical model's confines and turns the conversation away from the hierarchical structure toward the horizontal direction. Horizontal conversations mean that the two members of a couple are essentially equal. With this equality—and only with this equality—safe and empathic connecting, and thus a relationship between equal partners, becomes possible. This empathy fosters hope, and this hope is a gift that you, the therapist, have helped to facilitate.

What once seemed impossible now becomes possible for the romantic partners, including, first and foremost, the relaxation of the defensive structures that keep the other's messages out. Now that the conversation feels safe, those defenses are no longer needed; no defenses are necessary when we are not feeling threatened. In turn, speaking from a non-defended position brings each partner into a state of "presence" with each other, the state that is equated with true intimacy and original connecting. Simultaneously, this mutual experience of presence in the Space-Between restores the connectional rupture inflicted by emotionally or physically absent caretaking, thereby changing the past by restructuring the conversation in the present.

Once people shift out of the vertical into the horizontal position, they begin to approach each other from a different position, one of curiosity and of "power with," rather than judgment and "power over." This results in the dissipation of any danger in the Space-Between, which becomes permeated, instead, with safety. Once safety is established, what seemed impossible during the power struggle becomes possible. Most astonishing for couples is the promise of the restoration of their disrupted connection. Only when two partners encounter each other from a dialogical position—defenses down, hearts open—can they risk expressing their most vulnerable feelings to each other. Along with those feelings come long-forgotten thoughts and memories, denied impulses, and unmet yearnings, all of them remaining below the surface of our consciousness, until now. When the connectional rupture between partners is restored, the connectional rupture of each partner during childhood is also repaired.

This is precisely what the Imago Dialogue does: it becomes a container, a safe but powerful cauldron in which both the surface and depth of felt experience are symbolized and thus become integrated into our sense of self. In Imago Dialogue, we reach deep down into our storehouse of childhood pain and process it, and its meaning for us, with our partner in the role of a safe and nurturing substitute for the caretakers who, in one way or another, failed us. When the past takes on new meaning, so does the narrative of the present romantic partnership. By sharing our story using Imago Dialogue, both our past and our present are transformed, and we live in a new consciousness, a knowing "with" our partner rather than a knowing "about" them.

All this occurs not only at the psychological level but simultaneously at the level of our neurobiology, as a growing body of research demonstrates (Siegel, 2012; Siegel, 2020). As partners process their unlanguaged pain using Imago Dialogue, at the psychological level the material rises from unconsciousness into consciousness, and cognitively (at the mental level) from implicit to explicit memory. This cognitive shift from unconscious to conscious, from the ineffable to the languaged, brings our forgotten memories back into the light of our awareness, thereby revealing to us the truth, which enables us to become whole and free. Like the joy of finding something precious that we'd lost long ago, reconnecting with what has been forgotten and with our partner brings the heightened well-being that comes from the restoration of original connecting.

Accepting our partner without judgment—as different from us, but not wrong—comes with yet another shocking recognition—the otherness of the other. In other words, we "get" the otherness of our partner, and understanding this one crucial point: otherness has the power to transform how we live in the world of others. Our one-person reality turns into a two-person reality; curiosity replaces criticism, and we no longer need to be at the center, because we realize that, in actuality, there is no center for us to occupy. The only perspective left standing is the one that sees everyone, including ourselves, as in relationship with everything else.

The Benefits of Dialogue

Imago clinical practice focuses on helping couples change the structure and content of their conversation so that six essential ingredients of intimacy are established. These six elements are elaborated throughout the book. Here they are in summary:

1. Dialogue turns the conversation from an exchange of parallel monologues into a mutual sharing. People take turns talking and listening, and in so doing, they establish equality, safety, and connecting.

2. Dialogue facilitates differentiation by allowing each partner to become present to the other as a distinct person. Just as connection is ontological, so is difference. There is no true connection without the epiphany of the "otherness" of the partner and a gradual progression toward the important developmental state of differentiation. At some point in Dialogue, it hits them, "My partner is not me." As mentioned above, the work partners do to differentiate and reconnect will end up changing the chemistry of their brains.

3. Dialogue regulates negative exchanges by helping couples get rid of judgment—the destroyer of intimacy. This means eliminating all negativity, since negativity stimulates anxiety, signals danger, and thus activates defensiveness, which is the greatest barrier to intimacy.

4. Dialogue replaces judgment with curiosity. You can't be negative when you are curious. Wondering and wanting to know more is antithetical to judging and criticizing.

5. Dialogue is a structured way to acknowledge and work through conflicts. Partners now have a safe way to bring concerns into the relationship so they can be heard and handled.

6. Dialogue provides a structure for infusing relationships with positive feelings. Successful intimate partnerships are characterized by safety and passion, comfort and excitement, plus appreciation, admiration, acceptance, humor, and just plain fun.

In a therapeutic situation, Imago Dialogue is deployed carefully for the purpose of restoring connecting. If the rules are followed and the technique is actively practiced, Imago Dialogue will be the engine of transformation that leads to conscious partnership. Just as no one would expect to be a good tennis player without diligently exercising the muscles that get the ball over the net, no one can expect a complete change in perception and communication without dutiful practice of the rules of Dialogue. Once learned, these conversations can be used for many purposes: establishing pleasant interactions, exchanging information, negotiating tricky compromises, airing grievances, and so on. With Imago Dialogue as the truck, you can take any cargo where you want it to go.

The Meta-Effects of Dialogue

In addition to the above benefits, Imago Dialogue offers couples impactful therapeutic outcomes:

- **Provides Safety:** The unholy trinity of negativity, anxiety, and defensiveness cannot survive inside the dialogical structure. The "rules of engagement" disallow any shame, blame, or criticism. The structure and sequence help partners predict what is coming next, and that ensures that each partner's voice will be heard, understood, and honored.

- **Breaks Symbiotic Fusion and Results in Differentiation:** Symbiotic thinking and the Dialogue process cannot coexist. The receiver internalizes the subjectivity of the sender, thus experiencing that "you are not me and that's OK." As symbiosis decreases, differentiation, the maturational pearl of great worth, emerges.

- **Facilitates Connecting and Wholeness:** Connecting is what we achieve when we provide our romantic partner with the kind of love and nurturing they were deprived of by imperfectly attuned caretakers. When we experience connection with our partner, we simultaneously experience our connection with the universe. When we stretch (i.e., move past our defensive resistance) to give our partner what is most difficult for us to produce, undeveloped capacities and strengths emerge that empower us to thrive in our relationships. Understanding what senders need (connecting) and stretching into meeting those needs (wholeness) are the profound outcomes of Imago Dialogue.

- **Promotes Brain Integration:** Dialogue, with its calming and centering measures, brings both sender and receiver back into a regulated state. Additionally, during the complex tasks of mirroring, validating, and empathizing, both left (cognitive) and right (affective) hemispheres of the brain are working together in a balanced and integrated way. The structure of the Imago Dialogue consciously guides the couple from the cognitive structure of mirroring to the dual cognitive and affective stance of validation to the affective experience of empathy.

Finally, Imago Dialogue utilizes frontal cortex processes such as concentration, attention, and the screening out of irrelevant stimuli. This focus on the partner's message is similar to the positive effects of "being present," mindfulness, or meditation. Thus, Dialogue strengthens the couple's ability to:

- hold the tension of the unknown;

- move from "lower brain" reactivity to "higher brain" intentionality (from a dysregulated to a regulated state);
- balance left and right brain hemispheres; and
- practice "presence."

The Ultimate Restoration

Imago Dialogue achieves all of these outcomes: safety, decreased anxiety, relaxed defenses, dismantled symbiotic fusion, enhanced differentiation, and the reciprocal exchange of restoring connecting, thus producing growth. Additionally, it sheds the confines of the vertical model. Couples share equal power and equal responsibility and begin to approach each other from a different position, one of curiosity and of "power with," rather than judgment and "power over," as they move into consciousness and intentionality.

With practice, Imago Dialogue begins to feel comfortable, like an old pair of shoes or an old but reliable vehicle that is guaranteed to get you where you want to go. Imago Dialogue can be used to discuss anything: to share the joys and sorrows of the day; to clear up a misunderstanding; to plan a vacation; and, among many other things, to discuss the couple's hopes and dreams. The structure itself moves from "practicing dialogue" to "being dialogical" or, more accurately, being relational. And when couples are relational, another profound thing happens: the new relationship restores connecting lost in the early childhood rupture. In that Space-Between, couples find their "ontological dimension," their reason for being, rather than their external or internal psychological dimensions.

Dialogue is the language of this Space-Between. And in the Space-Between, provincialism is dissolved by diversity. Opposition is replaced by partnership. The ME is replaced with an US. Isolation is replaced with a sense of belonging, and anxiety is replaced with full aliveness, joy and wonder.

THE RESISTANCE TO DIALOGUE

In addition to the challenges we mentioned in the individual steps, Dialogue itself will often be met with resistance. The two biggest complaints:

1. No one talks this way!
2. It takes sooooooo long!

Stilted structure: The set structure of the Dialogue is likely to strike some couples as an unnatural, even stultifying way to converse. And they may rebel against it. And that is ok. The challenge of the therapist in that moment is to use the mirroring process to deal with the objection and encourage the couple to experiment. We find it helpful to characterize the process as a skill, and like any other skill, it requires learning and practicing certain behaviors until they are integrated. To become proficient in keyboarding, coding, skiing, speaking a new language, or playing the piano requires consistent practice to achieve proficiency. With practice, Dialogue becomes less artificial and more natural and, eventually, the new language of the couple.

Takes too long: Actually, Imago Dialogue is the long way that makes the whole trip shorter. Couples have to find the time to fully listen rather than take the short cut of refuting and cutting the other off. And while it may take longer to have these conversations, they are ultimately more efficient, as small frustrations don't quickly spiral out of control into a period of prolonged, resentful silence. It also ultimately puts an end to the "core scene"— the reoccurring fight where the amygdala hijacks the prefrontal cortex.

Yes, Dialogue is awkward and tedious, at first. And it is also absolutely necessary, humbling, and transformational.

SUMMARY

We can summarize the overarching goal of Imago Relationship Therapy in these few words: to create a tectonic shift in the structure and content of the couple's conversations.

How is this done? The therapist facilitates Imago Dialogue, whose horizontal structure assures equality between partners. Changing the content of the structure to acceptance and curiosity inserts safety into the Space-Between. Through Imago Dialogue, we speak aloud what we haven't felt safe enough to say until now. What we put into words becomes transformed by our saying it, and once transformed, becomes part of our narrative. All of these shifts—from vertical to horizontal communication, from hierarchical to egalitarian, from the unlanguaged to the languaged, and from the past to the present—work toward a single goal, which is to make history, history. Seeing the present as the present also means that we see our partner as our partner and for who our partner truly is, right now. Once we are able to tell the difference between the past and the present, we will stop mistaking our partner for our parent.

We have seen that when couples practice Dialogue, they restore connecting. Yet Imago Dialogue has a potential impact that is far more significant: what it is capable of doing is no less than tearing down the structure of a couple's unconscious relationship and replacing it with a new structure— a conscious partnership. The Imago Dialogue now becomes a way of life, of being in the world; that is, like the Dialogue itself, life becomes conscious and intentional. While we say Imago Dialogue improves a relationship, really it creates a new structure for relationship, a transformation. When the relational structure changes, eventually so do the character structures of the partners. This leads to the potential for a broader societal transformation because when couples are transformed, so are their children and, eventually, their children's children. Ultimately, these transformations continue to emanate outward, leaving their impact on the greater community and the society in which the conscious couple lives, fomenting a new relational civilization.

Tips for Imago Dialogue

- Start the first session by introducing mirroring.
- People like to be mirrored in different ways. Some prefer word-for-word mirroring, while others like paraphrasing. Coach the receiver to mirror in the way the sender feels most heard.
- Pay attention to how much the receiver is able to hear at any one time. Advise the receiver to indicate when they are "full," and cannot take in any more information, by using a verbal or nonverbal cue (e.g., the "time" signal) and saying, "I would like to mirror what I have gotten so far."
- If partners get reactive, move them back into process as quickly as possible by calling a pause for one or both. Help them use deep breathing, mantras, safe-place visualization, or other centering techniques to reduce reactivity and promote tension release. Then gently bring them back into Dialogue. If necessary, go into the receiver role yourself and start to mirror, validate, and empathize, modeling the process and helping both partners to feel heard. Get partners back into connection with each other as soon as possible by engaging directly with each other.
- Help partners practice Dialoguing and provide between-session assignments with the goal that it becomes overlearned.
- Keep attuned for indications of hidden or unconscious triggers (such as nonverbal cues).
- Use deepening sentence stems such as:
  - And what that reminds me of from childhood is . . .
  - And when that happens, I tell myself . . ., and then I decide that . . .

You will learn more about these deepening statements in the coming chapters.

10

The Imago Therapist

Facilitator of Connecting

We therapists have been trained to help our clients understand their predicament and achieve their goals without the imposition of our assumptions and wishes, only our expertise. The prime directive is the facilitation of our client's natural progress toward their objectives, which they have been unable to sustain on their own. But the reality is that we do not see our clients objectively, nor do our clients see themselves accurately.

We cannot help but view others through the filter of our personal, psychological, and cultural assumptions, and they view themselves and their suffering through their same sort of lens. We all, consciously or unconsciously view the universe in which we live, how it works, and what we have to do to survive, and hopefully thrive, in it through a personal lens shaped by the culture. And we each hold a theory about human nature, and thus a theory of change. For example, with regard to human nature, do we have an essential nature hidden behind our actions so that our actions are expressions of our nature, making change difficult? Are we like the Newtonian atom that is uncuttable and impermeable, or like the quantum, in constant change with infinite potential? In other words, is what we *do* an expression of who we *are*? Or, is our nature what we *do* in any given moment, changing constantly in response to our environment? If so, we have no fixed nature and thus can change by altering our behavior? In other words, is what we *are* based on what we *do*? Or is what we do based upon what we are?

What is your theory of human nature and your theory of change?

In this same vein, we tend to see our clients through some sort of diagnostic lens. We may get some comfort, and perhaps confidence, in presuming to "know" what we are looking at and the problem to be solved. Whether we know it consciously or not, we have a "theory of everything" behind the interventions we select to move them toward some view of mental/emotional health, and we have a view of what that is. And we have a view of our role in that process. And, in our view, we should! Otherwise, we should not be in the chair! And we should hold it lightly, because our next interaction with this client or the next one may raise doubts about its veracity. However, since this is how the mind functions, it holds true for how couples look at each other and at the therapist, as well as how therapists look at couples.

While it may seem abstract and irrelevant, metatheory or worldview is the most concrete aspect of clinical work, because it determines our theory about people—whether it be that they are what they do or that there is a "nature" behind what they do that can be discovered. It also guides our interactions with them and the outcomes we anticipate or get: how we position them in our office (they sit side by side on a couch or face each other in separate chairs); what questions we ask them about their situation; whether we take a waiting, agentive, or responsive stance; how we answer their questions (or whether we answer them); and our ultimate assessment of their progress with us. But, we do not and cannot see what is *really there.*

Like the quantum observer effect, what shows itself to us depends upon how we look. We look at everything through an interpretative filter. While we cannot change that propensity of our minds, we can know that we have it and what our perspective is, and we have, in our view, a professional and moral responsibility to do so. And, practically, if something is not working, we cannot change it unless we understand why we are doing what think we are doing.

Despite the fact that this epistemological stance was prefigured when Copernicus theorized and Galileo confirmed that we live in a heliocentric solar system rather than a geocentric centered one, the impact of the interpretative nature of the mind did not impact the human sciences much until around the 1940s when Kurt Lewin developed his "field theory," which posited that human behavior is a function of its social context (Lewin, 1951). "Naïve realism," which described the human tendency to believe that we see the world around us objectively and that people who disagree with us must be uninformed, irrational, or biased, was introduced in social psychology in the 1990s (Ross & Ward, 1995). And symbiosis, which is a radically egocentric bias, has just been identified as the universal filter through which all things pass.

These scholars contend that our minds interpret rather than objectively observe what we see. They are attempting to put an end to centuries of reliance on the correspondence theory of truth—that there is a one-to-one correlation between observation and knowledge—and to establish, in all disciplines, the awareness that all mental functions are hermeneutical: all perceptions are interpretations rather than pure descriptions.

In Imago, we see a similarity, or perhaps an identity, between naïve realism and symbiotic consciousness. The latter, as you may recall, was created by ruptured connecting in childhood, which triggered the pain of anxiety that produced self-absorption, with consequent loss of "otherness," and with that the loss of empathy, resulting in objectification and the tendency toward judgmental predication without experiencing the isolation of experience from what is external to oneself. The emotional pain of disconnection that produces the symbiotic state amplifies our natural human tendency to believe that what we see, is there.

The case that our minds objectively are innately interpretative is also made by phenomenological philosopher, Maurice Merleau-Ponty (2002), and the contemporary tradition of phenomenological philosophy which challenged two thousand years of rationalistic philosophy which posited that, not only is what we see there, our rational minds can know it objectively. For phenomenology, our minds are hermeneutic by nature. We cannot NOT have our assumptions. Our minds automatically connect the dots of data we believe we are observing and weaves them into models of reality without our active participation. Merleau-Ponty states that we can know we have assumptions, and we can "bracket" them and change them in the face of new observations, but we cannot dispense with the fact that our minds are interpretative by nature rather than descriptive. Preceding him, the philosopher, Immanuel Kant (1999), argued that the "thing in itself" eludes us. Like quantum observation and symbiosis, we can only see what our minds put there. The structure of our brain and the quality of our experience filter what we see in such a way that "what is" is unavailable to us and, paradoxically, our client's actual experience is unavailable to them, directly.

As we indicated earlier, quantum physics added another layer to this discussion with the discovery of the "observer effect," which posits that observation/perception is not only interpretative but also impacts the behavior of what is observed and how what is observed shows itself to us. The impact of observation on behavior has also been demonstrated in another experiment called the Hawthorne Effect, the discovery that individuals alter their behavior in response to being observed. These discoveries have tremendous implications for relational theory and therapy, as well as for understanding the dynamics of intimate partnerships. To complicate things a bit more, it turns out, according to the neurosciences, that memory itself is a construction (Fivush & Haden, 2003). Given all of this, it behooves us to check our perceptions and be humble with our assertions regarding the "truth," and to invite our clients to be tentative in what they believe about their partners, and even about themselves, and to be tentative in what we believe about them—they may unconsciously oblige us by becoming as we see them or may sense the frame we put them in and resist us, or fire us.

DISCOVERING YOUR OWN METATHEORY

Since interpretation is unavoidable, we deem it essential that Imago therapists become conscious of their own metatheory—their fundamental assumptions—in the service of being intentional and self-aware in clinical practice. We presented Imago metatheory earlier, and now we invite you to discover yours.

When we know why we are doing what we are doing (our assumption behind our interventions), we protect our clients from unexamined assumptions and blind interventions. At the same time, we empower ourselves to invent new clinical interventions and test their effectiveness against the theory, refining and changing both in a creative oscillation between theory and practice. Theory guides therapy, and therapy informs theory in an ongoing process of cocreation. This has been the methodology of the construction of Imago theory and therapy from the beginning.

The first thing to do on the path to unearthing your metatheory is to reflect on what you believe about the nature of the universe—not a small topic. The second is to reflect on what you believe about human nature, which you may not think about very often; we may not think on it unless someone has done something horrible or wonderful that compels us to ask that question. The third is to reflect on your view of the source and cause of human suffering, which is operative in your theory of why relationships fall apart. The fourth part of your metatheory is your view of what constitutes a thriving relationship and, lastly, how it is created, since that is what you are up to.

What Do You Believe About the Nature of the Universe?
Since we suggest you think about this in the context of other views of the universe, not just your own opinion, you may want to start by remembering the discussion of Imago metatheory and comparing or contrasting what you believe in relation to it. Are the metatheories similar, identical, different, or incompatible? The answer may help you decide whether you want to practice Imago therapy!

You may want to look again at the Introduction and Chapter 1 to recall the history behind psychotherapy that we located in classical physics and the theory of the separate self with a focus on the Space-Within. That is the current universe in which most people live, including therapists, whether they ever think about it or not. You may or may not live there. Or you may live in the only other universe available, the quantum universe, and you may be engaged in its implications for life and therapy, as we are.

Imago therapy is looks at the universe and the human situation through this quantum view. We are conscious participants in a conscious universe in which everything is interacting and connecting with everything, all the way up and all the way down. That means that our interactions impact the field and the interactions of others impact us, since we are all in the field and it is in us. The isolation and determinism of the materialistic universe of Newton has been replaced with choice and responsiveness; his lifeless universe has been replaced with a universe that is a conscious organism.

Optimal living in a quantum universe is not only knowing we are a part of the tapestry of being; it is the sensation of full aliveness and joyful relaxation and the state of wonder that attends our experience of our citizenry there. This not only gives life the possibility of meaning but also endows it with an infinite potentiality that is limited only when a choice is made to actualize one of them.

In which universe do you live? Or practice therapy?

What Do You Believe About the Nature of Human Nature?
If we wish to be helpful to couples in distress, we need a good grasp on the nature of couplehood. In order to gain that understanding, we must, first and foremost, understand our internal convictions about the nature of the human condition in whatever universe we live in.

For example, are people essentially benign—having good intentions even while engaging in bad behavior? Or are they defined by their bad behavior? Or their good behavior? Does this apply to everyone, or not?

Likewise, can couples change and grow? Or do they live in unchanging circumstances which they can understand, to which they have to adapt but cannot change? Do we suspect that some people are just not marriage material, that some people simply cannot "do" relationships? Or would we argue that anyone who wants to make their relationship better can do so, given enough energy and determination and willingness to jump into the pool, head-first, come what may?

Our convictions about people's ability to change will hinge, in turn, on what we believe human beings are, that is: fundamentally sinful and rebellious, as in the Ptolemaic universe; or unchangeable, as in the Newtonian universe; or as having infinite potential, as in a quantum universe. On top of those assumptions, we build our assumptions about what makes us tick—or not tick! As therapists, do we see personality as being more or less set in stone early in life? Do we see people as products of their DNA, of the genetic inheritance they were given? Or do we, like personality theorist Alfred Adler, believe that what's most important is what we do with those "givens"? Or do we take a quantum view and see everyone in constant flow and oscillation between form and creativity until we make a choice and collapse potential into actuality?

What we believe about these and similar topics, like it or not, will profoundly influence how we go about working with couples. What we see is what they get.

Why Do Couples Fight and Relationships Fall Apart?

As we indicated earlier, Imago theory began with the question: why do couples fight? Why does the dream become a nightmare? Our answer, derived from clinical observation, clinical research, and factor analysis, evolved through many iterations to be as follows: *couples fight because they can't tolerate difference.* The reason they cannot tolerate difference is that they both live in a symbiotic consciousness as a result of their childhood challenges with their caretakers, challenges that were so impactful that they triggered anxiety, which disconnected them from their caretakers and, simultaneously, from the cosmos. The debris of their long- or short-term conflict and polarization, whether in active fighting or mutual passive aggression or one person fighting and the other fleeing or playing dead, is the phenomena most of us encounter immediately upon meeting a couple.

Maybe you have already been working with couples for years, and based on all you have witnessed, you're convinced that couples become and stay disconnected because they hyper-focus on the negatives to the exclusion of anything positive. You might see the essential problem as a lack of focus on what initially made them fall in love, things they have in common, such as their philosophy on life or their love of nature, politics, books, or the arts. If this is how you saw it, then what would you focus on during sessions with them? It would make sense to do things like listing and discussing what they like or love about each other, intensifying the enjoyable moments or experiences they are already having, and so forth. These and other pleasure-producing strategies would be logical to use, taking into consideration what you view as important to a couple's relationship.

Some therapists pay particularly close attention to findings in the clinical research on couple's therapy. If you are among them, when you are working with couples, you may focus on the factors found to predict relationship dissatisfaction or dissolution and those that predict relationship survival (at least) or relational thriving. These factors include characteristics like poor conflict resolution, but they also involve things over which the couple has little or no control—financial or job stressors, having an infant or young children in the home, health problems, and so forth.

Research-oriented therapists might focus especially on research findings that establish a relationship between marital satisfaction (happiness) or marital stability (staying together) and a whole host of variables, such as the partners' socioeconomic status, differences or similarities between the partners' personalities on variables like neuroticism (versus normalcy or stability) or introversion (versus extroversion), or historical factors, such as the success or failure of their parents' marriage.

What Is a Thriving Relationship?

What, exactly, does "a thriving relationship" mean? What does it look like? What are the essential ingredients, and where do you find them? Are they innate, or can they be acquired? Are they available to all, or only to the lucky few?

When you think of a therapeutic outcome, do you see that as anything the couple wishes, or do you have a theory of an ideal outcome you want to help them achieve? Is it personal, and did you get it from research, a marital system, or from your parents(!)? These views may or may not be pertinent to the couple in front of you. The goal of Imago is conscious relating.

To give you a wall to push against so you can clarify your own views, in Imago *a thriving relationship is safe enough for each partner to drop their defenses and become vulnerable so they can restore connecting. To sustain connecting, or restore it if it is ruptured again, they have a process called Imago Dialogue to restore and sustain connecting.* Connecting is the optional condition and, we believe, the foundational desire, and Imago Dialogue is the connecting process. That is all they need, for that restores them to their true nature and original connecting. In that state, where connecting with each other is the conduit to their cosmic identity, all their problems will be resolved or dissolved by collaboration, cocreation, and cooperation .

Even beyond your view of the ingredients of a thriving relationship, which among them are of greatest importance? What is needed in a relationship that, if absent, is a real deal-breaker? For a lot of people, the first thing that comes to mind is the quality of a couple's communication, or what happens between them when they are sending each other messages, particularly when those messages trigger the soft underbelly of our emotional pain body. Communication has, in fact, been cited by researchers as among the most important indicators of relationship quality.

Virtually every distressed couple seeking our help tells us that they have "bad communication." What, exactly, does that mean? If you feel good communication is the sine-qua-non of a happy relationship, then understandably, that is what you will have couples work on. Some therapists believe that, when it comes to having a thriving relationship, what matters most is who you are; others insist it's who you're with.

For you, as a couple's therapist, which is more important?

How Do YOU Do Couples Therapy?

The therapeutic approach of all therapists in working with couples largely hinges, as it should, on how we answer this and similar questions. What we say or don't say, do or don't do when we're interacting with couples is bound to be tied to our deep-down convictions about this mysterious entity called romantic relationship—especially, what makes them work and what causes them to fail.

Now, operating with this assumption, imagine Diana and Mark have just walked through your office door for the first time. Once greetings have been exchanged and everyone is seated, you, the therapist, are onstage. Your assumptive system is influencing the first thing they hear coming from your mouth. What will you say? Would you look for diagnostic clues? For example, how well they match in terms of their personalities, values, beliefs, or goals? Or would you engage them in exploratory questions, asking them to take turns talking about what their childhoods were like or to give their version of what went wrong in their marriage?

Or would you, instead, have them try to connect their past with their present? Would you examine their parent's marriage—whether they stayed together or not, or whether their relationships worked out? Or maybe you believe that what happened in the partners' own previous relationships is more important.

Or maybe you think it best to start with the present, the presenting problem, and say: "What kind of problems are you having?" As you listen to their story, you may decide to get a sense of their skill level, how well or how poorly they communicate, how often they fight, whether they have had sex recently, and other clinical data. Or perhaps you prefer to dive right in and observe how the couple interacts as they discuss an emotionally laden topic. Or, you may be inclined to start with the past by getting some history from them—how long they have been together, whether they are married, cohabitating, something about their parent's marriages, maybe even some childhood memories or other such details, and when all that happened.

Some therapists start with the future by asking couples what outcomes they want, helping them envision their dream relationship and understand what has to happen to make their dream a reality. Most Imago therapists start here and circle back to the past and the presenting problem when doing so seems useful to creating a thriving future together.

The choice of how to begin therapy should not be made lightly. As any experienced therapist knows, how you begin a session has a lot to do with how well, or how badly, the session will end. To illustrate: imagine yourself starting your first session with Fran and Alicia. They have been in a power struggle for the last six months, and they have come to you for something they have not been able to achieve. Based on your clinical experience, you have concluded that a happy relationship is pretty much finding the right person, more a matter of luck than skill, like being born with good looks or a fast metabolism.

The luck assumption would make up part of the metatheory that guides your beliefs about people and would, therefore, influence how you approach and treat the couples you work with in therapy, including Fran and Alicia. Would you try to infuse them with hope that their relationship can improve? Would you invest a lot of time trying to convince them that their relationship is worth saving? Or might it, instead, lead you to go through the motions of helping them while, deep down, you feel pretty hopeless, given your conviction that they simply aren't a good match?

Next, imagine, instead, that you agree with Imago theory's position about the nature of partnership and the underlying purpose of the conflict between partners: that Fran and Alicia, like other couples, are meant to come together so that their complementarity, which makes them incompatible, will generate conflict and thus the opportunity for relational transformation and internal cohesion. Assuming this were your perspective, how would it lead you to approach and treat Fran and Alicia's relationship? Obviously, these and the other convictions we hold about relationships will make a powerful impact on how we work with couples.

To reiterate: Each of us, as therapists and as human beings, carries around with us a working set of assumptions about life, human beings, and relationships. These assumptions serve as the building blocks for a more complex cognitive structure called a theory. The most important theory for those of us working with couples in relationship is, obviously, our (your) theory about the nature of romantic relationships. That theory, along with all of the explanations and recommendations that flow from it, serves as the embedded operating manual on which we will base our interventions with any given couple sitting in our office. Whether we are conscious of it or not, we rely on our theory whenever we are trying to understand and help a couple who is sitting in our office.

In Imago, couples therapy is a dialogical process facilitated by the therapist. That's all! Imago Dialogue is like a "truck"; when used appropriately and regularly, it can take any content to its destination.

THE PERSPECTIVE OF AN IMAGO THERAPIST

Now, let's look at the perspective of an Imago Relationship Therapist. Every Imago therapist has the same fundamental understanding of Imago theory: 1) that connecting is our essence; 2) that ruptured connecting is the basic human problem; 3) that, along with contemporary science, human beings have a physiological, emotional, spiritual, and cosmic need to be in relationship with others; 4) and that exposure to the tools and techniques of Imago therapy, especially Imago Dialogue, are transformational.

This is the "science" of doing Imago therapy.

The "art" of Imago therapy is what you learn to do from experience as you respond to the cues you receive from your clients. Your clients are trying to tell you how to help them. A good part of the Space-Between that exists between you and them must be filled with your respectful attitude as you listen receptively to what they are saying. And since every couple is different and you yourself are always evolving, the art of therapy is in choosing what to do and say, and when. You must navigate the rapids instead of just rowing the boat. Yours skill is required when your passengers are on their best behavior in sessions and you can't see how they really feel. This information may not come out until later sessions, after they've let their guard down.

As rough as the waters may be and as different as your approach to different couples may be, your attitude toward them is always the same. This is how the Imago therapist fills the space between themself and the couple. You believe that every person you see:

- is a point of connecting in a conscious universe in which everything is connecting to everything, all the time;
- is experiencing anxiety because of a childhood connectional rupture with their caretakers that is being reexperienced in their current relationship;
- is attempting to regulate their anxiety and restore connecting rather than an expression of their being unloving or evil;
- has lost the sensation of full aliveness and joy and the state of wonder that attends the "felt sense" of connecting;
- is longing for connecting with their partner and the recovery of the sensation of full aliveness and joy and the state of wonder;
- believes that what they yearn for is available in their relationship because their relationship is why they've come to therapy, but they do not know how to make it better, so they have come to you for help;
- is already able to start the reconnecting process because they've come with what they need;
- is doing the best they can, given their histories of their childhood challenges;
- is struggling with the fear of relinquishing the defensive strategies that have kept them feeling safe up to now; and
- needs a safe environment so they can relax their defenses and be open to new experiences.

We believe you will be an effective Imago therapist with this orientation and with your skillful attunement to the profile of the couple. With experience, you will be able to accurately gauge and effectively modify your therapeutic regimen to match each couple's unique circumstances. You will learn how to gather the fragments of their story—the partners' childhood challenges, their defensive styles, and their maturity levels—into a whole picture, and this vision will guide your methodology. But no matter the complexity of their lives and the severity of their childhood challenges, every couple is looking for one thing: to restore connecting and experience full aliveness, joy and wonder that accompanies such renewed connecting.

And they intuitively know that they are longing for reconnection. That is why they tend to say: we are just not connecting anymore. It is a desire stated as a complaint.

Imago therapists find that doing Imago work is not just a job, it becomes a way of living. In a wonderful symmetry, the therapist finds themself evolving in the same direction as the clients they are helping. Clinicians report that the attitudes, philosophy, and practices associated with Imago seep into other realms in their lives.

We call this the "Imago vortex."

The implications of this are profound, but the reason for it is simple: Imago therapy requires that Imago therapists develop the same high quality of consciousness and interpersonal attunement that their clients are learning to develop. As an Imago practitioner, your knowledge and skills are important, but not as important as the quality of the consciousness and attunement with which you use them. It is a skillful process and an important dialogical endeavor.

Important Note About Imago Diagnosis

Imago therapy is not based on the medical model used in most psychotherapy and, therefore, does not use the DSM-5, which lists 354 diagnosable and treatable mental disorders. One of the problems of diagnosing people with a psychological disorder is, as also occurs in a physical diagnosis, the patient becomes their diseases; their disease is located inside them, so their interior is "treated" with psychotherapy or drugs, and this changes people into objects. Our view is simpler. All of those 354 diagnoses are symptoms of one common problem: ruptured connecting. The problem occurs because, when we rupture our connections, we become at odds with one of the basic features of the universe: the rule of connecting, which when engaged results in the end of symptoms by the transformations in relational experience.

Given that, we call your attention to our intent, hopefully with success, to replace all medical terminology with terms consistent with our existential and quantum view of the human situation—exchanging, especially, words like "wounds" and "healing" with "challenges" and "transformation," respectively. This view informs how we engage with and guide couples.

The Imago Therapist as Practioner

At the top of the Imago therapist's agenda is setting up the right kind of atmosphere or environment, a certain unique context that allows partners to engage in true dialogue—perhaps for the first time in their relationship. We characterize this special context as "safe," "holding,"[10] and "dialogical." These are nonnegotiable. What makes this safe holding environment? What does this context look like? How does an Imago therapist go about creating the therapeutic context?

While we will continue throughout this book to make the connections between metatheory and clinical theory and practice, at this point we want to suggest how the relational paradigm shifts how Imago therapists engage in the therapeutic process.

To establish the special context necessary for doing effective Imago work, the therapist:

1. **Walks the talk.** Beyond the actual therapy skills needed to be effective, the Imago therapist must work on themself to achieve their own growth toward a high level of consciousness. The therapist must be safe if others are to feel safe. The Imago therapist must be conscious so that they can help others become conscious. And they must be empathic so they can model it for their clients. In other words, the Imago therapist practices what they preach.

   Given that all things are interconnected and, in fact, influence each other, the Imago therapist acknowledges that they unconsciously and unintentionally affect the dynamics in the therapeutic office. Thus, to become congruent, they immerse their own relationship in the Imago process and recognize that they are also relationally challenged, struggling with their own imperfections and striving to recover full aliveness, joy, and wonder.

2. **Engages in conjoint therapy only.** Given that relationship is the location of change and given that "individual selves" can only be defined in the context of a relationship, Imago therapists facilitate therapeutic procedures in the presence of both partners. They do not see partners separately. The conjoint structure is essential to preventing the deleterious effect of uneven growth and the dangers of triangulation, both of which interfere with the quality of connection within the couple. Additionally, they are able to observe the specific dynamics that become obvious only in the dyadic structure.

3. **Suspends judgment and moves away from diagnosing.** Because "truth" is relative to context and subject to personal

experiences, Imago therapists never take sides or engage in traditional interpretation, analysis, or diagnostic judgments. Such predication objectifies couples, putting them in a box from which they can never escape. It tends to focus both therapist and client on symptom alleviation rather the dynamics they have created. For similar reasons, they do not engage in any individual assessment or reporting from a partner (through individual therapy, prequestionnaire forms, emails, or phone calls). All information is gathered in the therapist's office with both partners present.

4. **Reframes problems as symptoms of ruptured connection.** Imago therapists understand that we cannot NOT be connected, but we can lose our awareness and experience of connection through the interpersonal developmental process. From mild to severe, all couples' problems and complaints are reduced to the experience of ruptured connection (caused in early childhood experiences and reactivated in the dynamic adult love relationship). In the Imago framework, we view insight as useful but secondary to connection. Connection is primary.

5. **Focuses on the Space-Between.** The Space-Between has a hyphen because it is a fundamental reality rooted in the quantum field. All injuries and transformations occur between people and take up residence within them. H. S. Sullivan (1953) wrote about what matters most in life is what happens between people, not what happens inside them. Imago therapists keep couples focused on how they manage the Space-Between because they know that what happens there becomes the furniture of the Space-Within. Each partner is responsible for the quality of the interactions that constitute the relationship, and both are encouraged to become partners and surrender their role as opponents.

6. **Views "incompatibility" as the grounds for marriage.** At the quantum level, the pairing of opposing energies demonstrates how everything is inherently dyadic and complementary. Each particle, as it jumps into space, is paired with another particle (e.g., electron–positron, muon–antimuon, proton–antiproton). Whereas many programs focus on incompatibilities as the problem and often recommend searching for a compatible partner or divorcing the one they have, Imago therapists see incompatibility as the natural structure of a dyad and, thus, grounds for a great relationship. Simply put, opposites attract, and when difference is valued rather than annihilated, opposites create a dynamic relationship that optimizes potential.

These six fundamental ideological shifts are driven by the relational paradigm, and they make Imago therapy unique from other clinical approaches.

Perhaps the most unusual feature of doing Imago work is that, sooner or later, it is likely to grow on you to become not just a way of doing therapy, but a way of doing life. The reason for this is simple but profound: Imago therapy requires the Imago therapist to develop the same high quality of consciousness and interpersonal awareness that their clients are learning to use. This implies that, as an Imago practitioner, your knowledge and skills, although important, are not as important as the quality of the consciousness and attunement with which you use them.

How do you, as the therapist, develop the necessary levels of consciousness and attunement to generate Imago's goals of healing, growth, and transformation, to become a master at teaching and coaching couples to use Imago Dialogue?

Ten Therapeutic Principles Guiding Imago Relationship Therapists
Over the years, we have experimented with processes that worked in therapy, and processes that did not. We abandoned many processes and added others until we could summarize our current view, which includes 10 processes which, to us, are non-negotiable.

Therapeutic Principle #1:
Safety first!
Safety is the essential, nonnegotiable condition for therapy, and the creation of the therapy office as a safe space is the first and paramount duty of Imago therapists. Safe conversation is the essential foundation for therapy.

The therapist is therefore charged with helping couples create and maintain enough safety between them so that connecting can be restored and sustained. In light of this priority, the therapist guides couples toward eliminating *all* negativity from their relationship. It is impossible to connect if partners are negative, because negativity creates anxiety. And the anxiety of one partner triggers the anxiety of the other. This means that the therapist does not allow sessions to be used for reenactments of the partners' trauma, as these kinds of exchanges are inconsistent with a safe atmosphere. By engaging in only safe and healthy interactions, both inside and outside the therapy office, couples gradually develop a new relational model to replace the negative models they learned in childhood.

The therapist's top priority is to create and foster a safe therapeutic environment. Since confrontation produces anxiety and shores up defensive patterns, the encounter between the therapist and the couple is intentionally nonconfrontational in order to provide the couple with a model of safety.

Therapeutic Principle #2:

Focus on the relationship, not the partners

The traditional role of the therapist as expert in a hierarchical system is replaced in Imago therapy by an egalitarian model of "therapist as facilitator." That makes Imago therapy relationship centered rather than therapist or partner centered, holding the relationship container as the transformational agent. Since all emotional pain is relational, its relief must be relational, as well. In fact, this is, in Imago's eyes, relationship's central purpose: to serve nature's agenda for our personal and collective transformation. Within the context of our relationship with our romantic partner, the person who most closely matches the person(s) who challenged us, is the context that is necessary for our well-being.

Imago therapists function therefore as coaches, not healers. They are facilitators of a dialogical process that helps partners create safety so they can connect and communicate about and beyond their differences. Imago therapists are not the ones that resolve the issue in the marriage; they are the ones who help facilitate the Dialogue that can build connection between two partners.

Therapeutic Principle #3:

Move the conversation from vertical to horizontal

The Imago therapist teaches couples how to speak to each other in a new way, replacing monologues with dialogues. Shifting the content of the conversation from negative judgment to curiosity about and acceptance of their partner's reality makes the relationship safe and transforms conflict into creative tension. This changes the axis of conversation from vertical to horizontal and the nature of the relationship from one of inequality to equality.

As couples exchange accurate (flat) mirroring back and forth, the Space-Between becomes infused with safety, respect, and equality. That is, the Space-Between becomes a horizontal relational structure, which is the sine qua non of the conscious partnership. This is why, in Imago processes, criticism and judgment—features of the vertical structure—are replaced with curiosity and acceptance. This also demonstrates why flat mirroring, which by design reflects nonjudgmental acceptance of the other's message, is such a key component of Imago Dialogue's infrastructure. Structure and predictability are essential for reliable safety.

Therapeutic Principle #4:

Make history, history

The principle lying at the core of Imago theory is that romantic partnership is the reenactment of childhood in the service of restoring the original condition lost in childhood. Neither partner will find themselves attracted to someone who does not resonate with their deep-down convictions about what it means to love and be loved, which is among the primary lessons they carry out of our childhood. Partners are bound to trigger both positive and negative feelings that they felt with their first lovers, their caretakers. This unconscious mix-up between the image of the partner and that of the caretakers does not cause any real problems—that is, until the "good parent" they have been projecting onto their partner is replaced by their projection of the "bad parent." Then, the image of the partner as a perfect parent gradually degenerates into its polar opposite during the power struggle. The bridge connecting them is you.

Knowledge is power: as you teach couples how to view their relationship through this new relational lens, they get a far more hopeful vision of their relationship, of what they are going through now, and of their possibilities for the future. History can become history once couples become conscious of how the past influences the present.

Therapeutic Principle #5:
Hold the tension of opposites
At the quantum level, each particle is an oscillation between matter and energy (a wavicle). Likewise, relationship is neither static nor fixed, rather it is the oscillation between two (or more) subjectivities. Imago therapists hold this tension through a dialogical structure that teaches partners to "tolerate ambiguity" (Siegel, 2007) and invites the exchange of information to cocreate new outcomes and experiences. This difference between partners shows up in several relational and complementary dynamics and is useful for relational healing.

Recognizing the partners' complementary defensive styles, the Imago therapist validates both partners' perspectives until they shift out of an either-or position to a perspective that incorporates the values and desires of both. The therapist's modeling of boundary management helps couples move out of symbiosis and thus leads them toward recapturing their lost connection.

Therapeutic Principle #6:
Promote the "otherness of the other"
The Imago therapist emphasizes the importance of "otherness." Since differentiation, which includes the recognition of the "otherness of the other," is a prerequisite for restoring connection, the therapist facilitates the process of differentiation so that couples can shift from a state of symbiotic fusion to one of differentiated connecting.

Validation is the second step of Imago Dialogue. The validation step provides a structure that partners use to acknowledge that the other's reality makes sense, given the experience in which the other has framed it. The validation statement begins with the sentence stem, "You make sense, and what makes sense is . . ." which calls for the listener to confirm the validity (but not the objective truth) of the sender's perceptions.

How does validation bring about differentiation? As each partner discovers and accepts that their partner is "not me," their symbiotic bubble—in which you and I are one, and I am *the* one—finally bursts. What emerges in its place is differentiation—an authentic recognition by both partners that I am I, and you are you, and we are connecting. Differentiation is the precedent of connecting.

Therapeutic Principle #7:
Shift content from implicit to explicit memory
The Imago therapist helps partners transfer emotionally laden material from implicit memory into explicit memory. Since implicit memories have never been put into language and therefore are outside of awareness, they become merged with the present. Putting these memories into language facilitates their integration, which restores the partners' integration.

We know from recent neuroscience findings that certain areas of the brain—most notably, the cerebral cortex—are assigned to conscious mental functions, such as speaking, while others (e.g., the brain stem and limbic system) are engaged in unconscious processes—everything from our breathing and bodily temperature to our dreams and forgotten memories. Scientists who have explored the neurobiological effects of talk therapy have found evidence that applies equally well to dialogical processes: that putting unexpressed feelings into language changes the emotional meaning of those feelings, even at the level of brain functioning.[11] Furthermore, combining conscious language with primitive, unconscious, and emotional processes can facilitate neural integration (Cozolino, 2002). Imago Dialogue elicits in couples the kind of safe and intimate sharing necessary to invite implicit memory to emerge in the Space-Between.

Therapeutic Principle #8:
Facilitate the couple's dream relationship
The Imago therapist helps couples design and implement their dream relationship. By visualizing the relationship of their dreams and by using Imago process to actualize that vision, couples are able to shift out of the unconscious relationship into coproducing a conscious partnership.

The Relationship Vision Process is among the central processes used to reawaken the passion that almost always gets buried beneath the turmoil of the power struggle. Unlike the safety building exercises, which are designed to remove all vestiges of negativity from a couple's relationship, the Relationship Vision and other passion enhancing processes are what Imago uses to bring the initial positive energy back to their partnership.

Therapeutic Principle #9:
Help couples reclaim pleasure and joy
Many partners resist receiving the very pleasure they are seeking. To promote Imago's therapeutic goal of restoring connecting, full aliveness, joy, and wonder, the therapist engages them in processes for eliciting feelings of relaxation and responsiveness toward feelings of pleasure and joy.

It may be even more difficult to receive love than it is to give it. Partners' resistance to receiving love, to embracing the joy and pleasure that have now become possible, is often rooted in the negative messages of socialization, messages such as, "It's not okay to feel good," or "Nothing good lasts." These are the kinds of convictions that can, and should, be put into language and put on the table through the Imago Dialogue.

Therapeutic Principle #10:
Work collaboratively with couples to generate small behavior changes
Imago therapy is meant to proceed slowly, since the prospect of change can and often does stir up the partners' defenses.[12] Over many years of working with couples, we have found that although change at first comes in small doses, sooner or later, if a couple is motivated enough, the relationship becomes transformed. The good news is that this transformation occurs even if the couple has not been able to resolve their original impasse—that core issue arising from the partners' deepest hurts (and strongest defenses). This impasse, as intractable as it once seemed, dissolves in the warm connection that has reemerged in the couple's relationship.

Seeing Couples Through an Imago Lens
Since how therapists look at couples is what this chapter is about, let us address an aspect that is particularly important as far as its implications for how an Imago therapist approaches the couples they work with. This revolves around the viewpoint, the philosophical perspective, the Imago therapist holds toward couples. Of course, Imago therapists (like all therapists) have a view of couples. How is a couple viewed through eyes of an Imago therapist?

An Imago therapist considers:

- every partner as the human expression of a conscious universe in which everything is connecting with everything at all times;
- the partners' behavior to be a derivative of childhood challenges rather than evidence of their being deliberately unloving or evil;

- each partner to be deeply longing for connection with each other;
- the couple as already having all they need to begin the process of restoring connecting;
- the couple as doing the best they can, given their personal childhood challenges;
- each partner to be struggling with the same fear—that of relinquishing the defensive strategies that have kept them feeling safe up until now.

We recognize that, in combination, the above might be a lot for any therapist to be thinking about all at once. That is why each Imago exercise is based on these same perceptions and principles and why all of them are meant to promote the same ultimate ends: safety, connecting, full aliveness, wonder and joyful relaxation. That is a function of the quality of the relationship, and that is the outcome they seek.

But there is another role that may, at times, be the most important thing you will do for a couple—until they can do it for themselves: to be the container or holder of hope on behalf of a couple in despair. Indeed, there will be times when you will feel more hopeful than they do, and at those times, you will need to hold this vision for them while making sure to avoid invoking shame in them, due to their inability to be hopeful themselves.

There is, in fact, nothing wrong with the therapist, or one of the partners, (temporarily) holding (maintaining and expressing) a positive outlook for the relationship at those times when one or both partners are frozen in reactive patterns that make them unable to hold the hope for the relationship. This is what is known in Imago lingo as taking turns: when Mark and Diana are just starting to trigger each other, and, in this instance, Mark is the only one to catch himself reacting, so he is able to act intentionally to defuse a potential landmine. Here, Mark might say, "Let me try to mirror you, Diana, to see if I get it. If I got it, you're saying that . . ." Perhaps the next time around, Mark may be the one feeling too paralyzed to make a repair attempt, and then Diana could follow the principle of taking turns by reaching out to mirror Mark.

The Imago Therapy Process

Imago's 10 Therapeutic Principles	
Therapeutic Principle #1:	Safety first!
Therapeutic Principle #2:	Focus on the relationship, not the partners
Therapeutic Principle #3:	Move the conversation from vertical to horizontal
Therapeutic Principle #4:	Make history, history
Therapeutic Principle #5:	Hold the tension of opposites
Therapeutic Principle #6:	Promote the "otherness of the other"
Therapeutic Principle #7:	Shift content from implicit to explicit memory
Therapeutic Principle #8:	Facilitate the couple's dream relationship
Therapeutic Principle #9:	Help couples reclaim pleasure and joy
Therapeutic Principle #10:	Work collaboratively with couples to generate small behavior changes

We shift now from how you look at your couples and your relationship with them to what you will do to help them become whom they want to be and to experience what they want to experience by coming to see you.

11
The Imago Therapist
The Mechanics and Artistry of Connecting

There are three kinds of therapists: mechanics, crafts persons, and artists. Some therapists are born with innate instincts and abilities that make them good at helping others, but everyone begins as a mechanic; and if they pay attention to what is effective and repeat it, they become a craftsperson; and if they practice often and hard enough and integrate what they experience with their technique, they become an artist.

All of us need to be deepened by theory, honed by technique, and developed through practice. But no one can become proficient without practicing effective techniques. Education is essential, but mastery is a result of practice. Imago Relationship Therapy, rooted in clinical experience and relationship science and research, provides the evolving therapist with the opportunity to move through those three states of competence.

In this chapter, we present the mechanics behind the art and science of Imago therapy. Mastery of the mechanics of therapy, by consistent practice, will eventually transform any mechanic into an artist.

THE THERAPIST AS FACILITATOR

Although Imago clinical training is rigorous and helps a therapist transition through these three levels of competence, what happens in the therapy room depends less on what the therapist does and more on how the therapist helps the couple interact with each other. Remember, the primary goal is to focus on their connection, not to be the solution provider.

An Imago therapist helps couples become relationally competent by placing the therapeutic power in the hands of the partners rather than keeping them in the hands of the therapist. That assigns to the therapist a facilitative rather than an analytical, interpretive, or healing role. While this removes power from the therapist, it empowers the couples to cocreate a relationship that transforms their interactions in the Space-Between. Since the quality of their interactions is internalized as memory and becomes the content of their inner world (their subjectivity) it is important that their achievement be associated with their relational competence rather than the therapist's relational competence. This enables them to take charge of their future rather than leave it in the hands of the therapist. Paradoxically, to empower couples to engage in the cocreation of a conscious partnership, the therapist's competence must include the capacity to create and hold safety as the quality of the therapeutic space so that couples can cocreatively transform their unconscious relationship into a conscious partnership.

The transformational power of this reconfiguration of the therapy process lies in the unique meaning of partners for each other, a meaning that the therapist does not have and cannot earn. Because they are an Imago-Match, each has an expectation that the other will meet their need from childhood that has shown up in their relationship.

The significance of this is: the only person who can meet the unmet childhood need inhabiting the relationship is someone whose negative features are similar to the one who did not meet them in childhood. The need not met in childhood can be fully met only by a person who is a reasonable facsimile of the caretaker who did not meet it, and that person is the partner, who is similar to the caretaker. Since the Imago-Match unconsciously paired the just-right partners for optimal restoration of original connection, the role of the therapist is to create a safe space, unlike the childhood space, and facilitate a dialogical conversation between partners that should have occurred in childhood.

The listening and empathic therapist is tempted both to evoke awareness and insight or to become the substitute caretaker and offer what the caretakers were unable to give. But there are no receptors in the brains of their partners to receive from another what must come from a parental facsimile. The therapist may offer nurturing and empathy, and they should, but this is a substitute, and the supplies are limited. While ameliorative, the therapist as a resource for satisfaction of archaic needs is not deeply transformational at the unconscious level. And to offer this, instead of facilitating the process with the couple, disempowers them.

It is not the relationship with the therapist that brings about restoration of connecting; rather, the Space-Between is where the action is. It is in that space where the partners experience safety and recover the experience of connecting attended by the sensation of full aliveness and joy and the state of wonder. And the therapist's responsibility is to construct that space to include the therapist and the couple. The connection between the couple is the true power in therapy.

Thus, there is a coaching and facilitative quality to the work of an Imago therapist that in no way minimizes the crucial roles taken on by the therapist nor the importance of the skills the therapist brings to the table.

Let us take a look at the essential contributions the therapist makes as they move a couple toward conscious partnership.

Instill Hope

Hope is the imagination of things wished for. By the time couples first show up for therapy, many have run out of hope for their relationship, and some state that clearly, right at the outset. Therefore, starting with the first session, the Imago therapist's task is to inspire new hope in couples whose supply has gotten depleted.

One of the most powerful catalysts for inspiring hope is the immediate reduction in emotional pain and the beginning of feeling safer by immediate engagement in Imago Dialogue, which structures their conversation and regulates their feelings. When partners learn they can interact safely rather than with threats and in fear, this automatically brings on, for both of them, a new experience of their relationship. This is one reason why, in the chronology of the Imago Therapy process, engaging couples in Imago Dialogue is the first thing on the therapist's list, and it starts in the first session.

Encourage Attunement

Attunement and resonance are the elixirs of a thriving relationship. As we indicated earlier, an Imago therapist starts as a mechanic and proceeds through craftsmanship to artistry—meaning their skills increase incrementally. On the way, their beginning interventions are relatively simple and straightforward, while skills to come are "higher-level." One of the higher-level skills you'll develop on your way to artistry involves resonance and attunement; you will:

1. track the ebb and flow of the partner's interactions;
2. respond with attunement to any shifts that occur; and
3. model attunement so that the partners can achieve it.

This means that the Imago therapist must go beyond assessing the couple's initial dynamics—whether their challenges revolve around attachment or exploration issues or whether one or the other partner minimizes or maximizes—when they first present in therapy. The therapist's job involves more than teaching couples to Dialogue and facilitating safety in their interactions. Beyond all of this, the Imago therapist needs to stay attuned to what is going on in the Space-Between so that they can move the couple into attunement. That is the missing piece in childhood and the essential quality of a thriving relationship.

The longer you do this kind of work with couples, the more skillful you will become at selecting a specific Imago process to match what is going on between the partners—what is happening in the Space-Between—at any particular moment in therapy. After you have gained enough experience and expertise, you will find it easy to interrupt one Imago process to move into a different one—a movement we call *seamless flow*—without in any way diminishing the partners' growing sense of connection with each other.

This will get clearer once you learn the full range of Imago processes, but let us take a quick look at how an Imago therapist works this type of seamless flow. Imagine, for example, that Len and Ping are in your office and are engaged in an Imago Dialogue. While you are coaching them through the three steps of the Dialogue, Ping begins to talk about a painful childhood memory. She suddenly experiences a rush of deep sadness and starts to cry. At this juncture, by staying attuned to what is going on in the couple's Space-Between, you may choose to move Len and Ping into the holding exercise (see Chapter 14), which is achieved by Len literally holding Ping on his lap as she shares her strong emotions. Remaining therapeutically attuned and creating a seamless movement from one technique to another, when warranted, is not just good therapy practice, it also contributes to safety, the critical component that needs to constantly be present in the therapeutic space.

The power of attunement and resonance lies in the fact that they are the features of connecting that become the conduit to a connecting universe, the sensation of which is full aliveness and joyful relaxation and the state of wonder.

Model Integrity

Another way in which Imago is distinct from other approaches relates to its profound impact not only on couples but also on Imago therapists themselves—a phenomenon we refer to half-playfully as the "Imago vortex." This includes the common experience of Imago therapists that, as they increasingly enrich their understanding of Imago theory and processes, they are automatically integrating these same ideas and practices into the rest of their lives, both personal and professional. It is as though the intricacies of Imago theory, and its relevance to many aspects of our lives, seep into the wider realms of our experience.

An Imago therapist cannot effectively guide couples to a state of integration embodying the integrity the therapist is asking of them. So practicing as an Imago therapist can make a truly transformational impact on the personhood of the therapist—a side effect of practicing the therapy processes you are facilitating.

Offer an Invitation to Full Aliveness

The restoration of our original sense of full aliveness—no more and no less—is what an Imago therapist is aiming for and what the couple came to get. This is a tall order, but when couples learn to relax their defenses, to keep each other and their relationship safe, and to commit themselves to restoring connecting, their long-awaited return to the aliveness with which we were born becomes possible. In using the Dialogue process, which creates safety, full aliveness can break through the defensive walls and emerge once again, long after we lost touch with it in the romantic stage and, before that, during our childhood. As our original aliveness gets resurrected, it crowds out the pain and defensiveness of the power struggle, with which it cannot, and will not, coexist.

Another method used by Imago therapists to help couples reignite this inherent aliveness is introducing processes (e.g., high-energy fun) that elicit a high level of pleasurable nervous system arousal, such as laughter, touch, play, silliness, and so forth. (These and other process designed to re-stimulate passion in a relationship will be presented in Chapter 17.)

Keep a Balance Between Content and Process

Imago therapy is process rather than content oriented. There is an Imago saying: process is everything, content is optional. The process we refer to is Imago Dialogue. An Imago therapist spends the majority of time helping partners stay dialogical—to maintain a dialogical stance or attitude of listening, openness, humility, and empathy—no matter what topic they're discussing. If a couple starts to fall out of the process—for example, by mirroring inaccurately, interrupting or criticizing each other, accusing or blaming, and so forth—the therapist holds the space until they are able to return to safe engagement and to sustain it themselves. Here again, it is the *how*, not the *what*—the process rather than the content—that really matters.

But sometimes, the content of a couple's dialogue can be quite provocative, triggering difficult emotions in the therapist witnessing it and in the couple who is experiencing it, because it touches upon all their unfinished childhood issues at the same time. If the Imago therapist wants to be a safe and effective container for the couple, they have to be on high alert to stay conscious of their own reactivity and to have a process of self-regulation they can use while continuing the Dialogue process. An option that is very effective is showing vulnerability by sharing their experiences with the couple and partnering with them in regulating the energy in the therapeutic space.

Teach Couples Their Responsibilities

A great relationship requires the acquisition and practice of the skills that achieve relational competence in both partners. Neither partner can become an expert by themselves, they need the training of interaction with each other. To cocreate a conscious partnership, the Imago therapist helps couples understand that they have a responsibility to meet the conditions of therapy (Rogers, 1951; Siegel, 2006), which includes:

- showing up on time for all therapy appointments;
- staying in process (i.e., following the steps of the Dialogue);
- remaining open and curious about their partner's reality;
- taking responsibility for their contribution to the relationship nightmare (and to ending it);
- speaking honestly and responsibly about feelings and thoughts;
- interacting respectfully inside and outside of sessions;
- always making an appointment before expressing a frustration;
- converting frustrations into a wish and asking for a behavior;
- agreeing not to use any of the material brought up during sessions against the other;
- removing all negativity from all their conversations;
- being willing to attempt reconnecting should disconnection occur;
- caring for the relationship first so the relationship can take care of them;
- expressing appreciations and gratitude to each other on a daily basis; and
- advocating for their relationship's well-being.

Provide Psychoeducation

Although couples do not need to know as much as you do about Imago theory and how it applies to their relationship, we've discovered that sharing some Imago theory can significantly enhance their progress toward awareness and reconnecting.

In our experience, couples are often relieved to learn that their disconnection and conflict are nothing unusual and that the breakdown in their relationship is an almost-inevitable result of rupture to connecting in their past. By coming to understand their frustrations, disappointment, and suffering through the lens of Imago's theoretical framework, couples are often inspired by a new sense of hope that, because neither they nor their relationship are fatally flawed, transformation is possible, after all. When they are able to identify the root causes of their relationship breakdown—that both of them are developmentally challenged from their childhood and have developed opposite, and therefore clashing, ways of dealing with those challenges—they also discover that they are, deep-down, much more alike than different. That their relationship holds greater promise than they'd ever imagined. This is where the psychoeducational component of Imago therapy comes into play.

If we were to devise a list of all the theoretical elements that may benefit couples, we believe that they should know that:

1. First and foremost, they must become safe for each other.
2. The unconscious purpose of committed romantic partnership is to finish childhood.
3. Nature pairs us with just the right person we need to complete that purpose.
4. Unconsciously, we choose the partner(s) whom our unconscious recognizes as one who will provide us with the love, nurturance, and caring we've been longing for since childhood.
5. The first two stages of a committed relationship are unconscious and have a purpose.
6. Each partner's defenses trigger the wounds of the other.
7. When partners relinquish defensiveness and stretch to restore connecting, they are transformed by the process.
8. Incompatibility is inherent in romantic choice and is actually the grounds for a thriving and growth-filled relationship.
9. All negativity must be removed from the relationship and replaced with curiosity.
10. Pain delivered in the form of criticism and negativity cannot be received by the listening partner, whose defensive reactions cause temporary emotional deafness.
11. Daily affirmations of each other are absolutely essential.
12. Conflict is growth trying to happen.
13. No matter what they think they are fighting about, it is actually about restoring the original condition of connecting.
14. Relationships go through normal and predictable stages.
15. Disconnection and disappointment are normal in lasting relationships.
16. The sign of a thriving relationship is the quickness of restoring connecting.
17. The desire to terminate the relationship during the power struggle is normal, predictable, and usually temporary.
18. Anxiety about changes they are making indicates they are actually changing.

At some critical point in their evolution toward conscious partnership, the couple will experience a qualitative shift in the structure of their relationship—from unconscious relating to conscious connecting. With this shift, the old relationship, built on fantasy, projection, and coercion, will collapse and they will feel some mild or intense anxiety. If they stay with the process, a new relationship, built on authentic love, intentionality, and consciousness, will emerge. At that point, real love will become the foreground, and conflicts thereafter will be experienced as opportunities for further growth and deeper mutual understanding rather than as obstacles to be avoided or overcome.

THE CONDITIONS OF SUCCESSFUL THERAPY

There are three conditions of successful therapy: being present, establishing safety, and providing structure.

Being Present

Nothing is more counterproductive to successful therapy than a distracted and chaotic therapist. It replicates the childhood experience of the physical presence but emotional absence of the caretaker and replicates, in the therapist's office, the wounding of the childhood home. It may be better not to do therapy that hour or that day in order to prevent such a possibility, because only "presence" without judgment creates a coherent energy field that restores the original connecting. Physical presence with emotional absence creates anxiety, chaos, and disconnection.

Being "present" means you are emotionally in the room and attuning, every second, with warmth and acceptance.

Being Safe

Safety is the essential, nonnegotiable condition for therapy, and the creation of the therapy office as a safe space is the first and paramount duty of the therapist.

Safety is the primary agenda of the human race and is essential for thriving (Porges, 2003). It is an energy field that results from specific behavioral interactions between partners when facilitated by the therapist.[13] They cannot connect if they are negative, because negativity creates anxiety, and anxiety shuts partners off from one another. Without safety, nothing can happen in therapy, except the strengthening of defenses. With safety, therapeutic interventions work.

The couple needs an environment in which they can dream their dream rather than merely remember and recite their suffering and raise their defenses. To facilitate that, the Imago therapist resists pressuring clients to talk about the presenting problem or asking them to recite past abuses or allowing them to make negative remarks about each other in the session. In fact, because toxic exchanges imprint the therapist's office with associations of pain, these exchanges are not allowed. This may be just as much of a challenge for the therapist as it is for the couple seeking treatment.

Rather than diagnosing the pathology of a relationship, the Imago therapist facilitates the expression and actualization of desire, with which, if they had it, nothing would be wrong. But most couples will not understand this for a while. They will want to focus on content and outcomes and not process. And, more than likely, they will want to talk about their past, since that is all they have. This is natural because content is concrete and process is abstract. But, if you let them, they will stay there and forfeit their future. You yourself may be uncertain about the primacy of process over content and thus be tempted to accommodate their tendency and become interested in their story. That will entrap you in their old story and prevent a new story from emerging.

Providing Structure

Every therapeutic interaction is designed to facilitate safety and connecting and to integrate the upper and lower brain regions and the left and right hemispheres. This is achieved by providing structure through using the Imago Dialogue Process in all interactions. While the *proximate goal* of therapy is implementing the dialogue and constructing the couple's dream relationship, the *distal goal* is integrating Imago Dialogue into their lives and their living in a conscious and joyful relationship. It is a new way of being that is created by a new way of talking.

The orthodox Imago practice is to engage the couple, with their permission, in the Imago Dialogue Process in the first interaction and seldom engage in any other type of conversation.

THE MECHANICS OF DOING
IMAGO RELATIONSHIP THERAPY

It is paradoxical that the art of doing therapy is dependent on careful attention to specific details that convey messages to your couples about who you are and what they might expect to happen while they are with you. Remember, that the primitive part of their brains is constantly checking whether this is a safe or dangerous place.

Setting up your waiting room

Some things about therapy are mundane, like how to set up your waiting room. However, the way you do this sends a message to the couple about who you are and who you think they are. In Imago, the waiting room has a sofa and two chairs at the ends of the sofa. It has a chest or table with snacks, a coffee machine, and hot water for tea. Clients are offered some refreshments and given instructions on the whereabouts of the restroom. A sign requests them to leave their drink or food in the waiting room when they enter the office so they can be present to each other in the session.

Setting up your office

When couples enter the therapy office, they find two chairs facing each other and a third, where the therapist will sit, facing them in a sort of triangle as well as a couch against the wall, which will be used for specific therapeutic processes. The chairs and couch are comfortable and may be beige or brown leather or shades of blue with minimal patterns. It is warm, comfortable to the eyes, and shows a thoughtful arrangement. Some of the pictures on the wall represent couples, indicating your interest and taste. And you may have a sculpture or two of a couple, which shows that your commitment to couples therapy is central, not peripheral.

A camera is set up and permission is asked to record the session. You may want to assign viewing the recording as homework, on occasion, when you deem a particular session important for them to review, or the couple may themselves wish to view it.

The couple selects their seats, *then the therapist sits,* and the process begins. The length of an Imago session is usually one and a half hours.

Doing an intake

Imago therapists choose to know little if anything about the specifics of a couples lives except their demographic data. The reason they are there and the conditions behind their decision to come will be solicited from the couple and shared by them in the Dialogue process later. The data form indicates basic things like name, age, gender, ethnicity, and professional identity, if any. Also the form indicates whether each is in their first or second marriage or more, how long for each, whether they have children, who is the primary caretaker, and whether each has a full- or part-time career. It also indicates their therapy history, whether they have seen an Imago therapist, and, if not, what sort of therapist they had, as well as an evaluation of the therapy's outcome. The intake also asks if there is anything that might impede their engaging fully in the therapy process, such as physical health challenges, mental stress, addiction, unavailability because of work, etc. During the intake, the therapist would learn whether they have a spiritual practice and, if so, what kind. In no case does the Imago therapist use the standard *Diagnostic Statistical Manual* to make a diagnosis and a treatment plan and share that with the couple. The treatment plan will evolve from the details in the dream relationship they will describe in the first sessions.

Everything you need to know as a therapist will emerge in the process of the couple's engagement with each other through the Dialogue process. What couples need is a new story and the courage and skills to live it out in the real world with others. That is the purpose of therapy: to facilitate partner engagement—not to satisfy the therapist's curiosity. Partner engagement keeps couples open to infinite possibilities for their relationship and prevents collapsing that potential into a premature interpretation.

Create a working alliance

A working alliance is a buy-in between the couple and the therapist and will happen, or not, in the first 5 to 15 minutes of the first session. The couple should be able to leave the first session with a positive new experience that generates some commitment to the therapy process. They should know there is a way to start the journey home that is different from the way they got to your office.

This requires that the therapist has skills to establish the office as a safe space, has confidence in the process, has the courage to redirect all negative interactions toward connecting language, and can model connecting interactions to emulate until the couple integrates them into their behavior.

Facilitate commitment

Just like the first shoot of a plant will not emerge while the soil is still partly frozen, you cannot expect a single spark of healing in a couple unless both partners are committed to cocreating a safe, holding, and dialogical atmosphere. An important initial step of the Imago process, then, involves asking the couple to do their part in generating this essential atmosphere by making and keeping three commitments:

1. Commit to the Relationship: Remain (for now, not necessarily forever) in their relationship while postponing any decision to leave or stay in the relationship.
2. Commit to the Process: Participate in at least 12 Imago therapy sessions over the course of 3 months.
3. Commit to the outcome: Become conscious partners in the project of restoring connecting.

Many couples terminate therapy before their fifth appointment because unconscious issues that trigger anxiety tend to emerge between the third and fifth sessions. A tried and true method couples use for reducing anxiety is resistance and avoidance. Some couples react to their anxiety by claiming that therapy is making matters worse, and they fire the therapist. Others claim that they "can't find time" to keep their appointments. The reason for this is that change is not linear, but cyclical. Since Imago Dialogue is so immediately impactful, couples tend to feel safe quickly, to regulate their emotions, to drop their defenses, and to feel close. However, because the loss of closeness is so painful, they tend to pull back and return to their defended state in order not to lose it again. If the reason for making the commitment is shared with the couple, when the anxiety occurs, the therapist can reassure them that it was expected and that it means they are making progress. Most couples decide to stay in therapy if they know why they want to leave!

That establishes the importance of a commitment to the process that is concretized by the recommendation of an *initial 12-session contract.* The 12-session commitment does not mean 12 will be enough sessions for all couples. Those who are the most deeply conflicted may have to work for a year or longer. But, at the very least, the initial commitment creates the assurance that the partners will stay in therapy long enough to work through their initial resistance, weather their anxiety, and become fully involved in the therapy process.

Of course, not all couples are going to be willing to agree to the 12-session commitment. For example, partners who have felt polarized for a long time or who have already gone through therapy without success may be less than enthusiastic about committing to the full course of 12 sessions. Should you encounter this kind of resistance, we advise you to honor and respect the couple's current limits; then ask them if there is some alternative to which they might be willing to commit. Perhaps they will agree to attend just one more session or to discuss this at home.

We encourage accepting couples' ambivalence while gently informing them about its deleterious effects on therapy and their relationship. Our brains cannot work with ambivalence, and the anxiety of uncertainty tends to sabotage the process. In the final analysis, your policy should be to honor and respect whatever steps, however small, they are willing to take at this time. As they continue therapy, encourage couples to engage in dialogue and conscious connecting at home as well.

INITIATING THREE ESSENTIAL SKILLS

Positive change produces a new kind of threat. The old defense systems must be dismantled in the service of positive engagement. Letting old defense systems go triggers anxiety and arouses a whole new set of emotions and reactive behaviors. In other words, anxiety about positive change can produce an increase in negative exchanges. Because of that, it is important to introduce some key processes to clients early in the therapy sequence, to help them address these emotions in a safe way. The essential processes include 1) Imago Dialogue; 2) the Zero Negativity Process; and 3) the Affirmations Process.

1. Imago Dialogue

To sustain their skills, Imago therapists take care to help couple's transition from therapy to daily life by integrating Imago Dialogue into their lives as a new way to talk, about anything, anywhere, with anyone. That involves the use of the sentence stems informally in ordinary, daily conversation.

The integrative process can be started in the first session. For instance, the Imago therapist helps couples role play being at home talking with each other or one of their children or being at a social event or in the workplace and talking to someone. Instead of interrupting a conversation to talk, they make an appointment by saying "Are you available for me to share an opinion about that?" When someone is talking to them, instead of waiting for their turn, they instead use the mirroring process and interrupt the person speaking for a quick "If I got that, you are saying. . ." And of course, they can use the magic of curiosity and say to someone they have just mirrored, "Is there more about that?"

The core sentence stems are selected from the three-step structure. They include:

1. Ask for an appointment: "Are you available for a comment?" Or at home, a partner might say to another, "Is now a good time to talk about . . . (be sure to include the topic)?"
2. Mirror: "If I got that, you said . . ."
3. Check for accuracy: "Did I get it?"
4. Show curiosity: "Is there more about that?"
5. Validate: "That makes sense because . . ."
6. Empathize: "I can imagine you might feel . . . . about that."

Using these sentence stems in everyday life will bring magic—connection and safety—to every conversation.

As we indicated earlier, among all the things Imago is—a theoretical system, a therapy process and practice—Imago is a way of life—a conscious partnership—and Imago Dialogue is the language of this new reality. It contributes not only to making the Space-Between partners safe; it can make the Space-Between anyone safe.

2. The Zero Negativity Process

The second nonnegotiable is the Zero Negativity Process. Since the removal of negativity from any relationship is nonnegotiable, if the goal is sustaining connecting or establishing reconnecting when it has been ruptured, couples are invited to take a Zero Negativity Pledge. This begins the therapy process with a commitment to the quality of its outcome. The Zero Negativity pledge is the first step toward creating conscious partnership as the inhabitant of the Space-Between.

The steps toward a Zero Negativity relationship include:

1. Signing a Zero Negativity Pledge. We advise starting with a 30-day commitment, processing the experience; then add another 30 days followed by processing, and then another 30 with processing. Ninety days integrates the process into their lives, and then they should be prepared to commit to it forever.
2. Choosing a signal, like a word or gesture, that partners can use to indicate the experience of a put-down.
3. Committing to a daily monitoring process to reinforce it by using a calendar to keep track of put-downs and record progress toward the Zero Negativity state. See Appendices 21 and 22 for the Zero Negativity Pledge and calendar.

Choosing a signal to indicate the experience of a put-down is immensely important. Couples must be encouraged to do this, and they can have fun choosing one. One signal is so natural that you were able to do it before you learned how to talk: *saying ouch*. On the other hand, each partner may want to select their own, and they may want one they both can use. Some other options we have heard are "watermelon," "marshmallow," "oops," "wow," "whoa."

Using some signal they agree on prevents the couple from saying something else, something that might be the equivalent of a verbal nuclear bomb. If instead partners work collaboratively to accomplish reconnecting, they will then be able to promptly resurrect, like a phoenix rising from the dust, the steady background of safety and connectivity.

The signal, in whatever customized form the couple has chosen, is followed by several reconnecting processes, which are presented in detail in Chapter 15.

It is important to introduce the Zero Negativity Process in the first session and to invite them to sign the pledge and to introduce them to the Reconnecting Process.

3. The Affirmations Process

In addition to using the above strategies to neutralize negativity's effects when either experiences a put-down, we believe it is equally important that couples experience, as a counterbalance, heavy doses of the emotions falling on the positive side of the spectrum—feelings like excitement, enthusiasm, joy, amazement, even passion.

Affirmations can also include an "affirming" stance toward each other, amplified by specific behaviors such as daily appreciations, caring behaviors, monthly surprises, daily fun, and positive flooding.

The *Affirmations Process* creates a cocktail of pleasure-increasing neurochemicals, like endorphins and dopamine, and it decreases cortisol and adrenalin levels.[14] Whatever couples decide would effectively repair whatever damage has been done, they should do it (in some cases, in the private confines of their own home!), and quickly. It is important, if time allows, to introduce the affirmations process in the first session so the couple can begin the practice of replacing toxic interactions with connecting ones, exchanging cortisol for endorphins.

WHAT HAPPENS IN EVERY SESSION

In addition to removing negativity and engaging in affirming behaviors, every therapy session should:

1. **Provide a new experience.** In every session, couples should experience something different from what they are used to at home, including within the first 30 minutes of the first session. For example, the couple should be able to leave the first session with a new experience and some commitment to the process, even though they may not be fully convinced. And this something "new" should be an awareness they achieved from engaging in an interaction along with a tool they can practice at home. This begins a slow shift in the negative dynamics that brought them to the therapy office.

2. **Provide a little psychoeducation.** We indicated above that incorporating *psychoeducation* into our work with couples can sometimes significantly enhance their progress toward consciousness and increase their willingness to engage in new behaviors. In our experience, couples are often relieved to learn that their disconnection and conflict are nothing unusual and that the breakdown in their relationship is an almost-inevitable result of the unhealed wounds of their past. They are often inspired by a new sense of hope that neither they nor their relationship are fatally flawed, that there is something "normal" about their situation. We introduced some psychoeducation items above.

3. **Begin each session with an exchange of appreciations.** Facilitating couples to share appreciations with each other at the beginning of a session tends to decrease cortisol, which lowers anxiety, relaxes defenses, and increases endorphins, thus

allowing them to move to challenging topics. It also helps couples become mindful, between sessions, of the positive behaviors their partner is doing (rather than focusing on the frustrating behaviors) so they have something to share at the office. In sharing an appreciation, only mirroring is necessary.

4. **End each session with a homework assignment.** Since intrapsychic change occurs as a result of action in the interactive Space-Between, the focus of Imago therapy is on changing how couples interact with each other all the time. That means, the practice of new interpersonal behaviors is integral to the system and to the outcome of therapy. The therapist should indicate that homework is a part of therapy, that practice is the only way to integrate new behaviors, and that change is sustainable only if they practice until integration occurs and the behaviors become a new part of their lives. Awareness and insight are not enough.[15] Only one new behavior should be assigned at a time (building upon previously new behaviors), and it should be practiced daily. Some between-session assignments could include:

1. Practice mirroring each day on a safe topic, or on "mundane" items, using sentence stems such as, "Let me see if I got it . . . If I did you said . . ."
2. Send 1 to 3 appreciations a day to each other (and practice mirroring).
3. Reserve 15 minutes a day to practice mirroring on a neutral topic.
4. Ask the couple to evaluate the session.

    Since Imago Therapy is a collaborative rather than a vertical process (where the "therapist as expert" reigns), ask couples to share their experience of the session. The process includes these questions: "What were your body sensations during the session?" "What did you like about the session?" "What would you like more of?" "What would you like less of?" Engaging the couple in reflecting on the session removes the element of mystery from therapy and makes them partners in the process of their own transformation. In addition, your evolution from mechanic to artist will depend upon your willingness to allow your couples to teach you as they allow you to facilitate their process.

ENGAGE IN IMAGO'S BEST PRACTICES

If we do our level best to practice the dialogical attitude, which emanates with the safety, respect, and empathy engendered by Imago Dialogue, we will find that our work becomes more and more skillful and attuned. The behaviors of a skillful and highly attuned Imago therapist are those reflected in the list of Imago's "best practices." These are demonstrated when the therapist:

1. maintains good eye contact with and accurately mirrors both partners;
2. stays attuned to the (typically opposite) defensive styles of the partners, making sure to help both feel fully seen, held, and safe in the therapist's presence;
3. maintains a neutral stance while guiding the action between the partners;
4. gently persuades partners to discover and acknowledge their respective contributions to the power struggle;
5. uses sentence stems, verbatim (word-for-word) mirroring, or paraphrasing and other connection-building strategies;
6. allows enough time for partners to feel safe enough before moving them into regressive techniques (e.g., the Parent-Child Dialogue, the Holding Exercise, or the Behavior Change Request Dialogue);
7. understands the importance of both regression (slipping back into old patterns) and progression (making progress) as couples wind their way to psychosocial adulthood;
8. focuses on the couple's relational strengths and resources, encouraging couples to accentuate the positives while improving the negatives;
9. stays 100% present for the couple and helps partners be 100% present for each other;
10. envisions both partners as inherently well-motivated and as having positive or benign intentions and teaches couples to do this for each other;
11. sets clear boundaries, disallowing any exchange of criticism, shame, or blame;
12. explains theoretical ideas well enough for couples to understand why they are being asked to do a particular exercise in therapy; and finally,
13. helps couples build good relationship habits by assigning and checking up on homework (or between-session) assignments.

Now that we have described the features of personhood of Imago therapists and the mechanics and art of Imago therapy, we invite you to become acquainted with the six steps that lead to the conscious partnership we seek, in which the agenda of childhood and the relational dream will be fulfilled.

Part IV

IMAGO CLINICAL PRACTICES

SIX STEPS TO A CONSCIOUS PARTNERSHIP

The journey to conscious partnership is a six-step process, facilitated by the consistent practice of Imago Dialogue. You play a vital role as the facilitator of that Dialogue to create conscious connecting. Imago Dialogue is both the therapeutic intervention and the language spoken in the new collaborative and conscious partnership. Since Imago views suffering as ruptured connecting, the practice of Dialogue transforms suffering by creating consistent presence and resonance in the Space-Between. Dialogue is the means and goal of the therapeutic process (Figure A).

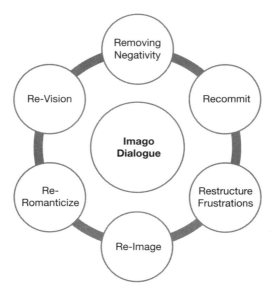

Figure A:
Six Steps to Conscious Partnership

The six steps are:

1. **Revisioning:** Couples imagine and cocreate their conscious partnership and their dream relationship. The Revisioning Process starts in the first or second session and may take several sessions, but it is of critical importance as an early intervention process because the vision becomes the map for the therapeutic process and the goal of therapy.

2. **Recommitting:** Couples mutually commit to their relationship and to their partner and to the use of the Dialogue process. This begins in the first session with the therapy contract and continues throughout the duration of therapy. It includes identifying and closing exits. Removing ambivalence is essential to creating and inhabiting a conscious partnership.

3. **Reimaging:** Couples rupture the symbiotic consciousness by differentiating and connecting. This involves discovering the "otherness" of their partner; seeing their partner and themselves as challenged by issues from childhood and as protecting themselves with opposite defenses; seeing the role each has in the transformation process; and seeing the Dialogue process as the vehicle of transformation.

4. **Removing Negativity:** Couples commit to removing all negativity from the relationship. They take a Zero Negativity Pledge and use the Reconnecting Process to restore connecting if either experiences a "put-down." Removing negativity is nonnegotiable, as it is essential to achieving a conscious partnership, so it is embedded in all sessions, starting with the first one.

5. **Restructuring Frustrations:** Couples discover that a frustration is a wish in disguise. They learn to convert their frustrations into wishes and to translate their wishes into specific behaviors they need in order to resolve their childhood challenge. Partners use the "stretching principle" to go beyond their comfort zone and meet their partner's unmet childhood need.

6. **Re-romanticizing:** Couples engage in specific high- and low-energy processes that trigger the release of pleasure neurochemicals that restore the experience of romantic love, which simultaneously restores connecting to each other and to the cosmos, the result of which is the sensation of full aliveness and relaxed joyfulness and the state of wonder. The exercises and behaviors include positive flooding, caring behaviors, laughter, hugging, surprises, eye gazing, orgasms—any activity that injects pleasure and passion into the relationship.

Quality of the Space-Between	Dialogical Process (the 6-Rs)	Imago Exercises
Table A: SAFETY IN THE SPACE-BETWEEN Creating a Conscious Partnership		
Intentional	Revisioning	• Global Vision • Individual Vision • Relationship Vision
Intentional	Recommitting	• Commitment Contract • Identify Exits • Commitment Dialogue
Empathic	Reimaging	• Differentiation Dialogue • Imago Profile • Childhood Challenge and Relational Need Exercise and Dialogue • Parent-Child Dialogue • Holding Exercise
Affirming	Removing Negativity	• Zero Negativity Pledge • Reconnecting Process • Space-Between Dialogue
Giving	Restructuring Frustrations	• The Frustration List • Core Scene Dialogue • Behavior Change Request Dialogue • Gifts of Change Dialogue
Passionate	Re-Romanticizing	• Appreciations • Caring Behaviors • Surprises • Fun • Positive Flooding
Restores the Experience of Connecting		

After revisioning and recommitting, the sequence of these steps is flexible. Revisioning and recommitting are essential commitments that make the rest of the journey possible. In fact, the therapeutic process is more spiral than linear; vision and commitment are implemented in the first sessions, and then it may be necessary to help them change a frustration into a wish so they can engage in a necessary behavior change, and then turn back to the vision. *The essential element is that couples learn Imago Dialogue and use it as the mechanism of progressing through all the steps in whatever order evolves.* Your wisdom and intuition as their therapist will help you decide whether to stay on the path or take a detour and come back.

NOTE: Each therapy process is designed to help couples transcend suffering by restoring connecting as the reality of the Space-Between. The precondition of experiencing connecting is safety, and that is the goal of the dialogical structure of the conversation and the facilitation of the dialogue process. When safety in the Space-Between is achieved and sustained, that is, it becomes their lifestyle, therapy is no longer necessary.

ACHIEVING CONNECTION
THROUGH THE IMAGO PROCESS

The success of the process is dependent on the process itself, and it is prudent to remember what we've learned: that the goal is for the relationship to heal the marriage through consistent, conscious relating via Imago Dialogue. As therapists, we must trust the process, so to speak, to see it through long enough for it to work, instead of inserting our own judgment or therapist-centric therapy.

The six processes create safety in the Space-Between and ultimately restore or enhance the felt sense of connecting (Table A), creating a conscious partnership. We will devote a chapter to each of these processes and provide tips, examples, and outcomes. In the Appendices, you will find corresponding worksheets and dialogue overviews for reference and to provide to couples as between-session assignments. Let us take a closer look at these six Imago processes to examine how these interventions move couples in the direction of creating a conscious partnership.

12
Revisioning

What: Guide couples to transform their implicit individual relationship dream into a joint relationship vision.

Why: The vision becomes the roadmap for therapy and shifts couples' focus from obsessing over what is not working in their relationship to imagining its potential.

When: In the first session and thereafter, assign specific behaviors to practice between sessions that will integrate session work with their daily life.

Most couples tend to think that a great relationship just happens, and they spend most of their lives waiting for it to show up. Without relational education and competence, couples unconsciously model their relationship after what they have witnessed and internalized from their families, staying in the illusion until their pain reaches the threshold of intolerance. But when couples become intentional and create their vision rather than focusing on their grievances, they become residents of their cocreated dream rather than prisoners in their cocreated nightmare.

The therapy office provides couples an environment in which they can dream their dream rather than merely remember and recite their suffering and practice their defenses. In a safe environment, couples can shift their focus away from the deficits to the strengths, from the problems to the resources of a relationship. This chapter will help you help them do that.

DEFINITION OF REVISIONING

The word "vision" usually refers to the future, but in Imago therapy, vision is defined as a transformed "present." Revisioning is an invitation for couples to shift from reviewing their painful memories to activating their imagination in the service of creating an alternative to their current relationship. Because our brains do not have the capacity to actualize something in the present if it is described as a future possibility, it is critical to help them describe their dream relationship in the present tense and engage in new behaviors that embody it. If it is "to come," it will always be "on the way" but never here. Revisioning, therefore, invites couples to replace their view of their current relationship with a new vision—to codesign the relationship of their dreams and act as if it already exists and to inhabit it immediately by engaging in new interactions.

The couple that arrives at your office may not know that they have to cocreate their dream and work at it. Or, that in order to get it, they have to live it. Thus, they may attempt to begin the first session with a presentation of their problem with some hope that you might "fix" their partner so they can remain as they are! But it is important that you resist the pressure of allowing them to talk about their presenting problem: recite past abuses and make negative remarks about each other so you will know where they problem lies. Instead, it is important that you move them directly into the design of their relationship, to start the therapy process talking about what they want and learn the process of translating desire into reality.

To focus on an outcome that fulfills their potential instead of revisiting the debris of a shattered dream is the way back to full aliveness, joy, and wonder in a conscious partnership. And accessing their mutual potential requires the intentional power of the cortical brain.[16] This requires you to help couples shift from reciting their memories—the library of their complaints—to activating their imagination to constructing something different. Exploring the pathways of memory helps people understand who they have been, but it does not help them access and develop who they can become.

THE REVISIONING PROCESS

Couples come to therapy with the raw materials to engage in the Revisioning Process and an implicit vision of their dream relationship, but they have neither the knowledge nor the skills to achieve it. The implicit dream includes the romantic stage of relationship as they remember it, and beneath that the primal childhood connection upon which it was built, but which was lost. Both are now buried beneath a mountain of mutual negativity that has isolated them from each other. Your role is to help them recover the implicit dream and make it explicit by creating an *operating manual* of daily practice to help them embody it as lived experience. You notice we do not speak of "curing," but co-constructing a new way of living together. That is the cure.

The steps for creating this manual include:

- recovering the implicit vision;
- describing the individual visions;
- sharing the individual visions through Dialogue;

- cocreating a relationship vision out of the shared visions; and
- developing strategies for implementing the vision with new daily practices.

In simplest terms, couples imagine and put into writing their dream relationship, share their respective visions using Dialogue, combine their visions into a joint relationship vision, and turn the vision statements into a set of goals and objectives and tactics that they, as a couple, will implement daily. In this way, the relationship of their dreams can come to fruition, not just an imagined vision, but a reality.

The first phase is to help them start implementing what they share in common, and later address what is different. When they both practice what they both want, they will increase their pleasure bond. When they later stretch into practicing together behaviors that represent different wants, they will experience differentiation and deeper connecting that will transform their relationship. The relationship vision becomes the therapeutic plan, and its achievement the therapy outcome. As a therapist, you know what they want, and you now know what to do. This is the therapy road map. This is ultimately why the Revisioning Process begins early in therapy, often in the very first session.

The First Session

As mentioned, it is critically important that the first session provide the couple with a new experience that portends the possibilities in their relationship.

We recommend that you start your first session with an Appreciation Dialogue, using the full mirroring process, paying strict attention to the sentence stems and their sequence. Remember, the goal of Imago therapy is to help couples become dialogical as a new way of living with each other and with everyone. Therefore, the purpose of the appreciation in the first session is for couples to learn the structure and sentence-stem flow of the Dialogue process. The reason we start with an appreciation, rather than a frustration or anything else, is that easy content has the most potential for the couple to succeed in their first attempt and it provides them with a new experience, as a preview of the potential they can realize in the sessions to come. It also motivates them to start with their vision rather than with their complaints. This shift from blaming, a mid-brain function, to imagining the positive possibilities, an upper brain function, contributes to brain integration, an essential for sustaining a conscious partnership.

Since this is their first training session, the appreciation needs to go both ways. For example, Diana asks Mark for an appointment, they make eye contact and take three deep breaths. And the therapist provides Mark with the sentence stems to begin sharing and provides Diana with the sentence stems for mirroring, checking for accuracy, and inviting more. When the appreciation is complete, the process is now repeated with Diana as the sender and Mark as the receiver.

After the Appreciation Dialogue is completed and processed, it is important to introduce the Zero Negativity (ZN) Process and Pledge and, if there is time and they are willing, to secure their signature on the ZN pledge and their agreement to give each other a daily appreciation as homework. (Details of this process can be found in Chapter 15.)

When both have sent and received an appreciation and committed to ZN, ask them to share their experience instead of asking questions so that they are ready to be guided to cocreate their dream relationship.

NOTES:
- Achieving all this may take the bulk of the session, and that is fine. However, be sure to leave enough time to offer them a between session assignment to begin thinking about their ideal relationship by filling out the revisioning worksheet (Appendix 3).
- In future sessions, appreciations can be a "one-way send" that is mirrored by the receiver, followed by "thanks for your appreciation" and "thanks for receiving it," thus lowering anxiety and relaxing the defenses of the receiving partner. This helps them listen to the sending partner with more accuracy and empathy and with less reactivity.

An Important Aside!

Before we proceed to the details of the Revisioning Process, we want to reveal the secret of its power and success. Its success has little to do with the content of the vision and everything to do with the process and quality of the conversation. The content is selected to address the couple's interests so they will engage in the process, but what transforms them is the quality of their engagement with each other as they discuss the content. And what enhances the quality of the engagement is the safety created by the structure and consistent practice of Imago Dialogue. Learning and practicing the Dialogue process is more important than the content of their vision, because practicing Dialogue is the engine of their new relationship. That is the structure that creates the safety which is a precondition of connecting. When the partners are safe enough, connecting happens.

Without safety, nothing happens in the therapy session except an increase in self-protective measures. When couples are safe, they relax their defenses and communicate about their needs, similarities, and differences without polarizing. That is what transforms the relationship, because it restores the quality of the original condition of resonant connecting in childhood before the "rupture."

Because content is secondary and Dialogue process is primary and the quality of their interaction is everything, any content can come up for discussion. Therefore, strict adherence to the Dialogue process, including the sentence stems, is essential. The power is in the structure and the sequence of the process. Please refer to the Imago Dialogue chapter (Chapter 9) for a detailed review of the process.

However, since content is what is processed in the Dialogue, let us begin with the mechanics of constructing and actualizing the dream.

Recovering the Implicit Vision

Everyone has an implicit relational dream that is qualitative and holistic. It consists of images in the right brain that can be accessed by the linguistic resources of the left brain with a question like: "What would your relationship be like if it were 'just right?'" The brain bases its survival on the visual ("Is it safe or dangerous?"), and visualizing is a powerful component to manifestation.

You can help couples achieve a relaxed state by taking them through a guided visualization. Invite them to focus on images rather than behaviors so that there is a picture, a tone, a color, a felt sense, a quality, rather than specific behaviors of the dream relationship. (You will find a sample script in Appendix 2.) You may want to give them a piece of paper to record the adjectives or draw their images. Have a stock of colored pens they can use if they want to draw something. The sentence stem you offer is: "In my dream relationship, we are . . ."

Of course, each partner will produce a different vision, but since the dream relationship is always built on the template of the romantic stage, which is built upon the childhood need, they will have different details but share core qualities. For some, the primal image of a dream relationship may be similar to "the golden embrace of two lovers." Or it might be "a diversity of soft green colors," a "rainbow," or a "valley with a stream running through." Adjectives we have heard have included safe, warm, playful, nurturing, joyful, and feeling connected. Smells may touch childhood memories of lavender fields, Italian sauce simmering on the stove, or fresh air brimming with salt, brine, and seaweed. All five senses can access images from the deep recesses of the unconscious, where our implicit vision of the perfect relationship lies. Each partner should be given time to share their dream images with the other partner.

IMPORTANT NOTE: As partners begin to design their vision, we invite you to listen developmentally. Although all of the issues all couples have are about ruptured connecting and their yearning for restoration of connecting, the rupture occurred at a specific developmental stage. Unconsciously, couples will create a dream relationship that includes relational needs that were not met in the particular developmental stage in which they were challenged. Needs that come from the stage before that are not an issue, but the issues of the next stage will become an issue once the presenting problem is resolved.

Keeping that in mind, you may want to listen for stage-specific clues as couples state their dreams. What you can predict is that the dream will include the vision and tactics to meet the stage-specific need. For instance, if couples share a connectional rupture in stage one connecting, their issues will include complaints about how clinging or absent the partner is, disrupting the security of the relationship. If the connectional rupture occurred as an exploratory challenge, their tension will be about rebelliousness and compliance. If the connectional rupture did not occur until the identity challenge, around ages 3 or 4, they will complain about rigidity and diffuseness in their process of decision making, but not about the security of the relationship. And, if it is about competence, their tension will likely be about competitiveness and manipulation.

Since the issues in their relationship originated in a specific developmental stage, and since their vision will be about the needs specific to that stage, those needs will become the agenda and goal of therapy. However, it is important to remember that the stage after the challenged stage has stage specific needs that were also not met in childhood and will show up after the couple resolves their presenting issues. In fact, those needs will start showing up as new issues and new frustrations as the preceding frustrations are addressed. That can be disturbing to both the couple and the therapist, tempting them to think they have made no progress.

This needs to be handled with some psychoeducation, some congratulations that they have completed one stage and are ready to take their relationship to the next stage, which repeats until they finish childhood and mutually achieve emotional and mental adulthood, which is essential for creating authentic love. Prior to that, the emotional bond is need-dependent.

As you listen to partners talk about their vision, the foundation will always be about restoring connecting, but we encourage you to listen developmentally to what must be resolved to create enough safety that connecting can actually be restored, authentically.

Describing the Individual Vision
What the brain can image, it can put into words; and what it can put into words, it can use to design actions that create the ideal experience that is

portrayed in the images. The next step in the Revisioning Process is turning the holistic image into explicit behaviors, moving from imagination to actualization. Actualizing the vision requires identifying actions and specific quantifiable behaviors that would give substance to the dream. You are now facilitating the couple moving from their right brains to their prefrontal cortex so they can put flesh on the bones to actualize their vision.[17]

For this part, you can ask them to take a few moments to write out short, descriptive, and positive sentences beginning with "We" to describe their personal vision of a deeply satisfying relationship they both can potentially inhabit.

This individual vision still lacks specifics but contains general descriptions such as "We have great sex together." "We co-parent together." The vision is always worded in the positive—how they *want* things to be ("We settle our differences peacefully") rather than how they do not want them to be ("We don't fight"), always pointing toward the possible. The vision is worded in the present tense, as if they have what they want right now. And it describes the actual behaviors that happen in their dream relationship, not abstract descriptions of desired relational qualities—such as more love or kindness, etc. You are the facilitator of their healing through your natural gifts.

Have them write only a few statements during the session. Their individual visions can be completed as a between-session assignment. A series of questions and a worksheet to help the process can be found in Appendix 3, along with specific instructions so they do not have to remember what you said. Please go over all the instructions with them and answer any questions. Since this process will be challenging, some couples may unconsciously sabotage the process by disagreeing about what they are supposed to do. To prevent this, you may want them to mirror you and write it down.

Sharing the Individual Vision
When each partner has completed writing 1 or 2 statements, ask each partner to share their dream relationship statements. This is another opportunity where you can provide them with psychoeducation around two people's subjectivities: inform them that they may not agree with what their partner shares and that is okay. The focus right now is on listening and mirroring accurately. Table 12.1 is an abbreviated chart of the sentence stems.

Mark and Diana: Sharing the Dream
Let us return to Mark and Diana. After exchanging appreciations and taking them through a guided visualization, they are invited to share one item from their dream relationship with each other.

Table 12.1: Mirroring Dream Relationship Statements (Overview)	
SENDER	**RECEIVER**
Asks for Appointment Is now a good time to share my vision of our relationship?	*Grants Appointment* I'm available now.
Connects Nonverbally *Makes eye contact and takes three deep breaths in sync.* *Sender shares one-way appreciation (receiver mirrors only)*	
Shares Dream Statement In my dream relationship, we _____ *Deepens* When I see this in our relationship, it makes me feel . . . And that feeling reminds me of . . .	*Mirrors and Checks for Accuracy* If I got that, in your dream relationship, we are . . . _____ Did I get that? *Expresses Curiosity* Is there more about that? *Summarizes and Checks for Accuracy* Let me see if I got ALL of that. In your dream relationship, we are . . . And when you imagine that, you feel . . . And when you feel that you remember when you were little that . . . Did I get all of that?
Continues sharing dream statements using the steps above.	
Optional: Validating and Empathizing	
Closings Thank you for listening. / Thank you for sharing. *Give each other a one-minute hug. Switch Roles.*	

THERAPIST: *Mark would you be willing to share your vision of your dream relationship with Diana as if it is happening now?* (Mark agrees.) *Although the vision is about the future, will you please describe it in the present tense and be inclusive of Diana by using "we" or "us" as appropriate? I will give you the sentence stems and you complete the sentences, as we did in the appreciation we just did.*

As the therapist you will prompt each of them with the sentence stems below (shown in **bold**.)

MARK: **In my dream relationship, we are** *travelling to exotic places together.*

DIANA: (Mirrors) *If I got that, in your dream relationship, we are travelling to exotic places together.*

(Checks for accuracy) *Did I get that?*
(Expresses curiosity) *Is there more about that?*

MARK: *Yes, you got it, and the more is that when I imagine that, I feel happy and excited.*
DIANA: (Mirrors) *And when you imagine us travelling to exotic places together, you feel happy and excited.*

(Checks for accuracy) *Did I get that?*
(Expresses curiosity) *Is there more about that?*

MARK: *Yes, and when I feel that, it reminds me that when I was little, in the summertime, my dad would take me on different hikes in the Catskills. Sometimes he would pull out the map and let me choose a new path. But we generally did a different one each time and made a day of it. It was just us. It didn't happen often but when it did, it was really special. I felt special. And I loved the sense of exploring with someone I loved.*

Diana mirrors, checks for accuracy, and invites more. When Mark says there is "no more," the therapist prompts Diana to summarize, check for accuracy, and share mutual gratitude.

THERAPIST: *OK, great work. Now let's change roles, and Diana, you are the sender and Mark the receiver. Is that ok?*

When it was Diana's turn, she shared with Mark her vision of co-parenting Jake together.

NOTE: While validating and empathizing are important pieces of the Dialogue Process, it may be difficult for couples to do those steps in the beginning of therapy. Whether you teach these techniques now or later, requires your clinical judgment about their capacity to do so. If you feel mirroring is all they can do, you can move to facilitate the closings. If they do the mirroring well, you may gently invite them to practice validating and empathizing. Remember, Imago Dialogue is a skill with "moves" that must be learned sequentially and practiced exactly to achieve the intended result of creating a safe context in which connecting can occur.

The dialogue about a specific behavior in contrast to a global picture gives them a sense of the difference between a quantity (the specific behavior) and a quality (the global image) in their relationship. Now, the process shifts to a between-session assignment to list, working separately (Appendix 3), all the behaviors they can imagine happening in their dream relationship and to bring the list to their next session.

COCREATING A JOINT RELATIONSHIP VISION

When they return for their next session, ask the couple to take turns reading the behaviors to each other and mirroring, briefly, each behavior (Appendix 4). When they have finished, ask them to compare their lists, checking off statements they both agree on. The checked items can be combined and put on a single list, Our Relationship Vision (Appendix 5). For the items they could not agree on, these statements should be moved to Our Relationship Potential (Appendix 6). Be sure to review the following to help them with the process:

- Identify what is the same and what is similar. The distinction between these two are often linguistic; the substance is often the same. These elements indicate the operative resources in their relationship, which can immediately be amplified.
- Discover what is different but could be included in their joint dream relationship. Some of these were just not thought of and could be included without stretching. Some are different enough that they would never have been considered, but they are acceptable and could be integrated as new behaviors. These elements offer the potential for new and exciting behaviors and opportunities for growth.
- What features, if any, are so different that either or both partners respond with something on the order of "no way in hell." While we generally take the position that "incompatibility is the grounds of a great marriage" and that the more different the individuals, the more potential for growth, it is usually wiser at this point to set these radical opposites aside for another day and return to them later in therapy. They should not be discarded, however, because they offer the couple the greatest potential for using their imagination to create new and adventurous behaviors and a thriving relationship. The disparate points go on a list called Our Relationship Potential. But for now, there is enough to work on. Reinforcing the same and similar elements will help stabilize the relationship and integrating those that are acceptably different will stretch the couple beyond their comfort zone and into relational growth.

While sorting out the matter of similarities and differences, sometimes partners are surprised by the way their separate visions intersect or are similar. Finding similarities is a powerful bond. When they find differences, the couple is more likely to consider the differences challenging or undesirable and perhaps an indication that their relationship may be a mistake rather than seeing them as beneficial or enriching. But that is the illusion of compatibility being preferable, if not essential, for a thriving relationship. This, too, is an important distinction to make. Just as opposites attract is a fact, the idea that our mate must be like us to be our chosen mate is a myth.

Nature, however, and counterintuitively, has decided that incompatibility is the grounds for a great relationship. The tension of opposites provides the energy for creative outcomes not available with compatibility. It is like the difference between monoculture and biodiversity. An environment with biodiversity is healthier and more likely to thrive. The discovery of Imago theory is that the more difference, the more growth, and the more satisfying the outcome. Ultimately the embracing and acceptance of difference facilitates differentiation—ending symbiosis—and becomes the hallmark of a conscious partnership.

The couple can complete this process at home, but if they do, it is important that you ask them to bring the cocreated Relationship Vision to the next session so they can take turns reading the joint relationship vision statements out loud with you as a witness. Keep a copy of their vision statement yourself, since it is the map for therapy and a means of evaluation. Also keep a copy of the items with which they were not in agreement (the Relationship Potential worksheet), so you can support them later, when they want to evolve their relationship to the potential embedded in their differences.

AT THE THERAPIST'S DISCRETION: You have two choices if partners can't agree on the nuances of the wording. You can ask them to dialogue in more depth about the item they are seeing differently; your goal would be to have them express in one or two sentences the essence of what they both want so they can both add it to their list. Or, you can have them put the item on the Our Relationship Potential list for a dialogue at some point in the future.

FROM THE RELATIONSHIP VISION TO SPECIFIC STRATEGY AND TACTICS

The last step in the Revisioning Process is creating specific strategies and tactics. To start this process, you ask each partner to describe the behavior in such detail that if it were recorded and shown to a stranger, the stranger would know how to do the behavior. That is, strategies should be SMART (**S**pecific, **M**easurable, **A**ttainable, **R**elevant, and **T**ime-limited) and include sensory experiences. For example, a vision statement of "We are healthy" can be converted into "We exercise together for thirty minutes each day for the next two weeks." Corresponding sensory experiences could be salty (taste); sweaty (smell), hot (touch), grunts (sound), sexy and energetic (feel; Appendix 7). While they can work separately to come up with specific behaviors and share in a Dialogue, partners can also work together to cocreate specifics around a vision statement. Again, the process is primary, outcome is secondary.

Once all the steps in the Revisioning Process are completed:

- Ask them to post their mutual Relationship Vision in a prominent place in their home (or elsewhere) where they will see it every day.
- Suggest couples take turns reading out loud the mutual Relationship Vision list every day for 90 days.
- Assign them to do behaviors from the vision list on a regular basis and to imagine those behaviors on a daily basis.
- Later in therapy, visit the Relationship Potential list.

The Features of the Wavicle Dream

While the process described above provides the mechanics of the Revisioning Process, it is also a fluid process between imagery ("wave") and concrete behaviors ("particle"). Couples are encouraged to move from imagining the general experience to verbalizing statements to creating specifics around behaviors, and then back to imagining engaging in those behaviors. For example:

Guided Imagery of Global Vision: Walking outside holding hands in a warm sunlit forest.

- Personal Vision Statement: We travel together.
- Joint Vision Statement: We travel together frequently to exotic places.
- Specific Strategy: We travel together to new places, outside our state, at least twice a year.
- Guided Imagery of Specific Strategy: We are walking the steps of the Parthenon under an Athenian summer sun.

Research has indicated that mental practices (such as visualizations and affirmations) are almost as effective as true physical practice and that doing both is more effective than either alone (Burton & Lent, 2016; Strong & Pyle, 2009; Ranganathan et al., 2004).

An Important Aside!

The Revisioning Process is not an assignment to complete, but a vibrant and evolving process that is woven throughout the sessions and the couple's life. To that end, it is essential for the couple to understand and hear this stated clearly, from you, the therapist. This is not an assignment offered in therapy but a new way of being.

The statements should be fluid and "tweaked" as the relationship grows, guiding partners in the day-to-day choices they make. It is their statements of intention, and it becomes a larger beacon the couple can look to when they stray off the path. And it is a left brain–right brain function. They dream and share in images, they translate those images into a behavior, they create strategies and tactics around that behavior and integrate them in their relationship, and they move back into imagining that behavior, all on a regular basis. What has been unconscious must become conscious and what has been instinctual must become intentional. So, this process, both the means—the incremental indices of progress gained through talking it out—and the ends—the measurable outcomes that are enshrined in the desires of the dream—may take a while. That's fine. Because, as mentioned, **the journey is the outcome**. In fact, it is important to caution against the vision becoming a list of "commandments" rather than a list of actions that help the relationship achieve its potential.

Table 12.2 lists behaviors Mark and Diana imagined would constitute that vision after completing therapy.

Pointers for the Therapist:
- Keep the partners in the ideal and out of comparisons with their current reality.
- Keep them experiencing the positive.
- Keep them in the present tense, as if their ideal were happening to them now.
- Keep them out of negating or shaming their partner. Maintaining a safe space is your number one priority.
- With some highly conflicted and deeply wounded couples whose hopes have been shattered over and over by many broken promises, you may choose to just have them come up with one or two items each that will then be the focus of the therapy.
- Always help them identify small concrete steps they can take to help them move forward just a little at a time.
- In addition to reading their Relationship Vision themselves every day, they can read it at the beginning of every therapy session.

Table 12.2: Mark and Diana: Our Relationship Vision	
• We travel together to exotic places twice a year.	• When the other is sharing something they are experiencing, we listen and mirror them back.
• We take turns reading to Jake every night.	• We take turns initiating a high-energy fun experience each day.
• We host extended family gatherings for at least one major holiday a year.	• When we have a special win, we celebrate it with high energy.
• We remove all negativity from our relationship by signing the Zero Negativity pledge.	• We ask for what we want rather than express a frustration.
• When we have a frustration, we ask for what we want rather than criticize.	• We take a walk each day as our schedule allows.
• When we experience a rupture, we will say "ouch," we mutually engage in reconnecting immediately.	• We have annual medical and dental checkups.
• We give each other three appreciations each day.	• We eat a healthy diet all the time.
• We begin each day with a smile and a warm gaze.	• We take time off each day to connect.
• We give each other a hug in the morning and whenever we see each other during the day.	• We contribute to a shared checking account for our living expenses.
• We make love at least once each week.	• We have a private account for our personal expenses.
• We put down our phones when the other comes into the room and connect.	• We discuss our differences and express respect for the other's point of view.
• We text each other at least twice a day.	• We cuddle each night as we go to sleep.
• We give each other a surprise once a month.	• When we are separate for any reason, we stay in touch by text each day.
	• We volunteer at a homeless shelter at least once each month.
	• When we are with others, we advocate each other's point of view.

DEEPENING THE REVISIONING PROCESS

We have said that the Relationship Vision can be used as a beacon for the couple, guiding them toward the creation of a conscious partnership. But it can also be used as a specific tool for the therapist and for the couple to see whether they are making progress toward their goals.

In addition, it can become a specific focus for additional effort. This exercise can be done during a therapy session or at home by the couple alone.

Here are the instructions for filling out the Shared Relationship Vision Scale (Appendix 8).

Step One: *Make a List:* Each partner, alone, writes down every statement from their shared Relationship Vision. Each of them separately rates each statement from 1 to 10 in terms of how satisfied they are today. 0 = No satisfaction; 10 = Very high satisfaction.

Step Two: *Share:* Partners share their ratings with each other, showing curiosity about places where there is discrepancy. Together, they choose one item to Dialogue about, paying particular attention to: (1) what they can each do (specific tactics) to raise their satisfaction by half a point, and (2) enumerating the challenges that might get in the way.

Step Three: *Check In:* After two weeks, the partners check in with each other and Dialogue about their successes and challenges. What specific actions did they take and how successful or unsuccessful were they? Why? What would help?

Step Four: *Repeat the Process:* Partners agree to choose another or the same item as a focus for trying to raise satisfaction over the next two weeks. After two weeks, they use Dialogue as a way of assessing their progress and addressing the problems.

OUTCOMES OF THE REVISIONING PROCESS

Creating the Relationship Vision provides a new experience from the onset of therapy. It helps couples:

- Learn a new way to talk and listen, through the Imago Dialogue process. This may be the first time, in a long time, that they have talked without polarizing. (Any attempt they make to engage in "I–It" language should be interrupted and redirected. "Would you be willing to try it this way?" becomes our constant refrain.)
- Uncover the unconscious wishes and identify a way to measure the progress of the therapy sessions.
- Shift their focus away from the past (blame) and toward a new future (hope). This translates negative complaints into positive desires (moving from the hippocampus to the prefrontal cortex). An important Imago lesson is "what you focus on is what you get." Focusing on the past keeps couples stuck in the past. Focusing on the future moves couples into living the dream.
- Cocreate shared meaning. Finding similarities helps couples to feel more bonded and connected. Practicing what is similar will *enrich* their relationship.
- Define differences, which, they will come to realize, are okay. It is the first lesson in differentiation and later becomes a lesson for growth and healing. Practicing what is different will *transform* their relationship.

- Become intentional. If they can imagine the relationship they desire and keep that image present in their awareness, they can create it by making choices that are consistent with their own intentions. Intentionality means living in alignment with the Vision rather than reacting in response to the moment.
- Foster curiosity through the whys that are inferred throughout the steps. Why is this important to you? Why is my behavior not consistent with the dream? The couple should be moving away from judgment (of partner and of the self) toward being inquisitive.
- Establish a doable between-session routine at home.

Takeaways for the Revisioning Process

- The Revisioning Process is introduced in the very first session. This becomes the therapeutic roadmap.
- As the therapist, it is important to resist any pressure to talk about their problems and/or complaints.
- Couples unconsciously model their relationship after what they have witnessed and internalized from their families. Thus, couples need to be intentional in cocreating a relationship vision to move from an implicit vision to an explicit plan.
- Revisioning accesses both left and right brain functions—oscillating back and forth between specific actions and visualizing.
- Revisioning is not an assignment to complete, but a vibrant and evolving process. Provide between-session assignments frequently.

TIP: Content is secondary; connecting is primary. It is the journey that is the outcome. Honor resistance, find common values, celebrate all achievements, and revisit your successes often. Creating the Relationship Vision in the first sessions of therapy gives you and your couple a map for the work you are doing together and a way of evaluating whether you are making progress. It is the place to come back to when your couple is wandering off into the weeds again. And it can be used as an integral part of a marriage or recommitment ceremony, should you recommend it and should the couple desire it.

FAQ for Therapists

Q: How should I handle a couple who is resistant to the process?
A: With some highly conflicted and deeply wounded couples whose hopes have been shattered over and over by many broken promises,

resistance is understandable. The first task is to honor the resistance. Second is to have them stretch a little, taking a small step forward. Shift the language so that it is more palatable, such as "Imagine how you are as a couple five sessions from now. What are you doing in the office?" Or you may ask them to recall one item from the past but put it in the present tense as if it is still occurring. A few sessions later, you can return and ask them to share some additional dream statements.

Q: Are there any instances where you do not introduce this in the first session?

A: Yes: When it is obvious that the couple is in a crisis and cannot access their prefrontal cortex and some remedial intervention is essential immediately (e.g., they are intoxicated, abusive, have physical bruises, etc.). In these cases—when there are obvious safety issues—you will need to attend with crisis intervention methods. Maintaining a safe space is your number one priority.

Q: What happens if a couple cannot find many similarities in their personal dreams?

A: This can be a common experience with couples in conflict. The Revisioning Process is an ongoing, fluid process. Normalize the experience with the couple and make a commitment to revisit the exercise regularly. Dreams will expand, change, and evolve as safety increases and connection deepens.

In the next chapter, we will visit the Recommitting Process, which takes us through restoring the necessary energy to the relationship rather than draining the energy to outside activities.

13

Recommitting

What: Couples commit to removing ambivalence from the relationship and closing exits.

Why: To increase trust, safety, and energy in the relationship.

When: Introduce after the Revisioning Process and provide between-session assignments throughout therapy.

Recommitting is an act of surrender, of letting go of any distraction that deprives the relationship vision of the attention it needs to materialize as a way of life. In fact, surrender is the core of commitment.[18] Everything that does not serve the optimal welfare of the relationship is excluded. The new commitment is first to the relationship, second to the Imago therapy process, and third to the partner—a paradox that serves both persons in the relationship and, in turn, the relationship itself.

Surrender also means letting go of ambivalence. Ambivalence means one foot in and one foot out of the relationship, whereas commitment is both feet in all the time. The only way to create a dream relationship is through unflinching devotion to the journey and to the process of getting there. Commitment without ambivalence is simple: keep all the energy that belongs in the relationship *in* the relationship, and do not invest intimate relational energy into anyone or anything else for any reason. In these sessions, the therapist helps the couple **discover and modify and/or remove** all emotional investments outside the relationship that might sabotage success on their journey to a conscious partnership. What is also important in Imago therapy is not only the commitment of both partners but the perceived commitment of each. If one partner doesn't perceive the other as committed to the relationship, anxiety ensues, destabilizing the relational foundation. In a recent longitudinal study that included over 11,000 couples, it was found that perceived commitment was the #1 predictor of relationship success (Joel et al., 2020).

THE SOURCES OF AMBIVALENCE

The emotional distress that feeds the ambivalence of partners replicates the pain they experienced with their neglectful or intrusive caretakers who were not attuned to their needs. That connectional rupture activated the intolerable sensation of anxiety, which manifested, in varying degrees, as anger or depression. Anger is a protest against relational rupture. Depression is a collapse into helplessness. Both mask anxiety triggered by the anticipation that their needs will never be met.

Since the needs reside in the part of the brain that is not connected to time, but are connected to survival, there is the deeper unconscious fear that if the needs are not met, one might cease to exist at all. This desperate situation fuels the enormous temptation to find substitute satisfaction to regulate the terrifying sensation of potential nonbeing. Given this universal story, a first response to frustration is to run toward activities, events, and people who represent pleasure and to run away from the partner, who is perceived as hurtful, like the caretakers who preceded them. For many people, the way out seems to be cultivating a relationship with a nonintimate person or a range of pleasurable activities—work, addictions, social media, etc.—as an attempt to fill the void.

Popular opinion tends to portray people getting themselves into this fix because they did not choose the right partner in the first place. In the cultural narrative, all you have to do to have a great marriage is to marry the right person, and you will live happily ever after.

The Imago perspective is completely different.

For the Imago therapist, the right person is chosen by the unconscious— and that person would not be chosen by the conscious mind. With them, conflict is inevitable, and is, in fact, growth trying to happen. If couples abandon the struggle that is taking place outside their awareness, they will miss the transformational potential present in their perceived incompatibility which, in quantum terms, are the poles of their complementarity. Partners don't have to be perfect for each other; they just have to be intentional and dedicated and present to the relationship as they interact in the tensions of the transformation process. That is what makes them perfect, for each other!

Your role as therapist is to guide the couple through the processes of containing reactivity, eliminating all the energy leaks in the Space-Between, refocusing on the needs of the relationship and keeping them in the process. During this process, the couple ideally will shift focus to conscious engagement as they begin to feel and experience hope. Paradoxically, nothing outside their relationship will be as interesting as what they will discover inside it, in time.

RECOMMITTING AS A PROCESS

The purpose of the Recommitting Process, like all the steps leading to a conscious partnership, is to create a safe emotional environment in which connecting can be restored and sustained. Remember the prime directive of the brain is safety. Safety is the ability to predict what is going to happen next. And that it will be good or great. Confidence in partner commitment is the primary source of predictability, and thus the quality of the relationship. Ambivalence won't work. You can't wait until you are certain to commit; you have to commit, then you are certain. A paradox, we know, but a fact nevertheless. When we take action and operationalize our intention, the brain can move beyond recycling and repeating the past. We can create new neural pathways that allow us to replace old habits driven by old fears with new actions that create safety.[19] The bottom line is that if the couple wants durability and joyful aliveness in their relationship, they will have to go beyond intention to action. No amount of understanding, insight, and desire changes behavior. Behavior is a risk that must become a choice in an anxious situation, without which no new forms can come into being.

As in Revisioning, Recommitting is a process rather than a single event. It does not happen in one session, nor is it a one-time thing. Engaging in the process may take several sessions, and it is renewed every day for the rest of the relationship. The process redefines commitment and facilitates awareness of energies that rightfully belong inside the relationship but are being expended outside. By identifying these energy leaks, called *exits*,[20] you help couples recommit to their relationship, recover safety, and develop the skills to restore and sustain connecting.

EXITS AND THE INVISIBLE DIVORCE

An exit is a form of "acting out" unspoken, painful feelings by finding satisfaction outside the relationship with another person (distraction or self-soothing activity) rather than talking about the feelings that are stimulated in the relationship. A relationship with an exit is like a tire with a tiny puncture that is slowly but steadily leaking air; sooner or later, it goes flat.

Exits are available everywhere, and relational pain makes use of them. People can show great creativity when it comes to avoiding being in each other's company! A partner may have hobbies that look perfectly reasonable, such as playing bingo or basketball, watching sports on TV, or going away for weekends with the girls. They seem harmless, except when they intrude on the sacred space of the primary relationship. Even necessary everyday activities can function as exits, although the exiting partner may not have intended them to be. They may have no choice about working overtime or taking a second job to make ends meet. There may be kids (or grandkids) to raise, bills to pay, homes to maintain, a circle of friends to keep in touch with, or relatives to keep happy. And, finally, there are exits that start out innocently enough but end up being deal breakers. Going out to lunch with a new coworker does not have to be an exit, but sometimes, it becomes one.

Over time, the emotional connection begins to shred until the relationship is hanging on by a thread. When the energy needed to keep a couple's relationship alive becomes the atmosphere of other relationships, they are living the "invisible divorce." In this state, couples remain in their relationship while breaking the cardinal rules of a committed relationship, often inflicting tremendous pain on each other in the process.

Paradoxically, when couples use the Dialogue process to talk about their fears and temptations rather than acting out with others, they effectively close the exit by "acting in."

In Imago therapy, we identify four different types of exits.

Functional. Any behavior becomes an exit if one partner consistently experiences it as an exit, even when the behavior is not intended to avoid one's partner. Examples: playing out of town with your rock band, going to school full time while also working full time, taking a promotion requiring frequent trips out of town, being a professional on call (like the medical profession or first responders), etc. In a functional exit, relational energy is invested elsewhere and may drain the relationship of the energy it needs, but the energy drain may not be intentional.

Motivated. Motivated exits are strategies that partners deliberately use to avoid interacting with each other. The behaviors may be benign, but the consequences are destructive. Examples: online gaming, watching TV, taking on an evening job to get out of the house, working late when it's not necessary, spending every free hour at the volunteer firehouse, focusing exclusively on the kids, getting increasingly involved in politics, etc.

Catastrophic. A catastrophic exit, when left open, will likely cause the demise of the relationship. Examples: Affairs, drug or alcohol addiction, excessive gambling, mental illness, and other relationally toxic and destructive behavior patterns.

Terminal. A terminal exit is the most calamitous. These are few in number, but they are deadly. Terminal exits include: divorce, murder, and suicide. They immediately, and irrevocably, end the relationship.

Terminal and catastrophic exits need to be addressed immediately and with great care. If divorce, suicide, or murder is on the table as an option, this calls for radical intervention that may involve frequent sessions, making behavioral contracts, sometimes medication, and always a commitment to at least 12 sessions to establish a bond and a process that stabilizes the relationship. If neither partner is contemplating terminal exits, then the therapist should discover whether partners are engaging in catastrophic exits.

Catastrophic Exits: Addictions

There are three main catastrophic exits: addictions, mental illness, and affairs. In a sense, addictions and affairs are the same, but, for the sake of simplicity and clarity, we will discuss them separately because they elicit different responses from the partner. Addictions tend to elicit frustration and despair, affairs tend to elicit anger and depression, and mental illness tends to elicit sadness and empathy.

NOTE: It is important that you, as a therapist, work through your own life experience with addictions, mental illness, and/or affairs so as not to unconsciously act out of bias with clients. This is what we are taught early on, however, it bears repeating.

Historically, addiction has been treated through the intrapsychic lens of the individual paradigm as an individual problem. The standard treatment model involves identification of the problem, referral to treatment, relapse prevention, and lifetime maintenance (Lemanski, 2001; White, 2014). Thousands of treatment facilities offer excellent treatment to addicts. The problems begin when addicts reenter their home environments with partners and other family members who have not had the opportunity to participate in the recovery process and grow and change along with the addict. Addicts are often referred to 12-step programs while their coaddicts are referred to ALANON. These programs offer individuals huge advances in personal growth, but unless an addict–coaddict couple is also growing together, they can easily grow apart.

In Imago theory, addiction is initially a compensation for a connectional rupture. The Imago theoretical premise is that the addictive use of drugs or certain behaviors is a replacement of a relationship with something else, like porn or social media, which compensates for the need not met in the relationship. The drug or activity becomes the lover that offers a substitute sensation of full aliveness or compensates for its absence in a context other than the relationship. The drug numbs the anxiety of relational rupture and serves as a substitute for the partner.

Imago therapy provides the context, tools, and expertise the couple needs to deal with recovery together, as a unit. Therefore, it follows that the deepest and most sustainable recovery will come from helping couples restore and sustain connection. To do that, you always see the couple together. While it is common for each partner to also be in individual therapy, we have discovered that separate sessions, even with the same therapist, is a parallel process that tends to create an imbalance in the growth process, and that parallel growth contributes to the possibility of further rupture. It is like taking tennis lessons in separate sessions. Partners learn different swings and practice them with the coach or another student. They learn the tennis dance with another person. When they come together to play tennis, they find they are playing with a stranger whose moves come as a surprise, and they have to learn to dance again with each other. If they had taken the tennis classes together, they would have learned the rules and moves of the game at the same time.

Partners need a context in which they can bond and grow together. This is challenged when individual recovery treatments are engaged in by each partner. A couple recovering together using the Imago tools has a greater chance of achieving the sense of full aliveness they are both seeking.[21]

Catastrophic Exits: Mental Illness

You may ask, "How can mental illness be an exit from a relationship?" since it is an expression of genes that have been inherited. Research that studies the impact of relational stressors on mental health suggests that relational stressors may activate genetic vulnerability. With new evidence of the impact of experience on DNA expression, it is conceivable that mental illnesses do not originate in the mind, but in the mind's interaction with its environment. It appears that the more accurate term for the most severe of these symptoms, schizophrenia and manic–depressive psychosis, could be "relational disorder."[22] That is why we prefer not to give anyone a diagnostic label of any kind, and because once labeled, it is nearly impossible to remove it from one's own mind as well as from the minds of others. Once a "schizophrenic," always a "schizophrenic." In Imago theory, this kind of labeling is considered abusive.

Whether the phenomena referred to by the terms schizophrenia and manic–depression are biological and genetic disorders or whether they compensate for the absence of a safe relational context in which connecting is predictable and sustainable depends on whether we look at them through the paradigm of the individual or the paradigm of relationship. If through the individual paradigm, then biology and genetics as cause and cure or regulation through medications make sense. Since the individual paradigm is still the dominant lens through which most research in medicine, psychology, and therapy look, it makes sense they would see suffering as intrapsychic stress in an isolated, separate self and healing as intrapsychic relief.

If we look at the same phenomena through the relational paradigm (grounded in the quantum field)—as Imago does—emotional and mental distress, at the level described as schizophrenia and manic–depression, are symptoms of an intolerable state of anxiety, which is loss of human connection and, through that intrinsic thread, the potential loss of experiencing connecting in the quantum field. It is not difficult to imagine that the potentiality of nonbeing would cause an amazing oscillation between mania and depression and the creation of an imaginary world that, for them, is safe.

In addition to the logic of paradigm consistency, Imago theory cites as its sources a list of distinguished and scholarly clinicians and researchers. Among them are Harry Stack Sullivan (1953), Ronald Laing (1969), Gregory Bateson, Don Jackson, Jay Haley, and John Weakland (1956), all of whom assigned these two severe mental illnesses to interpersonal stress caused by infectious anxiety and "problems in living" (Sullivan, 1953), anxious confusion caused by an epigenetic event (Bateson et al., 1956), and an "incompatible knot" (Laing, 1970) caused by the social cradle of the urban home (Laing, 1961, 1969). Imago takes the position, along with these clinicians, that although the predisposition toward mental illness can be inherited, its activation is triggered by negativity which in turn triggers anxiety that makes relational contexts threatening.

Obviously, this discussion is very old and controversial, and the objective opinion is to wait on more empirical research. However, because the questions researchers ask tend to originate in a paradigm, all answers have a paradigm bias that renders objective answers impossible. In the quantum field, the principle of uncertainty posits that when we choose what data to believe, all other options collapse and our choice will create the reality of the source and cure of mental illnesses which we will interpret as objective.

In the meantime, you will have to make up your own mind. Whatever you choose is what you will see. If you become an Imago therapist and look at your clients through the relational/quantum lens, you will see the source of suffering of human beings, including the mentally ill population, as a severe relational disorder, and you will see that disorder as a defense against an intolerable anxiety caused by relational stress that ruptures our sense of belonging to our social context and to the cosmos.

Catastrophic Exits: Affairs

Many couples come to therapy because one partner has discovered that the other partner is involved with another person, sexually or emotionally. Some affairs have already ended before the couple enters therapy, and the partners are there to deal with the remaining consequences. Some partners take turns having affairs while the other pretends not to notice. And there are other couples who agree to an "open" marriage and engage in outside relationships. Whether the affair is considered catastrophic or not depends on the kind of energy the affair has engendered in both partners. Affairs reflect developmental issues and the pattern of wounding and defense in childhood is re-created by both partners in the adult relationship.

Affairs are an obvious and serious exit from a relationship and indicate a profound lack of safety and intimacy. They are popular substitutes for missing intimacy. Partners use them to exit the pain in their relationship by discharging or avoiding feelings they cannot deal with in a safe and soothing way. There is an old saying that "no one walks away from love." Also, like for mental illness, the tendency toward affairs can be relationally inherited. Nine out of 10 people who have affairs also have extended family members who have had an affair. And affairs are gender complicated. If a man has an affair, the marriage is more likely to continue than if a woman has an affair. A man is more likely to consider himself happily married and to think of the affair as just sexual, whereas a woman is more likely to be emotionally involved and to have disconnected emotionally from the marriage by the time she has an affair.[23]

Affairs are relational rather than individual. They arise in the relationship because of the deficits there, rather than from the inner deficits of an individual. While this does not excuse an affair, it does explain its source. When any of us experiences a need deficit, it is important to remember that we can be "unfaithful" to our partners in many different ways: by talking with friends, by refusing sex, by developing greater emotional intimacy with a therapist than with our partner, or by violating the marital bed. Both partners contribute to the pain in the relationship and both act it out, although in different ways.

Both the "betrayer" and the "betrayed" may hold on to their own survival strategies, whatever they may be, for a long time in therapy. It is often much more difficult for the "betrayed" partner to own their contribution to the affair and to acknowledge the ways in which the diminished intimacy has been "working" for them. If the partner having the affair is in the romantic love stage with the new partner, the PEA (phenylethylamine) induced "altered state" may render them cognitively and psychologically unavailable to do the work of therapy.[24] Here's the choice as they see it: hard work versus the ease, spontaneity, and aliveness of romantic love.

Often the "betrayed" partner wants to know details about the affair. It is important to work very carefully with this. In exploring the details, the capacities of both partners should be held in balance: the capacity of the betrayed partner to actually hear the details, and the capacity of the betraying partner to contain the reactivity that the details unleash. If the details are asked for, and the partner then stretches into giving them but then gets attacked, shamed, or punished so that it is impossible to feel compassion for the hurt that was caused, the impulse toward secrecy is reinforced. The betrayed partner is wounded again through secrecy and the betraying partner is doubly sure that saying the truth brings punishment. "When I am in contact with you or express myself to you, your reactivity causes me pain."

Mistrust is the residual issue after an affair. It is important to balance the affairee's needs to know where the partner is and what they are doing, with the affairer's needs to feel safe from being annihilated, smothered, overcontrolled, and manipulated.

Just as in other catastrophic exits, Imago Dialogue is the process for dealing with affairs. Dialogue holds the couple in connection through the incredibly painful process of dealing with the "ultimate betrayal." Dialogue allows the therapist to create a safe Space-Between, where the partners can start to express all that needs to be expressed. Safety and neutrality are the nonnegotiable conditions that make it possible for a couple to deal with an affair in a productive and healing way. Instead of a traditional blame and release cycle where the one who didn't have the affair blames the other and it is sorted through, Imago focuses on the goal of safe conversations that lead to a conscious relationship.

Therapist neutrality is essential to safety. The therapist is often the only person in the couple's world holding a non-judgmental stance in the Space-Between. This makes it possible for partners to look at and own their contribution to the affair without focusing on the "bad behavior" of the other partner. This can be a delicate balancing act, requiring the therapist to be centered at the fulcrum of the relationship, holding both partners in equal respect and compassion. Constant use of the structure of the Imago Dialogue process helps partners listen with empathy to the other's experience, understand what is happening within the relationship that has contributed to the affair, own their own roles in the breach, and understand the affair in terms of childhood needs and adaptations.

For all catastrophic exits, when couples hang in there through the tough times, and many seem highly motivated to do so, they come out of therapy with a better and stronger relationship than they had before. Many report that they are spending time with each other and talking with each other in ways they have not experienced since the beginning of their relationship. The therapist holds the hope that the relationship crisis will be the catalyst that will motivate them to examine their relationship and do the work of growth and healing. Once a client shared at the end of therapy, "Even though it was hellishly painful, in some ways I'm grateful that it happened because we have a much better relationship now than we did before!"

THE RECOMMITTING PROCESS

The Recommitting Process is delicate and must be facilitated with great skill, otherwise the outcome could be more deleterious than the problem. Some exits are serious threats to the relationship, like affairs and drugs, and their disclosure can be shocking to the receiving partner. In some cases, a partner cannot promise to close one or more exits right away, even though they understand it is causing harm to their relationship. If forced, they may use a terminal exit, such as divorce. Always accept with grace whatever a partner is willing to offer. Except for terminal or catastrophic exits, in which someone's life may be in danger, the closing of a specific exit is not important. What is important is engaging in the exit closing process, and that means talking about feelings rather than acting them out. Focus on closing the exits that are achievable.

Partners should take small steps over time rather than making big changes that cannot be sustained. This allows them to get to know their partner's needs, to develop compassion for the exits their partner is using, and to understand that exiting indicates the need to work on making the relationship safe. For you the therapist, this process can offer a revealing glimpse into the complex dynamic of how partners with different energy expressions (maximizers and minimizers) manage their anxiety when connecting is ruptured. Sometimes, startling reversals happen and the intricate dance of growth, healing, and transformation becomes visible.

The steps for the Recommitting Process are as follows:

1. Draw up commitment contract (if this was not done in the first session).
2. Provide psychoeducation (teach couples about exits and how they have served an unmet need in the old relationship).
3. Identify exits.
   a. Use Imago Dialogue to share one exit they use that prevents the dream from happening, and to discover the underlying fear. (*NOTE:* If validation and empathy were not introduced earlier, this is the time to bring in the full Imago Dialogue.)
   b. Provide instructions for between-session assignments to identify all exits in the relationship.
   c. Share all exits in the following therapy session.
4. Close or modify exits (using the Commitment Dialogue).

Step 1: Drawing Up the Commitment Contract
The therapeutic map to a conscious partnership and to the dream both partners have of the relationship requires a commitment. Usually, we ask

couples during their first session to agree to stay through the turbulence and rupture of their homeostasis by making a Commitment Contract. The commitment is to attend all 12 therapy sessions together; make no long-term decisions about the relationship during the time period; and commit to the process practiced in therapy. Since closing exits will also rupture the homeostatic state of their brain, this time commitment becomes even more important. As each partner closes an exit and deepens their engagement with their partner, anxiety will increase, and the temptation to leave therapy or leave the relationship will increase. The Commitment Contract is usu-ally sufficient to stabilize this process. If the Commitment Contract was not done in the first session, it should be discussed and agreed to before begin-ning the next step. Without this commitment, ambivalence may remain, destabilizing the relationship.

Some couples may not be able to make this commitment right away, and others will be able to make it only if they are given more time. If there is resis-tance to committing to 12 sessions, honor and respect the resistance, explore it, and determine with the couple what they would be willing to commit to. Sometimes it's just for one more session. If this is the case, pay attention to this commitment process at the beginning of the next session—reminding them of the commitment, asking how it worked for them and if they are will-ing to commit to an additional 2 sessions, or 4 sessions, or the full 12 sessions.

Step 2: Some Useful Psychoeducation

The bridge from revisioning to recommitting is seamless. Couples can-not achieve the dream while necessary energy is leaking externally. These are the ideas the therapist will want to present to the couple in guiding the Recommitting Process:

- The relationship vision they cocreated requires a commitment to keep all the energy that belongs in the relationship *in* the relationship.
- Exits:
  - are behaviors that are expressions of relational ambivalence
  - tend to be unconscious attempts to compensate for relational stress
  - are an indication that the relationship has become unsafe for both partners
  - bring relief from anxiety and provide transient satisfaction or pleasure
  - compensate for, or substitute for, unmet needs in the relationship
  - sabotage one's ability to achieve their dream relationship
- Acknowledge that intimacy is scary to all of us because our hurts have been around ruptured closeness.

- Provide examples of all types of exits (catastrophic, terminal, functional, and motivated.)
- Suggest that rather than "acting out," we want to achieve "acting in," which essentially consists of **identifying** our exits and then **talking** about them.
- Assure the couple that you will not ask them to close exits immediately (except for catastrophic and terminal exits which must be addressed immediately). Introduce the idea of gradually closing exits to keep positive energy in the relationship.
- Acknowledge that the hardest exits to surrender are likely to be those that give intense pleasure or long-awaited gratification of desires.
- Ask them to trust the process.

Step 3: Address Exits

Step 3a: Identify an Exit

Closing an exit is a confessional process in which the exit must first be identified and owned. This process helps both partners become vulnerable to each other and prepares them for mutual empathy. Emphasize that this process is about each partner identifying their own exits, not identifying their partner's exits, and owning their individual contribution to the relational state.

After providing some psychoeducation on exits, you can ask the couple whether either of them can think of an exit they might use or are using that would sabotage their relationship vision. Then invite them to share that exit with their partner, as information only, using the Imago Dialogue.

Because exits are a way of behaviorally expressing feelings that have not been put into language, the way to start closing them is to start talking about them in a contained way. The structure of the Dialogue process makes it safe to speak and listen to each other's realities with a sense of openness, curiosity, and empathy rather than judgment and shaming. Expressing unspoken feelings rather than acting them out is an essential part of the exit closing process. The goal is to bring the energy back into the relationship so the relationship can become the source of satisfaction for unmet needs. When the exiting behaviors can be put into language, they no longer serve a purpose. Dialogical engagement makes the Space-Between safe enough for connecting to be restored and to mitigate the need for exits.

The therapist asks who wants to go first and then facilitates each fully sharing one exit using Imago Dialogue (see Table 13.1). Here you will want to uncover the feelings, fears, and childhood association underneath the activity, while coaching the receiver to mirror, validate, and empathize. (The full Dialogue can be found in Appendix 10.)

NOTE: It is important that both partners share an exit in the same session so that both know that each is using exits to manage their feelings in the relationship.

Step 3b: Identifying All Exits

Once both partners share an exit fully, the between-session assignment is to go home and write down all potential exits each partner engages in to avoid intimacy. Instruct them to put a check mark by the ones they are willing to close or modify and an X by the ones they are not yet willing to close.

NOTES:

1. ASK THEM NOT TO SHARE THE LISTS WITH EACH OTHER and to work alone.
2. Remind them that the focus is on the "I" and not the "you" (what

Table 13.1: Sharing an Exit in Dialogue: Sentence Stems	
SENDER	RECEIVER
One activity I use to avoid talking or being connected with you is _____ *Deepens* I do this when I feel . . . and what I am afraid of is _____ That reminds me of childhood when . . . _____	*Mirrors, checks for accuracy, invites more*
DEEPENING (Optional) *As an attuned therapist, pay close attention to body language and emotional tone of the exchange. Being sensitive to the nuances offers opportunities to deepen the process through additional sentence stems such as:* • *The way this behavior has served me well in my life is_____* • *The way this behavior has not served me well in my relationships is _____* • *I imagine my behavior affects you by _____* • *If I say goodbye to using this behavior, I might say hello to . . . and then I might feel _____* • *The story I tell myself why I need that exit is _____* • *What scares me about closing my exit is _____* • *While I was growing up, I saw my parents exited by _____* • *And that made me feel _____* • *I learned to protect myself from their exiting by _____*	
Listens to summary, validation, and empathy.	*Summarizes, validates, and empathizes.*

activities *I* might be using as exits rather than what activities my partner is using; this prevents negative exchanges).

3. A worksheet is available in Appendix 9 to provide to the couple.

Step 3c: Sharing Exits

In the next session, partners should alternate using Dialogue to share an exit (items that were written down) as information only. Neither partner comments on the exits of the other. The purpose is to mutually acquaint each other with the exits they use. Often, this process of *acting in* creates enough safety that each will start closing exits without a promise.

Divorce, affairs, addictions, mental disorders, and/or thoughts of suicide or murder are devastating to the relationship and need to be addressed as quickly as possible. You may suspect one of these behaviors is active in the relationship or it may have been the precipitating event that brought the couple to therapy. If a partner is considering divorce and/or is involved in an affair, talk with the couple about the necessity of commitment for a mutually agreed upon time period (i.e., 12 sessions). Ask them to postpone any further proceedings and to end the affair, if that is relevant, so they can provide full attention and intention during the committed time period.

Step 4: Closing or Modifying the Exits

We said earlier that closing exits is an act of surrender. It is a release of behaviors that might sabotage the dream. Therefore, this should be received and understood as a freeing process for the individual and the couple. The goal of the Recommitting Process is for couples to close exits gradually, thus restoring the necessary energy to the relationship. But if exits are closed too quickly, anxiety may spike and one or both partners may abandon the process. Closing exits often alleviates fear in one partner and exacerbates it in the other. It is a gradual process and it's important to start out slowly, with partners agreeing to close or modify an exit in doable ways.[25] One way to do this is to be time specific such as "As a gift to our relationship, I want to limit my TV watching for the next three weeks to only 1 hour, and I will do that after 8 p.m. and before our bedtime."

In the preceding exercise, partners shared their exits and became acquainted with the childhood sources of their needs and behavior. In the next exercise, partners will take turns closing or modifying an exit for a period of time, and this process will continue, either in the sessions or as homework, until all the exits are closed. Then the Space-Between will be safe. Once all exits have been shared, ask each partner to choose one exit they checked off as "willing to modify or close now." Using the Commitment Dialogue, partners collaborate in committing to repair the energy leaks in the relationship, one exit at a time.

The Commitment Dialogue begins the same way as Sharing an Exit but has an added step of committing to closing or modifying the exit and the receiver's invitation to support closing or modifying the exit (Table 13.2). (Full Dialogue in Appendix 11.)

Table 13.2: Commitment Dialogue (Additional Sentence Stems)	
SENDER	RECEIVER
What scares me about closing this exit is . . . And I am now ready and willing to close (or modify) that exit (immediately or date when.) If I feel inclined to use this exit, I will ask for an appointment for a dialogue to talk about it rather than acting out.	Mirrors, Checks for Accuracy, and Invites More If I heard you correctly, you said_____ Did I get that? . . . Is there more about that? Summary Mirror Let me see if I got ALL of that_____ Did I get all of that?
The support I think I will need to close it is _____	Is there anything you need from me to help close (or modify) that exit? Mirrors and checks for accuracy.
Validating, Empathizing, and Closings	

Here is an example, using psychoeducation with Len and Ping, the young couple we met earlier, of how a therapist can introduce and facilitate the Commitment Dialogue in the session.

THERAPIST: *In our last session, we talked about how the relationship vision you cocreated requires a commitment to your relationship and to the process. And we also talked about how we need to let go of some of our behaviors in order to bring the dream to fruition. You both shared some ways you avoid intimacy to protect yourselves, which make sense but cannot continue if you want the dream to happen.* (The therapist can remind them of the exits they shared in the last session. This shows the therapist is attuned to the couple's narrative.) *Your assignment for this week was to continue identifying, on paper, exits you might be engaging in.* (The therapist can do a brief check-in with both Len and Ping on how the identification process was for them.)

Identifying exits is the first part of this Recommitting Process. Identification alone helps bring the energy back into the relationship. The act of talking about an exit and your feelings behind the behavior with each other essentially closes the exit. You are choosing to "act in" to your relationship rather than acting out of your relationship. But we also want to take it a step further and modify or close the exit so that the energy is fully invested in the relationship to make the dream happen. Would that be okay with you both?

LEN: *Sure.*

PING: *Yes.*

THERAPIST: *Great. I will guide you through a Dialogue similar to what we did in the last session, but this time, after sharing your exit, I will ask you to close or modify the exit and I'll help you identify ways you might do that. So, Len, this week I would like you to start this Dialogue, knowing that Ping will also have a turn to share in this session.*

Guides Len and Ping, as in all Dialogues, through the opening steps:
    Ask for an appointment.
    Make eye contact and take five deep breaths in sync.
    Share an appreciation.

Len, can you review your list that you worked on at home and choose one item that you checked off that you are you are willing to close or modify at this time? You want to choose an activity that will stretch you slightly but not break you. That is, something you feel certain that you can commit to modifying or closing. (Gives Len some time to choose an activity. Once he has chosen, continues.) Great. Len, can you share your exit with Ping by saying: **One activity I use to avoid talking or being connected with you is . . .**

LEN: *Ping, one activity I use to avoid talking or being connected with you is going into the home office at night to catch up on emails.*

THERAPIST: Prompts Ping to mirror, check for accuracy, and invite more. Then prompts Len:

Tell Ping a little more about that behavior. Say something like, **"I do this when I feel _____. And what I am afraid of is _____."**

LEN: *I think I do this when I feel uncomfortable. What I am afraid of is losing my independence.*

THERAPIST: Prompts Len to deepen the feeling. *Say that again, "I'm afraid of losing my independence" or another way of saying that is, "I'm afraid of being dependent."* The therapist may also want to use some focusing techniques to deepen the send, such as "Where do you feel that fear in your body?" Then prompts Ping to mirror, check for accuracy, and invite more.

*Len, can you share with Ping more about that feeling of losing your independence? Does it remind you of something in childhood? Say something like, **"That feeling of losing my independence reminds me of childhood when _____."***

LEN: *Actually, it does bring up a childhood memory. Growing up, my parents had a very parallel marriage. My dad was not around much. My mom was a homemaker. For whatever reason, probably because of me and my brother, they stayed together. I know my mom was unhappy, and I think she really relied on me to make her happy. Even in my teenage years, I felt almost guilty if I went out with a girlfriend or my friends and left her behind with my younger brother.*

THERAPIST: *So, tell Ping about that feeling, "As a child, when my mom relied on me to make her happy, I felt _____."*

LEN: *Guilty. Smothered. Trapped.*

THERAPIST: Continues to prompt Ping to mirror, check for accuracy and invite more. *Can you share with Ping, **what scares you about closing or modifying this exit now?***

LEN: *What scares me about closing this exit now is that I will lose my independence. That you will rely on me, and I will lose what is important to me.*

THERAPIST: Prompts Ping to mirror, check for accuracy, and invite more. *Exits drain the relationship. It prevents you both from experiencing true intimacy. Len, are you willing to close or modify this exit for the duration of our therapy together?*

LEN: *Yes. I think I can modify it, not close it completely, as I sometimes do need to do some emails at home at night.*

THERAPIST: *So, try this. Tell Ping, **I am now ready and willing to modify this exit by** "blank" and the "blank" means coming up with a specific way of how you would modify the exit. What would it look like? Would that be okay?*

LEN: *Yes.*

THERAPIST: *And then say, **"If I feel inclined to use this exit, I will** ask for an appointment for a dialogue to talk about it rather than acting out."*

LEN: *I am now ready and willing to modify this exit by limiting how much I am in the home office every evening to no more than 15 minutes. If I feel inclined to use this exit, I will ask for an appointment for a Dialogue to talk about it rather than acting out.*

THERAPIST: Prompts Ping to mirror, check for accuracy, and invite more. When there is no more, the therapist prompts Ping to summarize everything.

PING: *"Let me see if I got ALL of that. . . . Did I get all of that?"* Once the summary is complete, prompts Ping to ask what Len needs from her to support his commitment, *"Is there anything you need from me to help modify that exit?"*

THERAPIST: The therapist then helps Ping validate and empathize with Len's send. For a closing, Ping thanks Len for sharing and for the gift to their relationship. *That was great Len and Ping.* (The therapist may want to take a little time to process the experience with sentence stems such as: *Ping, what did you experience inside when Len gave that gift to your relationship? Len, how do you feel gifting that to Ping?*) *Now I want to switch roles and Ping now will share an exit she is willing to close or modify at this time.*

Once the send is complete, the therapist congratulates both partners and also shares with them the possibility that tension might arise from closing or modifying the exits. *As a result of closing the exits, you may feel some increased tension in yourself and in your relationship. You may feel that your relationship is becoming more challenging or you might find that there is a lot of awkward silence. This is normal as you move toward a conscious partnership. Increased tension means that you are invested in the process of change. And as we continue therapy, we will be exploring ways to fill any voids. True intimacy can be scary to all of us because we all have experienced some sort of hurt relationally. But I encourage you both to trust the process. You have nothing to lose but a lot to gain.*

Again, it is important for each partner to be a sender in the Commitment Dialogue process *in the same* session.

The Commitment Dialogue and closing of exits should continue throughout therapy. If a partner fails to live up to their commitment to close or modify an exit, the process is to again put them into Dialogue to explore the resistance to and underlying fear of closing an exit.

OUTCOMES OF THE RECOMMITTING PROCESS

Closing exits (or even the thought of closing exits) can ignite tremendous anxiety in the relationship. It might also produce new dynamics. Ping, who complained that Len was never home, might now find it difficult that Len is home every Saturday. Anxiety, resistance, sabotage, new conflicts, etc. are to be expected and should be normalized. We often tell couples who experience renewed anxiety: "Stay in the canoe and paddle." That is, stay in the process and Dialogue. The process, not the outcome, is the focus.

Over time, the Recommitting Process:

1. increases safety, the essential and nonnegotiable ingredient, and decreases relational anxiety
2. brings necessary energy back into the relationship, which invites engaging in positive behaviors
3. increases intentionality and removes relational ambivalence
4. primes the Space-Between for differentiation to occur

The paradox of the exit process is that engagement in Imago Dialogue closes the exit because it brings energy back into the relationship so that the relationship itself becomes the priority. Because safe engagement with each other is the unmet need for which the exit is a compensation, talking closes the exit and removes the need to act out the feelings. With the dream relationship in place and the exit process initiated, couples are now ready to move to the Reimaging Process and discover each other's "otherness." Discovering the differences in their dream and identification of exits have already begun the differentiation–connecting process.

Takeaways for the Recommitting Process

- There are four types of exits: 1) functional (behaviors that may not be intentional); 2) motivated (strategies that partner's deliberately use); 3) catastrophic (activities that will likely cause the demise of the relationship, such as affairs, addictions, or mental illness); and 4) terminal (behaviors that end the relationship, such as divorce, murder, or suicide).
- Exits occur when couples act out their feelings rather than talk about unspoken, painful feelings. They are expressions of relational ambivalence.
- Using an exit not only provides compensatory satisfaction, it also regulates anxiety caused by the lack of safety.
- Usually, an exit is not a malicious act, but a desperate one, due to relational stress.
- The Recommitting Process includes committing to the relationship, process, and partner and identifying energy leaks (i.e., "exits") that drain the relationship and sabotage the realization of the dream.
- Terminal and catastrophic exits need to be addressed immediately and with great care.
- Except for terminal or catastrophic exits, the closing of a specific exit is not important. What is important is engaging in the exit closing process, and that means talking about feelings rather than acting them out.
- The Commitment Dialogue and closing of exits should continue throughout therapy.

TIPS:
Always accept with grace whatever a partner is willing to offer.
Focus on making several small steps over time rather than big leaps that cannot be sustained.

14
Reimaging

What: Partners reimage their partner as a separate, distinct, and challenged person.

Why: To surrender the symbiotic illusion of sameness, move into differentiation, and increase empathy.

When: Around the fourth or fifth session, but elements of seeing the partner as challenged and differentiated earlier, especially if touching childhood pain.

When couples fall in love, they fall into the illusion that they are like each other and forget that they are each unique, thus different. The sense of sameness is so intense that many feel they have found their soul mates, or more aptly, their soul mirrors—someone who inhabits a different form but feels and thinks exactly as the other. "We both want the same things," one might proclaim. Or, "Nothing will ever come between us," another might insist. People fall into the trap of believing that it is sameness that keeps them together, and the statements they use to communicate this may include: "I finally found someone who just wants to make me happy." "With you I am complete." "I can't live without you." It is as if the two are "one."

However, by the time a couple gets to therapy, this illusion has turned on them and started eating away at their relationship from the inside. Enough time has passed that the partner who once gratified their wishes, no longer does. Their explanation for this disintegration is that the partner has changed, did a bait and switch, which no amount of nagging, begging, criticizing, or threatening seems to be able to fix.

In Imago theory, we explain this as one of the consequences of being in the throes of a symbiotic consciousness that was constructed in childhood and reactivated in romantic love. In this consciousness there are no boundaries, and the two are merged into one. The real partner is merged with a fantasy partner, for whom they have searched since childhood. When they come for therapy, they have not differentiated this figment of their imagination from the real other, whom they will have to discover in order to construct a conscious partnership. But they have not come to therapy so you can help them with the differentiating process or to construct a conscious partnership. They are, instead, mired in the power struggle, the second phase of intimate relationships, and they want your help in keeping the real partner in the prison of their fantasy while remaining committed to freeing themselves from the illusion their partner has of them.

Each partner is understandably resistant to the demand to surrender their own reality and to conform to the fantasy of the other partner. They want acceptance for themselves and change for their partner. The core and consistent challenge of therapy is to facilitate differentiation by helping both persons wrestle with the necessity of knowing the otherness of their partner, accepting it, and coming to relish it.

The purpose of the Reimaging Process is to rupture symbiotic fusion by facilitating differentiation so both partners can see each other as they truly are—as an "other," warts, wounds, and all. Through the process of differentiation, which is facilitated by replacing judgment with curiosity, and practicing the Imago Dialogue process, each person discovers and accepts their real partner and grieves the loss of their fantasy. When both partners come to really know each other, the Space-Between becomes fertile ground for experiencing connecting, the sensation of full aliveness and joy, and the state of wonder which they both were born with, lost along the way and now needs to be restored. To summarize what has been done so far:

Step 1: In Revisioning, couples use their imagination to envision and design their dream relationship.

Step 2: In Recommitting, couples use their courage to overcome ambivalence and to commit to the dream by closing exits and focusing all their energy on positive engagement with each other.

And the next step:

Step 3: In Reimaging, couples practice using their curiosity to discover and differentiate their partner from themselves and to connect with the real person rather than their fantasy.

In traditional therapy, differentiation is a process of internal exploration that leads to self-discovery and self-declaration to others. "This is who I am." Self-knowledge precedes other-knowledge. The focus is first on the self rather than the other.[26]

From the Imago perspective, focus on self-discovery rather than the discovery of the other tends to maintain symbiosis rather than disrupt it.

Movement toward differentiation must come from engagement with another rather than exploration of oneself—from the outside in, not the inside out. One cannot know their partner better by getting to know oneself better first. Thus, differentiation is accomplished in relationship, not in reaction but in response.

In fact, the therapist's role is to help partners to "unknow" each other (given that their partner knowledge is based on symbiotic assumptions), to surrender all predication, and to become curious about each other. Curiosity is the engine of differentiation. Through it, one discovers the "other" and declares, *"You are not me, and that helps me to be clear about who I am. When I get clear about who you are, I know you are not me. Getting to know you helps me define me. For example, your complaints about my high energy have to be understood in relation to your low energy. My complaints about your laissez-faire parenting have to be seen relative to my need for more discipline. Our traits are complementary and exist in relation to each other, not as separate from each other."*

The goals of the Reimaging Process include:

1. rupturing symbiosis by helping partners shift from reactive judgment to genuine curiosity; and
2. deepening empathy by helping partners understand the role of childhood in their conflict with each other.

At this point in therapy, couples have practiced the full Dialogue process, a lot. They regularly express appreciations; they have a map in hand that they cocreated for their relationship; they have pulled the energy back into the relationship, and they can exchange information through a safe structure (i.e., Imago Dialogue). All of this has fortified the safety in the Space-Between, allowing the full expression of experiences and vulnerabilities so that the difficult process of differentiation can occur. But that is a challenging task that might be helped by the therapist's understanding a little more about the source, ubiquity, and function of the mental condition we call symbiosis.

SOURCE OF SYMBIOSIS

At the individual level, symbiosis is generated by connectional rupture during the course of childhood development (i.e., neglectful or intrusive parenting). Here is a brief review: connectional rupture caused by need-frustration triggers anxiety. The pain of anxiety generates such a high level of self-absorption that neural receptors of information from the outside world shut down and effectively insulate the self from others, producing an isolated self and the loss of the sensation of full aliveness. As a result, the self turns inward. The formerly interconnected self now lives inside a symbiotic illusion of separateness and, often, with a sense of alienation from others, from nature, and from the cosmos.

The inward-focused, self-absorbed self needs the outside world to be a certain way in order to maintain a sense of security. It achieves this by unconscious fusion of the self with the not-self, meaning that others and things in the external world are emotionally and mentally constructed in such a manner as to serve the survival needs of the self without reciprocation. There is no "relational" interaction with another; all others are merely utilitarian "objects."

In this self-constructed world, difference becomes a threat, and when discrepant information is encountered in the form of an opinion of another, the self goes into an alarm state that results in interpersonal conflict.

Conflict about difference is the source of all frustration. This is the human condition.

In romantic love, symbiotic consciousness rules the day. Unconsciously, lovers attempt to fuse their real partner with their fantasy partner and expect all their needs to be met by the perfect person of their imagination. The transition from "we are one" to the shock that "you are not me, nor whom I thought you were" begins quite soon after commitment. That shock is exacerbated by the desire of each partner to be seen as they really are while insisting that the other stay in character as a fantasy partner. Each criticizes the other for not being who they said they were or how they used to be. Unconsciously, these criticisms are meant to restore the romantic illusion of their merged imaginations. But these attempts at emotional coercion are strenuously resisted or resented, and the intensity of conflict increases. The only safe passage through this minefield of the power struggle is the conscious differentiation and connecting that is the agenda of the Reimaging Process.

THE FACE AND VOICE OF SYMBIOSIS

In individuals, symbiosis flourishes in the unconscious where there is no clear understanding of the self and no clear understanding of boundaries between the self and others, or that there are any boundaries.

The most obvious symptom of a symbiotic relationship is the belief that there is one RIGHT way of seeing, describing, understanding, and valuing what is going on. The inability to accept difference limits a person's capacity to be aware of, respect, appreciate, or comprehend the subjectivity of another. The symbiotic mind unconsciously manifests in different forms including:

- **Fusion:** "We want/feel/experience/value the same things. My experience is your experience."
- **Omniscience:** "You know what I need (without my having to tell you)."
- **Omnipotence:** "You have the power to meet all my needs and make me feel good."
- **Omnipresence:** "You must always be here with me."
- **Exclusiveness:** "I am your one and only."

The prime indicator of symbiosis is irritation or frustration with another for not sharing the same internal world script or for behaving in any way that is upsetting. When difference shows up, the inevitable consequence of these symbiotic attitudes is to derogate, put-down, distance, shame, or punish others when they disagree or, conversely, passively give in to the other person's thoughts, feelings, and memories, with deep resentment and fantasies of revenge.

Here are some examples of symbiotic frustrations collected from couples.

1. "I know what you really think/feel/want!"
2. "What do you know?!"
3. "You're too stupid to see what's right in front of you!"
4. "You're not as smart as you look!"
5. "Anyone in their right mind agrees."
6. "What do you mean, you don't like sushi?"
7. "How can you not like that movie?!"
8. "Come on, you've always liked visiting my family at Christmas!"
9. "I don't know how you can feel that way!"
10. "You're so different! What happened to you?"
11. "How can you feel/think that way!"
12. "You don't make sense!"
13. "That's crazy!" / "You're crazy!"
14. "I blame you for how I'm feeling!" / "It's your fault!"
15. "Everyone likes broccoli."
16. "If you loved me, you'd know what I need/want!"
17. "I know you know better."
18. "Whatever you think."
19. Eye-rolling, hand gestures, tone of voice, facial expressions, and body language.

All couples who come to therapy exhibit this fundamental human problem to a greater or lesser degree. The rigidity of their symbiotic thinking reflects the severity of their childhood wounding and the extent of their developmental arrest. This is the problem that Imago therapy is designed to address. Until partners accept that they are different, and that difference is reality, not a neurosis, they cannot experience connecting and they cannot begin the arduous journey to "real" love.

THE ROAD TO DIFFERENTIATION

Differentiation is the precondition of consciousness and connecting.

A conscious and differentiated person is aware that there are no absolutes, and even if there were, we have no clear, uncontaminated access to them. The attitudes and beliefs that underlie symbiosis, which claims access to absolute truth, stem from a lack of awareness that we live in a universe of diverse people, all of whom have a perspective that is "true" for them, and no one has access to a reality that is "true for all."

But nearly everyone tends to feel threatened when they encounter differences. They do not know that, in nature, otherness is foundational, and that difference is the *only* reality. There is no sameness. Two organisms may be similar, but none are ever exactly the same. Symbiosis puts them in a subjectively homogenous world, and they feel less secure when that world is not confirmed by others.[27]

Every person is doing the best they can to survive and restore the experience of connecting. But it is not until we break the symbiotic fusion that we can begin to heal the original connectional rupture, because fusion is not connecting!

Definition of Differentiation

In Imago theory, differentiation is a process that is practiced, not a concept that is merely recommended. It is acknowledging and accepting differences without judging the other in any way. Eventually, differentiated partners realize that tolerating the tension of difference grows them into their true selves where they can experience connecting and achieve the satisfactions of mature love."

The ability to differentiate is, once again, embedded in the structure of Imago Dialogue in which partners "mirror the other into being" with accurate, nonjudgmental listening and empathic curiosity. Every sentence stem is an act of differentiation. Each delineates that "I am not you. You are not me. And that is okay." In mirroring, one experiences the subjectivity of the other, which promotes curiosity and the discovery of the other as separate. Validating increases the understanding that two distinct experiences can exist side by side as equally valid. Empathy allows each partner to experience the feelings of the other—while remaining separate—and

Figure 14.1
From Symbiosis to Differentiation

From Symbiosis		To Differentiation
One way to see things	➡	Multiple, equally valid points of view
Conformity	➡	Diversity
Reacts to differences	➡	Curious about differences
Violates boundaries	➡	Honors boundaries
Closed	➡	Receptive

sets up the precondition of growth and healing (which we will explore later in the Restructuring Frustrations chapter). Dialogue builds safety, invites defenses to relax, breaks symbiotic fusion, and restores empathy.

The clinical task is to help couples move away from their subjective experience and toward the subjectivity of others with clear distinctions between the two (Figure 14.1).

Imago Dialogue as a Differentiating Process
Dialogue helps couples move from awareness of the need for differentiation to the experience of differentiation. Integration of Dialogue into every conversation makes differentiation a continuous process.

Mirroring and Curiosity
Each step in the Dialogue process achieves differentiation.

The first step is mirroring, which is *listening to*—as distinct from hearing—the other without distortion. You know you are listening rather than hearing when what the other person says impacts and changes you. Their reality becomes new content in your mind and reorganizes your inner world. If what we receive does not change us, then we are engaged in judgment and using an operating system that runs symbiosis and deflects the world of the other. Like all good operating systems, it runs continuously in the background, out of sight, out of awareness, but it is always there, determining the inner thoughts of the people involved in symbiotic relationships. In contrast, mirroring *is* the practice of withholding judgment, moving from "you" language to "I" language ("I feel"; "I think"; "my story about that is . . .").

Judging is thinking you already know the answer; curiosity is not knowing the answer accompanied by the humble belief that, in fact, you don't actually know anything and that the only way to learn anything is to become a listener. Suspending judgment and asking, "Is there more about that?" allows couples to move into genuine engagement, inviting the other to share their experiences. They stop fighting about their differences and start exploring them without the need to change them. Their attitude becomes "I'm not sure/I did not know that/maybe I should find out." This replaces certainty in all things.

The differentiation process has begun its transforming work when a breath of energy for inquiry and learning begins to infuse the therapeutic techniques designed to move couples from the prison of the self to the freedom and potential, and the constant oscillation between focus and flow, of the quantum energy field.

Curiosity, then, makes validating and empathizing possible.

Validating and Equality

Validating is the single most effective action that can be taken to achieve differentiation because it replaces authoritarian communication with equality. It is the expression of the fundamental tenet of differentiation: "I see you. I am contributing to an environment that feels safe enough for you to be able to express your authentic thoughts and feelings, knowing that I am going to trust that they make sense to you internally. I honor the ways you are different from me, and I accept those differences." When one validates, they "see" that the inner world of the other is distinct from one's own, that it has equal validity and is valued without an edit. It is not agreement; it is acknowledgement and acceptance of difference.

Validating has a profound effect. Slowly, over time, we assimilate the fact that our partner is distinct from us and, as such, all their desires, actions, vulnerabilities, and fears make sense internally. We cannot be saying, "I hear and validate your point of view," and "You and I are one, and I am *the* one" in the same breath. Partners begin to acknowledge the challenged experience of the other.

To facilitate this, therapists need to help couples practice validating in the office so they can use it as a tool for deep healing and growth as they reshape their interactions at home. The therapist may offer a bridge of words for examples, such as: "What you are saying makes sense to me." "I can understand that you feel this way, and why." "I appreciate it when you tell me what's on your mind because I can see why you made that decision." Through repeated validation of each other in the office, partners feel safe to speak more truthfully and to explore more deeply and vulnerably when they are alone at home.

Empathy and Connection

Empathy is the capacity to tune in to another's emotional experience without confusing it with our own, to visit the feelings of another but not own them as if they were ours. The loss of the capacity to experience empathy is perhaps the greatest tragedy we experience as human beings. Its loss is the major consequence of the anxiety of ruptured connecting that leads to objectification.

Empathy is what keeps differentiation from becoming an engine of dehumanization. It is not enough just to understand the partner is different. We must also have empathy for their differentness. We need to foster empathy in a situation where there has likely been anger or bitterness. Without empathy, "not me" can become "not human" and "not worth caring about." Empathy keeps alive the connection between people whose differences might otherwise typecast them as immoral, evil, useless, or the enemy. This is where empathy becomes connection.

When we are preoccupied with our own experience of living with the threat of nonbeing, it is too challenging, nearly impossible, to receive other persons' experiencing or to even care. Yet, empathy is the personal experience of connecting; it is the universal drive of the psyche, rooted in human nature, which is itself a manifestation of the universe. Our cosmic connection is experienced through empathy.

In the breaking of symbiotic fusion, differentiation occurs, and as a result, empathy can be restored. And as couples soften to each other by seeing their challenged nature that lies in the Space-Between, both partners move from cognitive empathy (imagining the feeling of the other) toward participatory empathy (experiencing the feeling of the other).

REIMAGING PROCESS

The Reimaging Process, the road to differentiation, has been embedded in Imago Dialogue from the beginning, and once enough practice has occurred to establish safety in the Space-Between, you can increase the tension of differences and acceptance and expand the couple's ability to empathize through specific exercises:

1. Practice sharing and honoring differences (Differentiation Dialogue).
2. Explore and share early childhood experiences (the Imago Profile, Parent–Child Dialogue, the Early Childhood Challenge and Need Exercise and Dialogue, and Holding Exercise).

Clinical Tool #1: The Differentiation Dialogue

The purpose of the Differentiation Dialogue below is to help partners who are experiencing a mild or intense frustration to engage each other and learn about each other when they see things differently. And, of course,

Table 14.1: Differentiation Dialogue (Sentence Stems)

Differentiation Dialogue (Sentence Stems)	
Sender 1 Something I have noticed about you is _____ *(you seem uncomfortable when I ask you about the money you've spent).* I interpret this to mean, or The story I tell myself is _____ *(you feel like I'm trying to control you).* The way this story is really about me is _____ *(I feel anxious about spending beyond our means).* The way this relates to my past is _____ *(as you know, I grew up with a real fear of losing our home because we never had enough money to pay the rent).* I'm curious about whether any of this fits for you.	**Receiver 1** *Mirrors throughout*
Switch roles.	
Sender 2 The way your story does fit for me is (or does not fit for me) is _____ *(I am worried that you are trying to control me).* What I can share with you around this topic is _____ *(I work hard and I want to be free to enjoy myself without checking with you for every item).* One way I make up that we are similar is _____ *(that I don't want to spend beyond our means as well).* I'd like to check to see if you think we are similar in this way.	**Receiver 2** *Mirrors throughout*
Switch roles.	
Sender 1 Yes, I see this in a similar way (or No, I don't see this in a similar way.) My experience is _____ *(It sounds like it would be good for both of us to sit down together and put together a financial plan so I can feel less anxious and you can feel free to spend within the budget).* Something I've appreciated about you in this Dialogue is _____ *(that you could hear that the thing I do that irritates you so much is actually coming from a place of concern for both of us).* I interpreted that to mean _____ *(that we will be able to work together on this difficult issue and maybe others).* That makes me feel _____ *(so relieved).* And my impulse is to _____ *(give you a hug).* Let me just make sure that this is what it meant for you.	**Receiver 1** *Mirrors throughout*
Switch roles.	
Sender 2 What that behavior (that was appreciated) did mean for me was _____ *(my irritation can become something more positive when I understand why you do what you're doing).* What I've appreciated about you in this Dialogue is _____ *(that you could see that I was irritated by something you were doing and you could hear the reason for my reaction without getting defensive).* I've interpreted this to mean _____ *(that we can talk about things without getting upset if we approach each other in a non-critical way).*	**Receiver 2** *Mirrors throughout*

to discover things about themselves that they did not know. Partners are guided to approach each other with attitudes of curiosity and respect as precursors to acceptance rather than judgment. The step-by-step process of Imago Dialogue encourages these attitudes to grow.

Table 14.1 lists sentence stems the partners will use in each step of the exchange. As in all Dialogue exchanges, the Differentiation Dialogue begins with asking for an appointment about the topic, "Is now a good time to have a Dialogue about _____?" Partners reciprocate sending and mirroring in an attempt to discover their similarities and differences on the subject. At the end of each exchange, the receiver should provide a summary mirror, validation, and empathy to complete the full Dialogue process.

Clinical Tool #2: Early Childhood Experiences

As we explored earlier in the book, the "Imago" is a psychological construct that refers to an internal image created during childhood. It is a composite image of the positive and negative traits of the people who are most significant to the child and the child's experience in response to these traits. It also includes the traits the child gave up through their experiences of repressive socialization. This image fuels romantic love in an attempt to recreate the childhood experience. An Imago-Match partner will carry the positive traits and, more importantly, the traits that were most painful to the child or will have the capacity to trigger similar painful feelings.

Imago therapists use a series of Dialogue exercises that help couples bridge the past and the present. These exercises enable them to see how their partner is triggered in their relationship by the intrusion of early experiences and to move from judgment to curiosity when that happens. These processes offer couples the opportunity to:

- increase awareness of the Imago-Match by discovering the similarities between partners and caretakers;
- see present conflicts and the energy behind them in the context of the past;
- experience or imagine their partner's feelings when they are triggered;
- gain awareness of their partners unmet childhood needs;
- reimage the partner as wounded and trying to survive rather than as a negative person trying to hurt them;
- transform the memories of being deflected and made invisible by a different experience of being heard, understood, and received by an Imago-Match partner; and
- restore the experience of connecting in the present by reconstructing a painful childhood memory.

The Imago Processes include:

1. **Imago Profile (Appendix 12):** This is a series of questions that help bridge past experiences with the present partner. The Imago Profile exercise can be provided as a between-session assignment and is meant as information only. This information helps couples shift from blame to curiosity and understanding.
2. **Childhood Challenge, Need, and Defense Exercise and Dialogue (applicable Appendices 13–17):** In this exercise, couples use a chart of wounding experiences and identify the type of caretaking they received (neglectful or intrusive parenting, the earliest and most challenging wound), discover their typical defenses in response (minimizing or maximizing), and then share this information in a Dialogue.
3. **Parent–Child Dialogue (Appendices 18–19):** The Parent–Child Dialogue is a regressive process that takes the sender back into their childhood experience. It invites the sender to consciously project the image of the parent onto the partner rather than unconsciously projecting it, as is often done in intimate relationships.
4. **Holding Exercise:** While not a regressive exercise (both partners remain in the present), this exercise accesses deep pain and often flows from an affective piece of work in which feelings of deep sadness or grief are being expressed.

The purpose of guiding couples into their childhood memories is to help them experience mutual empathy as they make the connection between past and present. However, it is equally important not to dwell on the past, because excessive exploration of the past is counterproductive to positive therapeutic outcomes. The more couples focus on their past childhood experiences, the more intense those experiences become.[28] What you focus on is what you get! This happens because of the brain's tendency to magnify the object of attention, and that often amplifies the childhood feelings beyond their original intensity. Since the goal of therapy is to live in the present (rather than the past) and experience connecting with each other, exploring the past beyond the functional value of making sense of the present puts the present in the distance. Connecting in the interactive Space-Between trumps self-knowledge.

Childhood Challenge, Relational Need, and Defense Exercise and Dialogue
In the Childhood Challenge, Relational Need, and Defense exercise, couples use a chart of wounding experiences and identify the type of

caretaking they received (neglectful or intrusive parenting), the earliest and most challenging wound and need, choose their defensive response, and then share this information in a Dialogue (Table 14.2). The charts and Dialogue are very effective in sessions and can also be used as between-session tools to provide the psychoeducational component to increase awareness of their early childhood wounding and the resulting need that was brought into the relationship. While this is not a regressive exercise, it tends to achieve the same result as the deeper Parent–Child Dialogue, described below, and is recommended as the first engagement of the couple with their childhood memories. After this process is completed, use your judgment as to whether the deeper dialogue is necessary. On occasion, you may also assign this process as homework by making a copy of the procedure available to the couple.

Table 14.2: Childhood Challenge, Relational Need, and Defense Dialogue (Sentence Stems) *(full template in Appendix 16)*

When I was a child, I lived with caretakers who were generally (Neglectful or Intrusive) and my relational CHALLENGE with them was _____.

And when I remember that, I FEEL _____

Instead of that challenge and feeling, what I NEEDED MOST from my caretakers was _____

And if I had gotten that, what it would look like as a BEHAVIOR is _____.

When I did not get that need met with that behavior, what SCARED me the most was _____ so I responded by (Maximizing or Minimizing) and tended to DEFEND myself by _____.

And, not getting that need met, I brought that NEED and that DEFENSE to my adult relationships.

The Parent–Child Dialogue

If the therapist feels deeper exploration will be useful, they use the Parent–Child Dialogue. In this Dialogue, the partner takes on the role of parent, both real and ideal. Real in the sense that the "child" will interact with the "parent" as they did in childhood. Ideal in the sense that this "parent" will listen with curiosity and empathy rather than as the actual parent probably did. The "child" can share with the "parent" their experiences of emotional hurt and frustration in an open and honest way, which they may not have had the opportunity or safety do to when they were young. The "parent" asks specific questions, prompted by the therapist, and then mirrors the "child's" response.

The sender may be experiencing strong emotions that seem out of proportion to the current event or that come up repeatedly as a hurt or frustration with the partner. After the current feelings have been accessed, expressed, and identified, the therapist may prompt the sender with a sentence stem such as, "What this feeling of _____ reminds me of in my childhood is _____." The therapist then helps the sender move into the role of child by going back in time and reexperiencing what it was like for them as a child, having these feelings with one or both parents.

Throughout the process, the therapist guides the "child" to go deeper into the effect of the childhood experience so that they connect with the unmet childhood need that is behind the pain and frustration. They are reexperiencing the pain of the past while being open to a new experience in the present. The therapist guides the "parent" to do a summary mirror at the end of each response.

The questions that the therapist feeds to the "parent" are:

"I'm your (mother, father, other caretaker). What is it like living with me?" (Or, if the parent was dead or not present, "What is it like living without me?")

This question helps the sender to go back to the time when they were living with the parent and to begin reexperiencing what that was like then, both positive and negative. It also helps the "parent" get a sense of what the partner's childhood experience was like. The "parent" mirrors the answers to the question.

"What is the worst part of all of that for you?"

This will prompt the sender to become aware of the childhood wound that keeps coming up in their current relationship. Many people respond to this question by describing the parent's behavior rather than their own internal pain. The therapist helps the sender get in touch with the feelings the parent's behavior generated. For example, if the sender says the parent never paid any attention to them, the therapist helps them express their hurt in more specific ways, such as feeling unloved, invisible, or overlooked. The sender may be prompted to say: **"When I experience that I feel _____, and when I feel that I think . . ."** This sentence stem accesses both the emotional and cognitive experiences behind the pain.

The "parent" mirror and then asks: **"What do you do when I hurt you that way?"**

However, the "child" responds, the answer will reveal which adaptive strategies were used, and both partners will notice the similarities between the survival strategies used then and the survival strategies used in the current relationship. Hearing the sender talk about this engenders compassion in both partners for the experience of that child. The "parent" mirrors.

"What are the good things you experience living with me? What is the best part of living with me?"

These two questions help the sender access the positive aspects of their childhood to balance with painful memories. It also helps the receiver hear information that they might replicate as loving behaviors in their relationship.

"What do you need from me most that I don't give you?"

This identifies the "child's" unmet need. This unmet need is at the core of their mutual frustration and central to the dynamic between them. In order to fulfill each other's unmet needs, they first have to know what those unmet needs are, and then both partners have to grow beyond their own childhood adaptations and into their own wholeness to be able to meet them.

The "parent" mirrors and then validates and empathizes with the "child's" experience. After these steps are completed, partners de-role and return to themselves, as partner and partner. The receiver then summarizes, validates, and empathizes—as the partner. The full Parent–Child Dialogue is in Appendix 18 with a summary worksheet in Appendix 19.

Some tips regarding the Parent–Child Dialogue:

1. Guide the couple to use the present tense, as if it is happening now.
2. De-role at the end of the Dialogue (move from "parent" to partner).
3. Be aware of any intense childhood memories that might resurrect deep emotional pain. In these instances, you will want to use shallowing techniques, engage with the prefrontal cortex (e.g., through deep breathing), or de-role and process on a cognitive level.

The Holding Exercise

The Holding Exercise normally flows from an affective piece of work in which feelings of deep sadness or grief emerge in the therapy session. It can be seamlessly woven into the session or it can be introduced as a specific, separate process. Since it involves physical holding, it is a good idea to have a couch in the office in addition to three chairs. At times it may flow from the sentence stem, "What this feeling of . . . (e.g., sadness, hurt, grief, loneliness) reminds me of from my childhood is . . ." The sender, who is experiencing the sadness, becomes the holdee, and the receiver becomes the holder. Use the Holding Exercise to:

1. deepen the empathy and connection between partners
2. provide the couple with a container for the expression of deep sadness and a process for this that they can use at home
3. meet needs for nurturing, nonsexual, physical closeness in the presence of strong emotions

The exercise begins with the therapist:

> **THERAPIST:** *Mary, would you be willing to let George hold you phys-ically in a particular way as you share more about those feelings?*
> **MARY:** *Yes.*
> **THERAPIST:** *George, would you be willing to hold Mary, inviting her to share more with you about the deep feelings?*
> **GEORGE:** *Yes.*

The therapist then helps the couple get into a position where the holder will be comfortable for at least 10 to 15 minutes (with the holder, for example, positioned against a chair or wall for back support or on a sofa). The holdee is cradled in the arms of the holder, fully supported, with the head on the holder's chest against the heart, able to make eye contact whenever they choose. It is similar to the position of a parent holding an infant child.

NOTES:
- While there will probably be some disruption of the feelings the first time the therapist moves the couple into this position, with familiarity, this disruption will lessen.
- This is not a regression exercise, although the position is regressive. This is done partner to partner, in the present tense.
- The therapist prompts the holdee using the sentence stems, doubling, focusing, silence, and directives to help the couple to deepen their emotional connection with their sadness so that they can express it with words or tears (Gendlin, 1982; Hudgins & Kiesler, 1987).
- The goal is to help the sender to stay out of the narrative ("thinking") and more in the emotion of the experience of the present or the past ("feeling").
- The therapist prompts the receiver to hold the partner in their emotions by making sounds of presence and encouragement like "Mmm" or mirroring just the feeling words—"lonely," for example.

The questions that the therapist feeds to the holdee include:

"Tell me about the pain and frustration of your childhood."
"What was the worst part of living with your family?"

The holder listens empathically, occasionally mirroring the feeling experience.

When it appears that all the feelings have been expressed with the affect associated with them, the therapist brings the couple out of the process by saying to the holdee something like:

"When you are ready, taking all the time you need, I invite you to come out of that position."

The couple may then choose to stay on the sofa or floor but in face-to-face positions or they may choose to move back to their regular chairs to process their experience using Imago Dialogue.

This exercise can bring up strong feelings of discomfort in both the holder and the holdee in response to earlier messages about their own nurturance needs, dependency, expression of feelings, shame regarding the longing to be held, and much more.

IMPORTANT NOTE: It is extremely important that the touch and intimacy experienced in this position never be sexualized. This exercise is designed to fill the unfulfilled adult to experience nonsexual touch. If there has been any history of sexual abuse or inappropriateness, touch may be considered unsafe. This exercise has strict boundaries so that both partners can relax and take in the tender experience, but the therapist should evaluate any potential for retraumatizing, given their respective histories, prior to engaging in this practice.

The Legacy of Wounding

Some couples are concerned that any talk about their challenges in childhood is a direct or indirect criticism of their parents. Others are happy to assign their suffering to their parents and to blame their partner for repeating their parent's abusive behavior. Should some resistance to talking about childhood discomforts come up for one partner, or if it is embraced too eagerly by the other, it is important to address that immediately.

Usually, the person most concerned about being loyal to their caretakers claims they had a happy childhood with wonderful parents who met all their needs, and they cannot think of any childhood challenges. They are more comfortable assigning their troubles to their partner's behavior and locating all their issues in the present. The other partner is all too happy to compare their complaints about their parents with their partner. And, both of their perspectives make sense, since it seems logically obvious that if certain childhood needs were not met, parents and/or other significant persons are involved in the deprivation, in some way.

Our position is that assigning adult relational issues to parents/

caretakers in childhood is never to assign blame—no one is to blame! Not even the most incompetent parent. The function of the exercises is to create awareness that repetitive relational patterns in the present emerged from negative relational patterns in the past. They are focused on the individual's unique relational experience, not the truth of what was.

The purpose of bridging the past with the present, therefore, is to draw attention to the tragic fact that relational suffering in adulthood is a universal human problem causally associated with childhood because the human race has not evolved to the point that caretakers know how to sustain the child's experience of connecting as they integrate them into the human family and society. No one is at fault because everyone in human history, thus far, has experienced some of their caretaker's limitations around specific survival needs whether they acknowledge it, amplify it, or deny it. The caretakers, through whom our clients experienced this universal tragedy as a personal experience, were also wounded by their caretakers, as was every caretaker preceding them, back through all the centuries humans have been trying to care for their young.

OUTCOMES OF THE REIMAGING
PROCESS: MARK AND DIANA

Let us revisit Mark and Diana. During an early therapy session Mark shared that sometimes, when Diana "gets emotional," he wants to shut down, leave the house, or, at the least, hide behind his computer screen until she "calms down." While Mark admits that Diana's expressiveness was one of the traits that initially attracted him to her, he is now wishing she could be more in control of her emotions. Diana's "excessive emotions" and Mark's "stoicism" were frequently a point of contention in their relationship. As they became curious about each other, they discovered their early patterns of defensiveness:

MARK: *Because of my parent's preoccupation with my brother's addiction, I learned early on to suppress my emotions. My parents had enough on their plate and it seemed that Jake's situation was a bit more precarious and took precedence, certainly over any pimple-faced teenage issues . . . I guess my deepest hurt from childhood was not having my parent's attention. I was frequently ignored but simultaneously praised when I was a "good boy," which, to me, translated to not having any needs. I think this led me to feel lonely or isolated. I remember spending endless hours by myself in our large expansive woodlands behind our house.*

DIANA: *Growing up the youngest in a family with 5 kids, I think I learned early on to get noticed by being impulsive, outgoing, expressive. I think my deepest hurt was feeling like I only got my parents' attention when I was emotional. That is, I had to have temper tantrums as a toddler, storm out of the house as a teenager, and, ultimately, threaten to end it all in order to get them to see me.*

As they continued to process in therapy, they began to accept each other as an "other"—two distinct people with different ideas, different memories, and **different ways of expressing themselves**. Curiosity replaced Diana's demands on Mark, which in turn allowed some of Mark's repressed feelings to safely emerge to the surface. Dialogue began to dissolve the symbiotic assumptions and increased their ability to "hold the space" without going into their turtle–hailstorm defenses. While differences can tear even a good relationship to shreds, a safe container to explore the complexity of differing emotions and experiences invites couples to become advocates for each other. Conflict can become an opportunity for strengthening the relational bond.

Over time, the Reimaging Process helps couples, like Mark and Diana, break the illusion that the other is an extension of the self and see that they are, rather, a separate being, worthy of our curiosity, understanding, acceptance, and empathy. Reimaging leaves partners with a clearer vision of themselves, of their wounding histories, and their unmet childhood needs. This makes their contact more genuine, more empathic, and more compassionate. Slowly the deleterious effects of the original rupture unravel, and the Space-Between becomes the safe container for the essential work of healing and growth. But before then, there is another necessary step: detoxing the relationship of the various forms of negativity that continue to linger in the Space-Between.

Takeaways for the Reimaging Process

- Connectional rupture caused by need-frustration triggers anxiety, which results in self-absorption, loss of empathy, and emotional symbiosis.
- The purposes of the Reimaging Process include:

  1. rupturing symbiosis by helping partners see the other as a separate, yet equal, being (differentiation)
  2. deepening empathy by helping partners understand the impact of childhood and its role in interpersonal conflict

- Reimaging is practiced through the Dialogue structure, which focuses on the other rather than the self. Mirroring promotes curiosity and the discovery of the other as separate. Validating increases understanding that two distinct experiences can exist side-by-side. Empathizing allows each partner to experience the feelings of the other.

TIPS:

Recalling early childhood experiences is not about assigning blame. It creates awareness that repetitive relational patterns in the present emerged from negative relational patterns in the past.

However, it is important not to let couples dwell on the past, but merely "visit" to understand the relational patterns and increase empathy for each other.

15
Removing Negativity

What: All forms of negativity are removed from the relationship.

Why: Negativity ruptures connecting, activates anxiety, increases defense mechanisms, and prevents relationships from thriving.

When: The first session, along with sender responsibility, the Zero Negativity Pledge, and the Affirmations Process. Other processes added as needed.

When the seductions and petitions of the romantic stage cease to work, romantic partners turn to mutual pain infliction in a turtle–hailstorm dance, which obscures their underlying need (the unmet childhood need) and its resolution. While some couples go to therapy as preparation and prevention, others go before they have reached an impasse. So when they show up at your office, they may or may not be on the brink of divorce, but their relationship has likely shown signs of trouble for years. Most couples take about 6-7 years from the time they start experiencing problems until they seek counseling (Gottman, 1994).

Negativity is the chronic background music that couples play to each other. In the presence of negativity, the old brain signals that the environment is not safe and, therefore, survival becomes primary. Only by relaxing the deep defensive structures can couples become vulnerable with each other and partner in transforming their relationship. Safety is nonnegotiable. Without it, human beings may survive, but they cannot thrive.

It comes as no surprise that highly negative relationships report lower marital satisfaction (Huston & Vangelisti, 1991; Fincham & Beach, 2010). What may be surprising is that a partner's dissatisfaction is influenced by their partner's negativity through a process called "emotional contagion" or catching the emotional state of the other (Hatfield et al., 1994). In quantum field theory, this is called "entanglement," a quantum situation in which the action of one particle simultaneously occurs in the other, no matter the distance between them. In other words, couples can feel each other's emotions even when they are not in the same place; even when they are far apart. One partner's anxieties, tensions, and worries are felt by the other and the relationship can quickly cascade into a nonregulated state (Gottman, 1993). Once emotional contagion takes hold, a battle of reactive behaviors ensues. Negativity is a punch to the psyche, spreads like a virus, and lingers indefinitely. Negativity begets negativity.

Removing negativity from the couple's Space-Between is an essential process that begins in Session 1 and evolves throughout the sessions to complete eradication by the end of therapy. A part of our job as therapists is to gently and nonjudgmentally coach couples to identify negativity and commit to its removal, engage in reconnecting when necessary, and expand positive interactions in their Space-Between.

Of course, eliminating negativity might be very difficult for some couples, especially those who have been using unskillful or non-dialogical methods of interacting for a very long time. But creating a Zero Negativity environment and encouraging a daily monitoring process is non-negotiable if partners want to move from surviving to thriving in their relationship.

WHAT IS NEGATIVITY?

We define negativity as anything that one partner *experiences* as a "put-down" by the other partner—an interaction, word, gesture, glare, eye roll, tone, or behavior. A key word in the definition is "experiences." That is, the intent by the sending partner may not have been negative, but whatever the vehicle—tone, word, look or behavior—if it triggered anxiety, a painful sensation that is recorded as a negative experience, that is negativity.

For some people, negativity is the air they breathe as well as their most ingrained habitual response to any anxiety or discomfort. Thus, like a fish that does not know it is swimming in water, they don't know they are doing it. One woman we know was not able to hear herself carp and negate until her granddaughter unwittingly videotaped her at a family wedding. She was incredulous. "I don't really talk like that, do I?" For her, it was the beginning of a long turn-around. We cannot see ourselves without looking!

The vehicles of negativity are easy to spot and tend to be pervasive: deflection, interruption, dismissal, anger, shame, blame, criticism, devaluation, contempt, guilting, withdrawal, aggression, tone, eye roll, and both language and gestures. Negativity ranges all the way from the gentle "Ouch!" to trips to the emergency room. A vast number of couples live with a kind of negativity that is cumulatively destructive. Imagine the effect on a partner who always has to walk on eggshells, who is afraid to voice an opinion or try a new recipe or change an established routine or go against a partner's preference? In this scenario, one possible effect is that the partner walking on eggshells will become passive–aggressive or depressed or will withdraw and engage socially with others, have an affair, take drugs—any way to get the pleasure that is unavailable with their partner. On the other hand, they may become a negative competitor and respond to anything their partners says, whether their partner is negative or not, by responding to a put-down with a counter put-down. Both become inflamed with negativity and defensiveness, and peace is absent from the home. Without a reprieve, one or both may decide the relationship is too toxic to sustain and take an exit option. In no case will they experience joyful aliveness, although its absence is the source of their mutual negativity.

Sometimes negativity can be subtle, its insidious erosion harder to detect. Put-downs and judgments flourish in many varieties, sometimes under the guise of "helpful" criticism. The person on the receiving end may not even be sure that what they just heard was meant to be negative. "You're not wearing that again, are you? You look so much better when you wear the other shirt." "How could you have forgotten to go to the store? Maybe we need to write out a To-Do list every day." "Stop complaining so much. You are making me sorry I came home from work!" "You're tired? Maybe you shouldn't stay up reading so late." "John's wife made the best lasagna last week. Maybe we could ask her to come cook for us!" But in the busy give-and-take, where such remarks are par for the course, their true effects may not be obvious to the people involved. Beneath awareness, the dorsal vagal system is busy monitoring what is going on and considering which defense to activate: fight, flee, or play dead.

In one of the sessions with Fran and Alicia, Alicia was relaying how she feels she contributes to the relationship. And in that exchange, Fran inserted a little "dig" that did not go unnoticed.

> **THERAPIST:** *Alicia, can you share with Fran how you feel you contribute to the relationship? Try saying something like, "One thing I do that I feel contributes to our relationship is . . ."*
>
> **ALICIA (PAUSES):** *One thing I do that I feel contributes to our relationship is doing all the grocery shopping to prepare our meals together.*
>
> **THERAPIST:** *Fran, can you mirror that back?*
>
> **FRAN:** *If I heard you correctly, one thing you do that you feel contributes to our relationship is doing all the grocery shopping . . .* **with my money** *. . . to prepare our meals together.*
>
> **THERAPIST:** *Fran, seems like you may have something to say to Alicia about this but let's save that for another dialogue when you are the sender. Could you mirror Alicia again but this time, just paraphrase what you are hearing without adding any of your own thoughts?*

Brain scientists say that human beings have a "negativity bias" left over from prehistoric times when our ancestors lived in the wild with no built-in security. And that left us with the paranoia of everyday life. Thus we humans seem wired to react negatively in conversation. Criticism is a habit of mind and therefore a habit of behavior. And its power comes from the accumulated weight of all the blaming and judging one has experienced during the course of their entire life. Most people do not set out to obliterate the ones they love, but it is inevitable when past experiences of criticism, judgment, shaming, and humiliation go unexamined and remain out of conscious awareness. Where there are criticisms and put-downs, connecting will be ruptured and full aliveness, joy, and wonder will be replaced with anxiety; anxiety activates angry or depressive behavior, which activates defenses to relieve relational stress, and this starts the cycle again.

THE ORIGINS OF NEGATIVITY

As we indicated earlier, negativity makes sense from an evolutionary perspective. Nature seems to have selected for negativity. In our evolutionary history, those who survived were more cautious and constantly on the lookout for danger and were less likely to jump into dangerous or fatal situations. Those survivors are our ancestors—because they were the survivors, we are here. They were good at retaining information about negative experiences like building a revulsion toward those berries that made you vomit or not being curious about the snapping sound of a branch that indicated the approach of a predator. Those who had a friendly attitude were vulnerable to being hurt by other people or eaten by animals, thus they had no children who survived them!

While we live in much safer times than our ancestors, we seem to have retained a "negativity bias" (Vaish et al., 2008) that may have made sense in the savannahs and jungles of our ancestors, but in modern day relationships, it does not work well. The negativity bias plays out in couple's tendency to speak before thinking. Defensive systems (old brain) fire at a faster rate than our thinking systems (new brain); negative thought often comes out of our mouth before our brains can stop it (open mouth, insert foot). In what Goleman (2005) called the "amygdala hijack," the reactive brain will respond emotionally before the thinking brain can think things through. It is a survival response that helps us escape dangerous situations, yet it often creates other negative situations when the brain reacts quickly to what it perceives as threatening (for example, a put-down).

Psychologically, negativity is rooted in the mind. Neurologically, negativity is rooted in the brain. Brain imaging studies indicate that negative information weighs more heavily than positive information (Ito et al., 1998). Relationally, negativity is an expression of symbiosis, the failure to differentiate, which has its source in childhood wounding. Pain turns us inward and we fuse what we find inside with the world outside. When others push back with their own reality, creating the trauma of "difference," we tend to amplify our efforts with criticism and negativity to annihilate difference. Obviously, this leads to conflict, both personal and global.

While negativity is toxic and destructive, it has a paradoxical goal. Its intention is to "negate" the partner's frustrating behavior and replace it with one that satisfies the unmet childhood need, thus removing the primal danger of need-frustration. In other words, negativity is a failed attempt to satisfy the desire for connecting that was frustrated in childhood. The tragedy is that the outcome creates an environment that guarantees that the needs will not be met, thus escalating anxiety and fortifying the defenses.

THE ZERO NEGATIVITY PROCESS

As long as the relational space is unsafe and fraught with negativity, the deep childhood issues will remain unresolved and couples will unconsciously continue to rewound each other. Without safety, connecting cannot occur, and the relationship will remain in a defensive posture, characterized by tactical and strategic interactions—aggression and avoidance rather than positive mutual engagement. Therefore, early on in the sessions, it is imperative that the therapist help couples:

1. commit to removing all negativity from all transactions in their relationship;
2. discover how to restore connecting when they fail; and
3. increase positive interactions.

Once the safety in the relationship becomes more pronounced, the therapist walks them through how to restructure frustrations in a way that is likely to meet the underlying needs.

The process of removing negativity is essentially focused on three exercises:

1. The Zero Negativity Process (Appendices 20–22) is a commitment to eliminate all negativity (i.e., blaming, shaming, accusing, and criticizing) in the relationship.
2. The Reconnecting Process helps couples move from rupture to restoring connection quickly when negativity is experienced by one partner.

3. The Space-Between exercise (Appendix 23) helps couples identify what behaviors they bring to the relationship that positively
contribute to the Space-Between.

All three of these exercises commit couples to the safety and well-being of
the relationship as a whole, and they shift the couple's focus from the self to
the Space-Between.

Zero Negativity Pledge
The ZN Pledge should be introduced and signed in the first session. The
pledge is a commitment made by both partners to eliminate any behavior
that would make either partner feel put-down. That means no negative or
harsh tone of voice, no negative descriptions of each other, no complaining
or blaming, no shaming, and no aggressive gestures like eye rolling, cold
stares, or aggressive hand gestures. While we suggest 30 days as a start, you
can also ask them to pledge for the full time that they are in therapy together.

Before asking couples to consider signing the ZN Pledge, you can do
some psychoeducation about the pitfalls of endemic negativity and the
necessity of removing it from their relationship. Here are some suggested
psychoeducation "gems" for couples:

- You cannot control your first thought, but you can control your
  second.
- Think before you speak.
- Curiosity may have killed the cat, but curiosity saves a marriage.
- The sign of a thriving relationship is how quickly you reconnect.
- Ask not what your partner can do for you, but what you can do for
  your relationship.

You can then facilitate a dialogue about the ZN Pledge in which the couple
shares their commitment to removing negativity from their relationship

Table 15.1: Zero Negativity Pledge Dialogue (Sentence Stems)
(full template in Appendix 20)

Shares Intention:
My intention is to remove negativity from our relationship and to commit to the
Zero Negativity Pledge.

Deepens:
When I think about eliminating negativity from our relationship, I feel . . .
And that feeling reminds me of . . .
And when I remember that, I think . . .

and their feelings about doing that and the signing of the pledge. Formalizing the pledge this way provides a stronger impact about its importance. You can provide the couple with some token reminder of their pledge, such as a Zero Negativity bracelet. Table 15.1 lists sentence stems for the ZN Pledge dialogue.

For Fran and Alicia, signing the ZN Pledge was not difficult. What was a learning process for them—and for many couples—is to understand that even when the intention was not meant to be a put-down, it may land negatively. And experience trumps intent.

One time, Fran and Alicia entered the office right after the holidays. They had a big blowup on Christmas over a gift Alicia gave Fran. This is how they recalled the incident as we facilitated a Dialogue between them:

> **THERAPIST:** *Fran, can you tell Alicia what happened for you when you opened your gift from her?*
>
> **FRAN:** *When I opened your gift, it was a nice watch, but I already had a watch, so to me, it was an unnecessary purchase. I appreciated the thought. I just really didn't need it and said you could take it back. I wasn't angry. That upset you so much that you burst into tears and stormed into the bedroom. I mean, you don't want me to pretend to love it, do you? Well, I can't be dishonest like that. And I'm practical. There are far more important things that money can be spent on.*
>
> **THERAPIST:** *Alicia, can you mirror Fran about her reaction to your giving her the watch?*
>
> **ALICIA:** *If I got that, when you opened the watch, you thought "I already have a watch, and this is an unnecessary purchase, and I could take it back . . ." Did I get you?*
>
> **FRAN:** *Yes, you got me.*
>
> **ALICIA :** *Is there more about that?*
>
> **FRAN:** *Yes. I really was not angry, just being practical.*
>
> **ALICIA :** *You were just practical, not angry. Is there more about that?*
>
> **FRAN:** *No, that is all.*
>
> **THERAPIST:** Prompts Alicia to do a summary mirror.
>
> **ALICIA:** *Let me see if I got it all. When you opened the watch that I gave you, you felt it was an impractical gift, since you have a watch, and you were not angry about the gift. You were just being practical. Did I get it all?*
>
> **THERAPIST:** Once Alicia got it all, prompts Alicia to validate and empathize. Then facilitates closings.
>
> **FRAN:** *Thanks for listening.*

ALICIA: *Thanks for sharing.*

THERAPIST: *Alicia, can you ask Fran if she is available to hear your response?*

ALICIA: *Are you available for my response?*

FRAN: *Yes.*

THERAPIST: *Can you share with Fran how her response to your gift felt to you? Try something like, "When you opened the gift and indicated that I could return it, I felt . . ."*

ALICIA: *When you opened the gift and indicated that I could return it, I felt . . . sad . . . and dejected.*

THERAPIST: Prompts Fran to mirror, check for accuracy, invite to share more.

ALICIA: *Well, I spent a lot of time picking out what I thought was the perfect gift. I probably went to five different stores, plus talking with our friends. Plus, I know the watch you wear now is from your former girlfriend, so I guess I wanted to remove the memory of her. I guess when you acted that way, I felt like all those efforts were unimportant. I felt like I wasn't important.*

THERAPIST: Prompts Fran to mirror, check for accuracy, and invite more. Then asks Alicia: *Can you say more about that feeling of being unimportant? Something like, "That feeling of being unimportant reminds me of childhood when . . ."*

ALICIA: *Well, I guess it was hard feeling important, being the middle child of four siblings.*

FRAN: Mirrors, checks for accuracy, and invites more.

ALICIA: *My older sisters often did their own thing, leaving me behind. And my younger brother and sister were 3 and 4 years younger than me and got all of mom's attention because they needed more care. I made a lot of effort to be good and giving and it was often unnoticed. I remember a time I drew a picture of the family. I wasn't much of an artist, but I spent a lot of time adding every family member—seven of us mind you! And a rainbow, the dog, and colorful flowers. When I presented it to mom, she just said, "That's nice." And nothing more. I guess I felt dejected then too. I often got overlooked. But I guess I felt a bit invisible no matter how much I tried to get noticed.*

THERAPIST: Prompts Fran to mirror, check for accuracy, and invite more. When there is no more, Fran summarizes, validates, and empathizes. Fran and Alicia thank each other for sharing and listening.

Deepening revealed that one of Alicia's core childhood issues was not being important enough in a family of five children. So, while Fran meant to be practical in her response to the gift, it landed negatively with Alicia, triggering a painful childhood experience.

Homework

One of the most important elements of successful therapy is that the couple continues the work between sessions. The ZN Pledge is a bridge that connects the structured experience of the office and the unstructured atmosphere of the home through a homework task that is specific and achievable. The ZN calendar helps them monitor their interactions on a daily basis. To inform couples of the value of daily monitoring, suggest the following tasks:

1. Buy a 30-day calendar (or you can provide a paper calendar, such as in Appendix 22).
2. Place the calendar in a prominent place where both partners can see it (e.g., on a bathroom mirror or wall).
3. At the end of each day for the next 30 days, decide together what kind of rating the relationship receives.
   a. Draw a frowning face on the calendar if either partner expressed or experienced a put-down that day.
   b. If neither partner felt a put-down, put a smiley face on the calendar for that day.
   c. If a put-down was experienced but connecting was successfully restored, write "RESET" on the calendar.

NOTE: The couple decides *together* what kind of rating the relationship receives at the end of the day, since they are monitoring the relationship itself, not individual partners.

4. Have a short check in each day about your progress and your feelings about the process.

Integrating Zero Negativity

Review the ZN Pledge as part of the check-in at the beginning of each session. This is especially important for the first 30 days of ZN practice. Most couples will have some difficulty remembering to practice consistently, but practicing consistently is the only way they will ultimately benefit.

NOTE: Near the end of the 30 days, each partner may begin to experience a high level of anxiety. Since negativity is a defense, when it is removed consistently for at least 30 days, the homeostatic balance of the brain is ruptured, because it removes the brain's primal and evolutionary defense system. Remember that for the millions of years when we lived in the savannahs and forests, our brains became paranoid as a survival tactic—you never knew if someone or something was coming to dinner or coming to have you for dinner! Given that couples tend to experience more negativity and/or leave therapy when they experience the loss of this brain homeostasis, it is essential that they share their experience in sessions so that you can help them normalize it. If they continue the ZN practice, their brains will re-stabilize at a higher level. But if they stop, they may be left with vulnerability to deep anxiety. A simple homework check-in at the beginning of each session can help them integrate the process.

It is possible that a 30-day commitment is too difficult for some couples, and you might only be able to get them to commit to ZN until the next session. Couples should stretch into new behaviors, but not stretch so much that it might break them. If they experience too much anxiety and become negative with each other again, at the end of 30 days it may be a good idea to evaluate the process with your couple and modify the agreement.

The full integration of ZN into their lives will require two more thirty-day periods of consistent practice.

The Reconnecting Process

Initially, most couples fail to keep the ZN pledge due to the pull of their evolutionary defenses. It is important to acknowledge this pull in the session. As couples work to eliminate negativity, when they fail, they also learn how to reset negative experiences quickly to reestablish connecting before they habituate to an attack–defend posture that may last for hours or days.

For example, if in the session the sender includes some criticism or negativity about the partner using "you" statements, you can help the sender by reminding them of the "I" statement responsibility. We have also developed a more formal Reconnecting Process that helps regulate emotions when a put-down is experienced. This Reconnecting Process is:

1. *Mutually Agree Upon a Signal.* Partners mutually select a signal to indicate they have experienced a put-down. The use of a signal helps the offended partner respond from their prefrontal cortex rather than their amygdala, thus replacing reactivity with a response that contributes to integrating the brain. The partners' signals can be the same or different. Some options couples have used include ouch, wow, whew, etc. One couple we worked with chose the word "marshmallow." For them, it was hard to stay negative with the word that stood for something soft and fluffy and that stirred memories of childhood campfires and Mr. Stay Puft from Ghostbusters.

2. *Explore Reconnecting Options.* After a signal that a partner has experience a put-down, it is important for them to reconnect as quickly as possible to avoid become habituated to the neuro-chemicals of disconnection. There are various options to help couples reconnect, including:

a. *Reconnecting Behaviors.* Sometimes all that is necessary is a quick, simple connecting behavior like an apology, a hug, a gift, etc. Again, what works for one, may not work for the other. (Apologies work for Helen but not for Harville. He wants a behavior change!)

b. *The Redo.* Take time out, start over, and redo the transaction. When one partner experiences a put-down, they can ask their partner to *redo* the message in a way that is not negative. "I felt a put-down by that comment. Would you send it to me again in a way that sounds affirming?"

c. *The Modeling Process.* The partner who received the put-down can offer to model how they would like the partner to resend the message. "Let me act it out for you, so you can not only hear but also see how I would like you to send your message."

d. *Imago Dialogue.* Sometimes the experience of a put-down is very painful and may require a formal Dialogue with a deeper emphasis on curiosity and empathy. See Table 15.2 for some key sentence stems that you can use to facilitate this Dialogue.

Table 15.2: Dialoguing Around a Put-Down (Sentence Stems)
I experienced a put-down and would like to Dialogue about it. Is now a good time?
Can you tell me more about that? What was it that made you experience a put-down?
When you did *[the put-down]* I felt _____ When I felt that, it reminded me of _____ *[childhood experience.]*
Please let me say it differently so it doesn't feel negative to you.
Let me model it for you so you can do it differently.
What I need from you is _____ *[a behavior, a redo, or a remodel.]*
Would you tell me (or show me) what I need to do to reconnect with you?

e. *Behavior Change Request.* Sometimes, the put-down activates a very painful memory that requires not only a deeper
understanding that can be achieved in a Dialogue, but a
change in behavior. The Behavior Change Dialogue will be
discussed in the next chapter.

Once you explain the Reconnecting Process, assign couples the following
homework:

1. Come up with a signal that each partner uses to register a put-
down (can be different for each partner or the same).
   a. The signal I will use when I experience a put-down is . . .
   b. The signal my partner will use when they experience a put-
down is . . .
2. Discuss things your partner can do that feel reparative:
   a. What removes a put-down for me and restores connecting
is . . .
   b. What removes a put-down for my partner and restores connecting is . . .

Space-Between Dialogue
Some couples flounder at the beginning of therapy when negativity is ban-
ished. It is like being deprived of oxygen. Not only will it be difficult for them
to give up the addictive power of negativity, but they may find an emptiness
in the relationship once they are successful. After all, one way to remove
negativity is by removing engagement. (For us personally, our marriage was
once so consumed with toxicity that when we went "cold turkey," we did
not have much to say to each other and an uncomfortable silence blanketed
our relationship until we discovered the need to show curiosity and express
appreciations.)

Most couples are generous about their complaints and parsimonious
about their appreciations. ZN helps remove behaviors that do not work from
our brain's defense system, but the brain needs a new set of instructions on
how to survive. Replacing negativity with curiosity and positive reflection
gives the brain a whole new way of being in the world, which, when practiced until integrated, assures not only safety and survival but also pleasure
and joy. Now, the brain becomes very interested and more integrated. For
this reason, while introducing the ZN Pledge, we simultaneously work on
increasing positive exchanges in the Space-Between.

We recommend introducing Appreciations in Session 1, and we recommend that every session begin with sharing an appreciation. To help couples

integrate appreciations into their relationship, we encourage them to begin a ritual of daily affirmations that creates safety and pleasure—expressing three appreciations at bedtime, sharing a gratitude in the morning, giving each other a one-minute hug each day. These simple, doable achievements can begin to tip the scale in the Space-Between from the red (negative) to the black (positive). If a negative transaction occurs, couples should work toward balancing any negative interactions they may have with positive ones, at a **minimum** ratio of five positives to one negative. Research shows relationships fare much better when there are at least five positive affirmations after a negative interaction (Gottman et al., 1998).

As a therapist, it is also important to convey positive observations about each partner and about the relationship as a whole. While we explore this further in the Re-romanticizing chapter, another simple process for infusing positivity into the relationship is using the Space-Between Dialogue (Table 15.3). There is also a worksheet that you can give your couple as a between-session assignment (Appendix 23).

Table 15.3: Space-Between Us Dialogue (Sentence Stems)
One of the best things I see you bringing to our relationship space is _____
When I experience you bringing _____ to our relationship, I feel _____
And when I feel that, I remember when I was a child _____
And when I remember that, I think _____

OUTCOMES OF THE REMOVING NEGATIVITY PROCESS

Negativity serves a purpose. Until now, it has been a survival mechanism (a paradox, given the relationship is dying from the toxicity). Therefore, eliminating negativity is difficult for most couples, especially those who have been using non-dialogical methods of interacting for a long time. It might be quite a while before they can decrease the level of negativity in their relationship, not to mention eliminating it all together. It is important that the therapist celebrates the small successes, validates the challenges, and encourages the couple to stay in the canoe and paddle together.

Over time, removing negativity:

- **Increases Safety.** Safety, of course, is essential and nonnegotiable. Without safety, the goal of therapy (restoring connecting) cannot happen.

- **Promotes Curiosity.** Replacing negativity with curiosity creates safety and facilitates differentiation and brain integration, which further reduces reactivity.
- **Breaks Symbiosis.** Zero Negativity removes the negative attributions of the symbiotic consciousness and promotes differentiation and connecting. Rather than "negating" the other because of difference, Zero Negativity accepts and celebrates the other's difference. This is a precondition of "real" love.
- **Shares Responsibility for the Space-Between.** Zero Negativity helps move from the "I–It" to the "I–Thou" and "Us" relationship.
- **Strengthens Intentionality.** You cannot control your first thought, but you can control your second. With daily practice, couples can strengthen their resolve to avoid negativity or quickly make a repair. Like a muscle being exercised, the thinking brain can take control of the reactive brain, over time.
- **Reveals Relational Patterns.** Under the frowny faces is a pattern of conflict that the couple can discover by moving into Dialogue and discovering the sensitive and painful childhood memories activated in each other when they engage in a negative exchange. This deepens empathic responding which contributes to restoring connecting.
- **Regulates Anxiety.** Providing a signal when experiencing a put-down helps identify the underlying anxiety quickly and safely. This process enables couples to move from ambiguity and confusion to clarity.

As you journey with your couples through the Removing Negativity Process, remember that this concept will be new to them. During their power struggles, they will not previously have thought that placing the relationship before the self, by implementing Imago Dialogue, would be beneficial to their relationship. Sharing with them the why behind the Zero Negativity process is as essential as facilitating the Dialogue between them. When we know the why and the what, we then become more interested in knowing the how. When we know how, we are able to adapt and practice more conscious connecting behaviors.

Takeaways for Removing Negativity

- Negativity is defined as anything that one partner *experiences* as a put-down coming from the other partner—an interaction, word, gesture, tone, or behavior.
- The symptoms of negativity include deflection, anger, shame, blame, criticism, devaluation, contempt, guilting, withdrawal, and aggression.
- Psychologically, negativity is rooted in symbiosis, the failure to differentiate that has its source in childhood wounding. Pain turns us inward.
- Negativity has a greater impact than positivity. Thus, couples should work toward balancing any negative interactions they may have with positive ones, at a **minimum** ratio of five positives to one negative.
- It is imperative to help couples throughout the sessions to 1) remove all negativity from all transactions in their relationship (the Zero Negativity Pledge); 2) discover how to restore connecting (the Reconnecting Process); and 3) increase positive interactions in the Space-Between (the Space-Between Dialogue).

16

Restructuring Frustrations

What: Discovering the wish embedded in the frustration and asking for what you want.

Why: Replacing the frustration with the wish invites partners to stretch into meeting each others' needs.

When: Any time during or after the Reimaging process.

Like all couples, their relationship started out great, and then it went bad, and they have spent a large part of their lives trying to make it good again. They are at an impasse. They have used up all their options, such as avoidance and fighting, and have failed to mitigate the pain, and now there are threats of divorce. They are delaying *that* action until after working with you.

When they arrive at your office, they bring with them a multitude of frustrations they have collected over the years. Each partner is seeking immediate relief from their suffering and hoping you will change their partner so their frustrations will disappear, and they won't have to change! But they do not know what the Imago therapist knows—that conflict is growth trying to happen and that the frustrations they wish to dispense with contain the secret formula for restoring the sense of belonging and the experience of joyful aliveness.

In Imago therapy, a frustration is viewed as a wish masked as a complaint. Embedded in every criticism is a desire, and that desire is a relic of unmet childhood needs. And, the complaint one partner makes to the other is a replication of the childhood cry that failed to get their caretakers to respond. The cry that failed to get childhood needs met became the adult complaint about those same needs not being met. And so far, it has failed again. But none of this is in the couple's awareness. They are under the illusion that all their troubles have to do with how their partner is frustrating them in the present and nothing to do with the past.

As their therapist, you will not take their frustrations away but use them as resources to discover what they need to change in their relationship.

Embedded in the frustration is the map to what they want. Your success in helping them get what they want will depend on how well you help them understand the function of this repetition between childhood and adulthood and how well you mine the gold hidden in the dross of their frustrations. You will be charged with communicating these principles so that they understand why they are participating in this dialogue rather than in a solution to their problems.

We have to get in our intimate relationship what we did not get in childhood. And we have to give what were unable to give previously. And we have to get it from and give it to an Imago-Match. It is a challenging process because it requires both partners to change in significant ways. Remember: what one needs, the other is least able to give due to similar wounding but complementary defenses. By now, hopefully, partners have removed the blinders, and the empathy restored by the Reimaging Process has helped them move from "having to meet my partner's needs" to "wanting to meet my partner's needs." They are now ready to transform existing conflicts into the foundation stones of a transformed relationship.

The Restructuring Frustrations process is simple:

1. state a frustration about a specific behavior;
2. convert the frustration into the embedded wish;
3. translate the wish into a specific behavior; and
4. enact those behaviors on a regular basis.

But simple does not mean easy, because what one partner needs most is what the other is least capable of giving, in the moment. That is what makes this process so challenging. Most couples fail in their early tries and need a lot of support to continue.

To facilitate their understanding of this complexity, provide some psychoeducation to teach them that conflict is:

1. the bifurcation point of either dissolution (in unconscious partnerships) or transformation (in conscious partnerships);
2. an opportunity for uncovering what is needed to live their dream relationship; and
3. growth trying to happen.

The process includes guiding couples into and through the transformation of conflict into connecting. If you do this process too soon, it sets the couple up for failure and they may give up on the relationship. Doing it too late, the couple might become frustrated and give up on you.

The goals of the Restructuring Frustrations process include:

1. identifying frustrations and the underlying feelings, childhood memories, and global desires;
2. sharing frustrations in a safe way that evokes empathy and invites change;
3. making a request for specific behavior changes that address the hurt and need;
4. gifting the relationship with new, specific behaviors that produce transformational growth.

A FRUSTRATION IS A HIDDEN WISH

When couples come to therapy, the challenges from the relational war of the power struggle has compounded the challenges from childhood. They are now doubly challenged by memories of hurts: from the immediate past to the echoes of long ago which seems also to be immediately present. Consequently, frustrations have grown in size and frequency. And with frustrations come the escalation of defenses. We call this the cycle of frustrations (Figure 16.1).

At the heart of frustrations (especially if they are chronic) is a disguised plea for the exact needs that a person did not get in childhood—affection, affirmation, protection, independence, connection, acceptance. The wish behind all frustrations is that the partner will morph into the idealized person whose vocation it to meet their childhood needs all the

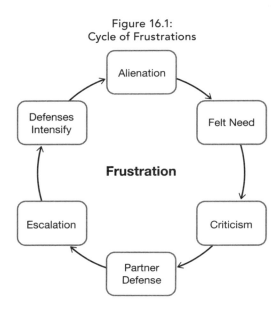

Figure 16.1:
Cycle of Frustrations

time. This wish is the golden nugget which, when properly translated, guides the couple to the outcome they are seeking.

The challenge to the therapist is to help couples dialogue long enough and well enough to cocreate a relationship that transforms tension into collaboration, conflict into connecting, and anxiety into joyful aliveness, because that will replace the challenges of the past with their dream of a safe and passionate future. That will require exploring frustrations and excavating the wish underneath—globally and specifically—in order to invite new behaviors that will become the bricks in the new house of their relationship.

THE STRETCHING PRINCIPLE

Stretching is the act of going beyond the comfort zone and caring absolutely and unconditionally for another in the exact way the other needs care, focusing less on the "I" and more on the "You." We call this the "Stretching Principle." It is not negotiation but transformation.

In the process of stretching to meet a partner's needs, the one who stretches simultaneously grows. Igniting the process requires the care of the other rather than care of the self. There is a profound spiritual beauty in this symmetry. Behavioral changes not only help the receiver (to feel safe/loved/visible) but also awaken the deadened areas of the giver, stretching them into undeveloped potential they could not otherwise optimize. Growth and transformation are the prizes of this relational journey.

UNCONDITIONAL GIVING

The restructuring process is not quid-pro-quo bargaining ("I'll do this if you do that"). That does not work and quickly degenerates into a power struggle with accusations about who broke the pact first. Instead, in the Restructuring Frustrations process, both partners commit to a behavior change as an unconditional gift to the partner and to the relationship. The unconscious mind is not interested in deals. In our view, it is basically instinctual, it has no negotiating capacity and wants what it wants!

But there is a more profound reason why behavioral changes need to be unconditional gifts. Neuroscientists recently discovered, somewhere in the unconscious mind, a pea size cluster of neurons that work 24-7. Together, they are called "the bullshit detector." It knows when a gift has strings attached and immediately sends out warning signals to the recipient, who promptly runs away. Only unconditional gifts transform the Space-Between into a zone of safety where transformation happens. This is an essential quality for couples to integrate into their behavioral changes, releasing all self-expectations.

RESISTANCE TO CHANGE

Resistance has been of interest throughout the history of psychotherapy. One of Freud's pivotal insights was that underneath every wish is a fear of having that wish come true, so every opportunity to satisfy the wish is sabotaged to retain the previous state of deprivation. The reason has to do with his view that the instinctual wishes of sexuality and aggression, which he later called the life and death forces, were forbidden by the superego, and to have the wish would cause anxiety and guilt—hence resistance shows up in therapy, and transcending it is a challenge most therapists have faced.

Imago states that since every frustration is an unconscious wish to have what one wants, partners have to identify the wish, then convert it into a request, and ask for a new behavior. Since Imago operates in the relational paradigm, the reason for the resistance is relational rather than instinctual, and there are two dynamics behind the phenomenon of resistance.

First, the wish embedded in the frustration is the desire for reconnecting rather than satisfaction of sexual and aggressive instincts. Connecting is the restoration of our original condition, the condition that was lost in childhood, and the moment of the rupture activated the desire for reconnection. But that presents a problem for the survival orientation of the primitive brain. Now there are two memories: 1) the original condition of full aliveness, joy, and wonder and 2) the anxiety created when connecting is ruptured. Rather than resistance being connected to the guilt about have a forbidden desire fulfilled (as in psychoanalysis), in Imago, resistance is fed by the anticipation that it will be ruptured again, triggering the intolerable pain of anxiety about the possibility of non-being, so the brain apparently says something to this effect: "It is better to want connecting and not get it than to get connecting and experience rupture again." To maintain that impasse, the complaint about disconnection is continually expressed, and the defense against reconnecting is chronically activated. That maintains awareness of the desire and protection from losing it absolutely. To move beyond this impasse requires a decision to engage in sustained connecting behaviors and to tolerate the anxiety of possible rupture until the brain's anticipation of pain and potential non-being is surrendered with the knowledge that reconnecting is always possible, and quickly, in the reconnecting process outlined in the preceding chapter.

The second dynamic for resistance has to do with our discovery that what one partner wants, their romantic partner is least capable of giving at the time of the request, and vice versa—which is usually early in the power struggle. To briefly review (see Chapter 6): an Imago-Match involves two people who unconsciously chose as an intimate partner a facsimile of the caretaker with whom they had the most difficulty getting their needs met.

Perhaps the childhood experience was unrequited love, disconnection, abandonment, harsh discipline, negative words, or some other rupture. Regardless of what it was, they have chosen a person as a potential partner to meet the need not met by their caretaker in childhood.

However, as a result of the unattuned parenting by their caretaker in childhood, that partner had to shut down the part of themselves they need access to in order to meet the need not met by their partner's caretaker. This dynamic has to do with the fate of the four functions: thinking, movement, sensations, and feelings. As a child, each partner was asked by their caretakers to shut down, or not activate, or limit certain functions in order to be acceptable in their family. For instance, the partner asking for a wish to be fulfilled did not experience warm emotional expressions from their caretakers, and since that was a need not met in childhood, they will want that need met by their intimate partner. *But*, the need has to be met by an Imago-Match, a person whose feeling function was shut down in childhood, not by a person who can naturally and easily do it. Since they ask for a response from a function that was not developed in their partner, this will be most challenging to the partner, and while in the Dialogue process they will come to understand their partner's need for emotional intensity, and with the addition of empathy about this need as missing in their partner's experience, they may offer to do it—but in most cases they will fail. The failure will be the result of two things: 1) the function was not developed (in this case, the feeling function), and 2) since it was forbidden to express feelings in the childhood home, to express feeling in the current situation triggers the unconscious fear of disobeying the caretakers and reactivating the rejection they experienced with their caretakers. Since this is mutual, the resistance creates an impasse that becomes a core scene to be reactivated over and over again.

To move through the impasse, each partner will have to stretch into the other partner's need and repeat the behavior until the brain sees the new behavior as a better defense than the archaic one. Not only will the anxiety wane, but each partner will recover an atrophied function and since they are responding to their partner's needs, they will recover original connecting.

On one level, what is happening at the impasse is nature's elegant design to keep us alive. It is a built-in resistance to change, a biological and psychological phenomenon. Homeostasis, from the Greek words for "same" and "steady," refers to any process that living things use to actively maintain an inner equilibrium necessary for survival. Any change to that balance is seen as a threat, and the survival mode goes into full gear, setting off a stress reaction cycle.

The problem with homeostasis is that it does not distinguish between a good change and a bad one. To the body, all change is threatening. And to the reptilian brain, psychological change is no different from physical change. While the body self-regulates in an elaborate system of feedback to protect the organism, the psyche can feel a looming death sentence. Therefore, when a partner is, for example, stretching into new behaviors (such as becoming more sexual, more emotional, more expressive), warning signals go up and often show up disguised as rational reasons not to continue on the particular path of change. "It's not working." "I can't do it." "It's not me, it's you!" "Why am I doing all the work??!!"

Throughout their lifetime, couples have carved an identity with their defenses. To be the "victim" who never gets what they need is familiar territory. Or to be "the hero" and "do it all" is the MO they are comfortable with. To give up those identities—no matter how conscious or unconscious—will be scary for your couples. Additionally, they do not have internal permission to *receive* what they need to heal or *give* what they need to grow or recover what they originally were. The unconscious sabotages both the giving (i.e., growth) and the receiving (i.e., transforming) aspects of the partnership. Ultimately their resistance to receiving is as crippling to the relationship as their resistance to giving (Hendrix & Hunt, 2004).

Here are some ways to help couples overcome resistance:

1. Coach them to expect and welcome resistance and to keep on with the process. Resistance means some movement toward homeostatic rupture has occurred. Let couples know to anticipate resistance and normalize it. (Provide examples such as, "I'm too tired today" or "I'm always doing for you. What about me?") Simply acknowledge resistance and move on.

2. Encourage them to focus on the practice, not the outcome. Put the experience into Dialogue. Use sentence stems such as, "When I stretched into that behavior, I felt . . ." "I think I deflected George's compliment because . . ." "I won't ask Mary for help because, if I did . . ." Explore together within a context of curiosity and empathy. Over time, the process itself will diffuse the anxiety. The Dialogue process itself is the focus, and its practice is the dedication.

3. Help them understand that they need to stretch beyond their comfort zone. Remind couples that stretching is not only in giving but also in receiving. Receiving, just as much as giving, threatens the homeostasis of the victim who never gets what they want. Encourage them to "allow" themselves to receive the unconditional gifts from their partner. Hold and tolerate discomfort as a way to move past the impasse.

4. Help them learn to ask for what they want, directly. Many of us have a difficult time asking for what we want or need for fear of rejection or, paradoxically, for fear of getting it, because that ends the basis of complaint and erodes our victim identity.

5. Help them continue the differentiation process by rupturing a little more of their symbiotic consciousness. Symbiotically, we have an illusion that the other knows, or should know, our internal world and what we need or want, and that we should not have to ask. "If you don't know what I want, you have not been listening." Tell couples that in order to have a conscious partnership, they need to give up this mind-reading fantasy.

If couples move through behavioral changes rather than back away from them, eventually anxiety will decrease because the brain will experience that the survival value of the new behaviors is more efficient than that of the old behaviors. Ultimately, the fear of absolute "death" (the possibility of nonbeing) will no longer be an inhibiting factor in the mutual campaign for joyful connecting.

Now we turn to a series of exercises designed to uncover the sources of frustrations and to turn conflict into connecting.

THE RESTRUCTURING FRUSTRATIONS PROCESS

At this point in the therapy process, the increased safety in the Space-Between allows challenge to old behaviors that need to be replaced with new ones. You can now work to address the recurring frustrations in the relationship and move from conflict to connecting through these clinical tools. The clinical process of restructuring frustrations is as follows.

1. **Psychoeducation**: Enough awareness has grown in the dyad for the couple to absorb some information about this process. Providing more psychoeducation now helps the couple understand the opportunity their conflicted relationship contains. Helping them comprehend the paradox of the embedded wish and the challenge of stretching could be your main points.

2. **Frustrations List** (written exercise and Dialogue): Both partners create their list of frustrations and a list of frustrations they imagine their partner has with them. Both rate the intensity of the frustrations (on a scale of 1–10) and, using the Dialogue process, share with each other. As with all Imago exercises, this furthers differentiation and diminishes symbiosis.

3. **The Core Scene** (written exercise and Dialogue): Most couples have a recurring fight that starts and ends the same way every time. The underlying feelings and the defensive outcomes are predictable, and they often say out loud or in their heads "here we go again." Frustration identification helps them identify the core scene, which helps decrease its potency by pulling away the layers to see its unconscious intent. There is no change in behavior, only in awareness—identifying and sharing feelings and defenses and visualizing doing something differently makes a difference!

4. **Behavior Change Request (BCR):** In this process, partners further peel back the layers of their frustrations and then make specific requests for behavioral changes from each other. The receiver unconditionally gifts a SMART change. The BCR process dismantles and rebuilds the foundations of the couple's relationship, moving them toward inhabiting a conscious partnership.

5. **Gifts of Change Dialogue:** This is similar to the BCR as a process but is a paradigm shift in practice. Rather than asking for a behavior change from the partner, in the Gifts of Change Dialogue, the sender identifies what *they* must remove from the Space-Between to benefit the relationship and gifts the relationship with specific behaviors to support the removal.

Each step of this clinical process is elaborated on below.

Clinical Tool #1: Psychoeducation
While education is not therapy, sharing information can help the therapy outcome by helping a couple understand the rationale and value of the therapeutic process, especially if the process is complex and challenging. Since Restructuring Frustrations is a foundational process, couples are helped by a little explanation—but not by *too* much.

These are the ideas you may want to present to the couple to guide the Restructuring Frustrations process:

- Review and praise the accomplishments they have achieved thus far in the relationship.
- Indicate that the relationship is safe enough now to deal with frustrations in the relationship in a healthy, collaborative way.
- Explain that the source of frustrations are due to the earlier childhood experiences and that conflict is an opportunity for transformation. A frustration is a wish in disguise.

- Explain the beautiful symmetry of mutual transformation. One partner's need is the other partner's gift. What one needs to receive in order to heal a childhood deficit requires the development of a capacity in the other that was shut down in their childhood. Thus, to exert that capacity in the service of a partner's need grows an undeveloped part of the self, activating potential, wholeness and connecting. Mutual transformation in the service of restoring and sustaining connecting is the reason they were brought together as an Imago-Match.
- Explain the stretching principle:

  - Change requires stretching beyond their comfort zone but only a little at a time so as not to arouse too much anxiety and prompt them to retreat to the original condition.
  - Start with small changes that will not break you.

- Indicate that they may experience resistance in both stretching and in receiving. Reassure them that resistance is normal. You will be there to encourage them to express their feelings using the Dialogue process and to discover the joy beyond the challenge of changing. Expression helps relieve their anxiety thus moving beyond the resistance.
- Offer the concept of unconditional giving. Explain that "gifting" the relationship means there are no strings attached. There is no keeping score. Emphasize that *only* unconditional gifts heal.
- Ask them to trust the process and have compassion for the challenge—in both giving and receiving.
- Remind them that they are under no obligation to make any changes they don't want to make, but also inform them that each change in behavior will help them to grow into a more complete human being, to heal their painful childhood experiences and to restore the experience of connecting in the Space-Between.

Clinical Tool #2: The Frustrations List

This exercise helps partners see the pattern in their frustrations and identify the core wound and need from childhood. Since the Frustrations List includes not only each partner's frustrations but also a guess at the frustrations their partner has with them, it continues the differentiation and connecting process by encouraging them to see the relationship through the other's eyes.

Most people can easily identify what their partner does that irritates, annoys, angers, or otherwise frustrates them. One reason for this is that our survival instinct is physically rooted in the primal brain, which reacts in a flash to whatever—in any way, shape, or form—seems threatening.

But it is not as immediately apparent to us how our behaviors frustrate our partners and trigger negative feelings in them. To identify this, couples need to activate the new brain, specifically, the prefrontal cortex. This relatively sophisticated brain region gives us a huge cognitive advantage over non-primate species: the capacity to see our impact on others and to reflect upon and change our thoughts, feelings, and behaviors.

The Frustrations List process can be done in the office or assigned as between-session work. If you ask them to make the list at home, be sure to ask them NOT to share their lists until they return to the office. The subsequent Dialogue should occur within a therapy session.

Step 1. Making the lists
Instruct and remind them that a frustration is a behavior, not a feeling or a trait or a memory. It is something their partner "does."

1. Ask both partners to write at the top of a sheet of paper: "My Frustrations" (Appendix 24) and list all the frustrations they have with their partner. When they finish the list, ask them to rate each frustration on a scale of 1–10, with 1 being the most mild and 10 the most intense.
2. Next ask both partners to write at the top of another sheet of paper: "My Partner's Frustrations" (Appendix 25) and make a list of frustrations they think their partner has with them, rating each on a scale of 1–10.
3. Next ask them to choose a mild frustration (under 5) and complete a series of sentence stems (Table 16.1). This process asks them to study the list of frustrations, feelings, childhood memories, and needs and to look for a common theme or pattern in each. While their Frustrations List may be long, their diversity can often be collapsed into one or more core themes.

As you might guess, many maximizers come up with a list that covers an entire page, while the minimizing partner often gets stuck after writing down one, two, or three items.

Step 2. Sharing the lists
1. Each partner shares their list of the ways they think they frustrate their partner, including the feelings, childhood memories, the need they had then that they still have, and how they rated it.

Table 16.1: Restructuring Frustrations (Sentence Stems)
My Frustrations With My Partner
When you *(describe a behavior)* _____ , I feel _____ And when I feel _____ , I remember that when I was little _____ What I wanted then and still need is _____
The recurring theme I see in my frustrations is that I tend to feel frustrated whenever someone *(does not keep their promise, when I feel invisible, no one answers my question, when I can't get their attention, etc.)* _____ The recurring feeling/s I see when I am frustrated is/are _____ My recurring childhood memory/memories are _____ My recurring need is _____
My Partner's Frustrations with Me
Complete this sentence stem for each frustration you think your partner has with you. I imagine you get frustrated with me when I *(describe a behavior.)* _____ _____ When I do that, I imagine you feel _____ And when you feel that I imagine you remember _____ What you wanted then was _____ And you still want _____
Identify the pattern you see in these frustrations using these sentence stem: The pattern I see in this list of frustrations is _____ The recurring feeling that I can imagine is _____ What you wanted in childhood and still want is _____

2. As in all Dialogue exchanges,
   a. The sender begins by asking for an appointment about the topic: *Is now a good time to share my list of the frustrations I imagine you have with me?*
   b. The partners connect while taking deep breaths and making eye contact.
   c. The sender expresses a one-way appreciation.
   d. The receiver mirrors the appreciation.
   e. The sender shares each frustration using the sentence stems: *I think I frustrate you when I . . . . The rating I give that is . . . . When I do that I imagine you might feel . . . and when you feel . . . I imagine your childhood memory is . . . and that what you wanted is . . . . And that you also want . . . now.*

f. The receiver mirrors each sentence, checks for accuracy, and invites more.

g. The sender says: *The pattern of frustrations I imagine you have is . . . and the recurring feeling I imagine is . . . . And the repetitive childhood memory is . . . . And what you still want is . . . .*

After the first partner shares the list and the second partner mirrors, they switch roles and go through the process again.

NOTE: Validating and empathizing are not necessary in this Dialogue exchange, although you may find them useful or necessary at times. Also, when listening and mirroring, receivers should resist verbal or nonverbal indications of whether the sender is "accurate" or not. This is purely about the sender's perception of the receiver's frustrations. However, once the process is complete, you may want to then move each partner to share with each other (dialogically) how accurate (or inaccurate) their perceptions were.

Step 3: Exchange the lists.
1. Make a copy of all four lists.
2. Ask partners to exchange their lists. Now each partner has their own Frustrations List, the list of frustrations their partner imagined they have, their partner's Frustrations List, and the list of what they imagined frustrates their partner, along with the ratings for each.

   NOTE: The ratings may be very different, but they help partners discover the inner world of the other and this distinction contributes to the differentiation process.

3. Each partner now compares the frustrations their partner imagined they have with the frustrations they actually have and adds the ones they actually have to their partner's list and removes the frustrations their partner imagined they have but they do not.
4. Each partner compares and edits the ratings of each frustration that matches theirs.
5. Using Imago Dialogue, they share their edits with each other.
6. Each partner then assembles from all this information a new list of the actual frustrations with any additions, as well as actual ratings.

NOTE: Remember, the intent of this exercise has little to do with the curated content. By listing the frustrations each partner has as well as the frustrations they think their partner has with them, they curate the impact of childhood on the relationship, promote differentiation, and contribute to the direction and content of the therapy process. The background achievement of making and sharing all these lists and creating a common list, and without realizing it, they are becoming conscious partners by collaborating on their discovery of mutual frustrations and designing outcomes that remove negativity and restore connecting.

Clinical Tool #3: The Core Scene
In the frustration analysis above, each partner has identified the material that constitutes the core issue in their relationship that shows up over and over again, which we call their "core scene." Now, with all this information, couples can begin their deep work, the first step of which is the construction of their core scene.

A core scene is any conflict that occurs three or more times and is attended with strong negative feelings. The pattern partners discovered in their Frustrations List and the unmet needs that trigger these frustrations are the material of a chronic drama that is played out over and over again with the same feelings, words, and interactions without resolution. They are the predictable and familiar same-old arguments. Be patient in facilitating. The reality is, the core scene keeps repeating itself over and over again because the brain is trying to achieve a different outcome, namely, to restore connecting. The core scene is a chronically failing attempt to address the symptoms of ruptured connection—not whatever topic they appear to be fighting about. The desire for reconnecting shows up in the content of their frustrations. For instance, one partner's disdain when the other wants more time to have fun or another partner's complaint about being neglected are unspoken wishes for connection. Behind the complaint are the challenges they experienced during childhood: the terror of being abandoned, the fear of being enmeshed, the hopelessness of feeling invisible, or perhaps the frustration of being considered incompetent.

The core scene has its roots in an unmet need from childhood, and it reappears in adulthood with devastating consequences. It is a replay of childhood scenarios with the addition of the current partner's defensive adaptation to them, including all the ways that primitive feelings are acted out. Once a core scene begins to be reenacted, each partner's defensive behaviors (e.g., the maximizer's slamming of doors or the minimizer's retreat behind a book) trigger pain in the other, who likewise reacts in ways that trigger the wounds of the first partner, and so on in an escalating experience of disconnection.

But, as in the popular adage attributed to Einstein: "We cannot solve a problem at the same level of consciousness with which it was created." The Core Scene Dialogue is the new consciousness that is needed to end this miserable and predictable repetition. Its goal is to identify the feelings, behaviors, and defense strategies—not to remove or resolve them. This is a part of the differentiation process that leads to empathy and connecting, rather than to polarization, if the exploration is done with curiosity and compassion. The tactic of this exercise is to use the patterns of frustrations and the underlying feelings and needs that constitute the dynamics of the impasse to highlight their developmental issues and stuck places so couples get a preview of the time when they will be invited to understand the source of the core scene. Learning about the genesis of their conflict will help them move through the conflict to connection.

Although couples will have practiced the Imago Dialogue process by now, we strongly suggest that you facilitate the Core Scene Dialogue in the office, since it is the source of their repetitive and intense negative exchanges. Ultimately, though, as is the case with all Imago exercises, the goal is for the couple to develop enough competence to engage in Dialogues at home.

Step 1. The List
Each partner should make a list of the behaviors, feelings, and defense strategies that come up over and over again in their relationship. The summary should be divided into three columns (Appendix 26). Column A describes one individual's behaviors (what they did), their feelings and defense strategies, starting with the first turn of the downward spiral—when they first felt triggered. Column B describes the partner's behavior (what my partner did) along the same lines.

Step 2. The Core Scene Dialogue
Using the Dialogue structure, partners take turns sharing a core scene (it does not have to be the same core scene). They should start with one that is "mild," a recurring behavior that does not have a lot of emotional intensity attached to it and use the same full Dialogue structure—asking for an appointment, sharing an appreciation, mirroring, summary mirroring, validating, and empathizing. The unique sentence stems are shown in Table 16.2.

Step 3. The Rewrite
In the office or as homework, each partner then rewrites the core scene script describing the new responses (words and behaviors) that would avoid triggering the partner's wound and that would stretch them into new behaviors that meet the partner's need and also benefit the relationship. Moving

backward through the previous script, they repeat this process for each identified trigger point. The sentence stems to help rewrite the scene are shown in Table 16.3.

Table 16.2: The Core Scene (Sentence Stems)
The Core Scene Dialogue
The one behavior I engage in over and over in our relationship is _____ I do that when I feel _____ And when I am feeling that, I protect myself by _____ And that feeling reminds me of _____
What I need from you when I do that is (do a behavior or express a feeling) _____, and then I would feel safe and connected.

NOTE: This process is what "I can do" rather than what "you can do."

Table 16.3: The Core Scene Rewrite (Sentence Stems)
When I am feeling this frustration, instead of _____, I can _____
When my partner is feeling this frustration, instead of _____, I can _____

Step 4. Visualize

Partners then visualize themselves doing the new behaviors every time the negativity of the Core Scene gets triggered. While they are not committing to these new behaviors, the act of visualizing will help plant the seeds for change, awakening the new brain activity to become aware of old brain reactivity.

Clinical Tool #4: Behavior Change Request

Constructing the Frustrations List (Appendix 24) also prepares the couple for another process, called the Behavior Change Request (BCR) dialogue, designed to help couples uncover the longing hidden in their frustrations and then assist them in the translation of that desire into a request for a specific and doable change in behavior. It operationalizes the discovery that "every frustration is a wish in disguise."

Step 1: BCR Flow Chart

You can provide couples with the Behavior Change Request flow chart (Appendix 27) for homework. Ask each partner to choose a mild frustration (rated under 5 from their "My Frustrations List") for this next exercise and to write the corresponding feelings, story, reactions, fears, childhood memory, and global desires into the flow chart. Please ask them not to share with each other. Given the complexity of the BCR Dialogue, the first Dialogue should be in the office.

Table 16.4: Behavior Change Request Dialogue (Sentence Stems)	
SENDER	RECEIVER
I get frustrated when _____ *Deepens* When I experience that frustration _____I feel _____ When I feel that, the story I tell myself is____ _____ And then, I react by _____ in order to not feel my fear of _____ When I feel _____ I remember when I was little that _____	*Mirroring,* *checking for accuracy* *and inviting more.*
SUMMARIZING, VALIDATING AND EMPATHIZING	
Global Desire	
What I desire from you all the time and forever is _____	What do you desire from me that would touch the pain and remove the frustration?
Behavior Change Requests	
State three positive and SMART behavior change requests. The behavior I want from you is: _____ _____	Tell me three behaviors that I can do that would help to satisfy that desire and remove that frustration? *Mirrors each request and checks for accuracy.*
The Gift	
Mirror the gift.	*Choose one request that you can do and say:* I will stretch and gift you by _____
Closings	
Thank you for being willing to give me this gift. It will begin to heal my childhood hurt of _____ And reduce my fear of _____ And help me feel _____	Thank you for giving me this opportunity to stretch for you. It will help me overcome my fear of _____ And help me grow back into being a more _____ person/partner.
Thank you for listening. / Thank you for sharing. *Give each other a one-minute hug. Eye contact on release.* Sender and receiver record the gift.	

Step 2: The BCR Dialogue

As in all Dialogues, the BCR is introduced with careful coaching on your part, to ensure that frustrations are expressed dialogically, in a safe atmosphere. There are important guidelines to put in place to make sure the couple learns how to use BCRs in the manner that's intended. Table 16.4 lists sentence stems for this dialogue. The full BCR Dialogue can be found in Appendix 28.

Invite the partners to select one of their lower-rated items from the list of frustrations they generated previously.

1. Invite the receiver to accept the other's frustrations with openness and curiosity.
2. Coach the sender to start sends with "I" rather than "you."
3. Send short; mirror long. This means that the sender's message should be short enough to allow the receiver to mirror it back fully and accurately.

   NOTE: Remind the couple of the Imago caveat: What your partner most needs from you is what is hardest for you to give. The most important aspect is the process and the integrating of small changes over time. Also remind them to give unconditionally and receive whatever gift your partner gives gratefully (Sheldon & Lyubomirsky, 2006).

An Example of a Behavior Change Request Dialogue

Because of their work in understanding how their respective childhoods played into their current relationship, Alicia and Fran learned that they both shared an earlier experience of feeling invisible and unimportant—for Alicia, though, it was because she grew up in a large family and for Fran it was because she was an only child and thus experienced smothering. In response, Alicia learned to exaggerate her need while Fran learned to minimize her need and stress her independence. Both needed, ultimately, to feel important to each other but in different ways.

   NOTE: The Behavior Change Request Dialogue requires at least 30 to 45 minutes and so should be introduced near the beginning of a session.

   ALICIA: *Fran, are you available for a Behavior Change Request Dialogue about a frustration I am feeling?*
   FRAN: *Sure.*

The therapist asks both partners to share an intention and an appreciation for this Dialogue.

> ALICIA: *I intend to stay connected to you during this Dialogue, and I appreciate your willingness to listen.*
> FRAN: *I also intend to stay connected to you during this Dialogue, and I appreciate your willingness to share your frustration with me.*

The therapist prompts Alicia to state her frustration in one sentence so that Fran knows what the subject is about. *"I feel frustrated when you . . ."*

> ALICIA: *I feel frustrated when I've asked for something from you, and I don't get it. Like last week, when we had a date to go out to lunch.*
> FRAN: Mirrors and checks for accuracy.

The therapist reminds Fran to move out of reactivity and into a place of undefended listening and curiosity. Other ways the therapist can help ground both partners:

- Having them put both feet on the floor, inhaling deeply, exhaling the tension out of the body, and making eye contact.
- Reminding Fran the hurt child underneath Alicia's frustration.

When they are both ready, prompts Fran to say, *"I am ready to hear your frustration fully."*

> FRAN: *I am ready to hear your frustration fully.*

Therapist prompts Alicia to share the feeling under the frustration.

> ALICIA: *And when I ask for something and don't get it, I feel unloved, not cared about, and rejected.*
> FRAN: Mirrors, checks for accuracy, and invites more.

Therapist prompts Alicia to share the story she tells herself.

> ALICIA: *When this happens, the story I tell myself is that I am not important, and I react by sending angry texts telling you how angry I am when I don't feel important.*
> FRAN: Mirrors, checks for accuracy, and invites more.

Therapist prompts Alicia to share what the underlying feeling(s) reminds her of from her childhood.

> ALICIA: *And when I feel unimportant, it reminds me of my father who was never there for me. He was always so preoccupied with other things, and he often forgot to attend my sporting events.*
> FRAN: Mirrors, checks for accuracy, and invites more.

The therapist prompts Alicia to share more about that childhood memory.

NOTE: Having an understanding of the childhood pain helps Fran empathically want to change behaviors to heal this childhood pain.

> ALICIA: *I remember when my lacrosse team was in the state finals. He said he would make it but never showed up. I made two goals. I thought he was there and was thinking how proud he must be. But he never showed up.*

Therapist prompts Alicia to mirror, check for accuracy, and invite more until there is no more. And then to provide a summary mirror.

> FRAN: *If I got it all, you get frustrated when you ask for something from me and you don't get, like last week when I did not remember our lunch appointment. When that happens you feel unloved, not cared for, and unimportant. And that reminds you of your dad's constant preoccupation, and specifically, about when he missed your lacrosse state championship. Did I get it all?*
> ALICIA: *Yes.*

The therapist prompts Fran to validate.

> FRAN: *Given the fact that your father was often preoccupied and forgot about your sporting events, it makes sense that when I don't show up when I promised it would remind you of your father's forgetfulness, and it also makes sense that you would be hurt and feel that you were unimportant and not loved. I get that now. Is that a good validation?*

Therapist prompts Fran to empathize.

> FRAN: *And I can imagine that you feel angry when you don't get what you wanted and expected, and also sad. Are those the feelings?*

Therapist prompts Fran to ask Alicia her global desire.

> FRAN: *What do you want that would remove the frustration?*

Therapist asks Alicia to share her global desire and encourages her to exaggerate the desire such as, *"What I desire is to have you by my side all the time!"* This is important because many of us were not given permission to state our needs when we were children.

> ALICIA: *What I desire from you all the time and forever is to know that I am important all the time, that I am always in your mind, and that I am more important than anything else, always.*
> FRAN: Mirrors and checks for accuracy.

Therapist prompts Fran to ask Alicia for three behavioral changes that would remove the frustration.

> FRAN: *Tell me three behaviors that I can do that would help to satisfy that desire and remove that frustration.*

The therapist asks Alicia to state two to three specific behaviors Fran could do that would help her feel more cared for, important, and loved. The requests need to be positive (what Fran can do rather than what Fran should not do) and SMART—small, measurable, achievable, relevant (to the frustration), and time-specific.

> ALICIA: *My first request is: I would like to be introduced to your coworkers when I come to your office for lunch next Thursday.*
> *My second request is: For the next 2 months, when we go out to dinner, I would like your cell phone to be left at home.*
> *My third request is: For the next 2 months, I would like you to reduce your hours at the office so that you don't work on Saturdays and Sundays.*

Therapist asks Fran to choose one request that would stretch her a little but that was achievable and to use the sentence stem, *"My gift to you and to our relationship is . . ."*

> FRAN: *My gift to you and to our relationship is that when you meet me at the office for lunch next Thursday, I will introduce you to my coworkers.*

Therapist asks both partners to thank each other and to indicate how this will help them.

> ALICIA: *Thank you for being willing to give me this gift. It will begin to heal my childhood hurt of being unimportant and reduce my fear of being unloved and help me feel important and loved by you.*
> FRAN: *Thank you for giving me this opportunity to stretch for you. It will help me overcome my fear of being close and help me grow back into being a more nurturing partner.*

Fran was able to easily move into a specific behavior change because she now understood that Alicia's frustration was not an attack on her "bad memory" but her pain around feeling unimportant. In the process, she grows into the ability to be nurturing and to overcome her fear of feeling controlled.

NOTE: Most couples have difficulty with this process. And that makes sense, because the adaption from childhood they each had to make atrophied the part of themself that their partner needs the most. So, they tend to fail and feel bad about it, especially if the partner or the therapist becomes legalistic about the couple's performance.

We have learned that when couples bring their failure to the session, we must celebrate that they tried. Then we facilitate a Dialogue about what happens when they try and what happens when they fail. In such Dialogues, each of them becomes aware of the fear that their partner has and develops empathy for the other.

Paradoxically, those empathic dialogues, in which each is present to the other's experience, become the transformation sought in the behavioral exchange. Actually, all challenges are about "presence" and its absence in childhood and in the relationship. Thus, "being present" to each other, in sharing the challenge of change and the anxiety it provokes, restores the connecting lost in childhood and in the relationship. That is the gold in the frustrations.

Clinical Tool #5: The Gifts of Change Exercise and Dialogue

The Gifts of Change exercise is an advanced process. It follows the pattern of the BCR dialogue with one significant difference: instead of bringing a frustration, each partner identifies three things they think should be removed from the relationship, selects at least one, initiates removing it and replacing it with a new behavior as a gift to the relationship. The therapist guides the couple through the written exercise and then facilitates the Gifts of Change Dialogue.

Step 1: Opportunities for Change Chart
The chart can be provided as a between-session assignment. Review all instructions and instruct couples to work separately and to bring the charts (Appendix 29) to the next session.

1. On the Opportunities for Change chart, each partner lists three things they need to remove from the relationship to help make the Space-Between safe. These should be behaviors that "I" can do, not what "You" (the partner) can do.
2. Ask each partner to check off at least one item they are willing to work on.
3. Next, ask them to write in the appropriate space a behavior change they can make (with some stretching) to gift the relationship. Make sure the change is positive and SMART:
    ✓ Small and specific (a behavior you can see)
    ✓ Measurable (an observer could count the number of times when it is happening)
    ✓ Attainable (a small step)
    ✓ Relevant (to the statement)
    ✓ Time limited (for example, once a day for two weeks)

Step 2: Gifts of Change Dialogue
In the next session, facilitate a Gifts of Change Dialogue, asking each partner to share their list. Though the structure is the same as previous dialogues (including validating and empathizing), Table 16.5 lists the unique sentence stems.

Table 16.5: Gifts of Change Dialogue (Sentence Stems)
I would like a Dialogue to share a gift of change I will bring to our relational space. Is now a good time?
I have decided to remove _____ from our relational space.
I want to remove _____ from our relationship because _____ *(Deepen the message by sharing how you contribute to this being in your relationship, keeping the focus on what you do—not on your partner).*
The gift I will bring to our relationship to replace it is _____.
When I do that, I imagine I will feel _____.
When I think about that feeling, it reminds me that when I was little, I _____.
In the Closings, include: This change will help me/us by _____ *(sender).* Thank you for that gift to our relationship *(receiver).*

Biweekly Review Process for BCRs and Gifts of Change

Changes in behavior are very difficult to achieve and equally difficult to sustain. Despite much good will, there is a very strong tendency to revert to previous behaviors or to never even implement the request or gift. The integration of new behaviors is a slow and laborious process, but a relationship will not improve if there are no changes in behavior. Insight alone is rarely enough. A formal BCR and Gifts of Change review every two weeks can help clients keep on top of this very important work. It provides accountability and an opportunity to explore resistance more deeply in the safety of Dialogue when the commitment has not been met. Keep a written record of clients BCRs and Gifts of Change from the work in session.

Takeaways for the Restructuring Frustrations Process

- Couples cannot address frustrations in their relationship until the Space-Between is safe enough and they have become sophisticated in their use of Imago Dialogue.
- Frustrations are unconscious wishes masked as complaints, relics of unmet childhood needs. What one needs, the other is least able to give, thus the therapeutic challenge.
- Unconditional stretching produces growth. Only unconditional giving heals.
- The goals of the Restructuring Frustrations process include:

  1. identifying frustrations and the underlying feelings, childhood memories, and global desires;
  2. sharing frustrations in a safe way that evokes empathy and invites change;
  3. asking for specific behavior changes that address the hurt and need; and
  4. gifting the relationship with new, specific behaviors that are healing and growth producing.

- Encourage small and sustainable changes that stretch partners beyond their comfort zone.
- Expect and honor resistance.

REMEMBER:

All childhood and adult challenges are about the absence of "presence." Thus, "being present" to each other in all sharings (the challenges, the requests, the discoveries) decreases anxiety and is the ultimate goal for restoring the experience of connecting.

17

Re-Romanticizing

What: Couples learn to initiate, amplify, and sustain affirmations by practicing specific processes that induce pleasure, well-being, full aliveness, joy, and wonder.

Why: To create memories of pleasure that alter how the relationship is viewed and experienced, that is, passionate and safe.

When: In every session. Express two-way appreciation in the first session and facilitate a one-way appreciation, or an alternative process, in every session. Some of the processes below should come later in therapy, once the relationship feels safe enough to be embraced.

Couples often ask whether it is possible to experience romantic love again, and the simple answer is, "Yes." We know that the experience of romantic love, the sensation of full aliveness and joy and the state of wonder, is our fundamental human yearning because it is our nature, thus its loss is life's deepest pain and the source of most of its suffering; and that the deepest desire of every person is to recover that original state of connecting and belonging, because that is who we *ARE*.

And, we view romantic love as a second experience of full aliveness, joy, and wonder with which we came into the world at birth. The capacity to experience the sensation of connecting is a function of the sympathetic and parasympathetic sides of our autonomic nervous system. That state of being is so intrinsically our birthright that our neurophysiology and neurochemistry are designed to experience it at the physical level which is the conduit to our feelings and thoughts. Since its loss seems universal, nature created romantic love as a reexperiencing of our original state by pairing us with a person who is similar to the caretaker with whom we had and lost the original experience of connecting: so that we could have again what we lost with them.

Romantic sentiments, pleasure, and passionate feelings all involve being fully open to the energy of life and cannot occur in a context of pain. Pleasure and pain cannot coexist. For couples to recover that exalted but natural state requires us to help them create a safe relationship so they can drop their defenses and become vulnerable to each other and reconnect as they did when they fell in love. When safety has become the backdrop of a relationship, the full aliveness, wonder and joyful relaxation that couples have been longing to experience can become the foreground. Love, at this stage, will be reality-based rather than fantasy-based; it is deeper and meant to last and can only occur when safety is established

Although this chapter is the last of a sequence, it could have been placed second, after the Revisioning Process because its focus is experiencing the sensations of the dream relationship. It is important to say that some of its content can and should be introduced at the beginning and present in every session along the way, and we have indicated that appreciations should be expressed at the beginning of every Dialogue.

However, we chose to place re-romanticizing at the end because, like full aliveness, joy at birth, and the bliss of romantic love, those sensations of our true nature tend to fade in the presence of challenges to our survival. To sustain our true nature as a constant experience requires information and skills training, which the preceding chapters have provided.

This chapter is about the final process of moving from the power struggle to the conscious partnership—from conflict to connecting. It is about moving from romantic love to real love. Through the preceding processes, couples have designed their dream marriage as the domain of perfect love, removed all ambivalence around commitment, cleared the space of negativity, practiced differentiation by reimaging each other, and learned to convert frustrations into opportunities for growth and healing. These Imago exercises are based on the premise that insight and behavioral change make powerful allies in restoring connection. While the last chapter focused on behavioral changes that arise out of conflict, this chapter involves behavioral changes focused on creating pleasure through affirmations. These practices are specifically designed to elicit and sustain the experience of full aliveness, relaxed joyfulness, and wonder.

INTENTIONALITY

In the beginning, love is free and easy. It is a feeling rooted in a fantasy that it can be sustained without effort and will last forever. But this open, unconstrained affection dies during the power struggle, when people hurt each other as they were hurt in childhood and erect archaic defenses against the pain they cause.

From the Imago perspective, love is a behavior, not a feeling or a quality of personality. It is not something you are; it is something you DO. Love is relational and consists of qualitative interactions in the Space-Between. Of course, we can "feel" love when we receive it, but feeling is the outcome of being loving. It is what you get when you give it! The act of behaving lovingly comes first and the loving feelings follow. Unfortunately, most couples believe that behaving lovingly before feeling loving is inauthentic. They want to wait until they feel loving before they act loving. But it is a gesture of real love and emotional maturity to behave lovingly when you are not feeling it. It means being willing to do things that you do not feel like doing and not doing things that you do feel like doing. This does not mean ignoring the feelings of anger and hurt but dealing with them in ways that are consistent with the intention to love.

For the Imago therapist, helping the couple reach the point of intentional behavior means working with a balance of pain and pleasure. It's not as simple as: help the couple work through the pain and the pleasure will follow. Both the therapist and the couple have a natural orientation toward problems, but as the pain ebbs, it is important to fill the void with pleasure, or the old conflict will flow back in. It is your job to interject pleasure into the therapy as soon as possible, so they can once again experience enjoyment in each other's company. At this point, they can no longer rely on spontaneity to fuel romance. Instead, they must become conscious partners and intentionally cocreate real love. That means reintroducing loving words and deeds into the relationship, and containing defensive reactivity when pain is triggered. That is the reason, starting in the first session, you invite the couple to exchange appreciations.

RESISTANCE

Reaching for fun, pleasure, and excitement would seem to be a no-brainer, and yet, many people are resistant to doing the things that will bring them these rewards. Why? A certain degree of resistance is to be expected. As we mentioned in the last chapter, our brains crave homeostasis and cannot distinguish "good change" from "bad change." But when it comes to loving behaviors, other resistances emerge. An obvious reason is that when partners have been treating each other like enemies for years, it's going to feel strange to engage in affirmations. It feels artificial and contrived. But deeper resistance finds its source in the early childhood messages.[29]

Not too long ago, we were having conversations with Imago therapists about the mysterious intractability of some couples in therapy. Imago practitioners were sharing about couples who were eager to heal, compliant in following the suggestions of their therapists, and demonstrably using the Imago tools. And yet no progress could be made past a certain point in the therapy. The typical scenario went like this: the wife wanted the husband to be more caring and involved in her emotional life. With the therapist's help, the wife was able to voice this desire and ask her husband for what she wanted. The husband said he understood and affirmed that he was willing to spend more time listening to his wife's thoughts and concerns. He also agreed to share more of his thoughts and feelings with her. The therapist helped the couple identify specific behaviors that would demonstrate the husband's emotional involvement. But when the husband did become more solicitous and engaged, the wife reacted by denying, trivializing, minimizing, or criticizing his efforts. He did what she asked for, but it did not seem to help. The wife continued to complain, and the husband eventually stopped trying to please her. The therapy stalled. The professional literature is replete with discussions on the importance of asking for what you want, and giving it, but the other half of the exchange—**the importance of learning how to receive**—has been neglected. The reason, from our perspective, is that it is so subtle that it is missed and so endemic that it seems normal. When we discovered this, we wrote a whole book about it called *Receiving Love* (2004).

The most obvious sign of difficulty with receiving is a partner turning away a compliment or rebuffing an attempt at affection or refusing to acknowledge a positive attribute or being afraid to take advantage of an opportunity. The language of refusal sounds like: "You don't mean that." "I wasn't that good." "Come on, you're exaggerating." "Well, what would you know about it?" "Not now, I'm busy." And it includes nonverbal behavior, such as looking down and shaking the head, changing the subject, or appearing not to have heard the positive remark.

Frequently, this resistance is rooted in the dynamics of childhood, all of which are laced with anxiety. Anxiety and pleasure cannot travel the same neural highway. When we were young, our life energy was boundless and intensely joyful. Unfortunately, our most exuberant moments were often cut short, either for safety reasons or because we needed to conform to social norms or because our high energy threatened the repressed state of our caregivers. After all, our parents had long ago given up diving into the lake, rolling down the hill, or skipping along the sidewalk. Limits, sometimes punitively imposed, created an association between pleasure and pain. When we experienced certain kinds of pleasure or perhaps a high degree of pleasure, we were ignored, reprimanded, or punished. On an unconscious level, we formed a powerful association between pleasure and anxiety. Eventually, we learned to limit our own pleasure so that we could reduce our anxiety and circumvent pain. We learned that to be fully alive was dangerous, but staying alive was essential, and we occasionally engaged in a variety of self-stimulation to feel alive. Gradually, we developed a built-in prohibition against the pleasure of full aliveness.

People who grew up experiencing a great deal of repression tend to have a particularly hard time receiving and thus struggle with the Re-romanticizing Process. They have difficulty coming up with any requests for caring behaviors or they sabotage their partner's efforts to carry them out. They find excuses to reject surprises and they don't find the time to engage in fun activities. They squirm uncomfortably and try to stop the flooding of positive infusions.

Another example of resistance is the partner who wants to cooperate but does not seem to have any needs or desires. This person is hiding behind the psychic shield they erected to protect themselves from overbearing parents. They discovered early in life that one way to maintain a feeling of autonomy from their intrusive parents was to keep their thoughts and feelings to themselves. These partners painfully eke out one or two requests in the Caring Behaviors exercise. And predictably (given the similar wounding but complementary defenses), the other partner furiously scribbles a long list of things "I want." To the casual observer it appears that a self-sufficient individual has few needs and the person with the bottomless pit has limitless desires. The fact of the matter is that both individuals have the identical need to be loved and cared for. Both are driven by anxiety and deal with it in different ways that sustain the deficient position. One withdraws, the other escalates. Both methods maintain the status quo.

The therapist plays an important role in this regard, being mindful of the various resistances. Upon observing deflecting positives or absorbing negatives behavior, the therapist can engage the couple in the dialogue process:

> **THERAPIST:** *Would you be willing to tell your partner what happens when she appreciates you?*
> **PARTNER 1:** *When you compliment me, I feel a tightness in my stomach and want to shut down.*
> **PARTNER 2:** Mirrors, checks for accuracy, and invites more.
> **PARTNER 1 WITH THERAPIST PROMPT:** *And when I feel like shutting down, I remember when I was little, my mother would always say something nice to me just before she told me what I had done wrong.*
> **PARTNER 2:** Mirrors, checks for accuracy, and invites more.
> **PARTNER 1 WITH THERAPIST PROMPT:** *Yes. I think I decided not to believe compliments, and I recall shutting down and trying to find my way out of the room.*

Along with observing, acknowledging, and exploring the resistance, our prescription is the same: Encourage the couple to keep doing the exercise exactly as described. Even if it causes anxiety, ask them to keep it up. Do it harder and more aggressively than before. Given enough time and enough repetition, the brain will adjust to a different reality. When it discovers that nothing bad is happening, the anxiety will go away. The person with low self-esteem can gradually carve out a more positive identity. The one with "little" needs has a chance to discover that sharing secret desires does not compromise their independence. The fear of new behaviors gives way to the pleasure the new behaviors stimulate, and the new behaviors begin to be associated with safety and life.

NOTE: Our relationship is what we remember, not necessarily what actually happened. We can say that a relationship is essentially "memories." Given the obvious truth of that statement, couples need to know that they created the memories their partner has of them, and if they want their partner to have a different set of memories, they have to create them. What works are memories of safety and pleasure. Memories of anxiety and the exchange of painful transactions tend to repeat themselves. But memories of pleasure tend not to reproduce themselves. Hence, helping couples intentionally engage in the creating of positive memories is a foundational process. That is the intention and goal of the Re-romanticizing Process.

THE RE-ROMANTICIZING PROCESS

The practice of affirmations began in the very first session with the introduction of the Appreciation Dialogue. In the Re-romanticizing Process, you now work to increase the positive interactions, with low and high energy, through these clinical tools:

Caring Behaviors (written exercise and Dialogue): A caring behavior is something you receive that you did not ask for. An appreciation is something you give that your partner did not ask for. This exercise is designed to educate partners about behaviors they have received in the past or are receiving in the present that make them feel cared about and loved. Acknowledging "what feels caring" lets the giving partner know the behavior has a positive impact and reinforces its repetition. What is not acknowledged tends not to be repeated. Each partner is encouraged to intentionally begin and/or continue engaging in these behaviors.

High-Energy Fun: Designed to infuse the relationship with positive intensity that promotes an immediate bonding experience.

Surprises: Developed to keep the relationship actively alive by encouraging partners to randomly create moments that match the desires of the recipient. These should be done monthly only. More frequency tends to diminish the element of surprise and the intensity of the pleasure, and thus negates the power of anticipation. Also, the brain tends to habituate to the new pleasure level and integrate it, so the sweetness of the intensity is lost.

Positive Flooding: Used by partners to take turns amplifying positive descriptions of each other. Partners make lists of what they appreciate or value in the other including: physical characteristics, character traits, behaviors, and global qualities.

Clinical Tool #1: Caring Behaviors

This exercise is a learning lab in which partners identify behaviors that make each other "feel cared about and loved." It provides a roadmap to the other's heart, inviting them to amplify the positive energy in their relationship and express their love and care effectively. By initiating a caring behavior, rather than responding to a request, partners say to each other "I see what touches you, and I give it without your having to ask." This is an act of being present and intentional with each other, reestablishing feelings of safety and pleasure, which sets the stage for increased intimacy.

The Caring Behaviors exercise asks couples to identify and share behaviors they actively receive from their partner (current behaviors) and behaviors that were present in their earlier romantic days together (past behaviors.) It does not ask for behaviors in the future; it is not a requesting process. But acknowledging the behaviors supports their repetition in the future.

Essentially, giving a caring behavior says: "I caught you liking something I did for you. I am going to repeat it until I learn that I am mistaken or you tell me you no longer want it." When couples begin to intentionally increase the loving behaviors toward each other, they begin to feel safer and more loving. One study by John Gottman found that healthy, long-term relationships had a ratio of five positive behaviors to every one negative behavior (Gottman et al., 1999).

Why is this simple exercise so effective? The obvious reason is that, through daily repetitions of positive behaviors, the old brain begins to perceive the other as "someone who nurtures me" and is thus on the side of my survival. Additionally, there is a part of the brain that cannot distinguish self from other, so the partner giving the caring behavior experiences the emotion of pleasure they intended for their partner, and since the pleasure is associated with the partner to whom the gift was given, that partner becomes associated with pleasure. Painful memories are overlaid with positive affirmations, and the partner is no longer categorized as a bringer of death, but as a wellspring of life. This opens the way for intimacy, which is only possible in a context of pleasure and safety.

But there are other, subtler reasons the exercise works so well. One is that it helps couples shed the infantile belief that their partners can read their minds. Whereas in the romantic stage, loving behaviors flow effortless in the Space-Between, during the power struggle stage, loving behaviors cease, and growing resentment fills the space. But in a conscious partnership, couples learn to tell each other exactly what pleases them, decreasing their reliance on mental telepathy.

Another benefit of this exercise is that it helps both partners understand that what pleases each of them is a product of their unique makeup and life experience and can be very different from what pleases their partners. It furthers the differentiation process of discovering they are demonstrably separate people. Whatever says "I love you" is idiosyncratic and learned from families and culture, just as the triggers for pain are personal, specific, and related to childhood experiences. Rather than the Golden Rule—"Do unto others as you would have them do unto you,"—in Imago we have the Platinum Rule: "Do unto others as they would have you do unto them." Caring behaviors are target behaviors, guided by the partner, based on what touches their heart. One cup of coffee in a favorite mug with just the right about of sugar tastes better than 10 too-sweet cups. One perfect peach-colored French tulip beats out a dozen long-stemmed roses in the "you-know-just-who-I-am-and-just-what-I-want" department. Being able to understand each other's love language, specific to their dialect, is a sign of healthy differentiation, while withholding information or assuming the other partner intuitively knows what they want is a sign of symbiosis.

The Caring Behaviors exercise can be provided as a between-session assignment or integrated into therapy sessions whenever it is appropriate, or it can be the focus of one or multiple sessions. Since this process helps restore the original condition of full aliveness, joy, and wonder, it is a crucial, not optional, process.

Step 1: Caring Behaviors Chart (written)
Ask both partners to list examples of caring behaviors in the two categories (see the chart in Appendix 30). The "Willing" column should be left blank for now. The categories are:

- **Caring Behaviors in the Present.** Have each partner make a list of caring behaviors they are currently receiving from their partner that they want to amplify and appreciate. The behaviors on the list should be specific, concrete, positive, and be happening with some regularity. Examples: *You stay by my side when we're at parties. You bring me coffee in bed on the weekends. You always remember to kiss me goodbye.*
- **Caring Behaviors in the Past.** Have the partners add to the list the caring behaviors that their partner used to give them in the past but no longer does. To help them come up with items, suggest

they go back in their minds to the romantic phase of their relationship, or to the period before their first child was born, or before they started in the jobs they have now. Examples: *You brought me flowers every week. You held my hand wherever we went. You said sexy things to me when we made love.*

Step 2: Caring Behaviors Dialogue
Facilitate a Caring Behaviors Dialogue by asking each partner to share their list. (*NOTE:* You can choose to have partners share just one caring behavior and assign the rest of the sharing as a between-session assignment or have partners share all of the caring behaviors in the office.) While the structure is the same as previous dialogues, Table 17.1 has some of the unique sentence stems for Caring Behaviors Dialogue. The full sample dialogue is in Appendix 31.

Table 17.1: Caring Behaviors Dialogue (Sentence Stems)
I would like to talk about one thing you do that makes me feel cared about and loved. Is now a good time?
I feel/felt cared about and loved when you _____
When you do/did that, I feel/felt _____
When I feel/felt that, it reminds me of something from my childhood which is _____ (*something similar happened/did not happen*).

Step 3: Implementing Caring Behaviors
Once all the caring behaviors have been shared in Dialogue, have partners:

- Thank the other for the present behaviors and ask that the behaviors be continued.
- When all the current ones are acknowledged, they can consider asking the other if the partner would consider reinstating the past behaviors.
- Exchange their lists. In the Willing column, they should put a check mark only by the items they are presently willing to do.

NOTE: Indicating the willingness to do a behavior is not the same as being committed to doing it. It is not necessary for the partners to explain why they indicated unwillingness to perform certain behaviors. The behaviors they commit to giving their partner should be those they are ready, willing, and able to do, beginning right now.

Advise couples to:

- Acknowledge, honor, and appreciate every caring behavior they receive; the simple rationale: human beings are more likely to repeat desirable behaviors when they are rewarded for behaving that way.
- Spend one minute per day reflecting on the positive aspects of their partner—their goodness, inherent wholeness, and original innocence.
- Give each other a minimum of one caring behavior a day.
- Remember that caring behaviors do not involve demands or obligations; they are unconditional gifts. But simultaneously encourage givers to do a little "stretching," even when they don't feel like it that day!

Date Night: A Special Type of Caring Behavior
It doesn't matter if couples have been together for only three weeks or if they've been married with children for 30 years: *dating* is about *two people being fully present with each other*. This implies setting up a special time and place for being alone, paying close attention to one another, and focusing on each other, and *only* each other.

Most couples say that their relationship is very important to them, but often, their behavior doesn't match their words. They pay attention only when they are about to head over a dangerous waterfall as, for example, when one of them has lost a job or when they start to have problems with one of their kids. Date nights are an opportunity to shine the light of their attention on themselves when they are *not* in a crisis. This kind of attention helps their relationship flourish in a way that makes the crises easier to handle. Encourage your couples to have regular date nights and to make dating a sacred ritual between them. They may spend time in sessions planning and sharing their experience of the dates.

Clinical Tool #2: High-Energy Fun
Imago therapy defines high-energy fun as any interaction between romantic partners that leads to a belly laugh or orgasm (or both!). It is a deep and free expression of utter joyfulness that promotes intentionally engaging in pleasure-producing activities together that increase intimacy and safety in the relationship.

Belly laughs and orgasms release endorphins and PEA in the body. When partners share this chemical rush together, their brains associate the other partner with the intense pleasure, fun, and passion they are feeling, thereby increasing a sense of bonding with the partner. Endorphins also boost the immune system and increase longevity. PEA is the excitement chemical, which we release at high levels during romantic love as well as during other exciting activities, such as driving fast and sky diving.

Both belly laughs and orgasms require safety and create safety, which means that defenses are down and controls are relaxed. While these activities may be peak experiences of blissful joy, this is not what we mean when we talk about our natural state of relaxed joyfulness. These are passing moments that cannot be sustained. But repetitive moments of intense pleasure followed by relaxation can reset our natural joy index. There is a more lasting sense of well-being, the oxytocin glow, and the full experience of being safe and satiated.[30]

It is true that belly laughs and orgasms contain an element of spontaneity, but it is possible to conscientiously create the conditions that increase the likelihood that they will occur. Imago therapists look for opportunities to model fun and laughter and weave fun activities into the regular therapeutic sessions at appropriate moments. They also inform couples about the value of pleasure-inducing activities, belly laughs and orgasms, and the need for intentionality in promoting them.

Most couples have sure-fire ways of making each other laugh, but some couples have been wounded around their core energy and have difficulty stretching back into their full aliveness. It is important to be sensitive to what is a doable stretch for each couple. In addition, it is important for therapists to explore their own resistance to experiencing high-energy fun, as it is hard to authentically persuade couples of the importance of participating in high-energy fun if the therapist has problems doing so.

As can the Caring Behaviors exercise, belly laughs can be integrated into therapy sessions whenever appropriate or they can be the focus of a single session. (Obviously, orgasms remain in the sanctity of the couple's privacy.) Some ways to encourage belly laughs in the office:

- **Suck and Blow:** Using a credit card, couples "suck" and "blow" the card with mouths about ½ inch apart.
- **Baby Talk:** Have couples practice mirroring with "baby talk," pig Latin, or some made up language. They can mirror exaggerated body gestures and facial expressions as well.
- **Jump-Start Belly Laugh:** Have couples face each other, bounce up and down, let out several grunts, and force a belly laugh until they are belly laughing naturally.

Step One: Fun Activities Charts (written)
Ask each partner to (separately) make a list of fun and exciting activities that they would like to do with their partner. Ask them to include face-to-face, physically vigorous, and emotionally intense experiences. Ask them

to include some activities that involve physically pleasurable body contact. These activities should need no skills, have no rules, cannot be done wrong, and often produce a "belly laugh." Examples: dancing, wrestling, showers together, sex, massage.

Step Two: Fun Activities Dialogue
Facilitate a Dialogue between partners (or assign this as a between-session assignment) to share the lists. For this Dialogue, sharing and mirroring the statements is adequate. After sharing, partners should compare lists and check off similar items. (Items that are not checked are most likely opportunities for healing and growth and should addressed if one of them becomes a frustration. Remind couples that what might be fun for one, may not be fun for the other. Tickling is a common example where one partner associates tickling as abuse from a parent or sibling.)

Step Three: Joint Fun List
As a between-session assignment, have partners create a joint fun list from the checked items on the previous lists and choose and engage in at least one item on that list before their next session. Couples should engage in fun activities at least once a week. Remind them that they will need to be intentional, such as scheduling a specific time to engage in the activity. And remind them that a belly laugh may take 5 minutes or less and that a belly laugh a day will keep the divorce lawyer away!

Clinical Tool #3: Surprises
Surprises protect the relationship from the boredom that accompanies our brain's innate tendency to habituate to almost everything, whether good or not-so-good. They are the hot sauce of relationships and their success and efficacy are based on the scientific principle of random reinforcement.

Our neuronal systems are wired from birth to respond both to familiarity and to novelty. Studies show that infants habituate quickly to predictable stimuli, such as the mother's face and smell, and they are aware of and stimulated by novelty or random reinforcement. Random reinforcement is the idea that a pleasurable action loses its effectiveness if it's repeated with predictable regularity. This concept was discovered accidently by a group of scientists who were training laboratory animals by rewarding them with treats. One day, the apparatus that dispensed the treats malfunctioned, and the animals were not rewarded for their efforts. The next day, the machine was repaired, and the regular reward schedule was resumed. To the trainers' surprise, the animals were even more highly motivated to perform than before.[31]

This information is insightful when working with couples. Unpredictable positive surprises can keep partners interested and engaged, while the most pleasurable experiences can lose their edge with repetition. Planned surprises can trigger dopamine release and convey: "I was thinking about you;" "You are worth making an effort for;" "I know you and what you would enjoy."

Your role as facilitator is critical.

Keep in mind, though, that some couples have had negative experiences with surprises. It is important that the surprise be something that the receiving partner actually wants, not something the giving partner wants to give, or wants for themselves or makes up that the other might want. The essential elements of surprises are that they should be: (1) offered randomly and unexpectedly; (2) something that the partner knows would please the other; and (3) something that the partner would be unlikely give to themself.

The following steps will help partners learn what the other partner would welcome as a surprise:

Step One: Invite them to ask each other about surprises that they would love to receive.
We have found that talking about this does not diminish the surprise when it happens—unless talking about it sets up expectations for fulfillment. In Imago, we maintain that only gifts heal, and people cannot be gifted when they expect certain things to happen. It is important to help clients let go of expectations, and if they cannot, to state these needs and desires as requests and use the Behavior Change Request Dialogue to deal with them.

Step Two: Encourage them to pick up "random ideas."
Random ideas are the little comments they make about things that they might like and want. These comments are not hints that are dropped with expectations attached, but they emerge as part of ongoing conversations. A husband mentioning a positive childhood memory of going to a baseball game with his dad might find Yankee tickets under his pillow one day. A wife who cherishes written letters might find a love note in her lunchbox. Random ideas also boost listening skills as partners express interests, preferences, secret wishes, and dreams in day-to-day conversations.

Clinical Tool #4: Positive Flooding

Criticism of others is often self-criticism, because negative comments are a projection of one's own self-hatred for the aspects of self that were denied, rejected, or shut away during childhood. But the opposite is also true. Because affirmations are actually positive projections of the self, flooding the partner with messages that they are loved is the same as flooding the self with the identical messages. Give and you shall receive.

The purpose of positive flooding is to experience intense positive energy that amplifies traits and characteristics of each partner. Many of us associate raised voices with anger—especially when it is directed at one person. Positive flooding is designed to help couples experience that intensity of energy but in a positive way.

Positive flooding is designed to help couples:

- amplify the positive energy in the relationship
- reconnect with the positive things they love and adore about each other
- associate intensity of emotion with the positive rather than the negative
- access more of their life energy and experience momentary joyful aliveness

You can introduce this into the therapy at any point it seems advantageous for the couple to put a lot of energy into the positive expression of their love for each other. This may be when they have completed a difficult piece of work and the therapist feels it would be good to balance this out with the positive, or it can be in response to the clients expressed desire to focus more on the positive aspects of their relationship.

Maximizing and minimizing partners generally have different experiences with this exercise. Those who tend to maximize more often love being the sender in this exercise. It gives permission for their expressiveness and a positive channel through which this can flow, which creates safety for them. They can often come up with whole lists of positives. Minimizing partners tend to have much more difficulty finding anything positive to say. But because of this, as minimizers learn to flood their partner in this way, the receiver of a minimizer's flooding is profoundly impacted, frequently resulting in tears, and expression of energy tends to break through the minimizers defense against expressing strong emotion.

Step One: Positive Flooding Chart (written)
Have the couple scribe various traits and behaviors they adore about each other on the Positive Flooding chart (full chart in Appendix 32.) You can assign this to the couple as a between-session assignment.

- **Physical characteristics:** aspects of the partner's physical appearance. Examples: *I adore your beautiful, long fingers. I love the little gray curls on the back of your neck, and the white at your temples.*
- **Character traits:** aspects of the partner's personality. Examples:

I admire your wisdom. I can always count on you to do the right thing. I love how smart you are.

- **Behaviors:** whatever can be observed and recorded, as on a video camera. Examples: *I love to watch you get down on the floor and roll around with the kids! I really appreciate how you always put clean sheets on the bed when I'm coming home from a trip!*
- **Global affirmations:** statements about how wonderful a person our partner is. Examples: *I feel like the luckiest woman alive to have you in my life! I think you are the most amazing woman on the planet. I just adore you!*

Step Two: Positive Flooding Exercise
The couple can decide who will send and receive first. The receiver sits on a chair. Maintaining eye contact, the sender walks around the receiver's chair while telling ("flooding") the receiver all the things the sender cherishes, etc., about the partner that they wrote on their chart, and anything else that comes to mind, increasing energetic intensity and exuberance with each category of items. When the sender reaches the last category, guide them to stand in front of the receiver and shout the global affirmations at a level of intensity equal to or surpassing expressions of rage or anger, jumping up and down if physically possible. The exercise should end with a 1-minute hug followed by a check-in with each partner about their experience.

The reason we invite the sender to walk around the receiver is that movement allows the sender to bring more of their whole-body energy, their life force, into the process than if they were sitting still. And the receiver reaps the rewards of this energy.

Step Three: Switch roles
Have the couple switch roles and repeat the process.

Special Tips on Positive Flooding
Surprisingly, for some couples, this can turn out to be the most challenging exercise of all. If partners have been stuck in the power struggle for a long time, they are almost certainly good at talking about how frustrated they are with their relationship. However, it is probably been quite a while since they have had any meaningful positive exchanges. Others who have experienced rage in childhood might also have a difficult time with this exercise. Discern whether couples need a softer start-up (such as, raising the voice to a gentler level) to build up to the new experience, develop new neural pathways for positive input, and increase the ability to receive.

An alternative to this exercise is for partners to write down how they want to be flooded in each of the four categories. This is where some people really "hit the wall." This may be because it touches the childhood messages to not feel good about oneself. It is therefore very important and valuable to coach couples in doing it this way also. It has great potential for transformation to allow a partner to ask for and get positive affirmations for aspects of themselves they have carried some shame about.

While coaching couples in this exercise, be sure to:

- Encourage "I" statements, as in "I love . . . ," "I admire . . ."
- Stay out of sight of the receiver when coaching the sender so that the receiver bonds to the sender and not to you. One of the reasons behind the circling of the receiver is the belief that this helps the receiver bond to the sender as the source of good things.
- Always allow enough time for processing this exercise after a couple has finished it, so that whatever feelings come up for them can be talked about, validated, and empathized with.
- Advise partners to monitor themselves for negative reactions toward their partner's or their own expressions of exuberant aliveness.
- Encourage the receiver to express gratitude for the sharing.
- Tell the couple that the exercise can be repeated with a focus of the receiver's choice; for example, only with comments from the behaviors category.
- Encourage the couple to do a positive flooding every week.

CASE ILLUSTRATION: PING AND LEN

Working with couples is, of course, not a straight line where you start with point A (Revisioning) in session 1, move to point B (Recommitting) in session 2, then to point C (Reimaging) in session 3, and so forth. As we have stated throughout, being an attuned therapist means listening with the third ear for the verbal and nonverbal cues that hint at the stuck, challenged, and unconscious areas, looking for the nuances where you can invite the implicit memory to explicit language, and knowing what the couple is needing and capable of doing at the moment. Being attuned is having the mastery to move spontaneously from one process to another in a seamless flow of insight and experience. Here is an example of how a simple check-in around Caring Behaviors uncovered resistance stemming from childhood wounding.

Ping complained that Len downplayed her job as a production assistant and never seemed to recognize her contribution to the household. In addition, she experienced him as sometimes cruel when he teased her. Early in their therapy, they both adopted the Dialogue structure quickly and were able to pinpoint how many of their earlier childhood experiences played out in the relationship today. In one session, we did a check in on the Caring Behaviors process.

THERAPIST: *Last session we worked on Caring Behaviors and I remember you both had several items on your checklist that you were willing to continue doing and/or reinstate. How did these past two weeks go? Len, let's start with you. Were you able to give Ping a Caring Behavior?*

LEN: *Yes—yes, the one that actually came up in session. The one about saying something nice and kissing her goodbye in the morning.*

THERAPIST: *And Ping, would you be willing to ask Len what was his experience giving that Caring Behavior to you?*

PING: *Sure. Len, what was your experience like giving that Caring Behavior to me?*

LEN: *Actually, it was really easy to remember to do it. The first time I was being playful, exaggerated a bit with, you know, singing to you, "You are my sunshine, my only sunshine" and such. The next time, I think it felt a tinge uncomfortable, I think because we both knew this was coming out of the session so felt a bit disingenuous. But after a while, I was getting into a rhythm. It got easier and I was doing it from the heart. It was feeling good, and I was enjoying doing something positive, like telling you how smart and beautiful you are and how lucky I am. But I think your response was weird.*

THERAPIST: *So Ping, before we check in with you around this, could you mirror what Len just shared about him giving you a Caring Behavior—what it was like for him and how he experienced your response?*

PING: *Yes. Well, if I heard him correctly . . .*

THERAPIST: *Try talking with him directly, rather than to me, "If I got it, you . . ."*

PING: *If I got it, you were talking about giving me the behavior of complimenting me every morning and how at first, it was a little awkward and you were exaggerating a bit. But then after a while, you noticed my response was weird. Did I get that?*

LEN: *Well, yes but also that I was enjoying giving you compliments.*

PING: *And so you also said that you enjoyed giving me compliments. Did I get that?*

LEN: *Yes.*

Therapist prompts Ping to ask Len more about the "weird response."

> LEN: *Well, you kind of brushed it aside. I think one time you said something like, "You're probably expecting sex tonight now." And then another time, really just physically pushed me away saying, "Stop, I'm going to be late for work." It was playful on some level, but it also felt a bit like you were serious as if you did not want me to do it.*

Ping mirrors, checks for accuracy, and invites more until there is no more.

> THERAPIST: *So Len, would you be willing to ask Ping what it was like that first day, when you intentionally came to her before leaving for work to give her a compliment?*
> LEN: *Ping, when I came to you in the living room to say goodbye before you left for work and give you a compliment, what was that like for you?*
> PING: *Well, I agree with you that it was playful at first. And I really liked that playfulness. It felt "light," you know? It felt safe and fun.*

Len mirrors, checks for accuracy, and invites more.

> THERAPIST: *So now Ping, I want you to try to remember the moment, kind of imagine it in your mind, when you pushed Len away that time. If you could put it in one word, what were you feeling when you did that?*
> PING: Thinking a bit. *Annoyed.*

Therapist prompts Len to mirror the feeling and invite more.

> LEN: Nodding head. *Hmmm . . . yes. Annoyed. Can you tell me a little more about that?*
> PING: *I don't know. I think I was annoyed because I was running late. But also, it felt fake. It felt like you really did not mean that.*
> LEN: *But I did!*
> THERAPIST: *So Len, rather than reacting to Ping, let's explore this a little bit more. Remember, her experience is her reality even if it does not match your intention. Would that be okay?*
> LEN: *Yes.*

Len mirrors and invites more.

PING: *Yes, there's more. I guess it's not that you did not mean it but rather I did not feel it. That I'm smart and that I'm important to you.*
THERAPIST: Using a quieter, softer tone. *Len, could you mirror that back—and remember, you're putting your story aside right now and just hearing Ping completely in what she is sharing right now.*
LEN: Mimicking the therapist softer tone. *So if I heard you correctly, you said it's not that I did not feel those things, but rather that you don't feel those things about yourself, like that you're smart and important to me. Did I get that?*
PING: Nodding her head yes and crying a bit.
LEN: *Is there more about that?*
THERAPIST: *So Ping, can you remember a time when you were younger when someone else said you were not smart or important or some other memory?*
PING: *When I hear you say I am smart it reminds me of my dad trying to help me with homework. I remember him shouting at me, "How can you be so damned dumb!"*
LEN: *So when you heard me say you are smart, it reminded you of when your dad yelled at you one time when helping with your homework, saying, "How can you be so damned dumb!" Did I get that? . . . Is there more about that?*
PING: *It just hurt. And I believed it. I guess I still do.*

The therapist continues prompting Len to mirror, check for accuracy, invite more, summarize, validate, and empathize.

This Dialogue shows how important it is for Ping's voice to be heard and to move into the affect rather than trying to correct her self-image. There are always opportunities for deepening to uncover the resistance. As long as the rejected part of the self remains unconscious, the more tenacious the resistance will be. One of the partners becomes stuck in places that prevent these opportunities for couples to connect deeply and authentically. On a simple level, it was impossible for Ping to believe that Len was telling the truth when he complimented her, because of her earlier childhood messages. On a more complex level, she could not let in, or receive, the idea that she could become her own person with her own talents and strengths.

When dealing with an affective piece, as in the case above, the goal is to have the partner step in as much as possible and engage directly with their partner (with the therapist prompting the sender and receiver). Transformation occurs in the dyad, and every effort should be made to keep the Dialogue within the dyadic structure of the couple.

There are several ways to process this experience further:

1. **Continue exploring the resistance in Dialogue:** "So Ping, it really does make sense to shut down that part of yourself. What would it feel like for you to believe that you truly are smart? And what would that look like?"

2. **Recap the sharing with some validation and psychoeducation:** "You did what you needed to do to get your father's approval. You believed what he said, and given what you have said about him previously, how harsh he was, you would not dare challenge that. And you are now an adult with the ability to reclaim that part of you that you shut down a long time ago."

3. **Highlight the opportunities for the receiver:** Len learned that, although in his mind "he was just teasing" Ping, sometimes his words triggered earlier experiences with her father, who was quick to criticize her when she was little. As a result, he became more conscious of removing the negative language from the Space-Between.

4. **Provide between-session assignments such as:**
   a. Ask both partners to write, separately, at least three specific items Ping has done to show how smart she is, and then share the lists with each other in the next session.
   b. Have Ping work on accepting compliments with an automatic "Thank you" and resisting the urge to turn away or deflect compliments.
   c. Explore together ways that Ping could further grow her "thinking self" by intentionally creating some specific goals.

The goal here is to help Ping understand that her rejection of that part of herself occurred early in life, through circumstances that were beyond her control, and that her self-rejection has compromised her functioning, with the consequence that she has not been able to bring all of herself into her relationship with Len and with others who are close to her (possibly including inadvertently passing on the same legacy of wounding to their children). In addition, she was pushing Len away when he was turning toward her.

In this one session, we touched upon elements of many of the Imago processes, such as re-romanticizing, removing negativity, and reimaging. It was not a "start here and end there" process but a seamless flow that embraced a fuller narrative of the "Len and Ping love story."

IMAGO AND SEXUALITY

You may have noticed that the Imago therapy process does not address sexuality. Our theory of sexuality is that sex is a normal and natural interaction in the Space-Between when safety reigns and connecting is experienced. In our view, sexual issues are symptoms of systemic issues, just like money, communication, anxiety, and depression, and their source is the anxiety caused by unrepaired ruptures in connecting. The anxiety gets localized to a topic area—money, sex, in-laws, etc.—which diverts attention from the intolerable sensation to a concrete problem. If we focus on the symptoms, we amplify the symptom and overlook its source.

This philosophy—that negativity ruptures connecting and triggers anxiety—is behind our focus in the first session on where the couple wants to go—their dream relationship—rather than where they have come from. That is also why we focus on the process—all sessions are facilitated dialogues—rather than the content. Couples first focus on their desired outcome and practice the skill of Imago Dialogue. Then the Imago therapist invites couples to share their frustrations, the wishes embedded in them, and the fears they have about intimacy.

Procedurally that means that an ideal sex life could be included in the Relationship Vision, followed by what would have to be included and excluded to make that happen. After that, couples are facilitated in making a commitment to their dream sexuality, differentiating their sexual differences, removing negativity from their sexual transactions, translating sexual frustrations into a wish and then into a behavior, and amplifying pleasure through caring behaviors, surprises, fun, and flooding. While focusing on a symptom amplifies it, engaging in Dialogue on all these levels transforms the symptom into a gateway to connecting. All other issues, such as money, children, in-laws, work, and vacations, are topics for the same process.

Whereas falling in love infused the body with a cornucopia of neurochemicals, such as PEA and dopamine, the power struggle replaced these euphoric feelings with stress chemicals, such as cortisol. The Re-romanticizing Process activates brain functions in both the anticipatory and pleasure centers and releases various neurochemicals. The predominating neurochemicals released in "real love" are oxytocin, the bonding chemical, and serotonin, the happy chemical. Real love is deep rather than high. It can be passionate and intensely spiritual.

Re-romanticizing helps couples restore some of the earlier positive experiences they felt—and freely gave—during the romantic phase of their relationship but with one modification. They are now intentional in the giving (output) and receiving (input) of behaviors; they made a decision to act on the information their partner shared: what touches their heart, what would be a wonderful surprise, what they interpret as fun. These intentional behaviors go beyond the romantic love phase, past the power struggle, and reside in the sacred Space-Between of real love.

Takeaways for the Re-Romanticizing Process

- Intentionality—to behave lovingly even when you are not feeling it—is the engine of real love.
- Re-Romanticizing practices can be the focus of a single or of multiple sessions or can be integrated into therapy sessions whenever it is appropriate.
- Pay attention to the nuances of resistance—such as a partner deflecting positives or absorbing negatives—and facilitate a Dialogue about your observations.
- Remind couples that they live in private worlds and neither comes with the ability to read minds. They must ask what they want to know, and share what they want their partner to know, about caring behaviors, surprises, and all sorts of pleasures.
- The daily repetitions of positive behaviors alters memories and brings new, joyful, and sustainable experiences to the relationship.

TIP:
Teach your couples: "Do unto others as *they* would have *you* do unto *them.*"

From the Clinic to the Culture

A t the conclusion of this ponderous tome, we introduce you to the next iteration of the Imago system and the application of Imago Dialogue. We extend its influence from the clinic as a couple's therapy to the culture as a social movement.

We know that Imago transforms couples who come to therapy. We also know that if they have children and practice the process with them, it also transforms their family. In the recent past, we asked whether Imago Dialogue would transform persons who are in non-intimate relationships and in non-intimate social systems larger than couples and families, like educational institutions, houses of worship, community organizations, and corporations. To push the question further, we asked whether Imago Dialogue could not only transform these institutions *in* the culture, but could it transform the culture *itself*.

To go from the institutions within a culture to the culture itself is an extension of our work with couples that focuses on changing the relationship—the Space-Between—rather than each partner. Changing the relationship is the prerequisite for changing the interior world of each partner—mirroring the shift from the individual to the relational paradigm. And that mirrors the particle–wave duality of the quantum field. For us, it is not a big leap from the specifics of couple's therapy to the dream of a whole culture, or global civilization, connected with positive energy and full conscious awareness. We naturally catch fire at the possibility of applying the principles of Imago Dialogue to a broader audience.

The question of the need for cultural transformation was raised when we discovered that behind their psychological problems, couples had another problem—the value system of the culture itself. The cultural context is the source of their relational issues. To be specific, couples live unconsciously in a cultural value system that extolls competition, control, domination, and winning at all costs. These dysfunctional behaviors are used unconsciously by couples to engage each other in the project of a better marriage, but because they focus on the individual rather than the couple, they reduce engagement in the relationship to transactions and negotiations rather than elevating the couple to safety and connecting. The power of these values lie in the fact that couples, as does culture, consider them as objectively real rather than cultural options, and the solutions available in that value system are passed on to the children and, through them, into the next generation of marriages/intimate partnerships as the "way life is." Couples not only live in these values in their personal space; they carry them to their places of work, worship, and learning—like a disease in every cell of the human body—rupturing the connecting essential for healthy functioning—and pass it on like transgenerational cultural DNA.

When we became aware of this impediment to connecting that is hiding in the cultural unconscious, and thus in the personal unconscious, we began to do a double diagnosis to discover the covert cultural problem behind the overt psychological problems that brought couples to see us. In every instance, they were attempting to manage their conflict with methods that created conflict. By engaging couples in Imago Dialogue, we were able to help partners replace competition, control, domination, and the need for excellence at all costs with collaboration, cocreation, and cooperation. They moved from being opponents to being partners.

Couples had difficulty counteracting the cultural factors behind their psychological issues, because the neurosis of the culture itself is considered "the way life is." Those hidden belief systems slowly begin to erode these gains. As time passes, couples tend to slow their practice of Dialogue and regress to the cultural drama of competition for the best outcomes for oneself. It is like working with an adolescent who returns to the family—which did not go to therapy and thus has not changed—and regresses to their former, troubled state. The lesson taken from family therapy is that the context in which couples live must be changed if they are to sustain their gains from therapy, which is why we place emphasis on the Space-Between, the relationship itself, rather than on symptoms. Our view is that until the culture, which breeds the pathologies that populate the clinic, is transformed, the clinic will always be full and mental health professionals will always be busy! It seems obvious that cultural transformation is a prerequisite for sustaining personal-couple gains, and in an oscillation of effects, couples who improve their relational space, as inhabitants of the culture, improve the relational quality of the culture. This oscillation of positive effect between the personal and the social will transform and sustain positive shifts in institutions, like schools, houses of worship, and the workplace.

So, how do we do this?

We have thought about that question a lot for the past several years. Our first thought was to reframe the culture as "client" and create a process by which we could bring Imago Dialogue from the clinic to the culture. The challenge we faced is that the relational sciences, upon which Imago

Dialogue is based, are hidden in the clinic and in research reports, journal articles, academic books, graduate school classrooms and therapy sessions, and that is a small population. And the resources that are delivered are limited to popular articles, blogs, social media outlets, and therapy sessions. While "some" is better than "none," it is barely, because the popular versions of this profound material, and their delivery systems, attract mainly individuals who want to be a better person or find a romantic partner, be more economically successful and fulfill their potential, all of which furthers the competitive value system of the culture which is the problem. And there is no comment whatsoever on the fact that a neurotic culture gives birth to neurotic individuals just as conflicted couples give birth to a neurotic child who then lives in and perpetuates the neurotic culture.

We think we can declare: *If the culture is not transformed, the clinic will always be full. And emptying the clinic does not transform the culture. It sustains the system it is designed to transform.*

From our perspective, the transformation of culture itself is the next challenge of the helping professions, but to do that, we need to unleash relational wisdom to the masses.

Imago therapists have been excited about the power of Imago Dialogue beyond the clinic. Because they experience Imago as more than a therapy, but also as a lifestyle, they have been committed to "transforming the world, one couple at a time" from the very beginning. Their vision was expanding the number of therapists helping one couple at a time until all couples were healed. But, because therapy is a resource for persons and couples with a defunct cultural value overlaying psychological problems created by that value system, that vision itself, while immense, commendable and unique for a therapy profession, was a part of the problem, not the solution. The solution is not the healing of the wounded only, but the creation of a context that is not wounding.

As if prescient about the question whether the teaching and practice of Imago Dialogue could be taken "from the clinic to the culture," some Imago therapists, with social, political and community interests, as well as interests in persons and couples, have facilitated Imago Dialogues in non-intimate situations—community organizations, group conflict, Israeli–Palestinian conversation, the Hutu–Tutsi conflict in Rwanda, businesses and classrooms and houses of worship, with compelling results. In all these instances, everyone has reported that diverse parties achieved connection when they practiced the Dialogue process, and the events evoked the same enthusiasm in these environments that couples experienced in workshops, seminars, and therapy. This seed has now grown into a global social movement with the goal of distributing Imago Dialogue to the planet.

However, to change any system requires reaching a tipping point. While doing the math of the world's population, the number of people who go to therapy, and the even smaller number of those who go to couple's therapy, it was painfully clear that if all the therapists in the world completely transformed all their clients, it would not change the world. They would have a minimal impact. We would need help.

Then we had an idea. Why not ask our distinguished colleagues—those with intellectual and therapeutic systems and researchers in the relational sciences—whether we might combine our visibility, intellectual and therapeutic systems and our collective prestige, and collectively deliver relational science information and relational technology to the culture. We envisioned curating selected information from the relational sciences that inhabit research journals and academic books and to bring it from the clinic into the culture through all the distribution channels that exist. In other words, we could collectively go "upstream" and attempt to prevent the conditions from developing that produced the necessity of "down river cleanup" in which we were investing our lives and careers. The outcome of such a project would replace the values of an individualistic culture—competition, control, domination, and a drive for excellence—with the collaboration, cocreation and cooperation that could effectively reduce, and perhaps remove, the conditions that produced the symptoms that bring our clients to us. And it would replace an individual culture with a relational civilization and move us toward the next stage in human evolution.

To our delighted surprise, they were all interested, and we met twice a year for four years as a think tank to discover the methodology of cultural transformation and employ it globally. Without going into all the details of implementation, that vision became housed in a nonprofit organization, brought to Dallas as a social experiment, and with the blessings and support of our peers, it has become a global social movement.

Since Imago Dialogue had proven effective in nonclinical situations, we decided to rename it Safe Conversations and rebrand it as the instrument of a social movement, rather than therapy, and offer it to anyone or organization, as relationship education—with the aim of helping its participants achieve relational competence which we see as a prerequisite for relational wellbeing, which in turn, is the prerequisite for emotional and mental wellbeing. We began with couples and families, which is our lane in the bowling alley, and eventually offered it to nonclinical and non-intimate populations. The "culture as client" consisted of everyone in all ecosystems: families, schools, corporations, houses of worship, and community organizations.

The work spread in Dallas and has become known internationally as Safe Conversations and is set for expansion. The vision is global, and the goal is specific: to help 3.8 billion persons, a tipping point of the world's population, become relationally competent by learning and integrating Safe

Conversations into their lives in the next forty years. (The theory goes that when a tipping point of 25%–30% of a system is changed, the rest of the system collapses and reorganizes at a higher level.) The strategy is face to face, digital workshops and personal and organizational training: 1) to train as many persons as possible to teach Safe Conversations in their ecosystem—home, community, their children's school, their houses of worship, and places of work; and 2) to augment these Safe Conversation leaders with a digital platform that is populated with digital products that can be accessed by anyone who has access to a digital device. We learned that the nonprofit organization could not contain a project of this size, so we have replaced it with a public benefit for-profit organization in order to secure the funds to create a digital platform that could deliver on a global scale.

There is a beautiful synergy in the fact that therapists and couples become interested in distributing Safe Conversations as a social movement and participants, who come for Safe Conversations training, or end users of a product, who need more than education, seek therapy from an Imago therapist to deal with their personal issues.

When we replace an individualistic culture with a culture that is comprised of persons who are relationally competent and experience relational wellbeing and who engage in collaboration rather than conflict, cocreation rather than competition, and cooperation rather than isolation, we will have fomented a relational civilization in which equality is universal, diversity is celebrated, and inclusion is total. With the transformation of culture and personal relationships, the safety that will exist in the Space-Between will constellate cohesion in the quantum field, bringing peace to our world. When the Space-Between becomes *safe* for everyone, we will have entered the next stage in human evolution!

Set in this context, the work of Imago is in service to a higher purpose. Educating, influencing, and facilitating more people into an awareness that high quality relationships can be considered a high calling, with social and political implications way beyond the personal. Being able to testify that that it is possible is life-giving.

The journey has begun and participation in the project is open to all interested persons.

APPENDICES

DIALOGUE: APPRECIATION

Make an appointment

SENDER: I would like to have a Dialogue about an appreciation I have for you. Is now a good time?

RECEIVER: I'm available now. (*If not now, state when and be available then.*)

Connect nonverbally

Sender and receiver make eye contact and take three deep breaths in sync.

Express an appreciation

SENDER: One thing I appreciate about you is . . .

Mirror and check accuracy

RECEIVER: Let me see if I've got that. You said . . . Did I get that? Is there more about that?

SENDER: Yes, you got me.

Resend or modify any parts not clearly received. "The part you got was . . . and I also said . . ."

RECEIVER: *Mirror until 100% accurate.* Let me see if I've got you. If I did, you said . . . Did I get that? Is there more about that?

Deepen

SENDER: When I experience that in you, I feel . . .

RECEIVER: When you experience that you feel . . .

SENDER: Yes, and it reminds me about something from my childhood which is . . .

RECEIVER: And it reminds you that in your childhood, you . . . Is there more about that?

If receiver feels overloaded, remember to use the hand signal and say: "I really want to hear all you have to say. Let me see if I got it so far. If I did you said . . . Is there more about that?"

SENDER: No, that is all.

Summarize

RECEIVER: Let me see if I got all of that. In summary, you are saying . . . Did I get it all?

SENDER: Yes, you got it all. *Resend if necessary. "The part you got was . . . and I also said . . ."*

Closing
RECEIVER: Thank you for sharing.
SENDER: Thank you for listening.

Give each other a one-minute hug, and breathe in sync for three deep breaths. Make eye contact on release.

When all the steps are completed, switch roles and repeat the process.

Appendix 2

SAMPLE SCRIPT: GUIDED VISUALIZATION

Some therapists use guided visualization to help couples relax and envision their dream relationship. It helps couples with full body experiencing through sensory visualizations such as tones, colors, smells, and sounds (Spangler, 2009). Sensory is also a key opening to the past: For example, a single waft of lavender can trigger a memory from our distant childhood. (Saive et al., 2014; Vermetten & Bremner, 2003).

After your couple expresses mutual appreciations, you can use a guided visualization as a prompt for the Revisioning Process. Below is a sample guided imagery. It is not necessary that you use it; it is optional based on your clinical judgment.

Let's take a few minutes to be fully present here in this time together today, to make the transition from whatever we have been doing before being here, and to be more connected with ourselves as we move into connection with each other. Let yourself go inward and focus on your breath. Breathe slowly and deeply. Let your body find its own natural rhythm. Notice. Notice the breath in and the breath out. With the breath in, notice the experience of taking in, of receiving, filling up, expanding. With the breath out, notice the experience of breathing out, expressing, of letting go, releasing, emptying. Slowly and deeply. Let yourself connect with your thoughts, preoccupations, worries, concerns, whatever is going on in your head. Notice. Notice the energy flow to your thoughts. And with the breath out, let go of any thoughts or concerns that you don't need to hold onto right now. Release. Breathe in quietness.

Let yourself connect with your feelings. Be aware of your emotions. Notice the energy to your feelings, the intensity. And with the breath out, let go of any emotions that you don't need to hold onto in this time and place, that don't belong to now. Release, empty. Breathe in calmness.

Let yourself connect with your body. Scan your body. Notice any places in your body where you may be holding pain or tension. Notice the energy flowing to your muscles. And again with the breath out, let go of any pain or tension that you don't need to be aware of right now. Scan your body again and notice any places in your body where you may be feeling calm or energized. Notice.

As you breathe in, let the breath fill those parts of you and let the calm or the energy spread through your body. Notice.

Let yourself connect with your sensory experience in this moment— notice the energy flow to your senses. Notice the colors, the movement, notice the sounds, the smells, the taste in your mouth, the touch of the air and your clothing on your skin. Notice. Then release that awareness. Let yourself connect with your core energy, your life force pulsating within you and radiating around you. Notice the quality of that energy.

Now I invite you to imagine you are with your partner, living the relationship of your dreams. Let go of any anxieties you might have and imagine yourself completely fulfilled and happy with your partner. You are laughing together. Everything is perfect. You feel completely and abundantly safe and loved and loving.

Notice how it feels in your body. Imagine the sensations of touch and smell—the sun caressing your face or the feel of your partner's hand in your hand. What smells are in the air? What sounds are you hearing?

Now I want you to take some time thinking about what kinds of things are in your relationship that make this perfect picture? What are you doing together? How do you play together? Let the images come to mind. (Pause.) Let the various images come to your mind.

Open your eyes now, slowly and gently. Look into each other's eyes and connect without words.

Appendix 3

WORKSHEET: MY RELATIONSHIP VISION

Instructions: Working separately, using short, descriptive, and positive sentences, describe your global dream of a deeply satisfying love relationship. Be sure to:
  - Include qualities that
    – are already present in your relationship that you want to keep.
    – you want to add to your relationship.
  - Write **ALL** sentences in the **present tense**, as if it were already happening. For example: *"We have fun together,"* and *"We are loving parents."*
  - Use **positive** words.
  - Positive wording vs. negative wording:
    – *"We settle our differences peacefully,"* rather than *"We don't fight."*
    – *"We trust each other,"* rather than *"We don't get jealous."*

Ignore the ✓ column for now.

The questions below may help you focus on aspects of your ideal relationship that you may wish to include on your list. Be sure to include other aspects you desire, even if they are not reflected in these questions.

What do you feel toward each other?
What do you do together?
How do you relate to each other?
Where do you live?
How do you live out your faith?
What is your sex life like?
How do you play together?
What do you do with your free time?
How do you relate around work?
How do you relate around money?
What is the status of your children, if any?
How do you relate to your children, and how do they relate to you?
How do you relate to mutual friends and friends of the opposite sex?
How are decisions made?
How do you resolve conflict?
What is your relationship to in-laws? Stepchildren?
How physically healthy are you?

	MY RELATIONSHIP VISION
	In my vision of our relationship, we . . .
✓	(Positive, short, and using present tense)

DIALOGUE: OUR RELATIONSHIP VISION AND OUR RELATIONSHIP POTENTIAL

As you did in the office with your therapist, use mirroring and take turns sharing your vision of your personal statements with your partner.

MIRRORING DREAM RELATIONSHIP STATEMENTS	
SENDER	RECEIVER
Asks for Appointment Is now a good time to share my vision of our relationship?	*Grants Appointment* I'm available now.
Connect nonverbally. *Make eye contact and take three deep breaths in sync.* *Sender shares one-way appreciation (receiver only mirrors).*	
Shares Dream Statement In my dream relationship, we . . . *Deepens* When I see this in our relationship, it makes me feel . . . And that feeling reminds me of . . .	*Mirrors and Checks for Accuracy* If I got that, in your dream relationship, we are . . . Did I get that? *Expresses Curiosity* Is there more about that? *Summarizes and Checks for Accuracy* Let me see if I got ALL of that. In your dream relationship, we are . . . And when you imagine that, you feel . . . And when you feel that, you remember that when you were little . . . Did I get all that?
Continue sharing dream statements using the steps above.	
Closings *Thank you for listening. / Thank you for sharing.* *Give each other a one-minute hug.* *Switch roles.*	

Compare the two lists, and put a check mark next to the statements you have in common.

If your partner mentions anything you agree with but did not think of yourself, add it to your list and put a check mark in the left column.

Design a mutual Relationship Vision by transferring all the qualities you had in common (checked items from your two lists) onto the Our Relationship Vision worksheet.

If your partner has written items with which you *do not* agree, do not discuss them at this time. Transfer these items onto the Our Relationship Potential worksheet. You can revisit these later, in your therapy sessions. As intimacy increases over time, revisit these statements. For any that continue to be a source of conflict, use the Imago Dialogue to work them through or bring them to therapy.

WORKSHEET: OUR RELATIONSHIP VISION

OUR RELATIONSHIP VISION

Appendix 6

WORKSHEET: OUR RELATIONSHIP POTENTIAL

OUR RELATIONSHIP POTENTIAL

WORKSHEET:
IMPLEMENTING OUR RELATIONSHIP VISION

Purpose: To achieve a relationship vision, it is necessary (as with any other vision) to become goal oriented. Each vision statement is a goal, and you have now completed the first two steps. This exercise will help you make the transition from goals to objectives and strategies.

Select a vision statement from Our Relationship Vision that you both share that you would consider easy to achieve. Translate this vision statement into a specific objective and strategy and complete the *Implementing Our Relationship Vision Worksheet,* as explained by your therapist and by referring to the example. After you complete the worksheet, put it in a prominent place where you will see it frequently. Repeat the process for each vision statement. It is a good idea to complete a Vision Worksheet weekly. Be sure to bring any challenges to and share any successes with your therapist.

EXAMPLE: IMPLEMENTING OUR RELATIONSHIP VISION		
Vision Statement	We have fun regularly.	
Objectives	Have high-energy fun once a week. Laugh together daily.	
Strategy or Tactic	Practice belly laughing once a day. See a funny movie once a week. Play a silly game each Sunday.	**Time Frame** 3 weeks
Sensory Effect	Taste: Sweetness Touch: Softness Smell: Perspiration Sound: Laughter Feel: Excitement and pleasure Emotions experienced: Happiness and joy	
Consequence or Payoff	Feeling safe with each other	
Progress Report	Laughed each day. Watched 9 movies.	
Revision of Plan	Play a silly game daily.	

IMPLEMENTING OUR RELATIONSHIP VISION	
Vision Statement	
Objectives	
Strategy or Tactic	
	Time Frame
Sensory Effect	Taste: Touch: Smell: Sound: Feel: Emotions experienced:
Consequence or Payoff	
Progress Report	
Revision of Plan	

Appendix 8

WORKSHEET: SHARED RELATIONSHIP VISION SCALE

Name _____ Date _____

Instructions:
1. Working separately, list each item on your Shared Relationship Vision below. Then rate each one in terms of your satisfaction with where you are in your relationship today by circling a number from 0 to 10. 0 = No satisfaction; 10 = Very high satisfaction.
2. Using Imago Dialogue, share your ratings with your partner. If there is a discrepancy, get curious about your partner's different experience. Together, pick one item and Dialogue about 1) what you can do (specific tactics) to raise satisfaction by ½ a point, 2) enumerating the challenges that might get in the way.
3. At the end of the two weeks, Dialogue about your successes and challenges, and make a new plan to raise the same or another item by ½ point. Remember you are on a journey toward living your vision.

Bring any successes and challenges to your therapist.

We _____
0   1   2   3   4   5   6   7   8   9   10

We _____
0   1   2   3   4   5   6   7   8   9   10

We _____
0   1   2   3   4   5   6   7   8   9   10

We _____
0   1   2   3   4   5   6   7   8   9   10

We _____
0   1   2   3   4   5   6   7   8   9   10

We _____
0   1   2   3   4   5   6   7   8   9   10

We _____
0   1   2   3   4   5   6   7   8   9   10

We _____
0   1   2   3   4   5   6   7   8   9   10

We _____
0   1   2   3   4   5   6   7   8   9   10

WORKSHEET: DEEPENING YOUR COMMITMENT BY IDENTIFYING EXITS

Purpose: To slowly increase energy and intimacy in your relationship by verbalizing feelings rather than engaging in activities or behaviors that are easier or more pleasurable for you to do.

An exit is acting out your feelings rather than expressing them in words in a way that is respectful to your partner and helps you connect. Any behavior or activity that allows you to reduce or avoid involvement in your relationship is an exit. These behaviors can be normal, positive, everyday activities, such as spending time with your children or working. These activities are not necessarily, in and of themselves, exits unless you are using them, at least in part, to avoid being with or talking with your partner about yourself and the difficulties that cause you to want to avoid spending time with your partner. They are behaviors that drain necessary energy from the relationship. We call this the *invisible divorce.*

If you are to create a conscious relationship with your partner, you will need to examine these activities. The first step is to begin identifying your current exits.

Instructions: Use the table below to begin identifying potential exits that you engage in that drain energy from your relationship. Put a check (✓) by exits that you are willing to eliminate or reduce at this time. (This does NOT mean you will eliminate or reduce it right now—only that you are willing.) Put an X by those that would be difficult for you to change or that you are unwilling to change at the present time.

Do NOT share the list with your partner. Bring the list to the next therapy session.

Willing to Close or Modify (✓)	I avoid closeness with my partner by . . .	Difficult to Close or Modify (x)

Appendix 10

DIALOGUE: SHARING AN EXIT

Ask for an appointment

SENDER: Is now a good time to share an exit with you?

RECEIVER: I'm available now. (*If not now, state when and be available then.*)

Connect nonverbally

Sender and receiver make eye contact and take three deep breaths in sync.

Express an appreciation

SENDER: First, I would like to express an appreciation which is _____.

RECEIVER: *Mirrors:* You want to express an appreciation which is _____. Did I get that?

SENDER: Yes. (*Or add what is missing*)

RECEIVER: Thanks for your appreciation.

SENDER: Thanks for receiving it.

Send the message / Mirror

SENDER: One activity I use to avoid talking or being connected with you is _____.

RECEIVER: Let me see if I've got that. I heard you say _____. Am I getting that? Is there more about that?

Deepen the experience

SENDER: I do this when I feel _____. and what I am afraid of is _____. That reminds me of childhood when _____.

RECEIVER: Let me see if I've got that. I heard you say _____. Am I getting that? Is there more about that? *Continue sending and checking accuracy until sender says: There is no more.*

Summarize

RECEIVER: Let me see if I got all of that. If I got that, one activity you do to avoid talking or being connected with me is _____. And you do this when you feel _____.

And what you are afraid of is _____.
And that reminds you of when you were a child _____.
Did I get all of that?

SENDER: *Listens to the summary and gives accuracy check.* Yes, you got me.

Resends if necessary. The part you got was _____ and I also said _____.

Validate

RECEIVER: You make sense, and what makes sense is that you (*exit behavior*) _____.
Because you feel _____.
And you are afraid to express your feelings of _____.
Because in childhood, you _____.
Is that a good validation?

SENDER: *Listens and receives validation.*

Empathize

RECEIVER: I imagine you might be feeling _____.
Is that the feeling?
Do you have more feelings?

Closing

RECEIVER: Thank you for sharing that with me.
SENDER: Thank you for listening.

Give each other a one-minute hug, and breathe in sync for three deep breaths. Make eye contact on release. Switch roles.

DIALOGUE: THE COMMITMENT

Purpose: This Dialogue is designed to help you continue the process of identifying activities (exits) you use to avoid intimacy and to begin closing or modifying the exit to bring energy back into the relationship.

Instructions: Choose one exit from the preceding list that you feel comfortable talking about and that is checked "willing to close or modify." Ask your partner for a Dialogue.

Ask for an appointment

SENDER: Is now a good time to share an exit with you that I am willing to close?

RECEIVER: I'm available now. (*If not now, state when and be available then.*)

Connect nonverbally

Sender and receiver make eye contact and take three deep breaths in sync.

Express an appreciation

SENDER: First, I would like to express an appreciation which is _____.

RECEIVER: *Mirrors:* You want to express an appreciation which is _____. Did I get that?

SENDER: Yes. (*Or add what is missing,*)

RECEIVER: Thanks for your appreciation.

SENDER: Thanks for receiving it.

Send the Message / Mirror

SENDER: One activity I use to avoid talking or being connected with you is _____.

RECEIVER: Let me see if I've got you. I heard you say _____.
          Am I getting you? Is there more?

Deepen the Experience

SENDER: I do this when I feel _____.
          and what I am afraid of is _____.
          That reminds me of childhood when _____.
          What scares me about closing this exit is _____.
          And I am now ready and willing to close (*or modify*) that exit (*immediately or state the date when*).

> If I feel inclined to use this exit, I will ask for an appointment for a Dialogue to talk about it rather than acting out.

RECEIVER: Let me see if I've got you. I heard you say _____.
Am I getting you?
Is there more about that?
When there is no more about that, ask: Is there anything you need from me to help close (or modify) that exit?

SENDER: The support I think I will need to close it is _____.
Or No, I will do it on my own, but thanks for offering.

RECEIVER: *Continue mirroring and checking accuracy until sender says there is no more.*

Summarize

RECEIVER: Let me see if I got all of that. In summary, you are saying _____.
Is that a good summary?

SENDER: *Listens to the summary and gives accuracy check.* Yes, you got me.
Resends if necessary. The part you got was _____ and I also said _____.

Validate

RECEIVER: You make sense, and what makes sense is that you (exit behavior) _____.
Because you need _____.
And are afraid to express your feelings of _____.
Because in childhood, you _____.
Is that a good validation?

SENDER: *Listens and receives validation.*

Empathize

RECEIVER: I imagine you might be feeling _____.
Is that the feeling?
Do you have more feelings?

Closing

RECEIVER: Thank you for sharing that with me and for the gift to our relationship.

SENDER: Thank you for listening.

Give each other a one-minute hug, and breathe in sync for three deep breaths. Make eye contact on release. Switch roles.

Appendix 12

WORKSHEET: IMAGO PROFILE

1. Take out a blank piece of paper and draw a large circle, leaving about three inches below the circle. Divide the circle in half with a horizontal line. Put a capital letter A above the line on the left side of the circle, and a capital letter B below the line on the left side of the circle. (See illustration below.)

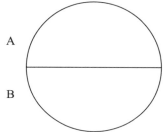

2. Remembering how you felt in child, list in the top half of the circle the *positive* traits of your early caretakers (i.e., the people who raised you and most influenced you) as you remember them from childhood (e.g., *loving, consistent, attentive, affectionate, funny, available*).
3. In the bottom half of the circle, list the *negative* traits of each of your early caretakers as you remember them from childhood (e.g., *angry, critical, depressed, abusive, withholding*).

REMEMBER: Recalling childhood frustrations does not mean blaming or criticizing parents or caretakers. Many basic, seemingly benign messages can be wounding to a child, such as "Stop crying. Everything will be okay" (which doesn't allow a child to fully express themself). The purpose of this exploration is to help us understand how past experiences may relate to our present functioning.

4. CIRCLE three positive and three negative traits that seemed to affect you the most.
5. COMPLETE this sentence:

What I **wanted and needed most** as a child and didn't get was (C) _____
_____ (e.g., *attention, love, support, time, information, nurturing*).

6. WRITE down three **positive** childhood memories you had with your caretakers and the corresponding feelings (column D). The memories can be specific or general (see examples below). Remember, feelings can be described with one word. If you are using more than one word, you are probably describing a thought, not a feeling.

Positive Childhood Memories	(D) Feeling(s)
Example (general):	
Christmas mornings.	*Excited*
Example (specific):	
My grandma cheering in the	
stands when I hit a home run.	*Proud*
1.	
2.	
3.	

7. Current frustrations with your partner mask unmet needs that often stem from childhood. WRITE down three **childhood frustrations** (using at least one "minor" frustration) **that you had as a child** and the corresponding feelings. The memories can be specific or general.

Childhood Frustrations	Feelings
Example (general):	
When my mother was away	
taking care of Grandpa all the time.	*Resentful and lonely*
Example:	
When my older brother forgot	
my birthday	*Unimportant*
1.	
2.	
3.	

8. Fill in the blanks below based on the answers above and in the previous page. This is your Relationship Agenda:

I am looking to find a person who is (B) _____

in order to get them to be (A) _____

so that I can get (C) _____

and feel (D) _____

WORKSHEET: MY CHILDHOOD CHALLENGE

Our past experiences with our caretakers shape the behavior and quality of our relationships in the present. This exercise will help you discover your early childhood challenge and connect it with the frustrations and desires you experience as you interact with significant others in the present.

Study the 14 items in the table below. **Select and CIRCLE the ONE (only select ONE)** that most represents your greatest childhood challenge.

If none of them describe your challenge, write one that does in the space marked "other."

MY CHILDHOOD CHALLENGE	
INTRUSIVE	**NEGLECTFUL**
• To get free from feeling controlled by others.	• To be seen and valued rather than ignored and invisible.
• To say what I think and feel rather what I should think and feel.	• To be included rather than excluded and abandoned.
• To be listened to while I am talking.	• To feel significant as a person.
• To have some privacy.	• To get support for what I think or feel.
• To have a say in what I am supposed to do.	• To get someone to show interest in what I want and like.
• To do what I wanted to do rather than what I ought to.	• To get someone to show up for events in my life.
• To be trusted.	• To get attention when I need it.
OTHER:	OTHER:

Appendix 14

WORKSHEET: MY RELATIONAL NEED

The early childhood challenge you identified on the previous page resulted in a relational need that you brought into your adult relationships. It is especially present in your adult intimate relationships, and it also shows up in all your significant relationships.

Study the 14 items in the table below. **Select and CIRCLE the ONE (select only ONE)** that best describes what you needed most from significant people in your childhood.

If none of them describe your early need, write one that does in the space marked "other."

MY CHILDHOOD NEED	
INTRUSIVE	NEGLECTFUL
• To have space and time to myself on a regular basis. • To be asked what I think and what I feel. • To experience genuine and reliable warmth when I need it. • To have the freedom to safely explore. • To experience that what I do and want is valued by others. • To be seen as I see myself and accepted and valued as that. • To experience trust from others in my thinking and decisions.	• To experience interest in me when I am talking. • To be responded to when I ask for it. • To ask me what I want, feel, and think. • To show curiosity about my experiences in life. • To be loved and gently touched without having to ask. • To feel important. • To experience the emotional presence of the caring other.
OTHER:	OTHER:

WORKSHEET: MINIMIZERS AND MAXIMIZERS

Instructions: When our early relational needs were not met, we felt threatened and tended to defend ourselves by escalating (maximizing) or shutting down (minimizing) our feelings. In childhood, each of us used both, but one of them worked better than the other, so the effective one was selected as our primary defense. We call them *Turtles* and *Hailstorms.*

Study the items in the two columns below. Check every statement, in both columns, that best resembles you. Now review the ones you selected, and CIRCLE the one that MOST describes you.

MINIMIZING (Turtle)	MAXIMIZING (Hailstorm)
• Tend to keep feelings in.	• Tend to let feelings out.
• Tend to be independent and not ask for help.	• Tend to depend on others and exaggerate needs.
• Tend to be private.	• Tend to be compulsively open.
• Tend to withhold feelings, thoughts, and behaviors.	• Tend to express feelings, thoughts, and behaviors excessively.
• Tend to have rigid self-boundaries.	• Tend to have unclear boundaries.
• Tend to be inner-directed; take direction mainly from oneself.	• Tend to be outer-directed and ask for direction from others.
• Tend to control others by force.	• Tend to control others by manipulating.
• Tend to be aggressive when passivity does not work.	• Tend to be passive when aggression does not work.
• Tend to take defensive positions.	• Tend to take offensive positions.
• Tend to be submissive.	• Tend to be assertive.

DIALOGUE: CHILDHOOD CHALLENGE, RELATIONAL NEED, AND DEFENSE

Make an appointment

SENDER: I would like to talk about my childhood challenge, the need not met in childhood that I bring to my adult relationships, and the defense I use when I feel threatened by that need not being met. Is now a good time?

RECEIVER: Yes, I'm available now. (*If not now, state when and be available then.*)

Connect nonverbally

Sender and receiver make eye contact and take three deep breaths in sync.

Share a one-way appreciation

SENDER: Before I start, I would like to give you an appreciation. Is that ok?

RECEIVER: Yes.

SENDER: One thing I appreciate about you is that _____.

RECEIVER: *Mirror:* If I got it. You appreciate _____.
          Check for accuracy: Did I get it?
          Thank you for sharing that.

SENDER: Thanks for receiving it.

Share your childhood challenge

SENDER: First I would like to share my childhood challenge. When I was a child, I lived with caretakers who were generally **Neglectful** or **Intrusive** (*circle one*) and my challenge with them was _____ (*challenge you circled on My Childhood Challenge worksheet*).

Mirror and check for accuracy

RECEIVER: *Mirror:* Let me see if I've got it. When you were a child, you lived with caretakers who were _____ and your challenge with them was _____.
          Check for accuracy: Did I get it?

SENDER: Yes, you got it (*or, "You got most of it. I also said _____."*)

RECEIVER: *Show curiosity and ask:* Is there more about that?

SENDER: And when I recall that challenge, I remember feeling _____.

RECEIVER: *Mirror the feelings:* And when you remember that challenge, you remember feeling _____.
Checks for accuracy: Did I get it?
Show curiosity: Is there more about that?

Share and mirror the early childhood need

SENDER: Instead of that challenge and feeling, what I needed most from my caretakers was (*item circled on MY RELATIONAL NEED worksheet*). And if I had gotten that, what it would look like as a behavior is _____.

RECEIVER: *Mirror:* If I got that, instead of the challenge of _____ and the feeling of _____, what you needed most from them was _____, and if you had gotten that, what it would look like as a behavior is _____.
Check for accuracy: Did I get that?
Show curiosity: Is there more about that?

Share and mirror the early defense

SENDER: When I did not get that need met with that behavior, what scared me the most was _____, so I responded by **Maximizing or Minimizing** and tended to defend myself by (*item circled on Minimizers and Maximizers worksheet*) _____.
And, not getting that need met, I brought that NEED and that DEFENSE to my adult relationships.

RECEIVER: *Mirror:* Let me see if I've got it. When you did not get that need met with that behavior, what scared you the most was _____, so you DEFENDED yourself by responding as a Maximizer/Minimizer and tended to defend yourself by _____.
And you brought that NEED and that DEFENSE to your adult relationships.
Check for accuracy: Did I get it?

SENDER: Yes, you got it. (*Or "Yes, and I also said . . ."*)

RECEIVER: *Show curiosity and ask:* Is there more about that?
Continue until there is no more about that.

Summarize

RECEIVER: *Summarize:* Let me see if I got ALL of that. In summary, your caretakers were generally _____ and because of that your CHALLENGE with them was _____. When you remember that challenge, you feel _____. What you NEEDED from them was _____, and what that would look like as a BEHAVIOR is _____.
Not getting that BEHAVIOR from them, you biggest fear was

_____ and you DEFENDED yourself by becoming a Mini-mizer/Maximizer and tended to defend yourself by _____.

And you brought that NEED and that DEFENSE to your adult relationships.

Check for accuracy: Did I get it all?

SENDER: *Listen to the summary and verify if accurate.*

Yes, you got me. (*Or "The part you got was . . . and I also said . . ."*)

Validation

RECEIVER: *Validate:* You make sense, and what makes sense is that if your caretakers were _____, your CHALLENGE would be _____ and you would feel _____. It also makes sense that your relationship NEED would be _____ and as a BEHAV-IOR it would look like _____.

And, not getting your NEED met in your early years, it also makes sense that your biggest fear would be _____ and you would DEFEND yourself by becoming a _____ who tends to _____ and, finally, it really makes sense that you would bring your need, your feelings, and your defense to your adult rela-tionships. It also makes sense that if your best childhood expe-rience was _____, you would feel _____.

Is that an accurate validation?

SENDER: *Receive the validation and verify if accurate.*

Empathize

RECEIVER: *Express empathy:* And given that, I can imagine that if your RELATIONAL NEED of _____ was not met that you would feel _____, and defend yourself by _____, and I can also imagine that if your childhood need was met in your adult rela-tionships as a BEHAVIOR that looked like _____, you would FEEL (*glad, relieved, happy, connected, heard, etc.*) and no lon-ger fear _____, nor have to defend yourself by _____.

Check for accuracy: Are those your feelings?

Check for additional feelings: Are there other feelings?

SENDER: Yes. (*Or, "I also feel . . ."*)

Closing

RECEIVER: Thank you for sharing with me your childhood challenge and need and defense and how you would feel if that need was met in your adult relationships.

SENDER: Thank you for listening.

Give each other a one-minute hug and then breathe in sync for three deep breaths. Make eye contact on release. Switch roles.

Appendix 17

WORKSHEET: CHILDHOOD CHALLENGE, RELATIONAL NEED, AND DEFENSE (SUMMARY)

Instructions:
Please fill out the form using the Imago Dialogue process; check with your partner for accuracy.

1. Summarize your partner's childhood challenge and feeling.

2. Summarize the relational need your partner brought to your relationship and what it would look like as a behavior.

3. Describe your partner's childhood defense when that need was not met.

4. Record what your partner would feel if that need were met in your relationship.

5. Summarize your relational challenge and feeling.

6. Summarize the relational need you brought to your relationship and what it would look like as a behavior.

7. Describe your childhood defense when your need was not met.

8. Record what you would feel if your need were met in your relationship.

Appendix 18

DIALOGUE: THE PARENT–CHILD DIALOGUE

Make an appointment

SENDER: I would like to have a Parent–Child Dialogue. Are you available now?

Connect nonverbally

Sender and receiver make eye contact and take three deep breaths in sync.

Express an appreciation

SENDER: First, I would like to express an appreciation, which is _____.

RECEIVER: *Mirror:* You want to express an appreciation, which is _____. Did I get that?

SENDER: Yes. (*Or add what is missing.*)

RECEIVER: Thanks for your appreciation.

SENDER: Thanks for receiving it.

Begin the dialogue

RECEIVER (PARENT):   I am your mother/father. What is it like living with me? *If the chosen caregiver was dead or was not present, say:* What is it like living without me? *or* What is it like to be my child?

SENDER (CHILD):   Living with you is _____ ; *or,* Living without you is

_____.

RECEIVER (PARENT):   Let me see if I've got you. If I did, you said _____. Did I get you?

SENDER (CHILD):   Yes. (*Or "Yes, and I also said . . ."*)

RECEIVER (PARENT):   Is there more about that? *Continue sending, mirroring, and checking for accuracy until there is no more.*

Identify the worst part

RECEIVER (PARENT):   What is the worst part of all that for you?

SENDER (CHILD):   The worst part of all that for me is _____. When that happens I feel _____.

RECEIVER (PARENT):   So your deepest hurt with me is when I _____. When that happens you feel _____. Did I get all that?

SENDER (CHILD):   Yes. (*Or "Yes, and I also said . . ."*)

RECEIVER (PARENT): Let me see if I got that. You also said _____.
Did I get it all now?
SENDER (CHILD): Yes, you got it all.

Identify the best part

RECEIVER (PARENT): What are the good things you experience living with/
without me?
SENDER (CHILD): The good things I experience living with/without you are

_____.
When I experience that I feel _____.
RECEIVER (PARENT): So the good part of living with/without me is _____.
And when you experience that you feel _____.
SENDER (CHILD): Yes, you got it all.
RECEIVER (PARENT): What is the best part of living with/without me?
SENDER (CHILD): The best part of living with/without you is _____.
When I experience that I feel _____.
RECEIVER (PARENT): So the best part of living with/without me is _____.
And when you experience that you feel _____.
Did I get all that? Is there more about the good part?
SENDER (CHILD): Yes, you got it all.

Identify the need

RECEIVER (PARENT): So, as your parent, what do you need from me the most
that I don't give you and what would it look like if you got it?
SENDER (CHILD): What I need from you the most is _____.
And what that would look like is that you would _____.
(Describe a behavior that would meet your deepest need.)
RECEIVER (PARENT): If I got that, what you need most from me is _____.
And what that would look like is that I would _____. Did I
get that?
SENDER (CHILD): Yes, you got it.
RECEIVER (PARENT): Given your experience of living with/without me and
your deepest hurt, it makes sense that what you need from me
the most is _____ and if I did that you would experience

_____.
I can imagine, if I did that, you would feel _____.
Did I get that?
Are there other feelings?
SENDER (CHILD): Yes, those are my feelings (or "And I also feel _____.")
RECEIVER (PARENT): So, those are your feelings (and you also feel _____).

I want you to know that I want you to have your deepest needs met. As your parent, I thank you for sharing all that with me.

SENDER (CHILD): Thank you for listening.

DE-ROLE

RECEIVER: I am no longer your parent. As your partner, I can understand that living with your caretaker was _____ and the worst part was _____.
Given that, it makes sense that what you needed in childhood is _____ and if you got that you would feel _____.
I am glad to know that. I also get it that the best part of living with your caretakers was _____.
Did I get it?

SENDER: I am no longer your child. I am your partner. Yes, you got it all. Thank you for listening and being present with me.

RECEIVER: You're welcome. What do you need in our relationship that would begin to meet that need?

SENDER: What I need from you now is _____.

RECEIVER: If I got that, what you need in our relationship is _____. Did I get that?

SENDER: Yes, that is what I need in our relationship.

RECEIVER: Thank you for telling me.

SENDER: Thank you for asking and for listening.

Closure:

Give each other a one-minute, full body hug and take three breaths in sync. Make eye contact.

This is an "information only" process and not an agreement of any other kind. When all steps are completed, switch roles and repeat the dialogue steps with your partner.

WORKSHEET: SUMMARY OF PARTNER'S CHILDHOOD CHALLENGE AND NEEDS

Recalling the Parent–Child Dialogue you have just completed, summarize the following:

1. The rupture your partner experienced in childhood with their caretaker(s) was _____

   _____

2. The rupture you experienced in childhood was _____

   _____

3. What your partner needed from their caretaker(s) was _____

   _____

   and what it would look like as a behavior was _____

   _____

4. What you needed from your caretaker(s) was _____

   _____

   and what it would look like as a behavior was_____

   _____

5. What your partner needs from your relationship with you is _____

   _____

6. What you need from your relationship with your partner is _____

   _____

DIALOGUE: THE ZERO NEGATIVITY PLEDGE

Ask for Appointment

SENDER: Is now a good time to talk about removing negativity from our relationship?

RECEIVER: I'm available now. (*If not now, state when and be available then.*)

Connect nonverbally

Sender and Receiver make eye contact and take three deep breaths in sync.

Share an appreciation

SENDER: One thing I appreciate about you is _____.

Mirror and check for accuracy

RECEIVER: Let me see if I've got it. One thing you appreciate about me is

_____.

Did I get that?

State intention

SENDER: My intention is to remove negativity from our Space-Between and to commit to the Zero Negativity Pledge.

Mirror and check for accuracy

RECEIVER: If I got that, your intention is to remove negativity from our relationship and to sign the Zero Negativity Pledge.

Did I get that?

Deepen

SENDER: When I think about eliminating negativity in our relationship, I feel _____ (*use one word, such as glad, scared, mad, sad*).

And that feeling reminds me of _____.

And when I remember that, I think _____.

RECEIVER: *Express curiosity:* Is there more about that?

Summarize and check for accuracy

RECEIVER: Let me see if I got ALL of that. When you express your intention to remove all negativity from our relationship you feel _____.

And when you feel that, you remember _____.

And when you remember that, you think _____.
Did I get it all?

Validate

RECEIVER: And what makes sense is that when you think about removing all negativity from our relationship, you would feel _____.
And that would trigger you to remember _____.
And that would cause you to think _____.

Empathize

RECEIVER: And I imagine what you're feeling now about signing the Zero Negativity Pledge is _____.
Is that your feeling?
Are there other feelings?

Closing

SENDER: Thank you for listening.
RECEIVER: Thank you for sharing.

Give each other a one-minute hug, and breathe in sync for three deep breaths. Make eye contact on release.
Switch roles and repeat the process.

Appendix 21

CONTRACT: THE ZERO NEGATIVITY PLEDGE

The 30-Day Zero Negativity Pledge

We understand that "negativity" is any transaction that ruptures our connection, whether intentional or accidental.

We pledge to make our relationship a **Zone of Zero Negativity** for 30 days. To that end, we pledge to avoid any transactions that could be experienced as a put-down, rupturing our connection.

If we experience a rupture, we will send a gentle signal (bing, ouch, oops, wow!) to communicate that we have experienced a put-down and then begin repairing the rupture by resending the message or redoing the action.

We pledge to gift each other with three appreciations each day, no matter what!

Signatures:

_____

_____

Witness:

_____

Date: _____

NOTES ABOUT THE ZERO NEGATIVITY PLEDGE:
- Signing the Pledge does not mean that you cannot bring up issues. But you will learn a better way of dealing with conflict in therapy. In fact, it is through the Zero Negativity process that you will be able to talk about the issues without drowning in a sea of negativity.
- Keep in mind that the pledge is to keep your relationship free of negativity. You will be assessing your relationship, not each other.
- Using a calendar, at the end of each day, you and your partner use mirroring to share whether your *relationship* got a "negative" that day. If YES, draw a "frowning face" on the day. If NO, draw a "smiley face" on the day.
- If either or both of you registered a put-down, use the reconnecting process. If you successfully reconnect, write "RESET" over the frowning face and give each other a one-minute hug.

CALENDAR: 30-DAY ZERO NEGATIVITY CHALLENGE

Sunday	Monday	Tuesday	Wednesday	Thursday	Friday	Saturday

Appendix 23

WORKSHEET: THE SPACE-BETWEEN

The Space-Between is the intangible space between you and your partner. The more positive behaviors and qualities between you and your partner, the greater the ability to work through conflict and increase connection. As you begin to remove negativity from your relationship, it is important to intentionally acknowledge the positive qualities that are already in your relationship.

Instructions: Work separately. Using words, images, drawings etc., describe your experience of the Space-Between to complete the sentences below before your next session. *Remember:* Use **positive** descriptors (examples below).

The Space-Between Worksheet
1. The positive qualities that describe the Space-Between me and my partner include: _____ _____
1. The interactive behaviors we do together that create and sustain safety in our Space-Between include: _____ _____
2. The best quality I bring to our Space-Between is: _____ _____
3. The best behavior I bring to our Space-Between is: _____ _____
4. Three things I see my partner bringing to our Space-Between are: a. _____ b. _____ c. _____

Positive Descriptors of the Space-Between		
Safety	Admiration	Sex
Love	Idealization	Truth telling
Confirmation of otherness	Adoration	Honesty
Exchange of information	Nurturing	Closeness
Dialogue	Communion	Sharing
Intimacy	Responsibility	Approval
Empathy	Being present	Reciprocation
Mutuality	Making the other present	Comfort
Trust	Disclosure	Holding
Tone	Vulnerability	Validating
Inclusion	Play	Forgiveness

WORKSHEET: MY FRUSTRATIONS LIST

Instructions:
1. List your frustrations with your partner, using the stem "I get frustrated when you . . ."
2. Rate each frustration on a scale from 1 (mild) to 10 (intense).

My Frustrations With My Partner "I get frustrated when you . . ."	Rating

Appendix 25

WORKSHEET: MY PARTNER'S FRUSTRATIONS LIST

Instructions:
1. List the frustrations you think your partner has with you, using the stem "I think my partner gets frustrated when I . . ."
2. Rate each frustration on a scale from 1 (mild) to 10 (intense). Leave the last column blank for now.

My Partner's Frustrations With Me "I think my partner gets frustrated when I . . ."	My Rating	My Partner's Rating

WORKSHEET: THE CORE SCENE

THE CORE SCENE					
Column A			Column B		
My behaviors	My feelings	My defenses	My partner's behaviors	My partner's feelings	My partner's defenses

FLOW CHART: THE BEHAVIOR CHANGE REQUEST

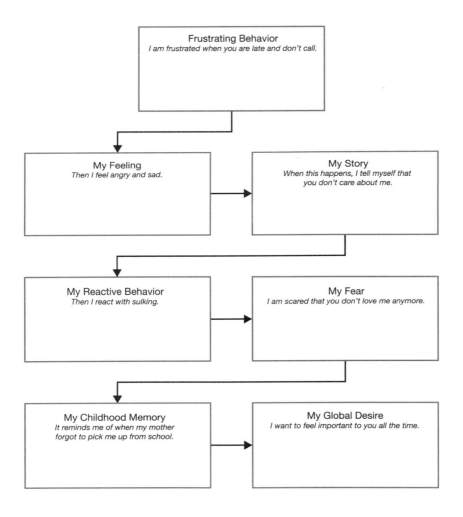

FLOW CHART: THE BEHAVIOR CHANGE REQUEST (CONTINUED)

Now list three behaviors that will satisfy the global desire.
Here, you generate three different requests, any of which would, if granted, help ease the frustration expressed earlier in this process. Not just any kind of request will do, however. All three requests must conform to the SMART formula:

- **S**pecific (an observable behavior)
- **M**easurable (you can count its frequency)
- **A**ttainable (do-able)
- **R**elevant (to the frustration expressed)
- **T**ime-limited (e.g., for the next month)

Behavior Change Requests
For the next three weeks, when you know you will be more than 30 minutes late, please give me a call at least 30 minutes before the time of our appointment to tell me. The request must be stated as a behavior, and it needs to be a SMART behavior.

_____

_____

_____

_____

_____

_____

NOTE: It is often the case that in the actual dialogue process, what you want as the three behaviors has changed. In that case, use the desired behaviors that arise organically in the dialogue.

Appendix 28

DIALOGUE: THE BEHAVIOR CHANGE REQUEST

Make an appointment

SENDER: I would like an appointment for a Behavior Change Request Dialogue about a frustration I am feeling. Are you available?

RECEIVER: I am available now (*or state when*).
Sender and receiver make eye contact and take three deep breaths in sync.

Intention

SENDER: I intend to stay connected to you during this Dialogue, and I appreciate your willingness to listen.

RECEIVER: I also intend to stay connected and appreciate your willingness to share a frustration with me using Imago Dialogue.

Express an appreciation

SENDER: First, I would like to express an appreciation which is _____.

RECEIVER: *Mirror:* You want to express an appreciation which is _____.
Did I get that?

SENDER: Yes. (*Or add what is missing.*)

RECEIVER: Thanks for your appreciation.

SENDER: Thanks for receiving it.

Express a frustration

SENDER: *State the frustration in ONE sentence. Remember, a frustration is a behavior your partner does which causes you discomfort.*
I get frustrated when _____.
Example: I get frustrated when I don't hear from you during the day and then you come home and watch TV without speaking to me.

RECEIVER: *Mirror:* Let me see if I've got you. If I did, you said your frustration is _____.
Check for Accuracy: Did I get that?
Takes a deep breath and says: I am ready to hear your frustration fully.

SENDER: *State the frustration fully, the feelings and thoughts you have, the story you make up.*
When I experience that _____.
I feel _____.

When I feel that, the story I tell myself is _____.

Example: When you don't call, I get angry and sad. When this happens, the story I tell myself is that you don't care about me.

Mirror the frustration

RECEIVER: *Mirror:* So, you are frustrated when I _____.

And when I do that you feel _____.

And when you feel that, the story you tell yourself is _____.

Check for accuracy: Did I get that?

Show curiosity: Is there more about that?

Sender: When you do that, I react by _____ (*describe a behavior or typical reaction you have*) in order to _____.

Example: When you do that, I react by withdrawing from you emotionally in order not to feel my fear of being abandoned.

RECEIVER: *Mirror only.*

The childhood connection

RECEIVER: Tell me what these feelings of _____ (*e.g., of abandonment, of being unloved, etc.*) remind you of in your childhood.

SENDER: *Take a minute to breathe deeply. When you are ready, recall a memory from childhood and the pain, hurt, fear, and anything else that comes up.*

When I feel _____ (*abandoned, alone, unloved, etc.*), it reminds me that, when I was little, my caretakers _____ (*describe a childhood memory or scene including your care-taker's behavior*).

And when that happened, I felt _____.

Receiver: *Give an accurate summary mirror from the beginning.*

You get frustrated when I _____.

The story you tell yourself is _____.

And then you react by _____.

In order to _____.

Those feelings of _____.

Remind you of your childhood when _____.

Did I get that?

Mirror any adjustments.

Validate the frustration

RECEIVER: You make sense and what makes sense is that when I frustrate you by _____.

You think _____ and feel _____ and react _____.

That reminds you of your childhood when _____.

Is that a good validation?

SENDER: Yes (or, *I want to add something*)

RECEIVER: I imagine that you might be feeling _____ or I imagine that you might have felt _____ Is that what you feel/felt?

Global Desire

RECEIVER: What do you wish would happen ALL the time instead of this frustration?

SENDER: *State your global, but unrealistic desire. Keep it large.* What I wish would happen ALL the time is _____.

Example: What I wish would happen all the time is that you would always love me in a way that makes me feel absolutely important and cherished.

The Behavior Change Request

RECEIVER: Tell me three behaviors that I can do that would help to satisfy that desire and remove that frustration.

SENDER: *State three behavior change requests. Make sure they are positive and SMART (specific, measurable, attainable, relevant, and time-limited).*

Example: For the next two weeks, I would like you to call me three times a week and tell me what you are doing and one thing you appreciate about me.

RECEIVER: *Mirror each request until it is 100% accurate.*

Then choose one request that you can do and say:

I will stretch and gift you by _____.

SENDER: *Mirror the "gift."*

Mutual gratitude

SENDER: Thank you for being willing to give me this gift.

It will begin to heal my childhood hurt of _____.

And reduce my fear of _____.

And help me feel _____.

Example: It will begin to heal my childhood hurt of feeling abandoned and invisible, reduce my fear of losing you, and help me to feel loved and valued.

Receiver: Mirror, then say:

Thank you for giving me this opportunity to stretch for you. It will help me overcome my fear of _____.

And help me grow into being a more _____ person/partner.
Example: It will help me overcome my fear of closeness and help me grow into being a more connected, considerate person and a more available partner to you.

SENDER: Thank you for listening.

Closing

Give each other a one-minute hug, and breathe in sync for three deep breaths. Make eye contact on release.

Be sure to record your requests and gifts in a journal or a separate piece of paper.

WORKSHEET: OPPORTUNITIES FOR CHANGE IN OUR SPACE-BETWEEN

OPPORTUNITIES
List 3 things that **need to be removed (or modified)** from your "relationship space." *Examples: social media, overworking, emailing, blaming, in-laws, reactivity, constructive criticism, television, preoccupation with children, etc.*
1.
2.
3.
Gifts of Change
I **will remove** (*list one of the opportunities for change above*) **from the Space-Between us:**   _____   **To do that, I will** (*list a positive and SMART behavior*):   _____
The SMART formula:
✓ Specific (an observable behavior) ✓ Measurable (you can count its frequency) ✓ Attainable (do-able) ✓ Relevant (to the frustration expressed) ✓ Time-limited (e.g., for the next month)

Appendix 30

WORKSHEET: CARING BEHAVIORS

Using the chart below, identify behaviors that your partner is already doing that make you feel cared about and loved. List as many as you can that are *specific, concrete, positive, and that happen with some regularity.*

Examples: *refill my coffee cup when it is empty; massage my back; tell me you love me.* In the time period column, write PR for present behavior. Ignore the "Willing" column for now. Continue by listing caring behaviors that your partner used to do in the past, especially in the romantic love phase of your relationship, but is no longer doing. Be specific, descriptive, positive, and quantitative (how much, how often). Examples: *wrote me love letters on special occasions; held my hand when we walked every morning; brought me flowers occasionally for no reason.* In the time period column, write PA for past behavior.

Willing ✓	Time Period PA (Past) PR (Present)	I feel/felt loved and cared about when you . . .

Appendix 31

DIALOGUE: CARING BEHAVIORS

Make an appointment

SENDER: I would like to talk about one thing you do that makes me feel cared about and loved. Is now a good time?

RECEIVER: I'm available now. (*If not now, state when and be available then.*)

Connect nonverbally

Sender and receiver make eye contact, soften eyes, and hold gaze for three deep breaths.

Send, mirror, and check accuracy

Focus only on the caring behavior and use "I" language and positive words.

SENDER: I feel/felt cared about and loved when you _____.

RECEIVER: *Mirror:* Let me see if I got that. If I did, you said _____.
          Check for accuracy: Did I get that?

SENDER: Yes, you got me.
          Resend or modify any parts not clearly received.

RECEIVER: *Show curiosity:* Is there more about that?

SENDER: Yes, when you do/did that, I feel/felt _____.

RECEIVER: *Mirror:* If I got it, you said when you experience/d that you feel/felt _____.
          Check for accuracy: Did I get that?
          Show curiosity: Is there more about that?

SENDER: Yes, and it reminds me of something from my childhood, which is _____.

RECEIVER: *Mirror, check for accuracy, and invite more.*
          Both partners continue the process until the sender agrees that the receiver has "got it" and there is "no more."

Summarize

RECEIVER: Let me see if I got all of that. In summary, you are saying

          _____.

          Did I get it all?

SENDER: Yes, you got it all.
          Resend if necessary: "The part you got was _____ and I also said _____."

Validate

RECEIVER: You make sense, and what makes sense is _____.
Is that a good validation?

SENDER: *Listen and receive validation.*

Empathize

RECEIVER: I imagine you might be feeling _____.
Is that the feeling?
Do you have more feelings?

Closing

RECEIVER: Thank you for sharing.

SENDER: Thank you for listening.

Give each other a one-minute hug, and breathe in sync for three deep breaths. Make eye contact on release.

When all the steps are completed, switch roles and repeat the process.

Appendix 32

WORKSHEET: POSITIVE FLOODING

POSITIVE FLOODING WORKSHEET			
Physical Characteristics	Personality Traits	Behaviors	Global Affirmations
I love your beautiful blue eyes!	*You are the kindest person I know.*	*You are immensely hard-working.*	*I have never loved anyone else the way I love you!*
I love the way your hair looks and smells.	*I adore your sense of humor.*	*I love it when you call me from work.*	*You are the only person I would ever want to be with!*

References

Ananthaswamy, A. (2018). *Through two doors at once: The elegant experiment that captures the enigma of our quantum reality.* Dutton.

Asch, S. E. (1946). Forming impressions of personality. *The Journal of Abnormal and Social Psychology, 41*(3), 258–290. http://doi.org/10.1037/h0055756

Atkinson, B. J. (2013). Mindfulness training and the cultivation of secure, satisfying couple relationships. *Couple and Family Psychology: Research and Practice, 2*(2), 73–94. https://doi.org/10.1037/cfp0000002

Atzil, S., Gao, W., Fradkin, I., & Barrett, L. F. (2018), Growing a Social Brain. Nature Human Behaviour, 2, 624-626.

Balon, R. (2016). Is infidelity biologically driven? *Current Sexual Health Report, 8,* 176–180. http://doi.org/10.1007/s11930-016-0084-z

Bateson, G., Jackson, D. D., Haley, J., & Weakland, J. (1956). Toward a theory of schizophrenia. *Behavioral Science, 1,* 251–264. https://doi.org/10.1002/bs.3830010402

Baumrind, D. (1971). Current patterns of parental authority. *Developmental Psychology, 4*(1, Pt.2), 1–103. http://doi.org/10.1037/h0030372

Becker, M., & Shalgi, B. (2013). On being, disappearing, and becoming: A journey of surrender. *Psychoanalytic Dialogues, 23*(4). http://doi.org/10.1080/10481885.2013.810499

Beier, J. S., & Spelke, E. S. (2012). Infants' developing understanding of social gaze. *Child development, 83*(2), 486–496.

Bennett, M. P., & Lengacher, C. (2008). Humor and laughter may influence health: III. Laughter and health outcomes. *Evidence-Based Complementary & Alternative Medicine (Ecam), 5*(1), 37–40. http://doi.org/10.1093/ecam/nem041

Berk, L., Tan, S., Napier, B., & Evy, W. (1989). Eustress of mirthful laughter modifies natural killer cell activity. *Clinical Research, 37,* 115A.

Berne, E. (1964). *Games people play: The basic handbook of transactional analysis.* Ballantine Books.

Bohm, D., & Hiley, B. J. (1995). *The undivided universe.* Routledge.

Bohm, David, (1996). *On dialogue.* Routledge, NY.

Bowen, M. (1978). *Family therapy in clinical practice.* Jason Aronson.

Bowlby, J. (1988). *A secure base: Parent-child attachment and healthy human development.* Basic Books.

Branden, N. (1983). *If you could hear what I cannot say.* Bantam.

Buber, M. (1947). *Between man and man. Routledge.*

Buber, M. (1958). *I and thou.* (R. G. Smith, Trans.). Charles Scribner's Sons.

Burton, L., & Lent, J. (2016). The use of vision boards as a therapeutic intervention. *Journal of Creativity in Mental Health, 11*(1), 52–65. https://doi.org/10.1080/15401383.2015.1092901

Buss, D. M. (2013). The science of human mating strategies: An historical perspective. *Psychological Inquiry, 24*(3), 171–177. http://doi.org/10.1080/1047840X.2013.819552

Calaprice, A. (2005). *The new quotable Einstein*, Princeton University Press, p. 206,

Carlson, R. (1996). *Don't sweat the small stuff and it's all small stuff: Simple ways to keep the little things from taking over your life.* Black Dog & Leventhal.

Carr, Laurie & Iacoboni, Marco & Dubeau, Marie-Charlotte & Mazziotta, John & Lenzi, Gian. (2003). Neural Mechanisms of Empathy in Humans: A Relay from Neural Systems for Imitation to Limbic Areas. Proceedings of the National Academy of Sciences of the United States of America. 100. 5497-502. 10.1073/pnas.0935845100.

Clore, G. L., & Huntsinger, J. R. (2007). How emotions inform judgment and regulate thought. *Trends in Cognitive Sciences, 11*(9), 393–399. https://doi.org/10.1016/j.tics.2007.08.005

Cobb, Matthew, (2020), *The idea of the brain.* Basic Books.

Conradt, E. (2017). Using principles of behavioral epigenetics to advance research on early-life stress. *Child Development Perspectives, 11*, 107–112. http://doi.org/10.1111/cdep.12219

Cory, G. A., Jr., & Gardner, R., Jr. (Eds.). (2002). *Human evolution, behavior, and intelligence. The evolutionary neuroethology of Paul MacLean: Convergences and frontiers.* Praeger Publishers/Greenwood Publishing Group.

Cox, B., & Forshaw, J. (2012). *The quantum universe: Everything that can happen does happen.* DaCapo Press.Cozolino, L. J., (2002). *The neuroscience of psychotherapy: Building and rebuilding the human brain.* W. W. Norton & Co.

Decety, J. (2010). The neurodevelopment of empathy in humans. *Developmental Neuroscience, 32*, 257–267. http://doi.org/10.1159/000317771

Doidge, N. (2007). *The brain that changes itself: Stories of personal triumph from the frontiers of brain science.* Penguin Books.

Eisberg, R., & Resnick, R. (1985). *Quantum physics of atoms, molecules, solids, nuclei, and particles.* John Wiley & Sons.

Erikson, E. H. (1959). *Identity and the life cycle.* International Universities Press.

Fairbairn, W. R. D. (1952). *Psychological studies of the personality.* Routledge & Kegan Paul.

Fenker, D. B., Frey, J. U., Schuetze, H., Heipertz, D., Heinze, H., & Duzel, E. (2008). Novel Scenes Improve Recollection and Recall of Words. *Journal of Cognitive Neuroscience, 20*(7), 1250–1265. https://doi.org/10.1162/jocn.2008.20086

Fincham, F. D., & Beach, S. R. H. (2010). Marriage in the New Millennium: A Decade in Review. *Journal of Marriage & Family, 72*(3), 630–649. https://doi.org/10.1111/j.1741-3737.2010.00722.x

Fisher, H. (2016). *Anatomy of love: A natural history of mating, marriage, and why we stray.* New York, NY: W. W. Norton & Co.

Fisher, M., Voracek, M., Rekkas, P. V., & Cox, A. (2008). Sex differences in feelings of guilt arising from infidelity. *Evolutionary Psychology, 6*(3), 436–446. https://doi.org/10.1177/147470490800600308Fivush, R., and Haden, C. A. (Eds). (2003). *Autobiographical memory and the construction of a narrative self: Developmental and cultural perspectives.* Lawrence Erlbaum.

Freud, S., & Breuer, J. (1895). *Studies on Hysteria. SE, 2,* 48–106.

Gause, G. F. (1934). *The struggle for existence.* The Williams & Wilkins Company.

Gavin, H. (2011). Sticks and stones may break my bones: The effects of emotional abuse. *Journal of Aggression, Maltreatment & Trauma, 20*(5), 503–529. https://doi.org/10.1080/10926771.2011.592179

Gendlin, E. T. (1982). *Focusing.* Bantam.

Genzel, L., Rossato, J. I., Jacobse, J., Grieves, R. M., Spooner, P. A., Battaglia, F. P., Fernández, G., & Morris, R. G. M. (2017). The yin and yang of memory consolidation: Hippocampal and neocortical. *Plos Biology, 15*(1), 1–26. https://doi.org/10.1371/journal.pbio.2000531Gergen, K. (2001). *Social Construction in Context.* London: Sage.

Gilligan, C. (1982). *In a Different Voice.* Harvard University Press.

Glass, S. P., & Wright, T. L. (1985). Sex differences in types of extramarital involvement and marital dissatisfaction. *Sex Roles: A Journal of Research, 12*(9-10), 1101–1119. https://doi.org/10.1007/BF00288108

Goff, P. (2019). *Galileo's error: Foundations for a new science of consciousness.* Pantheon Books.

Goleman, D. (2005). *Emotional intelligence: Why it can matter more than IQ.* Bantam Books.

Gottman, J. M. (1993). A theory of marital dissolution and stability. *Journal of Family Psychology, 7*(1), 57–75. https://doi.org/10.1037/0893-3200.7.1.57

Gottman, J. M. (1994). *What predicts divorce? The Relationship between marital processes and marital outcomes.* Psychology Press.

Gottman, J. M. (1999). *The seven principles for making marriage work.* Harmony House.

Gottman, J. M., Coan, J., Carrère, S., & Swanson, C. (1998). Predicting marital happiness and stability from newlywed interactions. *Journal of Marriage and the Family, 60,* 5–22.

Grande, D. (2017, December 6). Couples therapy: Does it really work? Psychology Today. https://www.psychologytoday.com/us/blog/in-it-together/201712/couples-therapy-does-it-really-work

Greenberg, L. S. (2004). Emotion–focused therapy. *Clinical Psychology & Psychotherapy, 11*(1), 3–16. https://doi.org/10.1002/cpp.388

Hamerman, S., & Ludwig, S. (2000). Emotional abuse and neglect. In R. M. Reece (Ed.), *Treatment of child abuse: Common ground for mental health, medical, and legal practitioners* (pp. 201–210). Johns Hopkins University Press.

Hardin, G. (1960). The Competitive Exclusion Principle. *Science, 131*(3409), 1292–1297. https://doi.org/10.1126/science.131.3409.1292

Hatfield, E., Cacioppo, J., & Rapson, R. (1994). *Emotional contagion.* Cambridge University Press.

Hendrix, H., & Hunt, H. L. (2004). *Receiving love.* Atria.

Horgan, J. (2018, June 6). *Do our questions create the world?* Scientific American. https://blogs.scientificamerican.com/cross-check/do-our-questions-create-the-world/

Hudgins, M. K., & Kiesler, D. J. (1987). Individual experiential psychotherapy: An analogue validation of the intervention module of psychodramatic doubling. *Psychotherapy: Theory, Research, Practice, Training, 24*(2), 245–255. https://doi.org/10.1037/h0085711.

Huston, T. L., & Vangelisti, A. L. (1991). Socioemotional behavior and satisfaction in marital relationships: A longitudinal study. *Journal of Personality and Social Psychology, 61*(5), 721–733. https://doi.org/10.1037/0022-3514.61.5.721

Ishikawa, M., & Itakura, S. (2018). Observing others' gaze direction affects infants' preference for looking at gazing- or gazed-at faces. *Frontiers in Psychology, 9*(1503). https://doi.org/10.3389/fpsyg.2018.01503

Ito, T. A., Larsen, J. T., Smith, N. K., & Cacioppo, J. T. (1998). Negative information weighs more heavily on the brain: The negativity bias in evaluative categorizations. *Journal of Personality and Social Psychology, 75*(4), 887–900. https://doi.org/10.1037/0022-3514.75.4.887

Iwamoto, S. K., Alexander, M., Torres, M., Irwin, M. I., Christakis, N. A., & Nishi, A. (2020). Mindfulness Meditation Activates Altruism. *Scientific Reports, 10,* 6511. https://doi.org/10.1038/s41598-020-62652-1

Jarius, S., & Wildemann, B. (2015). And Pavlov still rings a bell: Summarising the evidence for the use of a bell in Pavlov's iconic experiments on classical conditioning. *Journal of Neurology, 262,* 2177–2178. https://doi.org/10.1007/s00415-015-7858-5

Joel, S., Eastwick, P., Allison, C.J. Arriaga, X.B., Baker, Z. G., Bar-Kalifa, E. . . . Wolf, S. (2020). Machine learning uncovers the most robust self-report predictors of relationship quality across 43 longitudinal couples studies. *PNAS,* https://doi.org/10.1073/pnas.1917036117

Johnson, S. (2017). The new era of couple therapy – innovation indeed. *Person-Centered & Experiential Psychotherapies, 16*(1), 39–49. https://doi.org/10.1080/14779757.2017.1298050

Joshanloo, M. (2018). Fear and fragility of happiness as mediators of the relationship between insecure attachment and subjective well-being. *Personality and Individual Differences, 123,* 115–118. http://doi.org:10.1016/j.paid.2017.11.016

Kafatos, M. & Nadeau, R. (1990). *The conscious universe: Part and whole in modern physical theory.* Springer.

Kant, I. (1999). *Critique of pure reason.* (P. Guyer & A. W. Wood, Trans. & Eds.). Cambridge University Press.

Keng, S. L., Smoski, M. J., & Robins, C. J. (2011). Effects of mindfulness on psychological health: A review of empirical studies. *Clinical Psychology Review, 31,* 1041–1056. http://doi.org/10.1016/j.cpr.2011.04.006

Klein, M. (1952). *Some Theoretical Conclusions regarding the Emotional Life of the Infant.* In: The Writings of Melanie Klein, Volume 8: Envy and Gratitude and Other Works, Hogarth Press, London, 61-94.

Kohut, H. (1971). *The Analysis of the Self: A Systematic Approach to the Psychoanalytic Treatment of Narcissistic Personality Disorders.* Chicago, IL: The University of Chicago Press.

Krauss, L. M. (2012). *A universe from nothing: Why there is something rather than nothing.* Free Press.

Kubala, K. H., Christianson, J. P., Kaufman, R. D., Watkins, L. R., & Maier, S. F. (2012). Short- and long-term consequences of stressor controllability in adolescent rats. *Behavioral Brain Research, 234*(2), 278–284.

Kubler-Ross, E. (1973). *On death and dying.* Routledge.

Laing, R. D. (1961). *The self and other: Further studies in sanity and madness.* Quadrangle Books.

Laing, R. D. (1969). *The Divided self: An existential study in sanity and madness.* Penguin Books.

Laing, R. D. (1970). *Knots.* Penguin Books.

Lally, P., Van Jaarsveld, H. M., Potts, H. W. W., & Wardle, J. (2009). How habits are formed: Modeling habit formation in the real world. *European Journal of Social Psychology, 40*(6), 998–1009. https://doi.org/10.1002/ejsp.674.

Lange, B. C. L., Callinan, L. S. & Smith, M. V. (2018). Adverse Childhood Experiences and Their Relation to Parenting Stress and Parenting Practices. *Community Mental Health Journal, 55,* 651–662. https://doi.org/10.1007/s10597-018-0331-z

Lasch, C. (1978). *The age of narcissism: American life in the age of diminishing expectation*. W. W. Norton & Co.Laureys, S. & Tononi, G., (2008). *The Neurology of Consciousness: Cognitive Neuroscience and Neuropathology*. Academic Press.

LeDoux, J. (1996). *The emotional brain: The mysterious underpinnings of emotional life*. Simon and Schuster.

Lemanski, M. (2001). *A history of addiction and recovery in the United States: Traditional Treatments and effective alternatives*. See Sharp Press.

Lewin, K. (1951). *Field theory in social science: Selected theoretical papers* (D. Cartwright Ed.). Harpers.

Linehan, M. M., & Dimeff, L. (2001). Dialectical behavior therapy in a nutshell. *The California Psychologist, 34,* 10–13.

Mace, David R. (1960). *Marriage, East and West*. Doubleday.

Mausbach, B. T., Moore, R., Roesch, S., Cardenas, V., & Patterson, T. L. (2010). The relationship between homework compliance and therapy outcomes: An updated meta-analysis. *Cognitive Therapy and Research, 34*(5), 429–438. https://doi.org/10.1007/s10608-010-9297-z

McCarthy, G., & Maughan, B. (2010). Negative childhood experiences and adult love relationships: The role of internal working models of attachment. *Attachment & Human Development, 12*(5), 445–461. https://doi.org/10.1080/14616734.2010.501968

McKenzie, S. & Eichenbaum, H. (2011). Consolidation and reconsolidation: two lives of memories? *Neuron, 71*(2), 224–233. https://doi.org/10.1016/j.neuron.2011.06.037

McTaggart, L. (2011). *The bond*. Free Press.

Merleau-Ponty, M. (2002). Phenomenology of Perception: London: Routledge. (Original work published in 1945).

Miller, J. B., & Stiver, I. P. (1997). *The healing connection: How women form relationships in therapy and in life*. Beacon Press.

Misner, C. W., Thorne, K, S., & Wheeler, J.A., (1973). *Gravitation, Part 3*. New York: McMillan.

Mitchell, S. A., & Aron, L. (Eds.). (1999). *Relational perspectives book series, Vol. 14. Relational psychoanalysis: The emergence of a tradition*. Analytic Press.

Mitchell, S. A., & Black, M. J. (1995). *Freud and beyond: A history of modern psychoanalytic thought*. Basic Books.

Montag, C., Gallinat, J.,& Heinz, A. (2008). *Theodore Lipps and the Concept of Empathy, 1851-1914. American Journal of Psychiatry, 165(10), 1261.*

Numan R. (1978). Cortical-limbic mechanisms and response control: a theoretical review. *Physiological Psychology, 6*(4), 445–470. https://doi.org/10.3758/BF03326750

O'Neill, N., & O'Neill, G. (1972). *Open Marriage: A New Lifestyle for Couples.* M. Evans & Co.

Panksepp, J (2002). Foreword "*The Evolutionary Neuroethology of Paul MacLean*" (G.A Gory & R. Gardner, eds), Praeger, London.

Parker, S. C., Nelson, B. W., Epel, E., & Siegel, D. J. (2015). The science of presence: A central mediator in the interpersonal benefits of mindfulness. In K. W. Brown, J. D. Creswell, & R. M. Ryan (Eds.), *Handbook of mindfulness: Theory, research, and practice* (pp. 225–244). Springer.

Pavlov I. P. (1927). Conditioned reflexes. An investigation of the physiological activity of the cerebral cortex. (G. V. Anrep, Trans.). Oxford University Press.

Peterson, C., Maier, S. F., & Seligman, M. E. P. (1995). *Learned helplessness: A theory for the age of personal control.* Oxford University Press.

Ploog D. W. (2003). The place of the triune brain in psychiatry. Physiologic. Behavior. 79, 487–493.

Porges, S. W. (2003). The Polyvagal Theory: Phylogenetic contributions to social behavior. *Physiology & Behavior, 79*(3), 503–513. https://doi.org/10.1016/S0031-9384(03)00156-2

Porges, S. W. (2011). *The polyvagal theory: Neurophysiological Foundations of emotions, attachment, communication, and self-regulation.* W. W. Norton.

Price J. (2002). "The triune brain, escalation, de-escalation strategies, and mood disorders," in The Evolutionary Neuroethology of Paul MacLean. Convergences and Frontiers, eds Cory G. A.

Prochaska, J. O., & DiClemente, C. C. (2005). The transtheoretical approach. In J. C. Norcross & M. R. Goldfried (Eds.), *Handbook of Psychotherapy Integration* (pp. 147–171). Oxford University Press.

Quiller-Couch, A. T. (1919) *The oxford book of English verse.* Clarendon. Online edition, 1999 by bartleby.com. https://www.bartleby.com/101/536.html.

Ranganathan, V. K., Siemionow V., Liu J. Z., Sahgal V., & Yue G. H. (2004). From mental power to muscle power—gaining strength by using the mind. *Neuropsychologia, 42*(7), 944–956.

Rogers, C. (1951). *Client-centered therapy: Its current practice, implications and theory.* Constable.

Rogers, C. (1959). A theory of therapy, personality and interpersonal relationships as developed in the client-centered framework. In S. Koch (Ed.), *Psychology: A study of a science. vol. 3: Formulations of the person and the social context, pp. 184-256.* McGraw Hill.

Ross, L., & Ward, A. (1995). Psychological barriers to dispute resolution. In M. P. Zanna (Ed.), *Advances in experimental social psychology, Vol. 27* (pp. 255–304). Academic Press. https://doi.org/10.1016/S0065-2601(08)60407-4

Roth-Hanania, R., Davidov, M., & Zahn-Waxler, C. (2011). Empathy development from 8 to 16 months: Early signs of concern for others. *Infant Behavior and Development, 34*(3), 447–458.

Rush, F. (1980). *The Best Kept Secret: The Sexual Abuse of Children*, New York: Prentice Hall.

Rutherford, E. (1911). The scattering of α and β particles by matter and the structure of the atom, *The London, Edinburgh, and Dublin Philosophical Magazine and Journal of Science, 21*(125), 669–688. https://doi.org/10.1080/14786440508637080

Saive, A. L., Royet, J. P., & Plailly, J. (2014). A review on the neural bases of episodic odor memory: from laboratory-based to autobiographical approaches. *Frontiers in Behavioral Neuroscience, 8*, 240. https://doi.org/10.3389/fnbeh.2014.00240

Schnarch, D. M. (1991). *Constructing the sexual crucible: An integration of sexual and marital therapy.* W. W. Norton & Co.

Schnarch, D., & Regas, S. (2012). The crucible differentiation scale: Assessing differentiation in human relationships. *Journal of Marital & Family Therapy, 38*(4), 639–652. https://doi.org/10.1111/j.1752-0606.2011.00259.x

Schwartz, G & Woollacott, M. H. (Eds). (2019). Is consciousness primary? Advances in Postmaterialist Sciences, Vol. 1.

Seligman, M. E. P., & Groves, D. P. (1970). Nontransient learned helplessness. *Psychonomic Science, 19*(3), 191–192. https://doi.org/10.3758/BF03335546

Sheldon, K. M., & Lyubomirsky, S. (2006). How to increase and sustain positive emotion: The effects of expressing gratitude and visualizing best possible selves. *The Journal of Positive Psychology, 1*(2), 73–82. https://doi.org/10.1080/17439760500510676

Siegel, D. J. (2006). An interpersonal neurobiology approach to psychotherapy: How awareness, mirror neurons and neural plasticity contribute to the development of well-being. *Psychiatric Annals, 36*(4), 248–258. https://doi.org/10.3928/00485713-20060401-06

Siegel, D. J. (2007). *The mindful brain: Reflection and attunement in the cultivation of well-being.* W. W. Norton & Co.

Siegel, D.J. (2020). *The developing mind: How relationships and the brain interact to shape who we are.* The Guilford Press.

Siegel, D. J. (2012). *Pocket guide to interpersonal neurobiology: An integrative handbook of the mind.* W. W. Norton & Co.

Skinner, B. F. (1938). *The behavior of organisms: an experimental analysis.* Appleton-Century.

Skirry, J. (n.d). *Rene Descartes: The mind-body distinction.* The Internet Encyclopedia of Philosophy. https://iep.utm.edu/descmind/#H4. Retrieved August 3, 2020.

Slatcher, R. B., Selcuk, E., & Ong, A. D. (2015). Perceived partner responsive-ness predicts diurnal cortisol profiles 10 years later. *Psychological Science*, 26(7), 972–982. https://doi.org/ 10.1177/0956797615575022

Spangler, D. (2009). *The laws of manifestation: A consciousness classic*. Red Wheel/Weiser (Original work published 1975).

Staub, E. (1987). Commentary on Part 1. In N. Eisenberg & J. Strayer (Eds.), *Cambridge studies in social and emotional development. Empathy and its development* (pp. 103–115). Cambridge University Press.

Stein, M. I. (1947). The use of a sentence completion test for the diagnosis of personality. *Journal of Clinical Psychology, 3*, 47–56. http://doi.org/bn5sjk

Storbeck, J., & Clore, G. L. (2008). Affective arousal as information: How affec-tive arousal influences judgments, learning, and memory. *Social and Per-sonality Psychology Compass, 2*(5), 1824–1843. https://doi.org/10.1111/j.1751-9004.2008.00138.x

Strong, T., & Pyle, N. (2009). Constructing a conversational "miracle": Exam-ining the "miracle question" as it is used in therapeutic dialogue. *Jour-nal of Constructivist Psychology, 22*(4), 328–353. https://doi.org/10.1080/10720530903114001

Sullivan, H. S. (1953). *The interpersonal theory of psychiatry*. W. W. Norton & Co.

Sullivan, J.W.N. (1931, January 25). Interviews with great scientists. *The Observer*, p. 17.

Sullivan, R., Wilson, D. A., Feldon, J., Yee, B. K., Meyer, U., Richter-Levin, G., . . . Braun, K. (2006). The International Society for Developmental Psy-chobiology annual meeting symposium: Impact of early life experiences on brain and behavioral development. *Developmental psychobiology, 48*(7), 583–602. doi:10.1002/dev.20170

Symonds, P. M. (1947). The sentence completion test as a projective technique. *The Journal of Abnormal and Social Psychology, 42*(3), 320–329. https://doi.org/10.1037/h0054808

Tierney, A. L., & Nelson, C. A., 3rd (2009). Brain development and the role of experience in the early years. *Zero to three, 30*(2), 9–13.

Vaish, A., Grossmann, T., & Woodward, A. (2008). Not all emotions are created equal: The negativity bias in social-emotional development. *Psychological Bulletin, 134*(3), 383–403. https://doi.org/10.1037/0033-2909.134.3.383

Vermetten, E., & Bremner J. D. (2003). Olfaction as a traumatic reminder in posttraumatic stress disorder: Case reports and review. *The Jour-nal of Clinical Psychiatry, 64*(2), 202–207. https://doi.org/10.4088/JCP.v64n0214

Vischer, R. (1873). *On the Optical Sense of Form: A Contribution to Aes-thetics. In Empathy, Form, and Space. Problems in German Aesthetics,*

1873-1893. Harry Francis Mallgrave and Eleftherios Ikonomou (eds., trans.). Santa Monica, California: Getty Center for the History of Art and the Humanities. 1994.

Visual Perception (n.d.). In Wikipedia. Retrieved August 3, 2020, from https://en.wikipedia.org/wiki/Visual_perception#:~:text=In%20humans%20and%20a%20number%20of%20other%20mammals%2C,for%20the%20conversion%20of%20light%20into%20neuronal%20signals.

Wald, G. (1957). *The origins of optical activity.* Annals of the New York Academy of Sciences, 69: 352-368. doi:10.1111/j.1749-6632.1957.tb49671.x

Waldinger, Robert (November 15, 2015). What makes a good life? Lessons from the longest study on happiness. Retrieved from https://www.ted.com/talks/robert_waldinger_what_makes_a_good_life_lessons_from_the_longest_study_on_happiness?language=en

Wheeler, J.A. (1986). How Come the Quantum?[a] Annals of the New York Academy of Sciences, 480: 304-316. doi:10.1111/j.1749-6632.1986.tb12434.x.

Wheeler, J. A. (2001). "John Wheeler", In The Voice Of Genius: Conversations With Nobel Scientists And Other Luminaries , Brian, D. (ed). New York:Perseus.

White, W. L. (2014). *Slaying the dragon: The history of addiction treatment and recovery in America* (2nd ed.). Chestnut Health Systems.

Winnicott, D. W. (1960). The theory of the parent-child relationship, The *International Journal of Psychoanalysis. 41,* 585–595.

Zeman, A. (2004). *Consciousness: A Users Guide.* Yale University Press.

Züst, M. A., Colella, P., Reber, T. P., Vuilleumier, P., Hauf, M., Ruch, S., & Henke, K. (2015). Hippocampus is place of interaction between unconscious and conscious memories. *Plos One, 10*(3), 1–19. https://doi.org/10.1371/journal.pone.0122459

Resources

Bell, J. S. (1987). *Speakable and unspeakable in quantum mechanics.* Cambridge University Press.

Biglan, A., Flay, B. R., Embry, D. D., & Sandler, I. N. (2012). The critical role of nurturing environments for promoting human well-being. *The American Psychologist, 67*(4), 257–271. http://doi.org/10.1037/a0026796

Binetti, N., Harrison, C., Coutrot, A., Johnston, A., & Mareschal, I. (2016). Pupil dilation as an index of preferred mutual gaze duration. *Royal Society of Open Science.* http://doi.org/10.1098/rsos.160086

Capra, F. (1975). *The Tao of physics: An exploration of the parallels between modern physics and eastern mysticism.* Shambhala Publications.

Clauser, J. F., Horne, M. A., Shimony, A., Holt, R. A. (1970). Proposed experiment to test local hidden variable theories. *Physical Review Letters, 24*(549). https://doi.org/10.1103/PhysRevLett.24.549

DePaulo, B. (2017, February 02). What is the divorce rate, really? *Psychology Today.* https://www.psychologytoday.com/us/blog/living-single/201702/what-is-the-divorce-rate-really

Domes, G., Steiner, A., Porges, S. W., & Heinrichs, M. (2013). Oxytocin differentially modulates eye gaze to naturalistic social signals of happiness and anger. *Psychoneuroendocrinology, 38*(7), 1198–1202. http://doi.org/10.1016/j.psyneuen.2012.10.002

Farroni, T., Csibra, G., Simion, F., & Johnson, M. H. (2002). Eye contact detection in humans from birth. *Proceedings of the National Academy of Sciences of the United States of America.* http://doi.org/10.1073/pnas.152159999

Freud, S. (1937). Analysis terminable and interminable. *The International Journal of Psychoanalysis, 18,* 373–405.

Goldberger, N. R., Tarule, J. M., Clinchy McVicker, B., & Belenky, M. F. (Eds.). (1996). *Knowledge, difference, and power: Essays inspired by "women's ways of knowing."* Basic Books.

Gottman, J. M. (1995). *Why marriages succeed or fail: And how you can make yours last.* Simon & Schuster.

Guntrip, H. (1969). *Schizoid phenomena, object-relations, and the self.* International Universities Press.

Hendrix, H. (1996). The evolution of Imago Relationship Therapy: A personal and theoretical journey. *The Journal of Imago Relationship Therapy, 1*(1), 1–18.

Hendrix, H. & Hunt, H.L. (2019). *Getting the love you want: A guide for couples.* Henry Holt & Co. (Original work published 1988).

Hendrix. H, & Hunt, H. L. (2013). *Making marriage simple: Ten truths for changing the relationship you have into the one you want.* Harmony.

Hunt, H. (2001). Relationship as a living laboratory. *The Journal of Imago Relationship Therapy, 5*(1), 1–17.

Lally, P., Wardle, J., & Gardner, B. (2011). Experiences of habit formation: A qualitative study. *Psychology, Health & Medicine, 16*(4), 484–489. https://doi.org/10.1080/13548506.2011.555774

Love, P. (2001). *The Truth about love: The highs, the lows, and how you can make it last forever.* Touchstone.

Luquet, W., & Hendrix, H. (1998). *Imago Relationship Therapy. In case studies in couple and family therapy.* (F. Datillio, Ed.). Guilford Press.

McTaggart, L. (2002). *The Field: The Quest for the Secret Force of the Universe.* Harper-Collins.

Negriff, S., Susman, E. J. & Trickett, P. K. (2011). The Developmental Pathway from Pubertal Timing to Delinquency and Sexual Activity from Early to Late Adolescence. *Journal of Youth and Adolescence 40,* 1343–1356. https://doi.org/10.1007/s10964-010-9621-7

Nelson, C. (2009). Appreciating gratitude: Can gratitude be used as a psychological intervention to improve individual well-being? *Counselling Psychology Review, 24*(3/4), 38–50.

Numan, R. (2015). A prefrontal-hippocampal comparator for goal-directed behavior: the intentional self and episodic memory. *Frontiers in Behavioral Neuroscience, 9,* 323 doi:10.3389/fnbeh.2015.00323

Perry, W. (1970). *Forms of intellectual and ethical development in the college years: A scheme.* Holt, Rinehart, and Winston.

Rank, O. (1924). *The trauma of birth.* Robert Brunner.

Schacter, D. L., & Addis, D. R. (2007). The cognitive neuroscience of constructive memory: Remembering the past and imagining the future. *Philosophical Transactions of the Royal Society of London, B, 362*(1481), 773–786. https://doi.org/10.1098/rstb.2007.2087

Smith, C. A. (1997). Factors associated with early sexual activity among urban adolescents. *Social Work, 42*(4), 334–346. https://doi.org/10.1093/sw/42.4.334

Spangler, D. (2009). *The laws of manifestation: A consciousness classic.* Red Wheel/Weiser (Original work published 1975).

Stewart-Williams, S. (2010). *Darwin, god and the meaning of life: How evolutionary theory undermines everything you thought you knew.* Cambridge University Press.

Swanson, A. (2015, June 23). 144 years of marriage and divorce in the United States, in one chart. *The Washington Post.* https://www.washingtonpost.com/news/wonk/wp/2015/06/23/144-years-of-marriage-and-divorce-in-the-united-states-in-one-chart/

Sweatt, J. D. (2016). Neural plasticity and behavior—sixty years of conceptual advances. *Journal of Neurochemistry, 139*(S2), 179–199. https://doi.org/10.1111/jnc.13580

Teilhard, P. (1961). *The phenomenon of man* (B. Wall, Trans.). Harper & Row. https://doi.org/10.1111/j.1468-2265.1961.tb00246.x

Wolf, F. A. (1989). *Taking the quantum leap: The new physics for nonscientists.* Harper and Row.

Notes

1. As you'll discover in the later chapters on Imago Relationship Therapy, one of Imago's therapeutic processes, the Imago Profile, is designed to do just that: it helps partners unearth the contents of their imago and to trace the overlap between the caretaker's and partner's traits.
2. Although empirical research on the comparative prevalence of wounding at the childhood development stages is still lacking, many Imago clinicians have commented that most couples seeking Imago Relationship Therapy are "early wounded," that is, they show signs of wounding at one of the three earliest developmental stages (attachment, exploration, and identity).
3. A colleague related that her romantic partner has a full head of long, curly white hair—the same type of hairstyle worn by her beloved maternal grandmother, who lived with the client's family during childhood. It is this grandmother whom her partner most reminds her of!
4. According to John Gottman (1994, *Why Marriages Succeed or Fail*, New York, NY: Fireside Books), stonewalling is one of the "four horsemen of the apocalypse" found to predict relationship failure (the others are criticism, defensiveness, and contempt). Stonewalling, a prototypical minimizing strategy, is when one partner responds to conflict with the other using tactics like silence, unintelligible muttering, changing the subject, fleeing the scene, or other "shutting-down" behaviors.
5. In 1972, in a best-selling book entitled *Open Marriage*, married co-authors George and Nina O'Neill suggested that marriages could benefit from the partners having extramarital romantic liaisons. Ironically, the authors themselves eventually divorced, and Nina O'Neill retracted her endorsement of open marriage.
6. Gottman (1999) refers to such "below-the-belt" behaviors as "fundamental violations of the marital contract." (Gottman, J., *The Sound Marital House*. In Berger, R. & Hannah, M. T. (Eds.), Preventive Approaches in Couples Therapy (p. 322). Philadelphia, PA: Brunner/Mazel.).
7. The use of sentence stems was first used as a projective test by military personnel (Stein, 1947) and then used as a projective personality test to determine unconscious trends and motives of the individual (Symonds, 1947). Sentence completion tests were used to unveil deeper meanings in therapy sessions. Nathaniel Branden (1983) later used sentence stems to help couples reveal deeper meanings and unspoken feelings to each other. When couples are able to become vulnerable with each other through these emotional connections, there is a deepened empathic connection (Johnson 2017).

8. Eye contact plus deep breathing invites the dissolution of stress and superiority. Often times couples in distress will look away or glare at the other.
   Glares are a way of expressing superiority or disdain for the other and are
   interpreted by the brain as a threat. Studies of couples in a strong love relationship show that their eye contact occurs in a gaze as opposed to a glare
   (Rubin, 1970; Goldstein, Kilroy & Van de Voort, 1975). These gazes are loving
   and curious about the other, tender and nonthreatening, and also increase
   the pupil size (another sure sign to the brain that the other is "safe").

9. Direct scientific evidence of empathy did not emerge until the mid-1990s
   with the discovery of the mirror neuron (Rizzolatti, Fadiga, Fogassi, &
   Gallese, 1996). Discovered quite serendipitously when observing the firing
   of a neuron of a small monkey eating peanuts, the scientist observed that
   the neuron also fired when the monkey watched him eat a peanut. It fired
   as if the monkey was eating the peanut himself. The monkey was having a
   mirror response—a connection with the scientist. This discovery has led
   to a flood of research on how these mirror neurons help us do things like
   imitate behavior, understand others' intentions, and empathize.

10. Holding is a psychoanalytic term referring to the infantile longing to be
    entirely dependent and perfectly cared for—that is, held—by his mother.
    The great British psychoanalyst, D. W. Winnicott, made use of a similar
    term, the holding environment, to describe the safe psychic space infants
    need their caretakers to provide for them.

11. Considerable research has been undertaken recently on how consoli-
    dated memories—those memories that are entrenched, myelinated, and
    once thought to be hard wired—can be reconsolidated by bringing up the
    memories and changing the story behind them. Any new information or
    emotion can change the memory. Research by McKenzie and Eichenbaum
    (2011) seems to indicate that memory consolidation and reconsolidation
    is an ongoing process that continues to change memories and the emo-
    tional processes associated with them over the lifespan.

12. Behavior changes fall under the umbrella of habit formation. Studies have
    indicated that new behaviors become automatic over a sustained period
    of time. In one study of habit formation, it took a group of 96 volunteers
    an average of 66 days for the new study behaviors—eating fruit with din-
    ner, drinking a bottle of water with lunch, or running 15 minutes before
    dinner—to become automatic, with a range of 18 to 254 days. "For the
    majority of participants, automaticity increased steadily over the days of
    the study supporting the assumption that repeating a behaviour in a con-
    sistent setting increases automaticity" (Lally et al., 2009).

13. Polyvagal theory illustrates the necessity of working with automatic body
    responses when working with couples. The vagus nerve in humans has
    two branches, one that keeps us calm in the face of meeting others, and

one that puts us on the defense. When a person is in a safe space, they can access higher cortical functions and respond rationally. When a person is in an unsafe space, they are on the defense and in protection mode. Persons who are traumatized in their younger lives may stay in a heightened protective state and misinterpret faces of the other as aggressive and dangerous. Porges focuses on how we interpret the eyes of the other as cues to safety. Therapists working with couples should focus on helping couples develop kind eyes, relaxed bodies, and comfortable breathing so they can appear safe to the other (Porges, 2003; 2011).

14. In a large couple study by Slatcher et al. (2015) couples who had higher partner responsiveness—the extent to which respondents felt understood, cared for, and appreciated by their romantic partners—exhibited lower negative affect with correspondingly lower cortisol levels.

15. A meta-analysis of 23 studies involving 2183 participants on homework and its effect on therapy outcomes indicates a direct effect of compliance to homework and positive therapy outcomes (Mausbach et al., 2010). Compliance to homework also correlated with increased alleviation of symptoms, including anxiety, depression, and substance abuse.

16. The cortical brain communicates with the hippocampus in a similar mechanism as the hippocampus embeds memories in the cortical brain. Numan's comparator theory (1978) has been verified by fMRI studies stating that the prefrontal cortex develops an action plan and transmits a small copy to the hippocampus. The hippocampus holds this plan in memory to compare it to expected behaviors and actual outcomes. The hippocampus serves as an unconscious project manager checking to see if desired outcomes match actual outcomes (Robert, 2015). This process is the basis for goal directed behaviors.

17. The hippocampus is continuously recording events, forming memories in their space–time context. These memories are stored in various parts of the brain to form a consolidated memory. The hippocampus and the prefrontal cortex later work together to stitch together unconscious memories to conscious memories, which become the foundation of intentional actions. fMRI research by Züst et al. (2015) "supports the notion of synergistic interactions between conscious and unconscious relational memories in a common, cohesive hippocampal–neocortical memory space."

18. Psychoanalysts speak of "surrendering to the no-thing"—to find oneself, one must lose oneself. In other words, they must forget what they think they know because it gets in the way; ". . . presence is essentially entwined with absence and that the capacity to be a full self must go hand in hand with the capacity to lose any sense of self (Becker & Shalgi, 2013).

19. Recent research on neuroplasticity shows new behaviors change the neural pathways in the brain. The premise is that where intention goes, neural

firing occurs. Where neural firings occur, new connections, and thus new behaviors, are made to get past old behaviors that recycle themselves, behaviors must become intentional. Neurons that fire together, wire together. Intentionally participating in new positive behaviors changes the basic structure of the brain and creates new consolidated behaviors (Seigel, 2006).

20. Exits are similar to "escape hatches" in transactional analysis by Eric Berne (1964). But while Berne identified hatches as activities people use to escape their own responsibility, we define exits as activities people use to regulate interpersonal anxiety by avoiding intimacy in the relationship.

21. Millions of people have benefited from recovery and co-dependent support groups, such as 12-step programs. And many couples who enter conjoint therapy attend 12-step meetings on a regular basis, and these are a core support for their continued recovery. While we do not recommend the individual to stop attending these meetings, we encourage therapists to invite partners in the session to share with each other using prompters such as, "What did you learn about yourself?" "What do you feel you gain from this support group that you cannot gain elsewhere?" "What can I do to help in the recovery process?" This helps recovery be a relational journey. Additionally, these support groups can often become exits themselves (either functional or motivated). If this is the case, treat it like any other exit by bringing it into Dialogue and going through the steps of closing or modifying the exit.

22. Epigenetic research states that while a person may have a genetic predisposition to a mental illness, the gene may not express itself if the individual is raised in a low stress environment. Stress and trauma at an early age affect individuals differently, but for those who have a gene for a particular mental illness, stress can be the tipping point for gene expression. Lowering relational stress may be an epigenetic preventative measure for decreasing inherited gene expression for mental illness (Conradt, 2017).

23. Extensive research has been done on the causes of affairs. Evolutionary psychologist David Buss sees affairs as part of an overall short-term mating strategy—men seeking variety and spreading their genes and women seeking resources and emotional relationships (Buss, 2013). Consequently, men's affairs tend to be more sexual and women's affairs more emotional (Glass & Wright, 1985). Men will express less regret for their affairs because they see them as just sexual, while women will experience more guilt and regret for their emotional affairs (Fisher et al, 2008). Balon (2016) reports that affairs make little sense from an evolutionary point of view and may be biologically driven.

24. Fisher (2016) writes that humans are capable of three stages of love: lust, attraction, and attachment. Each of these has their own chemical

reaction in our brains. Lust increases testosterone and estrogen and is mostly related with sexual desire. Many people have several lust reactions per day when they see someone attractive. These typically do not result in anything other than a visual moment and a quick chemical high from the sighting. While lust and attraction can be separate, often affairs occur after a lusty moment and when there is availability and proximity to the other. Attraction increases dopamine and norepinephrine levels while decreasing serotonin levels. These chemicals affect the reward system of the brain and cause it to be highly focused on the person to the point of obsession. Phenylethylamine rounds out the chemical cocktail of attraction producing a cocaine like high when in the presence of the other. When an affair reaches the attraction level, it is difficult for the participants to remove themselves from the relationship because of the good feelings produced. Often these unfaithful partners enter into what is referred to as an affair fog. They find it difficult to end the relationship feeling they have found the perfect partner. Finally, with time the relationship enters the attachment phase where the couple feels closely connected and comfortable with each other. Hormones responsible for this comfortable feeling are oxytocin and vasopressin. At this point the affair is very difficult to end because it has moved past the physical and sexual and has moved into emotional connection. For an interesting and simple explanation of the chemistry of love, see http://sitn.hms.harvard.edu/flash/2017/love -actually-science-behind-lust-attraction-companionship/

25. According to Prochaska and DeClemente (2005) behavior change is a process that goes through stages from no desire to change to contemplating change to change to maintaining change. Relapses can be expected and can be used to solidify positive change when the person returns to the change process. Small, doable changes allow the person to become used to the new behaviors, and they increase the probability of permanent change.

26. Based on Murray Bowen's systems theory (1978), differentiation of self states that the person in relationship who can take a strong "I" position and declare their self to the other will have lower emotional reactivity. Traditionally used to help clients differentiate from their family of origin, differentiation of self was later utilized in couples therapy to promote anxiety tolerance and individuation through taking a strong "I" stance with the partner while working to stay in relationship (Schnarch,1991; Schnarch & Regas, 2012).

27. In ecological studies, Gause's Law (1934) and the Competitive Exclusion Principle (Hardin, 1960) state that two similar species cannot occupy the same space. The one with the competitive edge will win or will evolve into a different species. The same principle might be able to be applied to

human relationships as couples work to maintain their self in relationship while living in the same competitive space.

28. A major focus of Emotionally Focused Therapy (Greenberg, 2004) is called arriving and leaving. One cannot leave a place until one has arrived at it, so it is important that couples acknowledge and deal with past emotions so they can be dealt with and understood before the emotion loses its power.

29. At its extreme, those who fear pleasure may suffer from one of two phobias: hedonophobia, fear of pleasure, and cherophobia, aversion to happiness. Fear of happiness researcher Joshanloo found a positive relationship between those with insecure attachments and their fear of happiness who believed that happiness should be avoided because it may cause bad things to happen. They also believed that happiness is fragile and would soon be replaced by less favorable states (Joshanloo, 2018).

30. A study of endocrine levels of individuals watching a humorous film found a drop in their cortisol levels. Cortisol is an immunosuppressant, so a decrease in cortisol may be related to better long-term health (Berk et al., 1989). Decreases in cortisol levels are immediately related to muscle relaxation, with a corresponding decrease in heart rate, respiratory rate, and blood pressure (Bennett & Lengacher, 2008).

31. Familiarity provides little stimulation to the brain, while novelty awakens the hippocampus as it notices difference. During sleep, the novel experience is consolidated into memory. Positive surprises stimulate the hippocampus because of pattern difference and is consolidated into memory as a positive experience (Fenker et al., 2008; Genzel et al., 2017). Conversely, negative surprises can consolidate as a trauma.

human suffering
perspective on (*see* suffering)

id, 22
idealist(s), 42–43
idealization
in relationships, 135–37
identity(ies)
cosmic, 46
relational, 7–10 (*see also* relational identity)
identity-challenged couple
attuning to, 182
characteristics of, 180–82, 181*t*
identifying, 181
identity stage (3–4 years), 115*t*,
117–18
in developmental journey, 92*t*,
94–95
I–It relationship, 101, 114
illusion(s)
Descartian, 52
symbiotic, 17
image. *see* Imago
Imago. *see also* Imago Relationship
Therapy; Imago therapy; specific elements, e.g., connecting
basic tenet of, 10
characteristics of, 126–29
comprising childhood experiences, 127
defined, 124
described, xi, 2–3, 124–26
in Imago Relationship Therapy,
124–25
impact on present time, 128–29
new experiences impact on,
127–28
nonnegotiable conditions for
restoring and sustaining connecting, 10–11
perspective in, 3–5
psychosocial journey of childhood
development, 85–91, 92*t*, 98*f*
quantum field and, 48–54

relational identity in, 7–10 (*see
also* relational identity)
safety in, 239
search for original connecting,
124–49 (*see also under* Imago-Match; original connecting;
relationship(s))
sexuality and, 383–84
transformation in, 59–60
Imago clinical practices, 263–389,
392–441. *see also specific types*
recommitting, 284–303, 405–9
reimaging, 304–23, 410–22
removing negativity, 324–38,
423–27
re-romanticizing, 363–84, 438–41
restructuring frustrations, 339–
62, 428–37
revisioning, 267–83, 392–404
Imago clinical processes, 187–262
Imago clinical theory, 65–186
Imago diagnosis
important note about, 236
Imago Dialogue, 166–68, 172, 175,
190–225, 232, 234, 241–43, 248–
50, 254, 258, 261–62, 265, 270–
71, 275, 281, 305, 309, 385–88
basics of, 193–96
benefits of, 220–21
in breaking symbiotic fusion,
222
childhood challenge, 315–16,
316*t*, 415–18
coach couples in onramp
sequence in, 198
commitment, 408–9
in connecting, 190–225
as connecting process, 216–18
by conscious partners, 157–60
in dealing with affairs, 292
described, xii–xiii, xv, 158–60,
193–216
determining sender–receiver
sequence in, 196–97
as differentiating process,

ruptured connecting (*continued*)
  defensive styles across develop-
    mental spectrum, 114–20, 115*t*
    (*see also specific stages and
    defensive styles*)
  desire and, 108–9
  minimizing and maximizing
    maneuvers related to, 106–8
  nurturing deficits and, 102–3
  repressive socialization and, 103–
    6, 105*f*
  self-absorption and, 109
  sequence of, 121–23, 121*f*
  symbiosis and, 109–14 (*see also*
    symbiosis)

Safe Conversations
  described, 388–89
safety
  brain in, 72–73
  in children's relational journey,
    87–88, 92*t*
  in conscious partnership, 157
  emotional, 87
  in Imago, 239
  Imago Dialogue and, xii–xiii, 157,
    222
  by Imago therapists, 239, 253–54
  physical, 87
  removing negativity and, 336
  as requirement, xv
  search for, 8
  in Space-Between, 265*t*
seamless flow, 249
self(ves)
  basis of, 63
  cultural, 15
  defined, 83
  described, 53, 56
  differentiated, 85
  differentiation of, 461*n*
  as discrete entity, 37
  in Imago theory, 83–85
  psychological, xv, 22
  quantum (*see* quantum self)

  relational, 23
  relational essence of, 24–25
  relational features of, 7, 23–33
  as relationship, 2–3, 7, 23, 83–84
  separate, xv, 3, 6
  significant others in sense of, 28
  social environment in shaping, 68
  as source of suffering, 19
  "substantial," 83
self-absorption
  defined, 109
  ruptured connecting related to,
    109
  self-defense and, 109
"self as relational," 23
"self as relationship," 23, 83–84
self-awareness
  in quantum field, 46
self-defense
  self-absorption and, 109
"self-in-relation," 31–32
"self-in-relationship," 34
  of interpersonal and intersubjec-
    tive theories, 83–84
self-knowledge
  from engagement with others, 84
self psychology, 217
  Kohut and, 29–31
self-system, 28
sender(s)
  in empathizing, 215
  in mirroring, 202
  in validation, 209–10
sender–receiver sequences
  determining, 196–97
sensation(s)
  anxiety as most important, 71
sensing
  partners having opposite or com-
    plementary blocks in, 130,
    134–35
  in relating, 97, 98*f*
sensory information
  RAS in, 71
sensory visualizations, 394–95

structure (*continued*)
  defined, 89
  Imago therapist providing, 254
subjective knowledge, 172
"substantial self"
  of Individual Paradigm, 83
suffering
  anxiety and, 19, 20, 28
  changing views of, 19–20
  described, 20
  in first stage of human social evo-
    lution, 20
  Imago view of phenomenal expe-
    rience of, 19
  location of source of, 19
  new view in psychotherapy, 22
  outside as source of, 19
  perspective on, 18–22
  in quantum universe, 58–60
  reasons for, 5–7
  relational thread and, 27–33
  in second stage of human social
    evolution, 21–22
  self as source of, 19
  solution to, 19
Sullivan, H.S., xv, 28–29, 31, 119,
    191–92, 238, 290
superego, 22, 24
support
  in children's relational journey,
    91, 92t
surprise(s)
  positive *vs.* negative, 462n
  in Re-romanticizing Process,
    368–69, 374–75
surrender
  described, 284
"surrendering to the no-thing," 459n
Surrey, J., 31
survival directive, 71
sustaining connecting, 150–73. *see
    also* conscious partner(s); con-
    scious partnership
  in child–caretaker relationship, 82
  core development needs of child

in, 85–91, 92t (*see also specific
    needs and* relational journey)
  described, 82
  nonnegotiable conditions for,
    10–11
  in relational journey, 89, 92t
symbiosis, 139, 172, 227
  adulthood manifestations of,
    112–13
  childhood manifestations of, 111
  defined, 109, 110
  described, 109–11
  to differentiation, 310, 310f
  emotional, 109–10
  examples of, 112–13
  face and voice of, 307–9
  generation of, 306
  Imago Dialogue in breaking, 222
  indicators of, 308
  loss of empathy related to,
    113–14
  manifestations of, 111–14
  objectification and, 114
  removing negativity in breaking,
    337
  ruptured connecting related to,
    109–14
  source of, 306–7
symbiotic consciousness, 110–11
symbiotic frustrations
  types of, 308
symbiotic illusion, 17
symbiotic relationship
  symptoms of, 307–9
systems theory
  Bowen's, 461n

"taking turns talking"
  described, xii
  three-step process of, xii–xiii
talking
  taking turns, 193–94
"talking cure"
  Freud's discovery of, 25–26
tension of opposites, 241

Harville Hendrix, Ph.D., and **Helen LaKelly Hunt, Ph.D.**, are cocreators of Imago Relationship Therapy and a social movement called Safe Conversations. Internationally-respected as couple's therapists, educators, speakers, activists, and New York Times bestselling authors, their 10 books, including the timeless classic, *Getting the Love You Want: A Guide for Couples*, have sold more than 4 million copies. Harville appeared on the Oprah Winfrey television program 17 times! Helen was installed in the Women's Hall of Fame and the Smithsonian Institute. They have six children and seven grandchildren.

The Imago intellectual system is the foundation for various learning opportunities including training, public education, and clinical research. For more information about:

- Harville and Helen, including their speaking schedule, please visit HarvilleandHelen.com.
- Clinical and Professional Imago Training, including becoming a Certified Imago Therapist® or Imago Facilitator™, please visit ImagoTraining.org.
- Imago resources worldwide and our communities of practice, please visit ImagoRelationships.org.
- Increasing relational competency through online relationship wellness training, please visit SafeConversations.com.